Massimo Rospocher, Jeroen Salman, Hannu Salmi (Eds.)
Crossing Borders, Crossing Cultures

Studies in Early Modern and Contemporary European History

―――

Edited by
FBK - Istituto Storico Italo-Germanico /
Italienisch-Deutsches Historisches Institut

Volume 1

Massimo Rospocher, Jeroen Salman,
Hannu Salmi (Eds.)

Crossing Borders, Crossing Cultures

—

Popular Print in Europe (1450–1900)

DE GRUYTER
OLDENBOURG

ISBN 978-3-11-063951-3
e-ISBN (PDF) 978-3-11-64354-1
e-ISBN (EPUB) 978-3-11-063989-6
ISSN 2629-3730

Bibliographic information published by the Deutsche Nationalbibliothek
The Deutsche Nationalbibliothek lists this publication in the Deutsche Nationalbibliografie; detailed bibliographic data are available on the Internet at http://dnb.dnb.de.

© 2019 Walter de Gruyter GmbH, Berlin/Boston
Printing and binding: CPI books GmbH, Leck
Cover illustration: Charles Jameson Grant, The Penny Trumpeter! (1832, Cover of The Penny Magazine of 20 September 1832, published by Gabriel Shire Tregear in London); Rijksmuseum Amsterdam, RP-P-2015-26-1919.

www.degruyter.com

Contents

Massimo Rospocher and Jeroen Salman
Introduction: Crossing Borders, Crossing Cultures —— 1

I. Media, Intermediality

Daniel Bellingradt
The Dynamic of Communication and Media Recycling in Early Modern Europe: Popular Prints as Echoes and Feedback Loops —— 9

Rebecca Carnevali
Iconographies and Material Culture of Illustrated Cheap Print from Post-Tridentine Bologna —— 33

Andreas Würgler
"Popular Print in German" (1400-1800). Problems and Projects —— 53

II. Markets, Prices, and Collections

Francesca Tancini
The Railway Library and Other Literary Rubbish that Travels by the Rail —— 71

Goran Proot
Shifting Price Levels of Books Produced at the Officina Plantiniana in Antwerp, 1580–1655 —— 89

Flavia Bruni
Faraway, So Close: Frontier Challenges for Inter-National Bibliographies —— 109

III. Transnational Approaches

Jean-François Botrel and Juan Gomis
"Literatura de cordel" from a Transnational Perspective. New Horizons for an Old Field of Study —— 127

Alice Colombo
The Translational Dimension of Street Literature. The Nineteenth-Century Italian Repertoire —— 143

Jordi Sánchez-Martí
The Printed Popularization of the Iberian Books of Chivalry across Sixteenth-Century Europe —— 159

Julia Martins
The Afterlife of Italian Secrets: Translating Medical Recipes in Early Modern Europe —— 181

Niall Ó Ciosáin
Popular Print in Unofficial Languages. Ireland, Scotland, Wales, and Brittany —— 199

IV. Genres and European Bestsellers

Claudia Demattè
The Spanish Romances about Chivalry. A Renaissance Editorial Phenomenon on Which "The Sun Never Set" —— 217

Elisa Marazzi
Crossing Genres: A Newcomer in the Transnational History of Almanacs —— 227

Reinhart Siegert
The Greatest German Book Success of the Eighteenth Century. Rudolph Zacharias Becker's "Noth- und Hülfsbüchlein" (1788/1798) as the Prototype of Printed Volksaufklärung and its Dissemination in Europe —— 245

Rita Schlusemann
A Canon of Popular Narratives in Six European Languages between 1470 and 1900. The "Griseldis"-Tradition in German and Dutch —— 265

Contributors —— 287

Index —— 289

Massimo Rospocher and Jeroen Salman
Introduction:
Crossing Borders, Crossing Cultures

Although scholars have studied popular print culture intensively since the 1960s, this was done mainly with a regional or national focus, based on the assumption that popular print in the vernacular had a limited geographical reach. Within this broad and well-established historiographical vein, there have been excellent histories in many different areas of Europe, in particular Germany, England, Denmark, the Low Countries, and France[1]. In recent decades, Spanish *pliegos sueltos* and Italian *stampe popolari* have also been investigated more thoroughly[2]. Despite these welcome new contributions to the field, however, recent research has also suggested that popular print should be studied within a wider, European, perspective[3].

While we now have a clearer view of the European landscape of this cheap material also thanks to the technological aid of online resources and catalogues, still missing is a general interpretation of this cultural phenomenon and a more substantial comparative analysis of its social and economic dynamics. In 2016, a group of international researchers in the field started a collaborative network to initiate and stimulate transnational research concentrating on the "European Dimensions

---

[1] Some examples: R. Mandrou, *De la culture populaire aux 17e et 18e siècles. La Bibliothèque Bleue de Troyes*, Paris 1964; R. Schenda, *Volk ohne Buch. Studien zur Sozialgeschichte der populären Lesestoffe 1770–1910*, Frankfurt a.M. 1970; M. Spufford, *Small Books and Pleasant Histories. Popular Fiction and its Readership in Seventeenth-century England*, Cambridge 1981; J. Raymond (ed.), *The Oxford History of Popular Print Culture*, vol. 1: *Cheap Print in Britain and Ireland to 1660*, Oxford 2011; N. Ó Ciosáin, *Print and Popular Culture in Ireland, 1750–1850*. Dublin 1997; H. Horstbøll, *Menigmands Medie. Det folkelige bogtryk i Danmark 1500–1840. En kulturhistorisk undersøgelse*, Aarhus 1999; J. Salman, *Populair drukwerk in de Gouden Eeuw. De almanak als lectuur en handelswaar*, Zutphen 1999.
[2] For instance, in the recently published monographs and edited volumes on cheap print in early modern Italy: L. Carnelos, *I libri da risma. Catalogo delle edizioni Remondini a larga diffusione (1650–1850)*, Milano 2008; S. Minuzzi. *Il Secolo di carta. Antonio Bosio artigiano di testi e immagini nella Venezia del Seicento*, Milano 2009; R. Salzberg, *Ephemeral City. Cheap Print and Urban Culture in Renaissance Venice*, Manchester 2014; L. Braida / M. Infelise (eds.), *Libri per tutti. Generi editoriali di larga circolazione tra antico regime ed età contemporanea*, Milano 2011. On Spain, see J. Gomis, *Menudencias de imprenta. Producción y circulación de la literatura popular (Valencia, siglo XVIII)*, Valencia 2015; for more exhaustive bibliographical references, see the article by Juan Gomis and Jean-François Botrel in this collection.
[3] See, for example, D. Atkinson / S. Roud (eds.), *Street Literature of the Long Nineteenth Century. Producers, Sellers, Consumers*, Cambridge 2017; A. Pettegree, *Broadsheets. Single-Sheet Publishing in the First Age of Print*. Boston / Leiden 2017; N. Moxham / J. Raymond (eds.), *News Networks in Early Modern Europe*, Boston / Leiden 2016; J. Salman, *Pedlars and the Popular Press. Itinerant Distribution Networks in England and The Netherlands 1600-1850*, Boston / Leiden 2014; R. Harms / J. Raymond /

of Popular Print Culture (EDPOP)"[4]. The key question of this joint venture was: how European was popular print culture in the period 1450–1900? Suggesting a transnational and comparative approach to the dissemination of print in the early modern and modern period, this book intends to contribute to a better understanding of one of the most important issues in European communication history.

The definition we use for popular print in this project is inclusive, meaning that we do not focus on popular print as a clearly defined product, but rather as spectrum in a dynamic popularisation process. This leads to interesting questions about the intensions and strategies of the producers and distributors on the one hand and the demands and tactics of the consumers on the other. What is more, the close attention paid to this process, facilitates and enhances a dialogue between a group of researchers that study popular print from very different angles. The range of genres and categories of print that can be studied in this field comprises, among many others, broadsheets, pamphlets, almanacs, prose novels, ballads, penny prints, history prints, newspapers, and jest books. Aside from the origin, the translation, adaptation, and dissemination of these genres and their contents, the project also addresses the transnational infrastructure behind the production, distribution, and consumption of this material.

One of the first steps in this ambitious endeavor is to develop theoretical and methodological instruments to make Pan-European, long-term, comparative research possible. Many bibliographical, conceptual, linguistic, source-related, genre-theoretical, and technical problems have to be solved or at least discussed. This volume, based on the contributions of an EDPOP-conference held in 2017 in Trent, offers some innovative methodological and conceptual reflections as well as concrete case studies that can facilitate and stimulate further comparative research. We have divided the volume in four sections, each addressing important methodological and conceptual issues and at the same time presenting new research and case studies: 1. Media and intermediality; 2. Markets, prices, and collections of books; 3. Transnational approaches; 4. Genres and European bestsellers.

The first section approaches print culture from a wide, media-theoretical perspective, focusing on the interaction between print and other media. Recent historiography on pre-Industrial Europe has demonstrated that it does not make sense to separate printed from oral, acoustic, performative, and handwritten modes of communication, because all these means were bound together in a multimedia system[5].

J. Salman (eds.), *Not Dead Things. The Dissemination of Popular Print in England and Wales, Italy, and the Low Countries, 1500–1820*, Boston / Leiden 2013; R. Chartier / H.-J. Lüsebrink (eds.), *Colportage et lecture populaire. Imprimés de large circulation en Europe XVIe–XIXe siècle*, Paris 1996.

4 This Internationalization Project was funded by The Netherlands organization for Scientific Research (NWO). For more information on this project, its activities and participants see: https://edpop.wp.hum.uu.nl/.

5 R. Darnton, *Poetry and the Police: Communication Networks in Eighteenth-Century Paris*, Cambridge MA 2002; D. Bellingradt, *Flugpublizistik und Öffentlichkeit um 1700. Dynamiken, Akteure und Strukturen*

Currently, scholars are paying much attention to the intermediality integral to *Ancien Régime* communicative systems, based on the assumption that, then as now, communication was conveyed in and to countless combinations of intended and actual publics, meanings, and effects, and in myriad forms, including images, performances, rituals, objects, and spoken, sung, manuscript, and printed words interacting with each other[6]. Acknowledging that print culture was only one part of the wider *media ensemble* produces interesting insights into processes of recycling, adapting, and relocating news or texts. The notion of intermediality allows us to reconstruct how "printed echoes" reverberated through other media (Bellingradt). Focusing on print as a diverse medium that depended on different means of communication, techniques, and material supports, the case study of illustrated cheap print in Post-Tridentine Bologna also stresses the significant interplay between text and image in many popular printed genres and sheds new light on the social differences among their target audiences (Carnevali). And, finally, arguing for a less restricted notion of print and for greater attention to be paid to consumption, a historiographical overview of German scholarship addresses a fundamental question about the materiality of the sources and the need for advanced bibliographical research (Würgler).

The second section focuses on "Markets, prices, and collections of books" and it offers semantic, empirical, and bibliographical explorations of the concept "cheap", which is strongly associated with the notion of popular print. Research on the specific category of mass-produced railway literature draws attention to the marketing strategies of nineteenth-century publishers and booksellers to reach a broad and new audience and to maximize sales (Tancini). A long-term (1580–1655) overview of the actual prices of books produced by the famous Antwerp print house Plantin-Moretus, the *Officina Plantiniana*, provides us with unique evidence of the relation between format, price, and commercial considerations (Proot). If the study of book prices is essential to understanding European print culture, the dispersal of books across national boundaries is one of the main obstacles for a comprehensive reconstruction of the early modern print world. And precisely the more popular or ephemeral printed materials are subject to the highest rate of dispersion within contemporary national collections; what was once widely available has become extremely rare today. As

---

im urbanen Raum des Alten Reiches, Stuttgart 2011; F. Deen, *Publiek debat en propaganda in Amsterdam tijdens de Nederlandse Opstand*, Amsterdam 2014; A. Fox, *Oral and Literate Culture in England, 1500–1700*, Oxford 2002; S. Dall'Aglio / B. Richardson / M. Rospocher (eds.), *Voices and Texts in Early Modern Italian Society*, London / New York 2017.

6 For an historiographical overview on the history of early modern communication, see M. Rospocher, *What is the History of Communication? An Early Modernist Perspective*, in "Jahrbuch für Kommunikationsgeschichte", 20, 2018, pp. 9–15; D. Bellingradt, *Annäherungen an eine Kommunikationsgeschichte der Frühen Neuzeit*, in "Jahrbuch für Kommunikationsgeschichte", 20, 2018, pp. 16-21; P. Palmieri, *Interactions between Orality, Manuscript and Print Culture in Sixteenth-Century Italy: Recent Historiographical Trends*, in "Storia della Storiografia", 73, 2018, 1, pp. 135–148.

such, recovering these lost books is one of the challenges of international bibliographies (Bruni).

Section three on "Transnational approaches" is among other things a strong plea for including translation studies into our field of research. The great mobility of cheap texts via translations or adaptations, as is shown by these contributions, is often underestimated and therefore hardly examined. Several case studies present challenging approaches to analyzing and mapping the transnational diffusion of religious, medical, chivalric, and other entertaining texts. The Spanish "Literatura Cordel" includes many popular genres that in form and content present a strong European dimension. Gallows literature, for instance, is a rich and methodologically interesting field to explore the possibilities of comparative research. It demonstrates clearly that a transnational scope and related taxonomical discussion does not only lead to new insights into international phenomena, but reveals undiscovered national print cultures as well (Gomis and Botrel).

The European dimensions of chivalric novels or books of chivalry are considered evident but seldom studied systematically and in detail. The different strategies (size, paper, serialization, illustrations) that were deployed in Spain, France, Italy, and England from the second half of the sixteenth century onwards, made the early, elitist and expensive editions (often in folio) of chivalric texts available for a larger public. The case study in this volume analyzes different business models and tries to explain the long-term success of this genre in Europe as a whole (Sanchez).

The European phenomenon of printed books of secrets (recipe compilations) started in 1529 in Italy with the publication of *Dificio di ricette* and remained popular until at least the end of the eighteenth century. The popularization history described here shows how this medical genre was reshaped and transformed to fit into national publication strategies – such as integrating them into the French *Bibliothèque bleue* – and how it catered for new audiences. Contrary to common assumptions, this transnational journey often started with a translation from Italian into Latin before it was translated into other vernacular languages (Martins).

It has become clear that the approaches and methodologies of translation studies and book history must be combined in order to reach new insights into the translation strategies of European publishers of chapbooks and broadsides. New and unexplored methods are needed to at least determine if a cheap text, with usually very little paratext, is a translation, a pseudo-translation, or no translation at all, let alone to identify what the original language was. Interdisciplinary research can help us to discover how genres, themes, titles, and characters crossed borders and languages (Colombo). A whole new dimension of "popular" is explored in a contribution that focuses on print produced in non-official languages such as Breton, Welsh, Scottish Gaelic, and Irish Gaelic. Here the challenge is to analyze the features of these specific genres (e.g. almanacs and ballads), their audiences, and the interaction of these non-official idioms with material in the official languages (Ó Ciosáin).

The fourth and final section ("Genres and European bestsellers") addresses the intriguing question of how to define a bestseller, and discusses the complex connection between the concept of popular print and bestsellers. As demonstrated by the rapid and widespread diffusion of Spanish chivalric romances among different social classes, many European editors and publishers intuited the potential of this editorial phenomenon which became both a literary fashion and a commercial success (Demattè). If the so-called *libros de caballerías* are undoubtedly a recognized European bestseller of the sixteenth century, the Italian Barbanera almanac, issued from at least 1762, is an often-neglected example of a long-term bestseller. The almanac was one of the most widespread and popular genres in Europe in the early modern era. One of the intriguing features of the almanac, illustrated by the Barbanera, is its ability to adjust and respond to new cultures, languages, audiences, and worldviews. The fact that the almanac was not only used to read but, due to its practical function and structure, also to write and make notes, made these booklets less ephemeral than we would expect. The copies that have survived are unique witnesses to contemporary reflections on daily life and beg for further comparative research (Marazzi).

A remarkable bestseller of the German popular enlightenment was Rudolph Zacharias Becker's *Noth- und Hülfsbüchlein* (1788–1798). Different from many other popular works discussed in this volume, this genre aimed from the start at an audience of the uneducated and poorest in German society. Exceptional is also the fact that the production and distribution of this successful work was so strategically planned (Siegert).

An example of a long-term, comparative study of a canonical bestselling title, *Griseldis*, demonstrates the obstacles as well as the fruitfulness of a European-wide, book historical approach. *Griseldis* is a well-chosen case study because of its ancient origin – it was one of the stories in Boccaccio's *Il Decamerone* (1349–1353) – and the fact that it was translated, adapted, and printed in more than twenty languages up until the end of the nineteenth century. Interestingly, narrative stories that were already popular in the Middle Ages, were first published in German and were relatively short or part of a collection of tales, seem to have been the most successful ones in terms of longevity and geographical spread. We need more research to explain this fascinating pattern (Schlusemann).

As will become clear after reading the fifteen chapters, by moving across national, historiographical or linguistic boundaries, this volume offers multiple approaches, methodologies, sources and additional questions to facilitate and stimulate future comparative and transnational research on European popular print.

The editors wish to thank the Netherlands organization for Scientific Research (NWO) and the Fondazione Bruno Kessler for funding the international conference "Crossing Borders, Crossing Cultures" (held at the Istituto Storico Italo-Germanico of the Fondazione Bruno Kessler in Trento on June 15 and 16, 2017) of which this volume aims to represent a synthesis. We are grateful to the director of the Institute Christoph Cornelißen, for supporting this project, and this gratitude is extended to the staff,

Elisabetta Lopane, Moira Osti, and Antonella Vecchio, and to the editorial office of the Fondazione Bruno Kessler, in particular Friederike Oursin, for the care which they took in the publication of this volume.

I. **Media, Intermediality**

Daniel Bellingradt
The Dynamic of Communication and Media Recycling in Early Modern Europe: Popular Prints as Echoes and Feedback Loops

1 Introduction

Discovering the popular within the printed words and images of early modern Europe is often difficult. "Prints" are a paper-based material artefact resulting from complex and specialized publishing processes that are, in sum, a capital-intensive business. The so-called "print culture" was expensive and generally not economically accessible to large communities. Moreover, "print culture" is only one part of the wider "media ensemble", which also includes all other aspects of communication, be they verbal, written, visual, acoustic, or performative (i.e. through gestures). Searching for the popular in the early modern era is therefore a journey into past intermediality. Nevertheless, "popular" prints, when viewed as embedded entities in this network of communications, provide significant perspectives on intermedial aspects of the dynamics of communication. A focus on media recycling provides clarity on follow-up communications: that is, the most typical and constant processing of observed media-flows into new streams of media. In this chapter, I will refer to these follow-up communications as echoes and feedback loops. With regard to "print culture", these echoes and loops are called "printed echoes" and "printed feedback loops".

Focusing on the communicational dynamics of media recycling is one methodological path for the benefit of "book history" and the history of communication in early modern Europe. In order to better understand the transregional appearances, flows, and cycles of certain media topics and themes within Europe, such a focus is helpful in re-evaluating questions of past communication. In fact, a history of communication in early modern Europe, and therefore a "book history" that is part of this historiographical scope, must pay attention to the appearances, flows, and cycles of (printed) media – in text and image – that cannot be measured by boundaries of language, religion, law, or politics. Communication flows did not stop at borders, in fact communication flows moved without respect for any boundaries. We need to understand the many forms of borders within Europe as transparent and semi-permeable. This openness of borders between European communities and territories has been a primary focus for many years in several interdisciplinary fields of early modern communication history – including the so-called "transnational book history", and the growing numbers of studies on news(paper) history[1]. In these approaches, transre-

---

[1] The history of newspapers was traditionally written from the perspective of national history but it has been internationalized in the last few decades: J. Raymond / N. Moxham (eds.), *News Networks*

gional flows of news media and various book formats, whether handwritten or printed, are addressed by highlighting commercial, learned, and collecting activities, and by focusing on their publication, transportation, and distribution strategies. In these studies that deal with border-crossing communications, "entangled" histories of the book and news trades are already implicitly included.

The present case studies on border-crossing communications (or border-crossing media) ought to be developed into an "entangled history of early modern media". As is often the case, book history as an interdisciplinary field may profit from methodological transfers and ideas from other scholarly traditions that have already been engaging with questions of how an entangled (or shared, or connected) history may be designed[2]. Within the historiographical perspectives of the so-called "entangled history" or *histoire croisée*, the basic assumption centers on interconnectedness, interaction, and circulation processes that go beyond national perspectives[3]. Here, the legal, lingual, and political borders of early modern Europe are not taken as dividing markers that constitute particular isolated entities (or containers). As we are interested in the flows, cycles, and appearances of printed matter, we need to highlight the connections and motivations behind media appearances. By doing so, we are offered a more open horizon in considering these flows and their possible entanglements/connections. A future history of communication has to be firmly rooted in perspectives on transregionality, and this history has to be written as an entangled, inter-connected history.

In order to write an entangled history of early modern media, some general methodological considerations and explanations of the chosen case studies are needed. To begin with, the concept of "media recycling" needs clarification. In order to investigate early modern media recycling with regard to popular print culture, it seems fruitful to build on recent studies about the dynamics of a mainly commercially driven, serial, and periodical media producing early modern media system. In these studies,

---

in *Early Modern Europe*, Leiden / Boston MA 2016; P. Arblaster, *From Ghent to Aix. How They Brought the News in the Habsburg Netherlands, 1550–1700*, Leiden / Boston MA 2014. For an introduction to the richness of transnational approaches of early modern book history, M. McLean / S. Barker (eds.), *International Exchange in the Early Modern Book World*, Leiden / Boston MA 2016; C. Berkvens-Stevelinck et al. (eds.), *Le magasin de l'univers. The Dutch Republic as the Centre of the European Book Trade*, Leiden 1992; I. Hofmeyr, *The Portable Bunyan: A Transnational History of the Book*, Princeton NJ 2003; R. Chartier / H.J. Lüsebrink (eds), *Colportage et lecture populaire. Imprimés de large circulation en Europe, XVIe XIXe siecles*, Paris 1996.

2 Entangled history, or "shared history", has mainly been discussed in the context of global (modern) history and was developed mostly in colonial studies, for example.

3 On the concept of entangled history and its sister terms (shared history, connected history, often overlapping perspectives like transfer history, transnational history, Atlantic history, borderland history, *histoire croisée*), M. Werner / B. Zimmermann, *Beyond Comparison: Histoire Croisée and the Challenge of Reflexivity*, in "History and Theory", 45, 2006, 1, pp. 30–50; W. Drews / C. Scholl (eds.), *Transkulturelle Verflechtungsprozesse in der Vormoderne* (Das Mittelalter. Beihefte, 3), Berlin 2016.

mainly influenced by Johannes Arndt's concept of an early modern processing media system, the focus lies on the typical managing and recycling of oral, scribal, and printed information into new streams – or "flows" – of printed media[4]. As will be addressed further in the section, "Periodical news as echoing media", a growing field of scholars, highlights such new streams as printed "follow up stories" and "feedback loops" (*Feedbackschleifen*). Here, we may follow Arndt by understanding this dynamic of re-using as a feedback-loop producing media system of serial and periodical publications.

With regard to a "print culture", we obviously need to broaden our perspectives and include all other relevant prints that result from this recycling dynamism – including occasional or ephemeral pamphlets, broadsides, small or cheap prints, and all other "bookish" formats (e.g. small romances, almanacs, history books; printed images in all forms and shapes, as the section "Images as echoes in the communication process" will refer). The processing of media observation into the production of new printed media as "paper echoes" has been stressed in recent years, especially for occasional, i.e. non-periodical prints. The section "Narrating media events" will address this in more detail, examining the ways in which early modern pamphlet culture has been described as an echo-producing machine par excellence. In early modern Europe during times of contested notions, it was common practice to address the real and true interpretation of an issue in an on-going "published battle". These printed battles followed a lively code of *actio* and *reactio* that could be described as a ping-pong effect[5]. Basically, each (printed) voice sought to maintain its own position and gain the upper hand in this ping-pong match and such a battle would result in a stream of (printed) echoes. Furthermore, such a printed pamphlet echo, or in the words of Rosa Salzberg, a "paper echo"[6], is the result of an active practice of media observation, processing relevant aspects of media flows into new printed media, and finally publishing and distributing these "paper echoes".

Theoretically, any historical investigation into the processes and moments of media flows should pay attention to the plurality of a communicative landscape – the media ensemble. As we know from recent studies on the interplay and the complementarity of oral, written, and printed means of communication, mainly put forward within studies on the early modern media logic of an urban culture, we should always

---

[4] J. Arndt, *Herrschaftskontrolle durch Öffentlichkeit. Die publizistische Darstellung politischer Konflikte im Heiligen Römischen Reich 1648–1750*, Göttingen 2013; J. Arndt / E.-B. Körber, *Das Mediensystem im Alten Reich der Frühen Neuzeit 1600–1750*, in J. Arndt / E.-B. Körber (eds.), *Das Mediensystem im Alten Reich der Frühen Neuzeit (1600–1750)*, Göttingen 2010, pp. 1–25.
[5] D. Bellingradt, *The Early Modern City as a Resonating Box: Media, the Public Sphere and the Urban Space of the Holy Roman Empire, Cologne and Hamburg c. 1700*, in "Journal of Early Modern History", 16, 2012, 3, pp. 201–240, esp. p. 234; D. Bellingradt, *Flugpublizistik und Öffentlichkeit um 1700. Dynamiken, Akteure und Strukturen im urbanen Raum des Alten Reiches*, Stuttgart 2011.
[6] R. Salzberg, *Ephemeral City. Cheap Print and Urban Culture in Renaissance Venice*, Manchester 2014, p. 164.

inquire about the connections of all relevant and observed media flows within the lively world of authors, printers, and publishers[7]. Whenever possible, taking into account the entire mediality of the unique chosen communicative setting means to historically "freeze" the observed situation in order to evaluate the traceable media in the context of all the other relevant data of the "frozen" moment of communication (examples of these include the specific communicators, intended and reached audiences, legal constellation, levels of censorship activity within the situation, as well as the existence and accessibility of infrastructure).

Building on the notions of echoing, feedback-looping, and interacting, it seems generally appropriate to analyze media appearances that cross borders as (predominantly) commercially-motivated media flows that predominantly follow the infrastructure, speed, and rhythms of the contemporary postal systems – in letters, newspapers, pamphlets, calendars, etc. And, as these postal routes did not stop at territorial borders, we see European media flows all over the informational networks. Whatever written or depicted component seemed worth publishing or re-using, was used – as inspiration, in quotation, in paraphrase, in adaption, in thematic response, in translation, or in modulation, for example.

2 Periodical news as echoing media: The most common dynamic of producing flows of feedback loops

In early modern Europe, the production of echoes and feedback loops was the standard business routine of the periodical news systems and its rhythmic processing of old news into new news. As mentioned in this chapter's introduction, recycling information from other oral, scribal, or printed sources was the most common practice of news production[8]. In this light, all early modern periodical and serial news formats – e.g. from the mainly weekly formats of handwritten/manuscript newsletters and printed newspapers to (bi-)monthly journals, and yearly almanacs

---

[7] The most relevant (theoretical and empirical) studies on this topic have derived from research on early modern European cities. Schlögl recently coined these approaches as investigations into the media logic of an urban culture of presence (*Anwesenheitsgesellschaft*); R. Schlögl, *Politik beobachten. Öffentlichkeit und Medien in der Frühen Neuzeit*, in "Zeitschrift für Historische Forschung", 35, 2008, pp. 581–616; F. de Vivo, *Information and Communication in Venice. Rethinking Early Modern Politics*, Oxford 2007; D. Bellingradt, *The Early Modern City*; R. Salzberg, *Ephemeral City*; D. Freist, *Governed by Opinion. Politics, Religion and the Dynamics of Communication in Stuart London 1637–1645*, London 1997; A. Farge, *Dire et mal dire: l'opinion publique au XVIIIe siècle*, Paris 1992.

[8] J. Arndt, *Herrschaftskontrolle*; G. Scholz Williams / W. Layher (eds.), *Consuming News. Newspapers and Print Culture in Early Modern Europe (1500–1800)*, Amsterdam / New York 2008.

or calendars – were to great extent compilations – recycled goods made of re-ordered details from other (news) media. In other words, periodicals and serials consisted of media echoes. And these echoes were both transregional and European in scope. The news-business routine of observing and recycling, including the selection, compilation, and re-ordering of relevant information into new streams of media (mainly in varieties of new printed media) is international from its beginning. As a mid-seventeenth century publication from the Habsburg-Netherlands put it, "to watch the affaires of one another", was an established practice of a growing public accustomed to consuming news[9]. As this processing was conducted with the transregional focus of those included (scribes, journalists, *Novellanten*, newsagents, news publisher), the news horizon was always, in the words of Cornel Zwierlein, a European news horizon[10]. Observations of Europe were a typical feature of the transregional news media networks that selected "useable" parts of the observed news reports for their own audiences, and translated, compiled, and fitted them into fresh streams of news media. Both the "fresh" information and longstanding topics of ongoing interest came into circulation from nearly all points of news collection which were connected to a postal system that did not stop at territorial or regional borders[11]. News components that seemed worth publishing were compiled and published in a variety of ways including in quotes, paraphrase, in adaption, in thematic response, in translation, and most often in bold copy (i.e. in identical words). Moreover, it is

---

9 Thomas Scott, *The Belgicke Souldier. Dedicated to the Parliemant*, Dort (London) 1624, p. 3. For an overview on the growing public interest in news: V. Bauer / H. Böning (eds.), *Die Entstehung des Zeitungswesens im 17. Jahrhundert. Ein neues Medium und seine Folgen für das Kommunikationssystem der Frühen Neuzeit*, Bremen 2011; A. Pettegree, *The Invention of News. How the World Came to Know about Itself*, New Haven CT 2014. For the best summaries on the connections between public spheres and (news) communication: A. Gestrich, *The Public Sphere and the Habermas Debate*, in "German History", 24, 2006, 3, pp. 413–430; M. Rospocher, *Beyond the Public Sphere. A historiographical transition*, in M. Rospocher (ed.), *Beyond the Public Sphere. Opinions, Publics, Spaces in Early Modern Europe*, Bologna / Berlin 2012, pp. 9–28.
10 C. Zwierlein, *Discorso und Lex Dei. Die Entstehung neuer Denkrahmen im 16. Jahrhundert und die Wahrnehmung der französischen Religionskriege in Italien und Deutschland*, Göttingen 2006, p. 252 ("Berichthorizont").
11 For the growing studies on the postal services of early modern Europe, J. Raymond / N. Moxham (eds.), *News Networks*. The best analysis for the connection between news distribution and postal services are still W. Behringer, *Im Zeichen des Merkur. Reichspost und Kommunikationsrevolution in der Frühen Neuzeit*, Göttingen 2003, and P. Arblaster, *From Ghent to Aix*. The differentiation between "fresh" news making headlines for the first time, and ongoing media coverage pertaining to certain topics – including wars, sieges, political tensions – is important. On long-term flows of information about particular topics, J.W. Koopmans, *The Early 1730s Shipworm Disaster in Dutch News Media*, in "Dutch Crossing. Journal of Low Countries Studies", 40, 2016, 2, pp. 139–150, and J.W. Koopmans, *The 1755 Lisbon Earthquake and Tsunami in Dutch News Sources: The Functioning of Early Modern News Dissemination*, in S.F. Davies / P. Fletcher (eds.), *News in Early Modern Europe: Currents and Connections*, Leiden / Boston MA 2014, pp. 19–40.

worth remembering that even foreign-speaking news media were usually on offer in all major European news hotspots. Dutch, German, French, and English-speaking news media not only appeared in translation but were also regularly offered and read in the original language as well. For example, in seventeenth century Hamburg, when entering the news stall of publisher-news agent-bookseller Thomas von Wiering, one could purchase both German-speaking news and Dutch-speaking news[12].

The business culture of sixteenth century (and later) European handwritten newsletters was mainly rooted in recycling, as the available research on this topic stresses[13]. These forms of news media were (partly multilingual) handwritten bulletins of compiled news reports which were divided into paragraphs and partly organized under headlines always consisting of a city plus a date. The bulletins were compiled by (semi)professional scribes and ranged from two to eight pages. As these scribes sold their media goods – textual passages, compiled and translated, if needed – often to colleagues including media collectors and scribes in other cities, the same, i.e. identical or incredibly similar, news packages circulated within the transregional communication networks of early modern journalism[14]. One basic pattern of early modern handwritten news transmission is that it is based on a practice of both writing down heard and seen event stories (first-hand accounts), and of re-using textual passages from other newsletters and available media on the same topic. As the printed newspaper developed out of this handwritten tradition of news-communication, the same practice of compilation – and of producing echoes – is to be found. In the seventeenth and eighteenth centuries, the newspapers of Europe, either weekly, bi-weekly or later in almost daily formats, were all characterized by a high percentage of identical or paraphrased news flows[15]. Although this feature is international[16], it appears more obviously within newspapers of certain language-communities, when for example new relevant printed news arrived via postal connections to the main centers of publishing, including Hamburg, London, and Amsterdam, and

---

12 W. Kayser, *Thomas von Wiering und Erben. Ein bedeutendes Kapitel hamburgischer Druckgeschichte*, in "Auskunft. Mitteilungsblatt Hamburger Bibliotheken", 10, 1990, 4, pp. 343–371.
13 Although a true pan-European perspective is yet missing, see the studies on Italy, Germany, and the Low Countries: M. Infelise, *Prima dei giornali. Alle origini della pubblica informazione*, Roma / Bari 2002; O. Bauer, *Zeitungen vor der Zeitung. Die Fuggerzeitungen (1568–1605) und das frühmoderne Nachrichtensystem*, Berlin 2011; C. Zwierlein, *Discorso und Lex Dei*; N. Lamal, *News from Antwerp. Italian Communication on the Dutch Revolt* (forthcoming); H. Droste / K. Salmi-Niklander (eds.), *Handwritten Newspapers as an Alternative Medium during Early Modern and Modern Times* (forthcoming).
14 C. Espejo, *European Communication Networks in the Early Modern Age: A New Framework of Interpretation for the Birth of Journalism*, in "Media History", 17, 2011, 2, pp. 189–202; for the German-Italian CASE, C. Zwierlein, *Discorso und Lex Dei* and P. Molino, *Connected News. Geman Zeitungen and Italian avvisi in the Fugger collection (1568–1604)*, in "Media History", 22, 2016, pp. 267–295.
15 Among others: M. Brétéché, *Les compagnons de Mercure. Journalisme et politique dans l'Europe de Louis XIV*, Champ Vallon 2015, pp. 152–196.
16 S. Schultheiss-Heinz, *Politik in der europäischen Publizistik*.

was published in one of the larger, widely circulating newspapers. Then, the usual feedback process among the rest of the newspapers of that same language community was activated. For example, in German-speaking Europe, a report placed in the influential Hamburg newspapers "Stats= u. Gelehrte Zeitung Des Hollsteinischen unpartheyischen CORRESPONDENTEN" or "Hamburger RELATIONS COURIER" usually made its way through the German news system – in identical or nearly-identical wording, phrases, and copied reports[17]. Due to having the same content-transmitting news networks and the same postal and carrier services which transported the observed news reports, seventeenth century media coverage appeared quite often in nearly identical terms and passages[18]. In other words, the newspapers were also, to a great extent, full of slightly varied feedback echoes which relied on a journalistic practice of recycling, access to information and sources, and the time-pressure created by the speedy rhythms of print news deadlines. The journalistic practice of systematically selecting and recycling useable sources (from other news media and the like) depended on access to the "raw material" – news or story-worthy content for new serial or periodical publications[19]. However, this access to relevant contents was mainly rooted in costly investments in newsletter correspondence (i.e. economic information networks) and in the time investments required to analyze other (mainly) printed sources, like history books or journals[20]. Building on the European research into early modern newspapers and their implicit discourse on continuous content use, Peter Brachwitz and Sonja Schulheiß-Heinz highlight such "follow-up stories"

---

17 For examples of such news flows: D. Bellingradt, *Flugpublizistik und Öffentlichkeit*, p. 339; J. Arndt, *Herrschaftskontrolle*.
18 G. Fritz / E. Strassner, *Die Sprache der ersten deutschen Wochenzeitungen*; J. Raymond / N. Moxham (eds.), *News Networks*.
19 The term "raw material" is used by R. Arblaster, *From Ghent to Aix*, p. 259. For serials like almanacs or calendars: K.-D. Herbst (ed.), *Astronomie, Literatur, Volksaufklärung. Der Schreibkalender der Frühen Neuzeit mit seinen Text- und Bildbeigaben*, Bremen 2012 (including my own, *Der wiederverwertbare Räuberhauptmann. Oder: Wie kam der Räuber in den Kalender der Frühen Neuzeit?*, pp. 413–430).
20 As an example of the most common practice of early modern journalist-publishers to derive inspiration and compile from other printed sources, see the case of Eberhard Werner Happel in late seventeenth century Hamburg. As a writer, journalist, and publisher of a journal ("Relationes Curiosae"), Happel was always looking for relevant sources, and in doing so, he made extant use of other German speaking journals and systematically filed foreign language (history) books that he had access to in the Hamburger Stadtbibliothek. In his preface of the *Relationes Curiosae* (1683) he openly announced his compiling practice from other European books "Viele Lesens- und Wissens-begierige Gemüther haben mir zu offtern angelegen/ [...] worurch eine so-genannte Curieuse Relation außzugeben/ umb dadurch manchen ehrlichen Teutschen/ deme in Ermangelung der Lateinischen und anderer fremb-bden Sprachen/ die Begierden dergleichen curieuse Materien zu lesen/ gewaltig anwächst/ einiger massen zu vergnügen" (Eberhard Werner Happel, *Größte Denkwürdigkeiten der Welt oder so genannte Relationes Curiosae*, Hamburg, Wiering, 1683, vol. 1, Preface). For more information on Happel's compiling, F. Schock, *Die Text-Kunstkammer. Populäre Wissenssammlungen des Barock am Beispiel der 'Relationes Curiosae' von E.W. Happel*, Köln 2013, pp. 44–45.

explicitly as "feedback loops" (*Feedbackschleifen*)[21]. As already discussed, Johannes Arndt describes this entire recycling dynamism as a feedback-loop producing media system of serial and periodical publications. In other words, the typical observations and re-use of other periodical news content in particular made early modern printed periodical newspapers echo-producing and feedback-loop-establishing media. A future entangled history of early modern media should highlight and address these transregional news flows more carefully.

3 Narrating media events: Echoes, loops, and feedback moments

As the entirety of media coverage regarding certain events can be described as flows of echoes, it is worth mentioning that these coverage processes were not only a business of periodicals. With regard to "printed" follow-up communications on particular events, the typical flows of these – scripted – media coverage were produced and recycled in various ways, and usually fitted into new, non-periodical, streams of printed publication as well. Media events were the result of many on-going multimedia reactions to an observed event or flow of communication[22]. Pamphlets and broadsides also carried follow-up communications – printed echoes that could and did produce feedback loops. These occasional printed information flows were often, but not always, interwoven with the periodical echoes[23]. When it comes to the media cov-

---

[21] S. Schultheiss-Heinz, *Politik in der europäischen Publizistik. Eine historische Inhaltsangabe von Zeitungen des 17. Jahrhunderts*, Stuttgart 2004; P. Brachwitz, *Die Autorität des Sichtbaren. Religionsgravamina im Reich des 18. Jahrhunderts*, Berlin 2011. Brachwitz's perspective is limited to journal reports. Brachwitz is building on the research on "Folgeberichterstattung", as coined by G. Fritz / E. Strassner (eds.), *Die Sprache der ersten deutschen Wochenzeitungen im 17. Jahrhundert*, Berlin / Boston MA 2010, esp. pp. 220–228.

[22] On the inaugural theories of (early-modern) media events, A. Nünning, *Making Events – Making Stories – Making Worlds: Ways of Worldmaking from a Narratological Point of View*, in V. Nünning / A. Nünning / B. Neumann (eds.), *Cultural Ways of Worldmaking. Media and Narratives*, Berlin / New York 2010, pp. 191–214; F. Bösch, *Ereignisse, Performanz und Medien in historischer Perspektive*, in F. Bösch / P. Schmidt (eds.), *Medialisierte Ereignisse. Performanz, Inszenierung und Medien seit dem 18. Jahrhundert*, Frankfurt a.M. 2010, pp. 7–29; N. Couldry / A. Hepp, *Introduction*, in N. Couldry et al. (eds.), *Media Events in a Global Age*, New York 2009, pp. 1–20. An example of the growing research pertaining to these concepts of "media events" in the early modern period is T. Weissbrich, *Höchstädt 1704. Eine Schlacht als Medienereignis. Kriegsberichterstattung und Gelegenheitsdichtung im Spanischen Erbfolgekrieg*, Paderborn 2015.

[23] See, for example, the case of early modern Hamburg around 1700. Here, local conflicts regarding the power-sharing arrangement of the city led to a pamphlets-only print coverage. After six years and a minimum of 259 different first-edition pamphlets, with an overall print run of an estimated 200,000 copies, consisting of on average a new pamphlet published nearly every week for six years before

erage of certain events, pamphlet-echoes had their own special dynamic. However, it is characteristic for the occasional print publications of a certain media coverage that such printed goods were produced out of two main, sometimes intertwined, motivations. First, in times of contested ideas, the ping-pong-dynamic of pamphlet-publishing occurred[24]. And, as each (printed) voice sought to maintain its own position and gain the upper hand in this ping-pong match, such a battle would usually result in a stream of new (printed) echoes. Secondly, the relevant publishing processes were moments of commercially driven media recycling that mainly helped create an early modern media event.

As an example of a media event that generated transregional flows of communication – and many thousand printed echoes that each stimulated further multimedia follow-up flows and moments of reception – I have chosen the media coverage that followed a murder case around the year 1700. Following the murder of a popular and high-ranking Lutheran cleric in May 1726 in the residential city of the Electorate of Saxony, Dresden, a process of intense media recycling was triggered. In fact, the publishing of the Dresden murder case in non-periodical publications, mainly pamphlets and broadsides, occurred in (translated) streams of recycled feedback and echoes amidst a larger European context[25]. Within weeks following the murder, an estimated 90,000 copies of about 70 Germanophone pamphlets – in first edition, with a total print run of roughly 90,000 copies (if calculated with an average edition of 1000 to 1500 copies each) – were available in (German) book markets. As referred to, these pamphlets were the material results of commercially-driven media recycling moments which helped create the news or media event. In order to best understand the German pamphlets, they ought to be viewed in the context of an entangled European history. In fact, the media coverage and (occasional) printed echoes of the 1726 Dresden murder case were thematically embedded into the media stream surrounding the broader issue of religious conflict between Protestants and Catholics in Europe. To be more precise, the printed echoes of the media event in Dresden were directly connected to the religious turmoil – and its European media coverage – which occurred two years earlier – in 1724 – between Protestants and Catholics in the Polish and Royal Prussian city of Thorn (Toruń). In short, amidst the aftermath of the religious turmoil between local (German) Protestants and (Polish) Catholics in Thorn several German Lutherans were sentenced to death and executed by decision of the Polish Supreme Court and with the approval of the King of Poland. And because the King of Poland

---

periodicals began to publish on the topic; D. Bellingradt, *The Early Modern City* and D. Bellingradt, *Periodische Zeitung und akzidentielle Flugpublizistik. Zu den intertextuellen, interdependenten und intermedialen Momenten des frühneuzeitlichen Medienverbundes*, in V. Bauer / H. Böning (eds.), *Die Entstehung des Zeitungswesens*, pp. 57–78.
24 D. Bellingradt, *The Early Modern City*, p. 234.
25 D. Bellingradt, *The Publishing of a Murder Case in Early Modern Germany: The Limits of Censorship in the Electorate of Saxony (1726)*, in "Quaerendo", 45, 2015, 1–2, pp. 62–107.

was also the Elector of Saxony – and in this position head of a Lutheran territory and titular leader of the *Corpus Evangelicorum* (the permanent Protestant league in the Holy Roman Empire of the German Nation) – the outcry in the Protestant territories of Europe was deafening[26]. The protest was, in part, publicly orchestrated by officials and was published verbatim in large print runs: the European-wide media coverage consisted of an endless stream of German, English, French, and Dutch pamphlets, newspaper reports, and journal articles[27]. In his recent PhD dissertation on the media coverage of the Thorn events, the embedded media campaigns, and the impact of the hundreds of translated and multilingual publications on the topic, Samuel Feinauer states that "[t]his tumult in 1724 turned from a local event into a subject that was able to dominate European press and politics at the same time"[28]. The outcry regarding the local conflict proliferated in the European echo chamber of media coverage on the topic. German-language pamphlets on the topic comprise at least 245 different publications in first edition alone (with a total print run of roughly 245,000–356,000 copies)[29] which appeared in German-speaking Europe within two years of the events at Thorn[30].

The European media coverage surrounding Thorn would not only be embedded in all publications about the Dresden murder case, but would also act as background noise, thematic reference, a horizon of shared experience, and function as the textual template for a "fresh" flood of pamphlet echoes on the broader issue of religious conflict between Lutherans and Catholics. The leitmotif of a concrete Catholic-Lutheran struggle during the 1720s was a primary dynamic for more and more follow up communications – on Thorn, Dresden, and so on. The explicit reference to the sorrowful city of Thorn (*betrübtes Thorn*) was worth good money – and so was often used. For example, German pamphlets of 1726 tried offensively to explicitly connect

---

26 M. Thomsen, *Das Betrübte Thorn. Daniel Ernst Jablonski und der Thorner Tumult von 1724*, in J. Bahlcke / W. Korthaase (eds.), *Daniel Ernst Jablonski (1660–1741). Religion, Wissenschaft und Politik um 1700*, Wiesbaden 2008, pp. 1–24; A.C. Thompson, *Britain, Hanover and the Protestant Interest, 1688–1756*, Woodbridge 2006, pp. 97–132.
27 S. Feinauer, *"Tragoedia Thoruniensis". Ein europäisches Medienereignis des frühen 18. Jahrhunderts und sein Widerhall in Diplomatie und Publizistik*, Dissertation, OPUS / Online Publikationen der Universität Stuttgart, 2017. On the European media coverage of what Thompson termed "an officially orchestrated publicity campaign" (A.C. Thompson, *Britain*, p. 101): D. Bellingradt, *Flugpublizistik und Öffentlichkeit*, pp. 307–368.
28 S. Feinauer, *"Tragoedia Thoruniensis"*, p. 10.
29 Calculated with an average edition of 1000–1500 copies each.
30 A full list of 245 titles is listed in D. Bellingradt, *Flugpublizistik und Öffentlichkeit*, pp. 462–481. These many German echoes can partly be explained by the general political importance of Catholic and Protestant tensions in the 1720s. The extensive and contemporary so-called *Religionsgravamina* between Protestants and Catholics of the Holy Roman Empire produced a high level of media coverage regarding these struggles of faith, power, and money, and were deeply interconnected with politics; P. Brachwitz, *Die Autorität des Sichtbaren*.

Thorn with Dresden[31]. More and more of these chiefly anonymous and pseudonymous editions connected the concrete events in Dresden to the Thorn occurrence, because both topics were bought and read by Lutheran audiences. In fact, newspapers from Hamburg placed advertisements for publications about Thorn alongside the coverage on the progress of the Dresden events[32]. As to content, the connecting of Thorn and Dresden in terms of battling religions occasionally led to drastic claims for Lutheran revenge. For example, one anonymous voice proclaimed that the dead and precious cleric Hahn had become a martyr, and that his death would surely soon cause crying and tears in Rome, because the blood shed by both the righteous pastor and in Thorn will call out for revenge[33]. As a feature of this radicalization of content we see an intense media recycling of mainly older printed texts on either the events of Thorn in 1725 or Dresden in 1726. In combining the re-usage of larger identical passages of older texts with the copy of both small text units of one to three sentences and single words, most of these small, cheap prints provide more or less identical echoes of the events and their interpretation[34].

As a result of this commercially driven media recycling most of these new publications were patchwork products – often hastily arranged compilations of other (partly translated) texts including their terms, interpretation, and details. Only a few publications exploited new sources in the process of arranging new content, and only in one case a manuscript (and not a print) was used[35]. The bestselling modulation of the well-known term, "sorrowful Thorn" into "sorrowful Dresden" connected the two events ideologically and functioned as an umbrella term for a general Catholic threat to Protestants. The printing and publishing industries used the terms to encourage sales, aiming for a broader audience. Other pamphlets fueled this interpretive

---

31 Valentin Ernst Löscher, *Das Wohl=redende Blut eines unschuldig=getödteten Abels*, 1726. Full details of this and all pamphlets listed in the following footnotes in D. Bellingradt, *The Publishing of a Murder Case*, pp. 96–107.

32 See, for example, "Hamburger RELATIONS COURIER", June 3, 1726, unnumb., and "Stats= u. Gelehrte Zeitung Des Hollsteinischen unpartheyischen CORRESPONDENTEN", July 17, 1726, unnumb.

33 [Avtoptus Geamoenus], *Ausführliche und wahrhaffte RELATION Von dem Den 21. Maji dieses 1726. Jahres*, 1726, p. 20.

34 All pamphlets were published anonymously in 1726: *Kurtze Doch umständliche Nachricht von der wohlverdienten EXECUTION*; *Beschreibung von demjenigen Tumult, so sich wegen Ermordung eines Lutherischen Predigers in den Königl. Residentz-Stadt Dreßden*; *Gründliche und wahrhafftige Nachricht von der Execution des Priester=Mörders*; *Gründliche und ausführliche Nachricht Von Der wohl verdienten Execution*; *Gründliche Nachricht von dem entsetzlichen Meuchel-Mord, welchen ein Königl. Reitender Trabant zu Drezßden an den dortigen Evangelischen Prediger Herrn Magn. Hahn verübet*; *Gewisse und zuverläßige Nachricht / Von dem Erschrecklichen und grausamen Priester=Mord*; *Gantz erbarmens=würdige und glaubhaffte Nachricht/ Von dem erschrecklichen und grausamen Priester=Mord*; *Nachricht von dem Verlauff Des an dem bewusten Priester=Mörders in Dreßden Vollstreckten Todt=Urtheils*; *Kurtze, jedoch gründliche Nachricht von dem zu Dreßden entstandenen Tumult*.

35 *Sichere und gewisse Nachrichten Von dem Seeligen Märtyrer=Tode HERRN M. Herm. Joachim Hahns*, 1726.

path by using the same phrases and themes over and over again. For example, the Lutheran cleric Heinrich Cornelius Hecker from the small Saxon city of Meuselwitz published a pseudonymous pamphlet at that time, in which the events of Dresden were interpreted as the logical consequence of the Thorn "bloodbath"[36]. In his eyes, Thorn's River Weichsel was in 1726 still colored red by pious (Lutheran) blood ("Der Weichsel=Strohm ist annoch roth Von der erwürgten Frommen Blute"), and the Catholic obsession to kill (*Mord=Sucht*) was now aiming to color Dresden's River Elbe red as well.

In short, all Dresden echoes occurred in both relation to and connection with the general (printed) discourse, or in other words, they reacted to other echoes in a European setting. Translated loops of arguments, references, and details produced an entangled echo-process that cannot be understood and analyzed from only one national perspective. As translations are adapted forms fitted to different political, religious, legal, and language environments, the to-be-observed echoed translation patterns open a fruitful perspective on the moments of designing messages to new readerships[37]. Such culturally sensitive adaptations of words and texts to new cultural climates (in order to have impact or to be more saleable within the addressed communities), can be described as a practice of "cultural translating"[38]. By highlighting the feedback moments and loops of echoed early modern media events, we will better understand this type of "cross-border interaction" as an entangled process of communication[39]. In order to trace and analyze the flow of ideas, words, and concepts across time and space, the historical view may profit immensely from the rich (printed) media footprints of early modern media events. Therefore, a future entangled history of early modern media should highlight the interconnectedness of European media coverage.

---

36 [Bellamintes], *Das Uber den blutigen Tod, Seines von einem Papisten ermordeten Lehrers*, 1726.
37 On the growing field of studies on early modern translations: K. Newman / J. Tylus (eds.), *Early Modern Cultures of Translation*, Philadelphia PA 2015; J.M. Fernandez / E. Lee-Wilson (eds.), *Translation and the Book Trade in Early Modern Europe*, Cambridge 2015.
38 P. Burke, *Cultures of Translation in Early Modern Europe*, in P. Burke / R. Po-chia Hsia (eds.), *Cultural Translation in Early Modern Europe*, Cambridge 2007, pp. 7–38, p. 7.
39 With regard to Enlightenment history and its needed re-evaluation of translated impact moments on the special European knowledge culture: S. Conrad, *Enlightenment in Global History*, in "American Historical Review", 2012, esp. p. 1001.

4 Images as echoes in the communication process

The visual is an integral part of communication history – of the (early) modern period[40]. Printed images, or "printed pictures" as contemporaries of the seventeenth century put it[41], were on the one hand an often copied good in early modern print industries. An image that sold well often became the inspiration for a stream of thematically varied adaptations of the original. These streams of follow-up images may be called "inspirational echoes". In his influential *Graphic History*, Philip Benedict referred to the intellectual recycling of previously printed images into new printed images around 1600 in Europe as an economic-driven production of inspired echoes in relation to each other[42]. When, for example, a painter's workshop produced many "originals" of a certain painting, these copies and replicas were regarded as typical products of an artistic routine. Like in the case of Rubens' workshop which regularly produced countless versions of the famous artist's originals (executed by different hands), contemporaries understood the many retailed echoes as "original copies" of an image[43]. Within the field of art history, recently the question of originality in early modern painted and printed images has been cast in a new light. By highlighting both the potential and actual exchanges between printed artworks and other media, the patterns of these exchanges are described as a communicative dynamic. The image, whether painted, hand-drawn, or printed, is mainly understood as an active agent, setting off "chain reactions" within other media[44]. I call these printed chain reactions "inspirational echoes". Paintings, woodcuts, and copperplate prints were both inspirational graphic goods and study material for early modern artists creating new painted, hand-drawn, or printed echoes[45].

---

40 H. Pierce, *Unseemly Pictures. Graphic Satire and Politics in Early Modern England*, New Haven CT 2008; W. Brückner, *Populäre Druckgraphik Europas. Deutschland vom 15. bis zum 20. Jahrhundert*, München 1975; M. Jones, *The Print in Early Modern England*; M. Hunter (ed.), *Printed Images in Early Modern Britain: Essays in Interpretation*, Farnham 2010; S. O'Connell, *The Popular Print in England. 1550–1850*, London 1999.
41 In the seventeenth century, we find the expression of a "printing press for pictures" (meaning a copper plate): Geo. Thornley, Gent., *Daphnis and Chloe. A Most Sweet, and Pleasant Pastoral Romance for Young Ladies*, London, John Garfield, 1657; D.J. Davis, *Seeing Faith, Printing Pictures. Religious Identity during the English Reformation*, Leiden 2013.
42 P. Benedict, *Graphic History. The Wars, Massacres and Troubles of Tortorel and Perrissin*, Genève 2007. Here, both text and images of the original publication were recycled and set off inspired textual and pictorial echoes. Benedict's sixth chapter is entitled "Echoes" (pp. 171–207).
43 N. Büttner, *The Hands of Rubens. On Copies and Their Reception*, in T. Nakamura (ed.), *Appreciating the Traces of an Artist's Hand*, Kyoto 2017, pp. 41–54, here p. 50.
44 S. Karr Schmidt / E.H. Wouk (eds.), *Prints in Translation, 1450–1750. Image, Materiality, Space*, London / New York 2017; especially the chapter by E.H. Wouk ("Toward an anthropology of print", pp. 1–18).
45 See the many cases listed in G. Knaus, *invenit, incensit, imitavit. Die Kupferstiche von Marcantonio Raimondi als Schlüssel zur weltweiten Raffael-Rezeption 1510–1700*, Berlin 2016, pp. 63–86.

With regard to seventeenth century single-leaf broadsides, John Roger Paas speaks of a typical European image production dynamic that resulted from practices of copying and adapting existing printed images (selling well or thematically fitting)[46]. This inspired adapting of ideas from extant images was a typical recycling practice and could be delayed by months, years, or decades after the initial "original" had been created or published[47]. An example which illustrates this dynamic of inspirational echo producing occurred in 1664 when a deformed Tartar was depicted on many European broadsides. See Figures 1 and 2[48]. This image appeared as a reflection of contemporary media reactions to the ongoing military tensions between Christian European states and the Muslim Ottoman Empire[49]. At this time, circa 1663 and 1664, the general conflict heated up and the media attention and coverage of the conflicting parties – the Habsburg Monarchy and the Ottoman Empire – and their military campaigns became more intense[50]. Fighting as allies of the Muslim Ottoman Empire, the Tartars of Northeast Asia were received as part of an urgent threat to Christian Europe. Depicting them as "monstrous" tartars – with long deformed necks – built on the one side upon resurgent rumors circulating in early seventeenth century Europe. According to these stories, Tartars often had physical deformities; a rumor that partly had its origin in the Greek word for a region of the hellish underworld (*tartarus*)[51].

---

46 J.R. Paas, *Die Verbreitung wundersamer Neuigkeiten in der Frühen Neuzeit: Flugblätter über den sonderbaren tartarischen Bogenschützen von 1664*, in C. Caemmerer et al. (eds.), *Flugblätter von der frühen Neuzeit bis zur Gegenwart als kulturhistorische Quellen und bibliothekarische Sondermaterialien*, Frankfurt a.M. 2010, pp. 1–24, here p. 11. On the typical inspired creation of new copperplate prints in the early modern period by studying other graphics available: G. Knaus, *invenit, incensit, imitavit*, pp. 105–122; E.H. Wouk / D. Morris (eds.), *Marcantonio Raimondi, Raphael and the Image Multiplied*, Manchester 2016.
47 See the many both quick and delayed (sometimes by as much as 20 years) "recycling" moments of the 1570 publication *Quarante Tableaux* by Jean Perrissin and Jacques Tortorel in small prints, single-sheet-publications, historical books, calendars documented in P. Benedict, *Graphic History*.
48 More references to European versions of this deformed Tartar in J.R. Paas, *Die Verbreitung*. A few European manuscript and print versions are documented in J.R. Paas, *The German Political Broadsheet 1600–1700*, 13 vols., Wiesbaden, Harrassowitz, 2007, vol. 9: *1662–1670*, pp. 434–441. For example, the Dutch and French broadside "Desen Tarter is gevangen van de Graef Serin in february 1664. Ce Tartare fut faict prisonnier par le Comte Serin en fevrier 1664" (Herzog August Bibliothek Wolfenbüttel, A: 260.13.5 Quod.).
49 J.R. Paas, *Die Verbreitung*.
50 K.P. Matschke, *Das Kreuz und der Halbmond. Die Geschichte der Türkenkriege*, Düsseldorf 2004; A. Wheatcroft, *The Enemy at the Gate: Habsburg, Ottomans and the Battle for Europe*, New York 2008.
51 For example, on the rumour regarding the 1636 statement by Donald Lupton ("The Tartarians are [the] most deformed of all men"), see the citation from M. Thornton Burnett, *Constructing "Monsters" in Shakespearean Drama and Early Modern Culture*, Basingstoke 2002, p. 43; and the conclusion regarding the construction of monstrousness by S. Davies, *The Unlucky, the Bad and the Ugly: Categories of Monstrosity from the Renaissance to the Enlightenment*, in A. Simon Mittman / P.J. Dendle (eds.), *The Ashgate Research Companion to Monsters and the Monstrous*, London / New York 2013, pp. 49–75.

Fig. 1: *Dis ist der Tarter den der Herr Grav Nicolaus von Serin gefangen bekomen Anno 1664* (This is the Tartar captured by Count Nicolaus von Serin in 1664), copperplate print, 1664, Nürnberg, Erlangen Universitätsbibliothek, H61/EINBLATTDRUCK.A-VIIII 14.

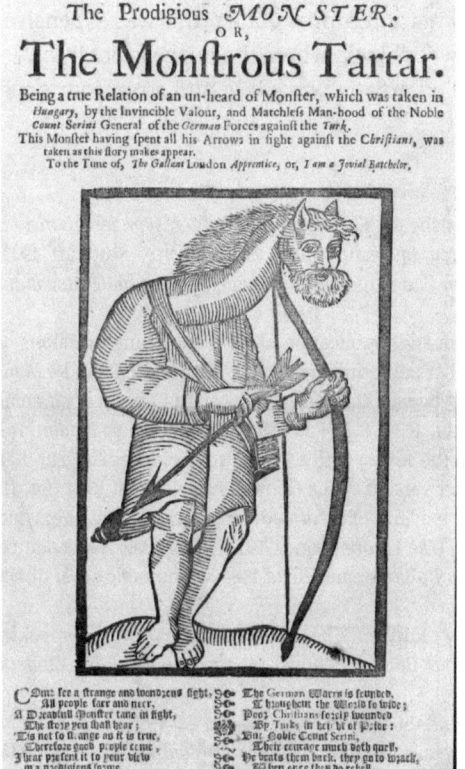

Fig. 2: *The Prodigious Monster. Or, The Monstrous Tartar*, copperplate print, 1664, s.l. London, British Museum, 1873,0712.923.

As demonized enemies, "The Monstrous Tartar", as an English broadside of 1664 phrased it (fig. 2), was part of the long-term cultural-religious communication process between Christians and Muslims, as well as the short-term military conflict of 1663/64, and contemporary media coverage of relevant news events that followed in response to assumed news-buyer demand by economic-driven publishers. On the other side, the depiction of an encountered Christian threat as a news-worthy (and good-selling) "monster" built on available images of deformed humans that were the direct source of inspiration[52]. In this case, likely the immediate sources of inspiration were published at the latest in 1660 (fig. 3) and in 1642 (fig. 4)[53]. Following Peter Burke, the cultural practice of depicting/imagining the "otherness" of the enemy led to deforming the other into beasts or monsters[54]. However, in 1664, these moments of depicting/imagining by woodcut and copperplate artists were inspired by the direct sources available within the contemporary book culture and markets.

In addition to the previously mentioned inspirational echoes of images that we find increasingly from the fifteenth century onwards, identical echoes produced using the original copperplate or woodblock also existed. Across early modern Europe, printed images, and the woodblocks and copperplates used to produce them, were being re-used, re-sold, and traded via the book trade channels. The main reason for these specialist trades of cut woodblocks and etched copperplates were the high costs of production. Producing ambitious woodcuts and copper plate prints was expensive, often too much so for most publishers. A woodblock, where the image is cut into vertically cut boards, was the result of a skilled artistic procedure and a precious good within the developing printing industries[55].

---

[52] On the lucrativity of deformed news on broadsheets, E. Holländer, *Wunder, Wundergeburt und Wundergestalt in Einblattdrucken des fünfzehnten bis achtzehnten Jahrhunderts*, Stuttgart 1921; I. Ewinkel, *De monstris. Deutung und Funktion von Wundergeburten auf Flugblättern im Deutschland des 16. Jahrhunderts*, Tübingen 1995.

[53] See, for example, next to the mentioned Aldrovandi publication of 1642, the printed versions of "monstrous" humans that stood in relation to earlier hand-drawn images by Ambroise Paré, *De Monstres et prodiges*, Paris, Gallimard, 1573; Fortunius Licetus, *De monstrorum caussis, natura et differentiis libri duo*, Patavium, Apud Paulum Frambottum, 1634. R.A. Paas, *Die Verbreitung*, p. 9 mentions at least one or two more French broadsides (from the 1650s) with a "monstre" from Madagascar that has a deformed long neck and looks like an earlier version of the German broadside of 1664 (fig. 1). Note, that older printed and hand-drawn template versions of deformed, long necked humans existed long before the seventeenth century. As R.A. Paas (*Die Verbreitung*, p. 10) suggests, the direct source for Aldrovandi's long necked human was likely an Italian broadside of 1585. On possible other direct sources, E. Holländer, *Wunder*, pp. 290–295.

[54] P. Burke, *Frontiers of the Monstrous. Perceiving National Characters in Early Modern Europe*, in L. Lunger Knoppers / J.B. Landes (eds.), *Monstrous Bodies. Political Monstrosities in Early Modern Europe*, Ithaca NY 2004, pp. 25–39.

[55] D. Landau / P. Parshall, *The Renaissance Print: 1470–1550*, New Haven CT 1994; P. Parshall / R. Schoch / D.S. Areford (eds.), *Origins of European Printmaking: Fifteenth-Century Woodcuts and Their Public*, New Haven CT 2005.

Fig. 3: *Abbildung einer sehr frembden Miß-gebuhrt / so neulicher Zeit auff der Insul Madagascar gefunden ...* (Depiction of a very strange freak, as recently found on the Island of Madagascar), copperlate print, c. 1660, s.l. Nürnberg, Germanisches Nationalmuseum, HB 15023/1283b.

Fig. 4: Ulisse Aldrovandi, *Monstrovum historia*, Benonia 1642, p. 14, Erlangen, Universitätsbibliothek, H00/2 ZOOL 55.

In fact, copperplate production was among the most expensive artistic and business practices of early modern print production, as copper was among the most expensive of commonly traded commodities[56]. The routine of buying and selling cut woodblocks and engraved copperplates lies at the heart of understanding the international pictorial flows and "image echoes" that we find within early modern book culture. In this light, the circulation of popular printed images is only partly a story of artistic innovation and cultural taste, it is mainly a history of business related re-usage.

The lucrative business of producing and selling woodblock prints is evidenced by the hundreds of thousands of printed copies with images sold during the fifteenth century[57]. As most woodblocks could be used to produce up to 25,000 prints[58], the blocks were not only re-used within the same printing office, i.e. in other publication projects of the owner or publisher running the printing shop, but were often re-sold and even rented within the marketplace[59]. For example, a woodcut heading popular broadsides in the sixteenth century could easily make appearances in different regions of Europe at various times. For the given community and moment of communication, these images were "new images" in the observed – often language bound – media ensemble[60].

Although research on the buying, selling and lending of copperplates and woodblocks between the fifteenth and eighteenth centuries lacks consistent data, it seems plausible to suggest that the more printed images were published during the seventeenth and eighteenth centuries (especially in broadsheet formats, small pamphlets, and booklets)[61], the more business trades of older woodblocks and copperplates took place. When the longevity of rarely or slightly varied images in print is taken into account, the traditional focus on the production of newly created woodblocks and copperplates is not sufficient. From the time of the Reformation until the end of the

---

56 See J. Farr, *Artisans in Europe, 1300–1914*, Cambridge 2000, pp. 56–60; A. Stijnman, *Engraving and Etching 1400–2000: A History of the Development of Manual Intaglio Printmaking Processes*, London 2012.
57 R.S. Field, *Early Woodcuts: The Known and Unknown*, in P. Parshall / R. Schoch / D.S. Areford (eds.), *Origins of European Printmaking*, p. 12.
58 C. Reske, *Der Holzschnitt bzw. Holzstock am Ende des 15. Jahrhunderts. Aspekte der Arbeitsteilung, Kosten und Auflagenhöhe*, in "Gutenberg Jahrbuch", 2009, pp. 71–78.
59 "Drucker liehen Holzschnitte aus oder verkauften sie an ihre Kollegen in andern Orten, wo sie dann als ‹neu› betrachtet werden konnten. Holzstöcke wanderten auf diese Weise durch ganz Europa"; I. Kok, *Die Datierung von Inkunabeln durch Holzschnitte*, in "Gutenberg Jahrbuch", 2006, pp. 62–70, here p. 62. Further: O. Dunze, *Ein Verleger sucht sein Publikum. Die Straßburger Offizin des Matthias Hupfuff (1497/98–1520)*, München 2007, p. 68.
60 For a perspective of "new images" in Europe around 1500, H. Belting, *Bild und Kult. Eine Geschichte des Bildes vor dem Zeitalter der Kunst*, 5th ed., München 2000, esp. p. 458.
61 On the European broadsides, see A. Pettegree, *Broadsheets. Single-Sheet Publishing in the First Age of Print*, Boston MA / Leiden 2017; W. Harms / M. Schilling, *Das illustrierte Flugblatt der frühen Neuzeit. Traditionen, Wirkungen, Kontexte*, Stuttgart 2008; M. Schilling / D. Bellingradt, *Flugpublizistik*, in T. Dembeck et al. (eds.), *Handbuch Medien der Literatur*, Berlin / Boston MA 2013, pp. 273–289.

seventeenth century, many quite "popular" images often show little to no variation in their printed appearances on either a regional or international level[62]. A "good-fitting" image seems to have been used over and over again[63]. For example, in Malcolm Jones' *The Print in Early Modern England* hundreds of identical and slightly varied woodcut and copperplate prints are mentioned that indicate the international circulation of original cut woodblocks and engraved copperplates between printing offices in England and the German/Dutch speaking regions of Europe[64]. Following Jones, some of these adaptations, copies, and variation flows followed certain time regimes: after an initial publication, these "popular" flows often occurred within a time frame of only a couple of weeks and months, but sometimes took a decade, or even a couple of decades, for an existing printed image to be published again elsewhere. That there seem to have been regular business transfers within Northern Europe that not only built on exchanging publishing ideas and adapting inspiration or strategies for future publications from already existing publications is perhaps the most important of the many conclusions in Jones' book. The same appears to be true for the trade of Northern European cut woodblocks and engraved copperplates, too[65].

As an example that illustrates the aspect of producing identical echoes of images by using original woodblocks or copperplates, I have chosen the case of Thomas von Wiering, a news-publisher and bookseller of late seventeenth century Hamburg. Wiering (1640–1703) was one of the most experienced local bookseller-printer-publishers of his day[66]. He was a professional media networker within a city of ongoing media flows. Wiering was also an eager compiler and re-user of older woodcuts. In fact, Wiering's hometown of Hamburg, at the time one of Europe's most important points of production, collection, and distribution of all sorts of written information, was full of echoes that he could use. In effectively combining well established economic, postal, and trade networks, Hamburg was considered by contemporaries to be the German Amsterdam, or *florentissimum Emporium totius Germaniae* (the most greatly flourish-

---

62 For the longevity of popular printed images within a national context, M. Hunter, *Printed Images*. International flows, between Germany, England, France are mentioned in M. Jones, *The Print in Early Modern England*.
63 On this typical re-usage in illustrated broadsheets, D. Bellingradt, *Das Flugblatt im Medienverbund der Frühen Neuzeit: Bildtragendes Mediengut und Recycling-Produkt*, in M. Eberle et al. (eds.), *Das illustrierte Flugblatt im 16. Jahrhundert* (forthcoming).
64 M. Jones, *The Print in Early Modern England*. See further the case study of a sixteenth broadside that was published in England and The Holy Roman Empire with an identical image: S. O'Connell / D. Paisey, *This Horryble Monster. An Anglo-German Broadside of 1531*, in "Print Quaterly", 16, 1999, pp. 57–63.
65 See the conclusion in M. Jones, *The Print in Early Modern England*, pp. 381–385 and the lists of English prints that had German or Netherlandish originals: appendices II and III (pp. 397–401).
66 On Wiering's publishing activity in Hamburg and his very successful newspaper "Relations Courier" (1675–1813): E. Bogel / E. Blühm, *Die deutschen Zeitungen des siebzehnten Jahrhunderts*, 3 vols., Bremen 1971, vol. 1, pp. 128 ff.

ing German city)[67]. Of its estimated 75,000 inhabitants in the late seventeenth century, about 15,000 were regular newspaper readers. Around 1700, the city had an extraordinarily productive publishing industry and was at the heart of both the European distribution of printed (periodical and non-periodical) news and the dissemination of these printed contents in oral, handwritten, and printed form[68]. For specialist like Wiering, the city was full of useful echoes that could be transformed into new printed publications. In 1683 Wiering was aware of the special historical setting and when the Ottomans, led by Sultan Mehmed IV, began besieging Vienna for the second time, he jumped at the chance to launch a new periodical on the topic. His "Türckischer Estaats= und Krieges=Bericht" was designed to focus mainly on the increasing conflict between the Ottomans and the Holy Roman Empire in South-Eastern Europe[69]. A specialized weekly newspaper on the topic seemed like a good investment as in 1680 the political and media attention of the Holy Roman Empire had already been focused for decades on the potential threat of the Ottoman Empire. Ever since the fall of Constantinople in 1453, and especially during the many minor and major conflicts between the Ottomans and the Holy Roman Empire in South-Eastern-Europe that followed, the media monitored the political, religious, and military conflict lines[70]. Grounded in a growing public interest on topics related to the threatening and fascinating "Turk" archetype that had developed over generations since the mid-fifteenth century[71], the demand for such news triggered the economic-driven news markets. Yet, the content of Wiering's periodical, especially the descriptions of Ottoman culture and the various political contexts of the conflict, were the products of intense recycling of other printed sources that had covered the Ottoman-Habsburg conflicts since the fifteenth

---

67 M. Lindemann, *Patriots and Paupers: Hamburg 1712–1830*, Oxford 1990, pp. 33–47.
68 On the printing world of early modern Hamburg, H. Böning, *Welteroberung durch ein neues Publikum. Die deutsche Presse und der Weg zur Aufklärung. Hamburg und Altona als Beispiel*, Bremen 2002; H. Böning, *Periodische Presse. Kommunikation und Aufklärung. Hamburg und Altona als Beispiel*, Bremen 2002; F. Schock, *Die Text-Kunstkammer*, pp. 34–46; on the pamphlet culture of the city D. Bellingradt, *The Early Modern City*.
69 The newspaper "Türckischer Estaats- und Kriegsbericht" appeared with a grand total of 137 issues between 1683 and 1684. See the complete facsimile edition of all issues by Hansebooks [Eberhard Werner Happel, *Türkischer Staats- und Kriegsbericht. Eine kurze und gründliche Beschreibung des türkischen Kaisers* (1683) Hamburg 2016].
70 T.M. Barker, *Double Eagle and Crescent. Vienna's Second Siege and Its Historical Setting*, Albany NY 1967; K.P. Matschke, *Der Kreuz und der Halbmond*; A. Wheatcroft, *The Enemy at the Gate*.
71 H.J. Kissling, *Türkenfurcht und Türkenhoffnung im 15. und 16. Jahrhundert: Zur Geschichte eines 'Komplexes'*, in "Südost-Forschungen", 23, 1964, pp. 1–18; Y. Topkaya, *Augen-Blicke sichtbarer Gewalt? Eine Geschichte des "Türken" in medientheoretischer Perspektive (1453–1529)*, Paderborn 2015; G. Melville, *Die Wahrheit des Eigenen und die Wirklichkeit des Fremden. Über frühe Augenzeugen des osmanischen Reiches*, in F.R. Erkens (ed.), *Europa und die osmanische Expansion im ausgehenden Mittelalter* (Zeitschrift für Historische Forschung. Beihefte, 20), Berlin 1997, pp. 79–101; K.D. Döring, *Türkenkrieg und Medienwandel im 15. Jahrhundert*, Husum 2013, pp. 145–153.

century[72]. In fact, the "Türckischer Estaats= und Krieges=Bericht" only became a best-selling periodical because of its many thematic images of the foreign threat – the Turk. These images however, came from printing blocks that Wiering purchased in Hamburg – and some of which were many decades old[73]. As new copperplate and woodcut prints of "Turks" and Ottoman culture could be very expensive to produce and would need time for preparation, Wiering managed to recycle older printed images in order to fill his new publications with suitable illustrations. In the seventh instalment of his periodical, which appeared in 1683, Wiering used an identical image (fig. 5) to one created by the painter and printmaker, Melchior Lorck, around the mid-late sixteenth century[74]. When in 1626, long after the artist's death[75], Lorck's "Turkish publication" (*Deß Weitberühmbten, Kunstreichen und Wolerfahrnen Herrn Melchior Lorichs, Flensburgensis. Wolgerissene vnd Geschnittene Figuren, zu Ross vnd Fuss, sampt schönen Türckischen Gebäwden, vnd allerhand was in der Türckey zusehen. Alles nach dem Leben vnd der perspectivae Jedermann vor Augen gestellet ...*)[76] – was first published in Hamburg by Michael Hering (1570–1633)[77], these woodblocks seem to have been on offer in the city. In 1646, the local publisher, Tobias Gundermann, used the original printing materials (woodblocks) for a second edition[78].

---

[72] W. Kayser, *Thomas von Wiering*, esp. pp. 349–350; J. Hillgärtner, *Die erste illustrierte deutsche Zeitung? Thomas von Wierings "Türkischer Estats- und Kriegsbericht"*, in S. Geise et al. (eds.), *Historische Perspektiven auf den Iconic Turn. Die Entwicklung der öffentlichen visuellen Kommunikation*, Köln 2016, pp. 96–114.

[73] W. Kayser, *Thomas von Wiering*; J. Hillgärtner, *Die erste illustrierte deutsche Zeitung*.

[74] E. Fischer et al. (eds.), *Melchior Lorck*, 5 vols., Copenhagen 2009, esp. vol. 1: *Biography and Primary Sources*. Lorck published a lot of "Turckophobia" titles and other thematic publications on the Ottoman conflict.

[75] E. Fischer, *Melchior Lorck*, vol. 1 [esp. "The Life and Works of Melchior Lorck" (pp. 63–138) and "Hamburg" (pp. 117–119)].

[76] Melchior Lorck, *Deß Weitberühmbten, Kunstreichen und Wolerfahrnen Herrn Melchior Lorichs, Flensburgensis. Wolgerissene vnd Geschnittene Figuren, zu Ross vnd Fuss, sampt schönen Türckischen Gebäwden, vnd allerhand was in der Türckey zusehen. Alles nach dem Leben vnd der perspectivae Jedermann vor Augen gestellet ...*, Hamburg 1626, VD17 23:295451Z.

[77] Melchior Lorck travelled to Istanbul in 1555–1559, made hand-drawings of the city and carved woodblocks from these drawings. Lorck died before his "Turkish Publication" was set to print; at the time of his death, only 20 of the woodcuts were ready. In 1626, when the entire publication was first printed by the Hamburg publisher Michael Hering, 128 woodblocks had been produced from Lorck's hand-drawings. For more information on this, see E. Fischer, *Melchior Lorck*, vols. 2 and 3: *The Turkish Publication, 1626 Edition* and "catalogue raisonné".

[78] Melchior Lorck, *Deß Kunstreichen/ Weitberümbten und Wolerfahrnen Herrn/ Melchioris Lorichii Flensburgensis, Wolgerissenen und geschnittene Figuren/ zu Rosß und Fuß/ sampt schönen Türckischen Gebäwen/ und allerhand/ was in der Türckey zusehen : Alles nach dem Leben und der Perspectiva jederman vor Augen gestellet/ in Kupffer und Holtz Jetzo zum drittenmahl/ mit einem Register uber die Figuren/ auß dem Original Manuscripto ... an den Tag gegeben*, Hamburg 1646, VD17 23:250394H.

Fig. 5: *Türkischer Staats- und Kriegsbericht*, no. 7, 1683, p. 1v, Nürnberg, Germanisches Nationalmuseum, 2° G. 12791b, © Germanisches Nationalmuseum, Digitalisat: Laura Bock.

And before 1683, Wiering seemed to have bought these original 128 woodblocks, likely from Gundermann, and used them again, although he was very attentive in erasing all details (including years of print and Lorck's name) from the woodblocks. Because Wiering owned the original 128 cut woodblocks, he used them all extensively, mainly in his own periodical and in publications that were produced in his printing office[79]. For example, a woodblock from Lorck that produced an image of an Ottoman man was fit into a story of the fifth number of Wiering's "Türckischer Estaats= und Krieges=Bericht" published in 1683 and appeared again in 1688, in a book by the enterprising journalist-author Eberhard Werner Happel, who published

---

[79] For example: in 1685, as Fischer in his prefatory remarks to Wiering's Turkish Publication refers to correctly, Wiering published a full compilation of every issue of the *Türckischer Estaats= und Krieges=Bericht* combined with a few more fitting sources on Turkish culture as "Der Türckische Schau-Platz. Eröffnet und furgestelt in sehr vielen nach dem Leben gezeichneten Figuren [...]", Hamburg 1685. See E. Fischer, *Prefatory remarks*, in E. Fischer, *Melchior Lorck*, vol. 3, pp. 7–20, p. 11.

with Wiering at that time[80]. The systematic recycling of printing materials within a person's own business was common practice for Wiering and his contemporaries. As the re-use of images made from woodcuts or copperplates is an established practice of the publishing industries in early modern Europe, a future entangled history of early modern media should highlight both the moments of identical image echoes – made with re-used identical cut woodblocks or etched copper plates – and the inspirational echoes of printed images – inspired by already circulating (popular) images.

5 A future entangled history of early modern media

A history of (early modern) communication, written as "an entangled history of media", explores the feedback-loops, echoes, and recycling moments, and offers fresh insights to the interdependency of communicational acts and transregional media occurrences. By focusing primarily on the "printed" echoes resulting from media recycling and their corollary communications, my case studies are only the starting point for a future multimedia evaluation of the topic. As demonstrated in the case studies, these echoes are fundamental to understanding the media ensemble of the early modern period and its feature characteristic, the entanglement of the media. The European news businesses functioned as periodical recycling machines: observing, re-using, and then publishing in various formats on European topics, which appeared in other news media in the recent past. Deriving mainly from the same sources, occasional printings too had their own and interconnected impact on European media coverage. Included into this mainly textual processing, the visual echoes – appearing both separately and included in occasional and periodical prints – resulted from the recycling of older images, i.e. a re-usage of images in other thematic settings as the original designed setting. This re-usage of an artefact of past communication for inspiration or adaption in a new historical setting happened in over both short and long spans of time and may be understood as an activated "memory box" (*Erinnerungsschachtel*)[81].

---

80 The original woodblock was used in Eberhard Werner Happel, *Thesaurus Exoticorum. Oder eine mit Außländischen Raritäten und Geschichten Wohlversehene Schatz-Kammer [...]*, Hamburg, Wiering, 1688, p. 34. As Fischer ("Prefatory remarks", pp. 12–23) states, 123 of Lorck's 128 woodcuts appeared in this book, as did large (identical) parts of Lorck's text passages as well. On the business collaboration between Wiering and Happel, F. Schock, *Die Text-Kunstkammer*, esp. pp. 52–63. On Happel as an eager re-user and recycler of different media, U. Egenhoff's, *Berufsschriftstellertum und Journalismus in der Frühen Neuzeit. Eberhard Werner Happels Relationes Curiosae im Medienverbund des 17. Jahrhunderts*, Bremen 2008; G. Scholz Williams, *Mediating Culture in the Seventeenth-Century German Novel: Eberhard Werner Happel, 1647–1690*, Ann Arbor 2014; N. Detering, *Krise und Kontinent. Die Entstehung der deutschen Europa-Literatur in der Frühen Neuzeit*, Köln 2017, pp. 409–540.
81 According to Roeck's concept of *Erinnerungsschachtel*, a memory box is an "artefact, [...] a container which already contained legacies from the past when it was being made". Reaching back in

In my understanding, a future history of communication, written as an entangled history of early modern media, is needed. Such an approach might begin to answer questions regarding the "popularity" of certain media – especially written media – by first placing the very media format into a perspective of reaction. Understood as an "echo", the media format will be seen as a reaction to past communication, thereby opening historical awareness of the analyzed communicative setting. The examples in this chapter presented model aspects of such an approach with a special focus on printed echoes, but these are only the first steps in this direction. Secondly, building on the unique communicative setting of every historical observation considered, the analyses will then be enriched with views that incorporate questions of availability (of past media) and accessibility (infrastructure of circulation, social networks, etc.) more prominently. In the end, media recycling is only a useful category of historical analysis when we also shift our scholarly attention from the content level to questions regarding extant infrastructure and openness, social business-networking within the book trade, and legal constellations (like censorship efficiencies, copyright enforcement, clandestine trade, etc.). Measuring the "popularity" of early modern media within particular communities is bound to entangled historical perspectives.

---

time and with a provenance in different regions, these objects – be it works of art, clothes, pieces of furniture, books, documents and so on – "were filled with memories" and became to artists, artisans and thinkers in other geographies and times as a starting point for the production of completely new objects and thoughts (B. Roeck, *Introduction*, in H. Rodenburg, ed, *Cultural Exchange in Early Modern Europe*, 4 vols., Cambridge 2006, vol. 4, pp. 1–30, p. 11).

Rebecca Carnevali
Iconographies and Material Culture of Illustrated Cheap Print from Post-Tridentine Bologna

> Oh the nice paper fans, who would buy them, who would like them, with their graceful handles, there's plenty, they're all cheap, / come on ladies, come on misses, look at how they're pretty, so magnificently worked, all well painted, and well printed [...][1].

I

At the turn of the sixteenth century, these words by the poet and street singer Giulio Cesare Croce (1550–1605) may have lured audiences and passers-by on the streets and squares of Bologna into buying such printed fans, called "ventarole" or "ventole". These were flat, rectangular paper fans mounted on wooden handles, that people used to protect themselves from the sun and heat as well as from fire sparks and to chase away flies[2]. Because of this constant and heavy use *ventarole* rarely survive today, but when they do, they provide a privileged window into the everyday life and habits of inhabitants of early modern cities, especially in Italy where they were particularly fashionable between the sixteenth and eighteenth centuries. Moreover, they were not the only kind of cheaply printed object available to and avidly consumed by these urban audiences.

By discussing examples of illustrated objects that employed cheap print – booklets and single sheets, but also fans, furniture decoration, games, etc. – from post-Tridentine Bologna, this chapter seeks to show that cheap print was a diverse medium that depended on different means of communication as well as techniques and sup-

---

[1] "Ah, le belle ventarole, chi ne compra, e chi ne vole, col suo manico garbato, a piacer, e a buon mercato, / su, su, donne, su donzelle, ecco qua come son belle, nobilmente lavorate, ben dipinte, e ben stampate [...]"; Giulio Cesare Croce, *Barceletta piacevolissima sopra i fanciulli che vanno vendendo le ventarole per la città, et un capitolo e lode sopra la bella ventarola*, Bologna, Eredi del Cochi, 1639, Biblioteca Comunale dell'Archiginnasio of Bologna (BCAB), TREBBI. Cart. 41 06/2, c. π1v. I have modernized the spelling, capitalization, and punctuation in the transcriptions of Italian texts, and all translations in this paper are mine. On the life and works of Croce, see n. 4 below; here it is enough to say that the work, although printed after the poet's death, can be safely attributed to him: no. 20, *Catalogo*, in R.L. Bruni / R. Campioni / D. Zancani, *Giulio Cesare Croce dall'Emilia all'Inghilterra. Cataloghi, biblioteche e testi*, Firenze 1991, pp. 56–152.

[2] On printed paper fans of early modern Italy, see A. Milano / E. Villani, *Ventole e ventagli. Museo d'arti applicate, Raccolta Bertarelli*, Milano 1995.

ports[3]. Furthermore, it aims to show how such intermediality sheds light on the social classes that consumed cheap print and furthermore leads us to reconsider certain characteristics of early modern cheap print as part of the wider world of material culture.

II

Croce was undoubtedly the most prominent and successful vernacular poet from late sixteenth- and early seventeenth-century Bologna, and his works provide plentiful evidence of scenes and characters typical of the city at the time. Indeed, a well-established scholarship has focused on the literary and social elements present in his works, for instance on his use of the vernacular and dialect, his portrayal of the habits and life of the Bolognese social classes, and how he explored themes of popular culture more broadly, while his printing production in particular has been studied within the field of textual bibliography[4]. Here I will build on this scholarship in order to investigate Croce's printed works in a new and different light, for I will focus on their relationship with other kinds of cheap print that were associated with his oeuvre, such as official ephemera and printed everyday objects like fans or board games.

One striking characteristic of the penchant of local audiences for Croce's oeuvre is how this spread throughout the social spectrum. Already in his lifetime, people from the wealthier ranks of society owned and appreciated his works. Among Croce's enthusiasts were the scientist and naturalist Ulisse Aldrovandi (1522–1605), whose interest in the *cantimbanco* was not confined to scientific purposes, as in the case of his transcription of Croce's *Canzone sopra il mal mattone*. Among the works Aldrovandi owned, we find the distinguished poetic compositions of the *Descrittione del nobil palazzo* (Bologna, Giovanni Rossi, 1582) and *La gloria delle donne* (Bologna, Alessandro Benacci, 1590)[5]. Moreover, in his dedication of *La libraria* to Cardinal

---

[3] Here, I always use the term "media" (and the related intermediality or multimediality) in this twofold sense.

[4] On Croce's life, see O. Guerrini, *La vita e le opere di Giulio Cesare Croce. Monografia*, Bologna, Zanichelli, 1879, and more recently F. Bacchelli, *Alcuni documenti sulla vita di Giulio Cesare Croce*, in *Le stagioni di un cantimbanco: vita quotidiana a Bologna nelle opere di Giulio Cesare Croce*, Bologna 2009, pp. 11–33. For an analysis of Croce's themes, the best introduction is P. Camporesi, *La maschera di Bertoldo: Giulio Cesare Croce e la letteratura carnevalesca*, Torino 1976, while the most important bibliographical works on Croce are: M. Rouch, *Bibliografia delle opere di Giulio Cesare Croce*, in "Strada maestra. Quaderni della Biblioteca comunale Giulio Cesare Croce di San Giovanni in Persiceto", 17, 1984, pp. 229–272; R.L. Bruni / R. Campioni / D. Zancani, *Giulio Cesare Croce*; with some updates in R. Campioni, *"Una fatica improba": la bibliografia delle opere di Giulio Cesare Croce*, in L. Balsamo (ed.), *Libri, tipografi, biblioteche: ricerche storiche dedicate a Luigi Balsamo*, 2 vols., Firenze 1997, here vol. 2, pp. 399–420.

[5] Aldrovandi's transcription of the *Canzone sopra il mal Mattone* is the only form in which the text survives today and can be found in the Biblioteca Universitaria of Bologna (BUB), Ms. Aldrovandi

Giorgio Radzivill (Jerzy Radziwill, 1556–1600), a Polish diplomat who spent time in Bologna as a papal legate, Croce describes how the cardinal attended his performances on several occasions[6]. Although Croce consistently struggled financially due to the lack of an official or stable patron, he was praised in his profession by several contemporaries and commanded high prices for his private performances in noble households[7]. On the other hand, a wide range of cases demonstrates the consumption of Croce's works by the lower classes, above all the adaptation and dissemination of his editions in other Italian dialects, but also practices such as family readings of his works during nighttime working sessions[8].

At the same time, Croce's success among local audiences persisted long after his death in 1605, during and beyond the seventeenth century. For instance, we find Bolognese editions of Croce's works as late as 1717, when his *Smergolamento overo piantuori, che fà la zia Tadia del Barba Salvestr da Tgnan* was printed by the heirs of Benacci and Girolamo Cocchi (*fl.* 1644–1717), and even from 1771, as in the case of the *Le piacevoli e ridicolose simplicità di Bertoldino*, printed by Gaspare de Franceschi (1712–c. 1807)[9].

This enduring and socially widespread demand for Croce's works was deeply connected with the visual and material culture of cheap-print objects. Croce was clearly aware of the potential dissemination of his works in different printed media

---

6, vol. II, fols. 23v–28r. Croce's *Descrittione del nobil Palazzo* is now held at the Biblioteca d'arte e di storia di San Giorgio in Poggiale della Fondazione Cassa di Risparmio of Bologna, Ambr. 569; the copy bears Aldrovandi's autograph ownership note and subscription "f. 234", which corresponds to the item classmark of his personal inventory in BUB, Ms. Aldrovandi 147, fol. 246r. *La gloria delle donne* is now in the BUB, Tab. I.M.II.193/6. All information on Croce's copies owned by Aldrovandi comes from R. Campioni, *Giulio Cesare Croce nelle biblioteche dell'Emilia-Romagna: una prima ricognizione*, in R.L. Bruni / R. Campioni / D. Zancani, Giulio Cesare Croce, pp. 171–208.

6 *La libraria, convito universale, dove s'invita grandissimo numero di libri tanto antichi, quanto moderni, ritirati tutti in un sonetto, opera non men utile, che dilettevole*, Bologna, Giovanni Rossi, 1592, BCAB, A.V.G.IX.1/401, cc. A2r–v.

7 P. Camporesi, *Il palazzo e il cantimbanco: Giulio Cesare Croce*, Milano 1994, p. 27.

8 A. Pegoretti, *Dismembered Voices and Acoustic Memories: Dante and Giulio Cesare Croce*, in L. Degl'Innocenti / M. Rospocher / R. Salzberg (eds.), The Cantastorie in Renaissance Italy: Street Singers between Oral and Literate Cultures", Italian Studies Special Issue, 71, 2016, 2, pp. 225–237, reports family readings of Croce's works by the young men in the household in order to keep mothers awake while working. On the practice of adapting Croce's language as evidence for appealing to local audiences see D. Zancani with respect to Florentine editions: *Una "imperfettissima perfettione": scelta di testi di Giulio Cesare Croce conservati nella British Library*, in R.L. Bruni / R. Campioni / D. Zancani, Giulio Cesare Croce, pp. 209–246, especially pp. 236–237.

9 *Smergolamento overo piantuori, che fà la zia Tadia del Barba Salvestr da Tgnan, quand'Sandron sò fiol andò alla guerra l'altrdì. Con le parole confortatorie della Nastasia Scarpelada, sua vicina. In lingua del suo paese*, Bologna, Per li successori del Benacci ad instanza di Girolamo Cocchi, 1717, Biblioteca di Casa Carducci in Bologna, 3. l. 237; *Le piacevoli e ridicolose simplicità di Bertoldino, figliuolo del già astuto, ed accorto Bertoldo con le sottili ed argute sentenze della Marcolfa sua madre, e moglie del già detto Bertoldo*, Bologna, Gaspare de Franceschi, 1777, BCAB, A.V. G. IX. 1/80.

and works meant to appear on *ventarole*. In the afore-mentioned *Barceletta piacevolissima*, the *Lode sopra la bella Ventarola* praises the ability of the *ventarole* to entertain people by disseminating pleasant and funny sayings: "My name is wind-bearer, for by my simple action I bring solace and joy as I cause the air and wind to stir [...]"[10]. In the woodblock collection of the Soliani-Mucchi press in the Galleria Estense of Modena we also find matrices for *ventarole* depicting Zia Tadia, the character protagonist of the *Smergolamento*[11]. See Figure 1. Furthermore, the printer Bartolomeo Cochi (or Cocchi, *fl.* 1585–1621), Croce's main publisher during his lifetime, must also have printed *ventarole* on his own, judging from the fact that he sometimes subscribed his publications as "Bartolomeo dalle Ventarole".

Fig. 1: *Ventarola* with *Zovagnon* and *La Cia Tadea*, woodblock, Galleria Estense of Modena, Barelli collection, no. 6477, mm. 132 x 194 x 21. By kind permission of the Ministero per i Beni e le Attività Culturali, Archivio Fotografico delle Gallerie Estensi.

---

10 "Mi chiamo ventarola, che con l'opera sola do ristoro e contento portando l'aura e il vento [...]": *Barceletta piacevolissima*, c. π4v. Further works on *ventarole* by Croce are now preserved in BUB, MS 3878: caps. LI, t. VII/2; caps. LIII [formerly LII], t. XVI/5, /8, and /28; caps. LIII [formerly LII], t. XVIII/16: R. Campioni, *Giulio Cesare Croce*, p. 176. To these I would add the imprints in BUB, caps. LI, t. VII/3; caps. LIII [formerly LII], t. XVI/10–12, and /29.
11 Galleria Estense of Modena, Barelli collection, no. 6477, mm. 132 x 194 x 21; on this woodblock, see A. Milano, *no. 199*, in Soprintendenza per i beni artistici e storici di Modena e Reggio Emilia (ed.), *I legni incisi della Galleria Estense: quattro secoli di stampa nell'Italia settentrionale. Modena, giugno–settembre 1986*, Modena 1986.

Bartolomeo Cochi also printed board games associated with Croce. One of the most popular games of chance in early modern Italy, the "Gioco del Chiù" (pluck the owl) was a board game where players gain – or lose – points by casting three dice, and each total corresponds to specific figures on the board[12]. A version of this board game by Croce survives in print in the Biblioteca Universitaria of Bologna but woodblock versions survive as well, this time in the afore-mentioned collections of the Galleria Estense[13]. See Figures 2 and 3.

Fig. 2: Giulio Cesare Croce, *Il novo e piacevole Gioco del Pela il Chiù*, Biblioteca Universitaria of Bologna, ms. 3878, caps. LIV [formerly LIIIbis], t. XXV/25. By kind permission of the Alma Mater Studiorum Università di Bologna – Biblioteca Universitaria di Bologna. Total or partial reproduction or copies of this image are strictly forbidden by any means.

---

12 On early modern games, see A. Milano, *Giochi da salotto, giochi da osteria nella vita milanese dal Cinquecento all'Ottocento*, Milano, Mazzotto, 2012, especially pp. 11–28, and D. Domini, *Giochi a stampa in Europa: dal XVII al XIX secolo*, Ravenna 1985.
13 *Il novo e piacevole Gioco del Pela il Chiù*, BUB, MS 3878, caps. LIV [formerly LIIIbis], t. XXV/25. The woodblock is no. 6521 of the Soliani collection at the Galleria Estense of Modena, and measures mm 519 x 362 x 25; on it, see A. Milano, *no. 191*, in *I legni incisi*. Further woodblocks for *Chiù* board games survive as nos. 6527 and 6647, Soliani collection, respectively mm 476 x 353 x 23 and 489 x 356 x 23. For this collection of woodblocks, see also the *Xilografie modenesi* database at http://www.gallerie-estensi.beniculturali.it/ricerca-nel-database-museale, accessed March 21, 2018.

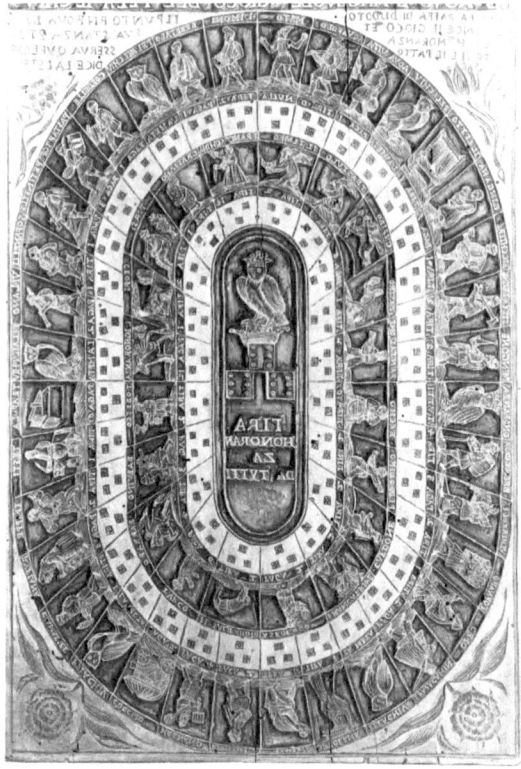

Fig. 3: *Gioco del Pela il Chiù*, woodblock, Galleria Estense of Modena, Soliani collection, no. 6521, mm 519 x 362 x 25. By kind permission of the Ministero per i Beni e le Attività Culturali, Archivio Fotografico delle Gallerie Estensi.

Some of the squares on such woodblocks depict, among other subjects, a woman selling *ventarole* (called a *ventarola*, too), Graziano, and Babuino, all characters from Croce's works.

All these printed objects depict scenes and iconographies from traditional folklore (the cycle of the seasons, trades, figures of the commedia dell'arte, etc.) that were the subject of Croce's works in the first place, as in the case of Graziano just mentioned. Yet, such examples also demonstrate the ability of content associated with a vernacular author to cross boundaries between different cheap-print media, between different products of the press and different printed objects in general. This intermediality is above all rooted in the constant exchange between written and oral culture typical of vernacular cheap print, as several scholars have noted[14]. Indeed, Croce performed his works, an activity testified to firstly by his nickname, "dalla lira", which refers to

---

14 Within the vast bibliography on the subject, see "Oral Culture in Early Modern Italy: Performance, Language, Religion. The Italianist Special Issue", 34, 2014, 3, and especially B. Richardson, *Introduction*, pp. 313–317; L. Degl'Innocenti / B. Richardson / C. Sbordoni (eds.), *Interactions between Orality and Writing in Early Modern Italian Culture*, Farnham / Burlington NJ, Ashgate, 2016; L. Degl'Innocenti / M. Rospocher / R. Salzberg (eds.), *The Cantastorie in Renaissance Italy*; S. Dall'Aglio / B. Richardson / M. Rospocher (eds.), *Voices and Texts in Early Modern Italian Society*, London / New York 2017.

the musical instrument he used to accompany his performances and which became an attribute of his persona. In addition, a strong component of the intermediality of Croce's oeuvre is the recurrent interplay between written and visual culture. For instance, Croce wrote satires of *iudicia* and *tacuina*, the official astrological prognostications released by professors of astrology of the Bolognese *studium*, and here he imitated their language and structure, as in the *Pronostico perpetuo sopra l'anno presente* (Bologna, Alessandro Benacci, 1584)[15]. Sometimes, the graphic layout alone was a parody of his models: the *Pronostico et almanacco stupendo e maraviglioso* (Bologna, Bartolomeo Cochi, 1617) mimics the broadside format and display of contemporary *avvisi*, or news reports, where each news item was reported under the heading of the city from which it came[16]. Only a public constantly exposed to such types of cheap print in their actual printed form would have been able to grasp Croce's puns and allusions – both in verbal and visual form[17].

Another example of intermediality between the oral and visual consumption of Croce's works can be found in his *Alfabeto de' giuocatori in ottava rima* (Bologna, Bartolomeo Cochi 1610). Here, each stanza of the nineteen *ottave* of the poem, dedicated to the theme of games, begins with the same letter to achieve the effect of alliteration, but eventually forms an acrostic of the entire alphabet. The chosen figures of speech and composition allow the potential audience to experience Croce's text at different times, as delivered orally during his public performances but also in its printed form, where the visual component becomes most effective[18].

The contribution of such visual features to the consumption of Croce's works appears even more prominent if one considers that his editions were not heavily illustrated, aside from certain adventures of Bertoldo and Bertoldino. His publishers most likely adopted this strategy in order to control costs, and for the same reason they printed his works in small formats, such as quartos and octavos of few leaves, or as broadsheets (as in the case of the mentioned *Pronostico et almanacco stupendo e maraviglioso* of 1617). In addition, they constantly reused and copied the few illustrative woodcuts[19]. Yet, the possibility of reusing woodcuts is further connected with the

---

15 On the production of astrological prognostications in Bologna, see E. Casali, *Le spie del cielo: oroscopi, lunari e almanacchi nell'Italia moderna*, Torino 2003. Of the *Pronostico perpetuo sopra l'anno presente*, I have consulted the later edition by Bartolomeo Cochi in 1607, British Library of London (BL), 11429.b.48.
16 *Pronostico et almanacco stupendo e maraviglioso sopra l'anno presente*, Bologna, Bartolomeo Cochi, 1617, BCAB, A.V.G.IX.1/426.
17 On the intertextuality and diversity of Croce's references, see A. Battistini, *La cornucopia letteraria di Giulio Cesare Croce*, in "Strada Maestra", 33, 1992, pp. 49–55.
18 *Alfabeto de' giuocatori in ottava rima*, Bologna, Bartolomeo Cochi, 1610, BCAB, A.V.G.IX.190.
19 For instance, the same woodcut landscape of Bologna was used in the *Breve compendio de' casi più notabili occorsi nella città di Bologna*, Bologna, Bartolomeo Cochi, 1606, BCAB, 17–SCR.BOL F.PO-ES.ITAL. 10, 020, and in the *Parentado del Ponte di Reno nella Torre degl'Asinelli*, Bologna, Bartolomeo Cochi, 1609, BL, 1071.h.42(6), while the woodblock appears worn out and broken on the *Per il rittrato*

potential of Croce's texts to cross boundaries between various cheaply printed products. In the edition of the *Barceletta piacevolissima* already mentioned, the title-page shows the figure of a so-called "Todesco" ("German", a character recurrent in games) accompanied by a number: there is a strong chance that the woodcut was cut from the block of some contemporary printed lotteries or games such as the *Biribisse* (another popular game of chance of the time), which were printed on sheets from which players cut or ripped off their numbered tickets, called "bollettini"[20]. See Figure 4.

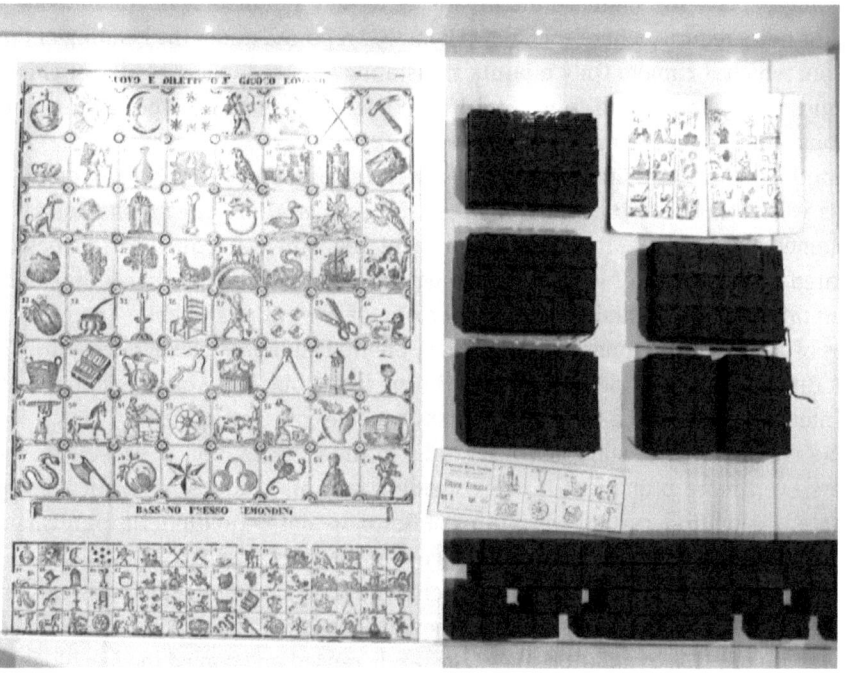

Fig. 4: *Nuovo e dilettevole Gioco Romano*, woodblock, Musei Biblioteca Archivio of Bassano del Grappa, Museo Remondini, MBAB Inc. Bass. 2909. By kind permission of the MBA Musei Biblioteca Archivio of Bassano del Grappa. Total or partial reproduction or copies of this image are strictly forbidden by any means.

---

della città di Bologna, Bologna, Eredi del Cochi, 1628, BCAB, A.V.G.IX.1/411. The broadsheet of the *Indice di tutte l'opere di Giulio Cesare dalla Croce*, Bologna, Bartolomeo Cochi, 1608, BUB, MS 3878, LI [formerly LIIIbis], t. XIV/13, and the *Scelta artificiosa di settecento cognomi*, Bologna, Bartolomeo Cochi, 1617, BUB, MS 3878, caps. LIII, t. XII/4, both bear a smaller copy of the same woodcut of 75 x 90 mm, more worn out in the latter case.

20 See the digital reproduction of the *Barceletta piacevolissima* in the repository of Giulio Cesare Croce's works at: http://badigit.comune.bologna.it/GCCroce/index.html, accessed May 11, 2018. An eighteenth-century woodblock matrix for the *Nuovo e dilettevole Gioco Romano* (New and fun Roman game) preserved at the museum of the Remondini press in Bassano del Grappa shows missing areas in the bottom part of the block where some of the images for the tickets have been cut out to be likely

That Croce's readership covered a broad spectrum of different social classes, as I mentioned earlier, can be further demonstrated via the *ventarole* and board games associated with his name. These printed objects were indeed "cheap print" from the viewpoint of production standards: they were printed from single large woodblocks that were reused by generations of printers, and paper was thus the main cost in their production. In the case of *ventarole*, they therefore became the low-end version of more expensive goods such as embroidered or lace fans. *Ventarole*, however, were bought and used not only by the middling – and potentially lower – classes, but also by patricians. Early-modern visual sources portray women from well-off families carrying paper fans, such as the Venetian noblewoman in Cesare Vecellio's *Habiti antichi et moderni di tutto il mondo*, and the aristocratic lady on an early sixteenth-century fragment of printed wallpaper found in 1887 in a little vault under the floor of the noble apartments of the Castello Sforzesco in Milan[21]. See Figure 5.

Fig. 5: Noblewoman with a *ventarola*, partially colored woodcut, Civica Raccolta delle Stampe Achille Bertarelli, Castello Sforzesco, Milan, Art. Prez. m. 285, mm 390 x 310.

---

reused in other imprints: Musei Biblioteca Archivio of Bassano del Grappa, Museo Remondini, MBAB Inc. Bass. 2909. On the Remondini matrices see C. Chiesura / R. Dalle Nogare, *I Remondini: matrici xilografiche a Bassano del Grappa*, in "Studi di Memofonte", 17, 2016, pp. 96–110, while specifically on the game of the Biribisse A. Milano, *Giochi da salotto*, p. 18.

21 Partially colored woodcut, Civica Raccolta delle Stampe Achille Bertarelli, Castello Sforzesco of Milan, Art. Prez. m. 285, mm 390 x 310; I would like to thank Mauro Alberti of the Bertarelli collection

On account of their very cheap price, *ventarole* were within the reach of poorer social strata, too. In the already mentioned *Barceletta piacevolissima*, some of the printed fans are on sale for a *bolognino*, and others for what then corresponded to a *quattrino*. At the end of the sixteenth century, the price per pound of common food items (such as an eel or a pint of wine with raisins and nuts) in Bologna was between two and five *bolognini*, roughly the same amount paid for a night's stay in an inn and a journey by boat between Ferrara and Bologna[22]. As a result, printed items such as the *ventarole* belonged to the everyday experience of almost every social class throughout early modern Italy.

III

Intermediality was not exclusive to the vernacular production, for illustrated cheap print also comprised devotional publications, such as prayers, booklets on miracles, or lives of saints, and above all printed images[23]. The various kinds and formats of these printed products do not merely tell of different devotional practices but of how their visual component and materiality were essential to the way that audiences experienced them. In this sense, and in order to draw a parallel with the consumption of Croce's vernacular cheap print, I will discuss examples of cheap religious printed items that come from the area of present-day Emilia and act as evidence for the most prominent devotions and pious practices of post-Tridentine Bologna.

In the collection of woodblocks at the Galleria Estense of Modena, a group of seventeenth- and eighteenth-century matrices depicts the miraculous icon of the

---

for his help in identifying the woodcut. See A. Milano, *Prints for Fans*, in "Print Quarterly", 4, 1987, 1, pp. 2–19, especially pp. 3–4, for other examples of visual depictions of *ventarole*. The "Nobile ornata alle feste" is at c. N4v of Cesare Vecellio, *Habiti antichi et moderni di tutto il mondo*, Venezia, Appresso i Sessa, 1598.

22 *Barceletta piacevolissima*, c. π1v, and F. Moryson, *An Itinerary Containing his Ten Yeeres Travell*, 4 vols., Glasgow, John Mac Lehose and Sons, 1907–1908, vol. I (1907), pp. 204 and 200–201. At the time, one bolognino was worth six quattrini, or sesini: G.B. Salvioni, *Il valore della lira bolognese dalla sua origine alla metà del secolo XVII*, Torino, Bottega d'Erasmo, 1961, especially pp. 558–559. In the *Lode sopra la bella Ventarola* of the same *Barceletta*, c. π3v, all social classes ("Da bassi, da mezani, e da gli heroi") take delight in *ventarole*.

23 Within the vast bibliography on devotional religious prints, special attention to the cheapest items has been paid by R. Cobianchi, *The Use of Woodcuts in Fifteen-Century Italy*, in "Print Quarterly", 23, 2006, 1, pp. 47–54; D.S. Areford, *Multiplying the Sacred: The Fifteenth-Century Woodcut as Reproduction, Surrogate, Simulation*, in P. Parshall (ed.), *The Woodcut in Fifteenth Century Europe*, Washington D.C. / New Haven CT 2009, pp. 119–153; S. Karr Schmidt / K. Nichols, *Altered and Adorned: Using Renaissance Prints in Daily Life*, Chicago / New Haven CT 2011, especially the chapter "Religious Prints as Substitute Objects", pp. 60–71; and the various items discussed throughout M. Corry / D. Howard / M. Laven (eds.), *Madonnas and Miracles: The Holy Home in Renaissance Italy*, London 2017.

Madonna di San Luca[24]. See Figure 6. The Bolognese faithful were particularly keen on this supposedly Byzantine icon, kept in a sanctuary in the city's hilly outskirts[25], and large-size single prints of this kind testify to this popular devotion. They could be posted outside churches and sanctuaries but also on the walls of private houses[26].

Fig. 6: Madonna of San Luca, woodblock, Galleria Estense of Modena, Soliani collection, no. 4620, 520 x 357 x 26 mm. By kind permission of the Ministero per i Beni e le Attività Culturali, Archivio Fotografico delle Gallerie Estensi.

---

24 Galleria Estense of Modena, woodblocks: Soliani collection, no. 4620, mm 520 x 357 x 26; Soliani collection, no. 4636, mm 396 x 242 x 24; Barelli collection, no. 4664, mm 257 x 179 x 20; Soliani collection, no. 4732, mm 236 x 171 x 26. Bologna is no exception to the intense early-modern consumption of devotional and religious printed items, and these materials have consequentially rarely survived. The woodblocks preserved at the Galleria Estense are therefore a remarkable source: they come from presses in nearby Modena, most notably the Soliani, and testify to the range of dissemination of Bolognese devotions; updated research on this collection can be found in M. Goldoni / D. Levi / M. Mozzo (eds.), *Le matrici della Galleria Estense. Alla riscoperta di un patrimonio nascosto*, numero speciale di "Studi di Memofonte", 2017.
25 M. Fanti / P. Angiolini Martinelli, *La Madonna di San Luca in Bologna: otto secoli di storia, di arte e di fede*, Cinisello Balsamo 1993.
26 Interesting cases of printed images connected to miraculous cults in fifteenth- and sixteenth-century Italy are, among others, discussed by R. Maniura, *The Images and Miracles of Santa Maria delle Carceri*,

Also holy images, or *santini*, another widespread kind of cheap devotional print, testify to the devotion to the Madonna di San Luca: in the same Estense collection two seventeenth-century woodblocks display the icon of the Madonna within a regular grid of holy images. Among these, as proof of the Bolognese destination of such prints, we can also identify the image of Bologna's patron saint, San Petronio[27]. See Figure 7. These holy images were meant to be distributed at sanctuaries and religious festivities; they were also posted on the indoor walls of homes as single prints, but on account of their dimensions they could also be pasted into books of prayers, family albums, boxes, and other small objects, or worn as amulets inside clothes[28].

Fig. 7: Holy images, woodblock, Galleria Estense of Modena, Soliani collection, no. 4922, 412 x 282 x 21 mm. By kind permission of the Ministero per i Beni e le Attività Culturali, Archivio Fotografico delle Gallerie Estensi.

---

in E. Thunø / G. Wolf (eds.), *The Miraculous Image in the Late Middle Ages and Renaissance*, Roma 2004, pp. 81–95, and L. Pon, *A Printed Icon: Forlì's Madonna of the Fire*, New York / Cambridge 2015.
27 Galleria Estense of Modena, woodblocks: Soliani collection, nos. 4922 and 4939, mm 412 x 282 x 21 and 394 x 315 x 20 respectively.
28 Specifically on early modern printed holy images, see E. Gulli Grigioni / V. Pranzini, *Santini: piccole immagini devozionali a stampa e manufatte dal XVII al XX secolo*, Ravenna 1990.

Cheap devotional print was furthermore particularly apt to be used in a variety of everyday devotional contexts: for instance, woodblocks for candle-bearing angels and decorative paper, surviving again in the Galleria Estense, could replace paintings or *ex votos* in private altars, especially in the homes of the less wealthy[29]. Scholars have suggested that large-size devotional prints may also have functioned as icons for private altars once pasted on hard surfaces and painted; even matrices could be hung and used for devotion, and some woodblocks in the same Estense collection present hooks and white paste filling in the carved parts of the figuration so as to make the outlines stand out[30]. See Figure 8. These last examples especially show how the early modern faithful experienced cheap devotional prints via their materiality and ability to traverse different media and objects. From this perspective, cheap devotional prints blended easily into a world of everyday objects, becoming of them.

Fig. 8: Candle-bearing angels, woodblock, Galleria Estense of Modena, Soliani collection, no. 4773, 192 x 271 x 25 mm. By kind permission of the Ministero per i Beni e le Attività Culturali, Archivio Fotografico delle Gallerie Estensi.

---

29 Galleria Estense of Modena, woodblocks: *Crucifixion with Angels that Collect the Blood of Christ*, Mucchi collection, no. 18004, mm 256 x 179 x 22; *Candle-bearing Angels*, Soliani collection, no. 4773, mm 192 x 271 x 25.
30 Galleria Estense of Modena, woodblocks: Mucchi collection, no. 18019 (eighteenth century), mm. 113 x 178 x 14; nos. 15745 and 15764 from the Mucchi collection, respectively mm 78 x 73 x 24 and 116 x 87 x 23, show the paste-filling but no hooks. On the matrices discussed in this paper see also M.L. Piazzi, *Manipolazioni e falsificazioni nelle matrici xilografiche Soliani-Barelli e Mucchi*, in M. Goldoni / D. Levi / M. Mozzo (eds.), *Le matrici della Galleria Estense*, pp. 134–158.

More specifically with respect to iconographic models, religious and devotional prints from more distinguished artworks could gain a wider audience once adapted and further circulated in the form of cheap print. Several devotional copperplate prints by established printmakers of the Bolognese school were later translated into lower-quality woodcuts, such as the Madonna del Carmine and the San Carlo Borromeo *d'après*, respectively, Franceso Brizio (1575–1623) and Giovan Battista Coriolano (1590–1649), both pupils of the Carracci and protagonists of Bolognese printmaking and book illustration during the seventeenth century[31]. Artistic prints, whose circulation was limited to the studios of amateurs and collectors, can be seen as just a phase in the life of some religious images and their consumption, which acquired a broader audience only via cheap print – broader consumption practices that are mirrored also in printed holy images and private altars.

IV

What broader considerations about cheap print emerge from these case studies offered above?

First, such case studies show that cheap print was at times deeply rooted in a world of everyday objects and consumption practices consisting only partially of texts. Devotional prints, vernacular booklets, and printed objects such as board games and fans all shared the same production procedures, too, coming off the printing press at the lowest possible cost. We should therefore think of cheap print as belonging to a wider category of low-priced material objects: the adaptability and functionality of cheap-print products mean that they were experienced and accessed not just as texts but as objects, and that such practices can be better assessed by using concepts from the study of early modern material culture.

This approach has various implications. One is that it further confirms that different social classes actively consumed cheap print. In this sense, I would like to stress that cheapness of price did not exclusively correspond to poorer consumers, but rather to a potential for such items to circulate widely and become accessible to all kinds of people[32]. Vernacular works in cheap print were collected by influential

---

[31] Examples of the transmission of the Madonna del Carmine are Franceso Brizio, *The Madonna of Mount Carmel with the Infant Christ and Angels*, Albertina Graphische Sammlung in Vienna, etching, 270 x 193 mm, as in V. Birke ed., *The Illustrated Bartsch*, vol. 40: *Italian Masters of the Sixteenth and Seventeenth Centuries*, New York 1982, no. B.5 (256); and the woodblocks in the Galleria Estense of Modena, Soliani collection: nos. 4579 and 4737, mm 254 x 169 x 22 and 256 x 174 x 23 respectively. On the two printmakers see A. Brogi, *Brevi su Francesco Brizio*, in "Nuovi Studi", 17, 2007, pp. 137–143, and N. Takahatake, *Coriolano*, in "Print Quarterly", 27, 2010, pp. 103–130.

[32] On approaches that stress accessibility as the main characteristic of cheap print see R. Harms / J. Raymond / J. Salman, *Introduction: the Distribution and Dissemination of Popular Print*, in R. Harms /

figures of the time and further disseminated via oral practices, as in the case of Croce, who himself performed simultaneously on the streets and squares of Bologna and in its noble households. *Ventarole* and printed decoration for the home are other telling examples of cheap-printed products considered fashionable and used by the lower and wealthier classes alike.

A second implication of a "material culture" approach is that we are led to reconsider the role of visual culture in cheap print. The figurative components in widely-distributed printed items undeniably helped to disseminate specific iconographies to a broader audience, and worked as direct visual counterpart to the texts for the less literate. Next to these acknowledged roles, the circulation of visual culture in and via cheap print also accounts for the particularly intermedial nature of cheap print itself, for it connected various ways of experiencing "texts" – from oral to written and more sensorial modes – and, above all, different objects. The same imagery, in the form of specific themes or characters, could be shared across numerous printed objects and in this way it reached even more disparate social groups at the same time. Early scholars of popular culture such as Achille Bertarelli and Alberto Milano placed this interpretation of visual culture at the core of their investigations[33], and recent research is revealing new evidence in this sense. For instance, collective practices of consumption (such as performances and group readings) could resort to images as stage props: Eugenio Refini has drawn attention to the painted banners that charlatans such as the sixteenth-century Modenese Iacopo Coppa used on their improvised stages to guide audiences through their shows[34]. As a result, the role of illustrations in cheap print can be better understood if we reposition them within the frame of wider dissemination and consumption practices, where a multimedial and sensorial experience of texts was more common than one based on binary correspondences between texts and images. Such a frame of experience would also explain the frequent mismatches between printed illustrations and the contents those had to portray, as well as the constant reuse of printed illustrations *per se*[35].

J. Raymond / J. Salman (eds.), *Not Dead Things: The Dissemination of Popular Print in England and Wales, Italy, and the Low Countries, 1500–1820*, Boston MA / Leiden 2013, pp. 1–29.

33 See A. Bertarelli, *L'imagerie populaire italienne*, Paris 1929, although somehow dated for his take on the concept of "popular", and for Milano his *L'immagine dei colporteurs*, in A. Milano (ed.), *Colporteurs: i venditori di stampe e libri e il loro pubblico*, Milano 2015, pp. 7–45. See also the comprehensive bibliography of Milano's writings published in *Le matrici della Galleria Estense*, pp. 17–27.

34 E. Refini, *Reappraising the Charlatan in Early Modern Italy: The Case of Iacopo Coppa*, in L. Degl'Innocenti / M. Rospocher / R. Salzberg (eds.), *The Cantastorie in Renaissance Italy*, pp. 197–211, especially pp. 200–201.

35 This aspect of early modern printed illustration is addressed by M. Rothstein, *Disjunctive Images in Renaissance Books*, in Degl'Innocenti"Renaissance and Reformation / Renaissance et Réforme", 14, 1990, 2, pp. 101–120.

In this light, intermediality explains the adaptability and possible reuses of printed images across cheap-print items and not only in a top-down direction from higher to lower publications. An example in this sense is the *princeps* edition of the *Amfiparnaso*, the opera by the composer and *Kapellmeister* of Modena's Cathedral, Orazio Vecchi (1551–1605). Published in 1597 in Venice by Angelo Gardano, the woodcut illustrating the prologue, portraying the carachter Lelio, was first copied, in counterpart, to likely appear on a title-page and later was reused in a *ventarola* with the addition of a rectangular frame[36]. Furthermore, the series of monstruous figures by the contemporary Bolognese artist Bartolomeo Passerotti (1529–1592) gave birth to an iconographic tradition that continued in the grotesque character appearing on the title-page of the 1617 edition of Croce's *Vita, gesti, costumi di Giandiluvio da Trippaldo* (Bologna, Bartolomeo Cochi). The same tradition was later adapted and further disseminated in rougher single prints whose woodblocks again survive in the Soliani press collection in Modena[37].

The intermediality of cheap print also reveals the distinctive visual literacy of early modern audiences. I have discussed the case of Croce's *Alfabeto de' giuocatori*, but *rebuses* and illustrated riddles were a very common form of cultural entertainment at the time and feature heavily in booklets and on printed fans, as another work by Croce, *Alle bellissime e virtuose gentildonne bolognese*, shows[38]. Such visual puns, also called *sonetti figurati*, often employed musical notation in the place of syllables,

---

[36] Orazio Vecchi, *L'Amfiparnaso comedia harmonica*, Venezia, Angelo Gardano, 1597, München, Bayerische Staatsbibliothek, 4 Mus.pr. 2426, c. Q3v; Galleria Estense of Modena, woodblock, Barelli collection, no. 6476, mm 160 x 120 x 22, on which see A. Milano, *no. 201*, in Soprintendenza per i beni artistici e storici di Modena e Reggio Emilia (ed.), *I legni incisi della Galleria Estense*. Croce was acquainted with Vecchi and allegedly wrote a part of the *Amfiparnaso*: see G. Merizzi, *Giulio Cesare Croce dalla Lira. Musica e testimonianze musicali nell'opera letteraria di un cantastorie*, in M. Privitera (ed.), *Theatro dell'Udito, Theatro del Mondo*, Modena 2010, pp. 171–210.

[37] A. Mazza, "Trascendendo in facetie, in motti, in rime, e in ridicolosi passaggi". "Pitture ridicole" a Bologna al tempo di Giulio Cesare Croce, in *Le stagioni di un cantimbanco*, pp. 97–131, especially pp. 107–108, and for the single prints A. Milano / M. Goldoni, *no. 249*, in *I legni incisi*. In his essay, Mazza discusses another group of grotesque figures on the title-pages of Croce's editions and their relationship with earlier models by artists such as Agostino Veneziano (active 1509–1536) and Leonardo da Vinci (1452–1519). For further woodblocks that disseminated printed images associated with Croce, see *ibid.*, A. Milano / M. Goldoni, *nos. 236, 248,* and *250–251*. The 1617 edition of Croce's *Vita, gesti, costumi di Giandiluvio da Trippaldo, arcingordissimo mangiatore e diluviatore del mondo* is in BUB, MS 3878, caps. LIII, t. XXI/8.

[38] Giulio Cesare Croce, *Alle bellissime e virtuose gentildonne bolognese*, Bologna, Girolamo Cochi, n.p., BCAB, A.V.G.I.X.1412; see its digital reproduction at http://badigit.comune.bologna.it/GCCroce/index.html, accessed May 11, 2018. On *rebuses*, see J. Céard / J.-C. Margolin, *Rébus de la Renaissance. Des images qui parlent*, vol. 1: *Histoire du rébus*, Paris 1986, and A. Sbrilli / A. De Pirro (eds.), *Ah, che rebus! cinque secoli di enigmi fra arte e gioco in Italia. Catalogo della mostra tenuta a Roma nel 2010–2011*, Milano, Mazzotta, 2010.

and thus add to the list of evidence for the interplay among the oral, written, and visual consumptions of a "text"[39].

A third outcome of an approach that examines cheap print as part of early modern material culture is that it enables us to reconsider the times and places where cheap-print consumption occurred. From a temporal point of view, cheap-print objects clearly illustrate the enduring appeal of certain themes and characters over decades and even centuries, and consequentially the influence of widespread demand for iconographic models[40]. Cheap-print consumption was strongly and increasingly tied to its production and distribution in a self-reinforcing cycle that both created and met local demand: several printers, as well as printing dynasties, thrived on the regular production of such materials, from devotional and vernacular illustrated booklets and single prints to printed objects such as board games, fans, and wallpaper. In seventeenth- and eighteenth-century Italy, examples of such families, aside from the Cochi in Bologna, include the Soliani of Modena and the better-known Remondini of Bassano[41]. See Figure 4.

Cheap-print products themselves also provide evidence of the extent to which they were consumed in domestic spaces and not only in the streets and squares of Italian cities. Croce's 1599 work *I parenti godevoli* describes the habit of reading and playing parlor games during all-night gatherings called *veglie*, during which servants and masters of a household would gather together, disregarding the usual social barriers[42]. Printed playing cards and games of chance were common domestic possessions, although gambling was not considered an appropriate pastime in respectable households, as reported in anthologies such as the *Cento giuochi liberali, et d'ingegno, novellamente da M[esser] Innocentio Ringhieri gentilhuomo bolognese ritrovati, et in dieci libri descritti* (Bologna, Anselmo Giaccarelli, 1551 – republished Bologna, Giovanni Rossi, 1580).

---

39 F. Alazard, *La musique dans la rue: Giulio Cesare Croce à Bologne, 1550–1609*, in L. Gauthier / M. Traversier (eds.), *Mélodies urbaines. La musique dans les villes d'Europe, XVIe-XIXe siècles*, Paris 2008, pp. 163–176, further argued for the hybrid nature of Croce's production by analyzing the traces of music in his works.
40 See again R. Harms / J. Raymond / J. Salman, *Introduction*, on the long life span of cheap-print products.
41 An overview of the respective print productions can be found in P. Bellettini, *Scienza e tipografie nel XVII secolo*, in *Alma mater librorum: nove secoli di editoria bolognese per l'Università*, Bologna 1988, pp. 156–161; E. Milano / A. Battini / A.R. Po (eds.), *Lavori preparatori per gli annali della tipografia Soliani*, Modena 1986; and L. Carnelos, *I libri da risma: catalogo delle edizioni Remondini a larga diffusione (1650–1850)*, Milano 2008.
42 *I parenti godevoli, opera piacevolissima nella quale s'introduce un riduto di gentilhuomini, e gentildonne a metter ceppo insieme, et a cavar la ventura, secondo che s'usa in Bologna le feste di Natale*, Bologna, Eredi di Giovanni Rossi, 1599, Bibilioteca Nazionale Braidense of Milan, IT-MI0185 RACC. DRAM.2002.

Later in the seventeenth century, more upmarket versions of such games by prominent printmakers appeared, and in Bologna the artist Giuseppe Maria Mitelli (1634–1718) established a successful career as an author of printed games, among other things[43]. Cheap devotional prints could be found in bedrooms but also in the common areas of less wealthy family homes: a drawing attributed to the Bolognese Annibale Carracci (1560–1609) shows a poor household hearth where an image of a Madonna and Child – most likely a print – is hanging on the wall[44]. Print could be used to replace and imitate more expensive furniture, for instance as a decoration on chests and boxes[45]. At the same time, printed furniture decoration also characterized ecclesiastical indoor spaces: in the Bagatti Valsecchi Museum of Milan, a mid fifteenth-century cathedra from the abbey of San Donato di Sesto Calende (in the Varese area) displays a woodcut decoration in black and red that imitates wood intarsia[46].

The domestic consumption of cheap print further supports scholarly research that has reconsidered the home as a dynamic environment, open to the outside; in this light, homes are seen as "a key site for cultural production and transmission alongside the court, the city, and the church"[47]. Cheap print worked as an intermediary between lower classes and elites, but it also connected private and public spaces in the same way. More precisely, I would suggest that the intermediality of cheap print is another example of the circularity Rosa Salzberg and Massimo Rospocher have talked about in their work on street singers when describing how vernacular works circulated in various forms between heterogeneous publics[48]. This circularity occurred between cheaply-printed objects and on account of their ability to permeate a multitude of spaces in different formats and to interact with different aspects of everyday life. Because they were cheap, certain printed items came to be ubiquitous.

Furthermore, the domestic dimension of cheap print particularly highlights how practices associated with it belong to a pre-industrial world, especially with respect

---

[43] I would like to express my gratitude to Naomi Lebens for her insight on the subject and for letting me read her PhD dissertation for the Courtauld Institute in London on Mitelli and his self-fashioning strategies via printed games.
[44] *Interior of a poor household*, whereabouts unknown, put for auction at Sotheby's in London on 11 July 1972, as in L. Miller, *Prints*, in M. Ajmar-Wollheim / F. Dennis (eds.), *At Home in Renaissance Italy. Catalogue of the exhibition*, London 2006, pp. 322–331, pl. 22.4.
[45] See the three *cassoni*, ibid., pp. 327–328, respectively from the Raccolte Civiche Palazzo Sforzesco of Milan, the Museo Civico of Turin, and the Museo Bardini of Florence.
[46] Partially colored and gilded wooden cathedra with applied woodcuts, *c.* 1469, Museum Bagatti Valsecchi of Milan, *no. 27*, as in C. Cairati, *no. IV.20*, in M. Natale / S. Romano (eds.), *Arte lombarda dai Visconti agli Sforza: Milano al centro dell'Europa. Catalogo della mostra*, Milano 2015. I would like to thank Silvia Urbini and Laura Aldovini for drawing my attention to this artefact.
[47] M. Ajmar-Wollheim / F. Dennis, Introduction, in M. Ajmar-Wollheim / F. Dennis (eds.), *At Home in Renaissance Italy*, pp. 10–31, especially p. 12.
[48] R. Salzberg / M. Rospocher, *Street Singers in Italian Renaissance Urban Culture and Communication*, in "Cultural and Social History", 9, 2012, pp. 9–26.

to its production and distribution. Pedlars and street-performers who sold pamphlets, single prints, and *ventarole* were not usually regulated by guilds and within recognized urban trades. Moreover, certain cheap-print objects were regularly customized by their purchasers: owners pasted board games on canvases or woodboards depending on their level of wealth, and colored and modified printed fans[49]. Audiences actively and materially contributed to their consumption experience by, for instance, applying color and other materials to the printed images, as in the case of *ventarole* and single commercial cheap prints, as well as cutting and pasting them into albums, especially for devotional purposes[50].

V

In conclusion, I have argued that the hybrid, intermedial nature of illustrated cheap-print items from post-Tridentine Bologna contributed to their increasing exposure to audiences of different social classes, on the streets and inside homes. Such items could therefore be potentially adapted throughout different media and objects and so their consumption took place not just every day but also everywhere.

---

49 A. Milano, *Prints for Fans*, n. 27, reports that in a 1791 sale catalogue of the Remondini press 100 sheets of *ventarole* came at different prices if colored or not: seven lire versus two lire. On domestic production and customization of goods in the early modern period, see J. De Vries, *Between Purchasing Power and the World of Goods: Understanding the Household Economy in Early Modern Europe*, in J. Brewer / R. Porter (eds.), *Consumption and the world of goods*, London / New York 1993.
50 In addition to the several examples considered in S. Karr Schmidt / K. Nichols, *Altered and Adorned*, see those in D.S. Areford, *The Viewer and the Printed Image in Late Medieval Europe*, Farnham 2010. In his chapter here "Acts of Viewing", pp. 64–103, Areford particularly focuses on the concept and practices connected with the agency of viewers onto printed images; see also the *Introduction: The Aura of the Printed Image*, pp. 1-23, for a discussion of ideas of hibridity, materiality, and adaptability of prints.

Andreas Würgler
"Popular Print in German" (1400–1800)
Problems and Projects

1 Introduction

This article addresses some of the problems and projects around the topic "Popular Prints in German" or in "Germany" from the general and media historians' perspective, with special focus on the so-called "German Language Area" (GLA) and the Early Modern period (c. 1400–1800). It will first analyze the semantic problems and the ongoing bibliographic projects around the terms "print", "German" and "popular", and then it will suggest future research options focusing on different cultural uses of popular print under the headline of "consumption".

2 Print

Prints are not necessarily texts or books. Print culture in Germany, or the Holy Roman Empire north of the Alps, started around 1400 with the emergence of woodcuts. The technique is the same for the printing of images and texts on paper as for textiles or parchment. Many academic disciplines concerned with printing focus on either images or texts, woodcuts or typographical "Gutenberg" books. Woodcuts and (metal) engravings produced since the late fifteenth century became more important in the sixteenth century and were used to illustrate typographic prints until the end of the eighteenth century[1]. Therefore, we should better combine the analysis of printed texts and images (and maps).

Of course, typography in the Gutenberg tradition changed many aspects of culture and, in this respect, seems to be a particularly European phenomenon. The polycentric structure of the printing landscape reflects the GLA's fragmented political structure and makes it difficult to establish comprehensive bibliographies. Only a few years after its beginnings in Mainz in the 1450s, the art of printing spread rapidly across Germany and Europe. The German book market, by far the biggest in the sixteenth century, was diffuse: Andrew Pettegree and Matthew Hall list 93 "printing centres" in what they call "Germany" during the sixteenth century, compared to 60 in Italy and 53 in France. These 93 included 22 "significant printing centres" that produced more than 30 books during the sixteenth century. This is the same as the total

---

[1] A. Würgler, *Medien in der Frühen Neuzeit* (Enzyklopädie deutscher Geschichte, 85), 2nd ed., München 2013, pp. 7–10, 28–30, 42, 110 f.

number of printing centers in the six countries of Italy (8), France (5) Spain (3), the Low Countries (3), Switzerland (2), and England (1)[2].

The GLA has no obvious and fixed borders so there are many boundary zones and pockets of German settlements outside the areas with considerable shares of German speakers. Prints in German can be found outside the GLA far to the north (Copenhagen, Stockholm, Riga), east (Warsaw, Krakow, Brasov, Cluj, Eger, Bratislava), and in other places. Typical border zones are located in the west: towards the Low Countries where high German, low German, and Dutch are intermingled and towards France where the mixed French-German belt stretches down from Luxembourg and Lorraine through Alsace to Switzerland. In the south we also find mixed zones between German and Italian, such as the Grisons (today Switzerland) or Trento (Italy).

If we change our viewpoint, we note that the majority of books printed in the GLA were not in German. The *Universal Short Title Catalogue* (*USTC*) offers the search option "country" for sixteenth century political entities like the "Holy Roman Empire" and the "Swiss Confederation" (although, in the sixteenth century, the latter was still part of the former), but not for linguistic areas. If we add up the two polities mentioned, we see that 53% of the prints were in Latin. Of course, Latin, and in much lower degrees classical Greek and Hebrew, were for a long time the dominant languages of learned printing, especially for scholarly and ecclesiastical purposes. But can books in Latin be popular? Apart from the learned languages of Latin, classical Greek and Hebrew, there were other vernacular languages besides German that were present in German production, as table 1, based on the *USTC16*, displays.

Tab. 1: Book production in the Holy Roman Empire and the Swiss Confederation 1501-1600 (USTC16)[3]

1501-1600	Holy Roman Empire	Swiss Confederation	Total	Language %
Latin	47,814	9,692	57,506	53.45
German	43,047	2,190	45,237	42.04
Greek	660	245	905	0.84
Dutch	585	5	590	0.55
French	424	1,977	2,401	2.23
Danish	180		180	0.17
English	151	23	174	0.16
Italian	99	131	230	0.21
Hebrew	93	125	218	0.20

---

2 A. Pettegree / M. Hall, *The Reformation and the Book: A Reconsideration*, in "Historical Journal", 47, 2004, pp. 785–808, here pp. 793 f. The figures are based on 10,000 consecutive items taken from the *Index Aurelianis*.
3 USTC search path: "1501–1600" plus "Holy Roman Empire" / "Swiss Confederation", http://ustc.ac.uk/index.php, accessed May 30, 2017. Of course, the French and Italian speaking parts of the Swiss Confederation are not part of the GLA and thus distort the results slightly (especially for the part of the French language). There are 290 titles printed in other languages than those on the list.

1501-1600	Holy Roman Empire	Swiss Confederation	Total	Language %
Swedish	57		57	0.05
Hungarian	42		42	0.04
Czech	23	1	24	0.02
Spanish	15	14	29	0.03
Total	93,190	14,403	107,593	100.00

From the point of view of printed languages, the GLA print market is multilingual and transnational. The same goes for the authors printed in the sixteenth century: among the bestsellers within the GLA we find the Dutch Erasmus, the German Martin Luther, and the ancient Roman Cicero. The transnational character is even visible in printing types used: German texts are printed in *Fraktur* (Gothic type, dark letters) but Latin, French or Italian expressions within German texts and texts entirely in Latin or French or Italian are set in *Antiqua*.

Fig. 1: Samuel Dilbaum, *FEBRVARIVS Anni 1597*, Rorschach, Leonhart Straub, 1597, VD16: D 1705. USTC16: 657379, Bayerische Staatsbibliothek München, Res/4 Hom. 1950, S. 1, urn:nbn:de:bvb:12-bsb00086840-6.

3 German

The term "German" means that the prints are designed "in German language" and hints at the other possibilities: "printed in Germany" or "printed in the German Language Area". If we are talking about popular print in German, we must accept that there is no central nor complete bibliography of German books, or in particular, of German "popular prints". The politically fragmented structure of the German speaking part of Europe during the Early Modern period comprises of the modern-day nation-states of Germany, Austria, Switzerland (German speaking parts) as well as German speaking areas or minorities in the modern-day states of France (Alsace), Belgium, Denmark, Hungary, Italy, Poland, Romania, the Czech Republic, and the Baltic States. As a result, we have several national projects engaged in establishing retrospective complete bibliographies. Correlating to the size of these political entities, the projects in the Federal Republic of Germany (FRG) are the most important.

However, as the federal German tradition survived even World War II, the FRG – not to mention the German Democratic Republic (GDR) – organized the national bibliography in a federal way. The FRG's national bibliography is called *Verzeichnis der im deutschen Sprachraum erschienen Drucke* (*VD*), in English: "Bibliography of the prints published in the GLA", but this bibliography is divided into centuries: the sixteenth, seventeenth, or eighteenth centuries as well as the *Gesamtverzeichnis der Wiegendrucke* (*GV*) – the complete bibliography of the incunabula (fifteenth century). The bibliographies are, however, not complete and are not constructed according to identical criteria of selection, as table 2, including online[4] and printed[5] bibliographies and collections[6], displays.

---

4 Websites: *GW* = *Gesamtverzeichnis der Wiegendrucke* [Incunabula]; *ISTC* = *Incunabula Short Title Catalogue*, British Library, http://www.bl.uk/catalogues/istc/, accessed January 8, 2018; USTC; *VD16* = *Verzeichnis der im deutschen Sprachbereich erschienenen Drucke des 16. Jahrhunderts*, Bayerische Staatsbibliothek, München, https://opacplus.bib-bvb.de/TouchPoint_touchpoint/start.do?SearchProfile=Altbestand&SearchType=2, accessed January 8, 2018; *VD17* = *Verzeichnis der im deutschen Sprachraum erschienenen Drucke des 17. Jahrhunderts*, http://gso.gbv.de/DB=1.28/, accessed January 8, 2018; *VD18* = *Verzeichnis der im deutschen Sprachraum erschienenen Drucke des 18. Jahrhunderts*, http://gso.gbv.de/DB=1.65/START_WELCOME, accessed January 8, 2018; *ZDB* = *Zeitschriftendatenbank*, Staatsbibliothek zu Berlin, http://www.zeitschriftendatenbank.de/startseite/, accessed January 8, 2018; * *Z17* = *Zeitungen des 17. Jahrhunderts*, University of Bremen, http://brema.suub.uni-bremen.de/zeitungen17/, accessed January 8, 2018, integration into VD17 (planned).
5 Printed bibliographies *GV* = *Gesamtverzeichnis des deutschsprachigen Schrifttums. 1700–1910*, 160 vols., München et al. 1979–1987; F. Blaser, *Bibliographie der Schweizer Presse mit Einschluss des Fürstentums Liechtenstein*, 2 vols., Basel 1956–1958; H. Böning (ed.), *Deutsche Presse. Biobibliographische Handbücher zur Geschichte der deutschsprachigen periodischen Presse von den Anfängen bis 1815*, 3 vols., Stuttgart-Bad Cannstatt 1996–2003; E. Bogel / E. Blühm, *Die deutschen Zeitungen des 17. Jahrhunderts. Ein Bestandesverzeichnis mit historischen und bibliographischen Angaben*, 3 vols., Bremen / München 1971–1985; E. Bogel, *Schweizer Zeitungen des 17. Jahrhunderts. Gallen und Solothurn*, Bremen, Schünemann, 1973; VE15 = F. Eisermann, *Verzeichnis der typographischen Einblattdrucke des 15. Jahrhunderts im Heiligen Römischen Reich Deutscher Nation*, 3 vols., Wiesbaden 2004; J. Kirchner, *Bibliographie der deutschen Zeitschriften des deutschen Sprachgebietes bis 1900*, vol. 1, Stuttgart 1969; H.-J. Köhler, *Bibliographie der Flugschriften des 16. Jahrhunderts*, Teil 1: *Das frühe 16. Jahrhundert 1501–1530*, 3 vols., (A–S), Tübingen 1991–1996.
6 W. Harms (ed.), *Deutsche illustrierte Flugblätter des 16. und 17. Jahrhunderts*, 7 vols., Tübingen 1985–2005; J.R. Paas, *The German Political Broadsheet 1600–1700*, 14 vols., Wiesbaden 1985–2017;

Tab. 2: Components of a "German National" bibliography 1400-1800. Bibliographies usually list [all] extant titles [library holdings], except those in bold. (Italics = not completed)

Centuries	Broadsheets, single leaves	Books 1450–1900	Pamphlets (Flugschriften)	Newspapers 1605–1900	Journals 1674–1815	Periodicals 1450–1815
15th	VE15 (2004) (typogr.)	GW ISTC				**Deutsche Presse (Böning 1996-2003)** – all periodicals (calendar, mess-relation, year book, newspaper, journal etc.) – For a few particular printing centers as Hamburg, Altona etc.
16th	Harms ed. (1985–2005) Strauss (1974/75)	VD16 USTC16	Köhler (1990–1999) USTC16			
17th	Harms ed. (1985–2005) Paas ed. (1985–2017)	VD17 USTC 17	VD17 USTC17	VD17 (*Z17) ZDB **Bogel/ Blühm (1971-85)** CH: **Bogel (1973)**	ZDB Kirchner (1969)	
18th		VD18 GV 1700–1910 (1969–87)	VD18	ZDB CH: Blaser (1956–58)	VD18 ZDB Kirchner (1969)	

- There is no clear definition of the geographic borders of the "German Language Area". The book historian Jürgen Beyer posits that the underlying map is from 1918 (which is not really relevant for the fifteenth to the eighteenth centuries)[7].
- These bibliographies only deliver a compilation of the existing books, not all the titles ever produced.
- They all explicitly exclude music sheets, i.e. also popular songs or song texts, as well as maps.

The following points, shown in table 3, are even trickier, because they do not concern all centuries alike.

Tab. 3: Comparing bibliographies: VD16, VD17, and VD18

	VD16 (2013: 104 000 titles)	VD17 (2017: 299 000 titles)	VD18 (2016: 170 000 titles)
Collaborating institutions	Libraries	Libraries	Libraries
Prints	Actually existing	Actually existing	Actually existing
Geography	Not defined (1918?)	Not defined (1918?)	"Historical GLA"
Language	Any in GLA	Any in GLA German outside GLA	Any in GLA German outside GLA
Explicitly excluded	German prints outside GLA Music sheets Maps Single leaf prints	Music sheets Maps	Music sheets Maps
Missing, because (often) not hosted in libraries, but in archives	Official printings Pamphlets Tracts Newspapers Journals	Official printings (Pamphlets) (Tracts) Newspapers* Journals	Official printings (Pamphlets) (Tracts) Newspapers

* Integration of newspapers (Z17) planned.

M. Geisberg, *The German Single-Leaf Woodcut 1500–1550*, ed. by W.L. Strauss, 4 vols., New York 1974; W.L. Strauss, *The German Single-Leaf Woodcut 1550–1600. A Pictorial Catalogue*, 3 vols., New York 1975.

7 J. Beyer, *How Complete are the German National Bibliographies for the Sixteenth and Seventeenth Centuries (VD16 and VD17)?*, in M. Walsby / G. Kemp (eds.), *The Book Triumphant. Print in Transition in the Sixteenth and Seventeenth Centuries* (Library of the Written Word, 15), Leiden / Boston MA 2011, pp. 57–77, here p. 61.

- The titles in German printed outside the GLA are not included in the printed edition of *VD16*, but they are now going to be included in the online version of *VD16*.
- Broadsheets are excluded from *VD16*, but included in *VD17* and *VD18*.

The last group, in italics, represents the greatest challenge.
- Official printings such as laws, police ordinances, edicts, proclamations, etc. have usually been stored in archives rather than in libraries. Many of them are broadsheets to nail at cities' doors, single leaf prints, or small booklets to be distributed to every household or even printed forms or receipts to be filled in or signed by hand. Based on the analysis of regional samples, Jürgen Beyer estimates that only 20% of the extant official publications are currently listed in *VD17* – that means that probably 80% are not[8].
- Tracts and pamphlets represent a similar case. Lacking the immaterial and material "value" of a book, tracts and pamphlets were not very interesting for libraries. Even if libraries stored tracts and pamphlets, they were typically squeezed into boxes or bound to volumes without listing all pieces one by one in a catalogue or bibliography[9].
- As official prints or tracts and pamphlets have been produced in the context of political communication, they are sometimes stored in archives. Archivists, however, treated prints like "neglected orphans" for a long time – just as museums did[10].
- The political context could also mean the authorities confiscated and even destroyed pamphlets or tracts for the reason of censorship[11].
- Prints in German produced outside Germany are missing from the *VD16*. During the sixteenth century, the Swiss city of Basel was among the five most important printing cities of the GLA and among the twelve most important in Europe. For Basel and Zurich the librarian, Urs B. Leu, involved with the Swiss libraries' e-rara-project and the *Index Typographorum Editorumque Basiliensium (ITB)*, has found up to 20% more titles printed than listed in the *VD16*[12]. Jürgen Beyer

---

8 J. Beyer, *How Complete are the German National Bibliographies*, p. 75.
9 A. Würgler, *Unruhen und Öffentlichkeit. Städtische und ländliche Protestbewegungen im 18. Jahrhundert* (Frühneuzeit-Forschungen, 1), Tübingen 1995, pp. 133–144, 146–153, 186–188; A. Würgler, *Medien*, p. 101.
10 J. Beyer, *How Complete are the German National Bibliographies*, p. 75. Cf. J. Odenbreit, *Einblattdrucke des 16. Jahrhunderts in Gedächtnisorganisationen. Erfassung und Erschliessung*, (Berliner Handreichungen zur Bibliotheks- und Informationswissenschaft, 369), Berlin 2014.
11 A. Würgler, *Unruhen*, pp. 234–236; D. Jones (ed.), *Censorship. A World Encyclopedia*, 4 vols., London / Chicago IL 2002.
12 U.B. Leu, *Die Bedeutung Basels als Druckort im 16. Jahrhundert*, in C. Christ-von Wedel / S. Grosse / B. Hamm (eds.), *Basel als Zentrum des geistigen Austauschs in der frühen Reformationszeit*, Tübingen 2014, pp. 53–78, here p. 53–55; U.B. Leu, *The Book and Reading Culture in Basel and Zurich During the*

estimates that *VD16* and *VD17* include only two thirds of the books still extant – the rest can be found in libraries outside the GLA and in archives[13]. The French case proves the relevance of this strategy: 30% of French books have survived only outside of France[14].

The *Universal Short Title Cataloque (USTC)* has become the most powerful database available and has finally surpassed the nationally and linguistically restricted bibliographies, but it exists only for the sixteenth century – the seventeenth is under construction – and faces some of the problems discussed above[15]. The explicit exclusion of broadsheets and maps by most general bibliographies and catalogues and the implicit or factual exclusion of single leaf prints (small size), official printings, and tracts is very much our concern: this exclusion regards popular prints insofar as they are of cheap price (single leaves, calendars), have a great audience (official printings), or address a largely public and political context (pamphlets, tracts).

There exists however, bibliographies that list specific genres of printings, such as particular kinds of illustrated broadsheets hosted in large collections[16]. These editions are mostly based on collections made by contemporary princes (or cities) for specific purposes, i.e., they are highly selective and usually favor high-quality images and "art", but not cheap or popular prints.

The lack of the most popular genre of seventeenth and eighteenth century texts, the newspapers, in all *VD's*, is, however, the biggest problem. The journals integrate into *VD18*, but not into *VD17*. For newspapers and journals, we again have specific, yet fragmentary bibliographies[17].

Sixteenth Century, in M. Walsby / G. Kemp (eds.), *The Book Triumphant*, pp. 295–319, here pp. 295 f.; A. Pettegree, *Calvin and Luther as Men of the Book*, in K.E. Spierling (ed.), *Calvin and the Book. The Evolution of the Printed Word in Reformed Protestantism*, Göttingen 2015, pp. 17–32, here p. 20. Cf. ITB http://www.ub.unibas.ch/itb/, accessed January 19, 2018.

13 J. Beyer, *How Complete are the German National Bibliographies*, p. 76.

14 A. Pettegree, *Field Work*, in http://ustc.ac.uk/index.php/site/about, accessed January 11, 2018.

15 The *USTC* has no problems with national boundaries, but, of course, depends on the uneven level of local or national library systems; it includes music printing, but excludes single-leaf and broadsheet prints; and it lists only extant books; cataloguing the "lost books" is in its beginnings, cf. A. Pettegree, *The World of the 16th Century French Book*, in https://www.st-andrews.ac.uk/~bookproj/resources/FVB%20-%20The%20World%20of%20the%20C16th%20Book.pdf, accessed January 11, 2018; F. Bruni / A. Pettegree (eds.), *Lost Books. Reconstructing the Print World of Pre-industrial Europe*, Leiden 2016. Even for the catalogued items, there remain leaks. For Berne, to give just one example, the *USTC* seems to have not included the prints of the category "ordinances and edicts" and "broadsheets", but it does include both categories for Zurich Cf. *USTC* search "Bern + Switzerland" and "Zürich + Switzerland". About these prints, C. Schott-Volm (ed.), *Repertorium der Policeyordnungen der Frühen Neuzeit*, vol. 7/1: *Orte der Eidgenossenschaft*, Bern / Frankfurt a.M. 2006, pp. 15 f., here p. 741.

16 E.g. W. Harms, *Deutsche illustrierte Flugblätter*, but no comprehensive bibliography containing all sorts of prints (on one page or leaf) – because *VE15*, is restricted to "typographic" prints.

17 *ZDB*, collaboration of 3,700 libraries in Germany and Austria; E. Bogel / E. Blühm, *Die deutschen Zeitungen*; E. Bogel, *Schweizer Zeitungen*; Z17; *Deutsche Presse*.

4 Popular

The term "popular" is not very popular in the GLA, because it incorporates many semantic problems. Unfortunately, Alisha Rankin's paper about Germany in the *History of Print Culture* does not discuss them[18]. The first problem is, of course, to know whether popular means "widely liked" in the sense of "widely sold, bought and consumed" or "cheap price", or whether it includes "the whole cloth of experiences and activities with and around books"[19].

Etymologically, the term popular is "difficult" to translate into German. We have today the word "popular" *(populär)*, but this is, according to the late eigteenth century dictionary of Johann Adelung, a word recently – and as Adelung underlines: without need – imported from the French *populaire* at the end of the eigteenth century. The German adjectives for "people", *Volk*, i.e. *völkisch, volkstümlich,* have not been in use since the National Socialist period *(völkisch)* or are not comparable to popular *(volkstümlich)*[20]. This might be the reason why there is not much research in Germany that is labelled "popular", except some seminal works from around 1970 typically written by cultural anthropologists[21].

Among the most popular – widely liked, sold, bought, read, heard – products of the early modern products of the printing press are newspapers[22]. Newspapers are periodically (at least weekly) printed news from Europe and beyond, written in a dry, standardized, and not too complicated language. Sold at a low price in bookshops, post offices, or by annual abonnements, they seem to have been read, heard, and discussed by persons from almost every social strata of seventeenth and eighteenth century populations. They were more easily accessible in cities than in the countryside and more common in wealthy milieus than among the poor but practices like public reading on the street or in taverns and inns, reading aloud in monasteries or in families, at work or at school, and even during or after church services helped to

---

18 She just offers a narrative of the invention of typography A. Rankin, *Germany*, in J. Raymond (ed.), *The Oxford History of Print Culture*, vol. 1, Oxford 2011, pp. 205–213.
19 J. Raymond, *Introduction*, in *The Oxford History of Print Culture*, vol. 1, pp. 1–14, here p. 14.
20 Popular music in the sense of "pop" music is quite the opposite of "volkstümliche Musik", which is probably nearer to "folk" music.
21 R. Schenda, *Volk ohne Buch. Studien zur Sozialgeschichte populärer Lesestoffe 1770–1910*, Frankfurt a.M. 1970; R. Schenda, *Die Lesestoffe der kleinen Leute. Studien zur populären Literatur im 19. und 20. Jahrhundert*, München, Beck, 1976; W. Brückner, *Populäre Druckgraphik Europas: Deutschland, vom 15. bis zum 20. Jahrhundert*, München 1975; R.W. Brednich / A. Hartmann (eds.), *Populäre Bildmedien*, Göttingen 1989; C. Lipp (ed.), *Medien populärer Kultur. Erzählung, Bild und Objekt in der volkskundlichen Forschung: Rolf Wilhelm Brednich zum 60. Geburtstag 1995*, Frankfurt a.M. / New York 1995.
22 V. Bauer / H. Böning, *Die gedruckte Zeitung und ihre Bedeutung für das Medien- und Kommunikationssystem des 17. Jahrhunderts*, in V. Bauer / H. Böning (eds), *Die Entstehung des Zeitungswesens im 17. Jahrhundert. Ein neues Medium und seine Folgen für das Kommunikationssystem der Frühen Neuzeit* (Presse und Geschichte. Neue Beiträge, 54), Bremen 2011, pp. IX–XVII, here pp. IX–XI.

popularize the newspapers and their contents and to shape everyday social conversation[23].

Newspapers emerged in the early seventeenth century by printing the handwritten news that had been in circulation through the expanding postal networks since the sixteenth century[24]. The first known printed newspaper was the "Relation", produced at Strasbourg by the printer and humanist Johann Carolus starting from 1605. The concept of the weekly printed newspaper was soon copied in Wolfenbüttel in 1609, Basel 1610, Frankfurt 1615, Hamburg 1618, Stuttgart 1619, Cologne 1620, Vienna 1621, Zurich 1622, Oettingen and Rostock 1625, and some 20 more towns in the GLA before 1650 when the first daily newspaper emerged in Leipzig[25]. The new genre spread quickly throughout the rest of Europe. Weekly papers emerged in Amsterdam in 1618, Valencia 1619, Antwerp 1620, London 1621, Paris 1631, Copenhagen 1634, Genova 1639, Barcelona 1641, Bologna and Naples 1642, Turin and Stockholm 1645, and so on[26].

These early journals did not yet form an opinion press, but they informed readers and hearers about wars breaking out and armies coming closer, prices getting higher, peace treaties being concluded, dynasties disappearing, and revolts being repressed by the authorities. The development of the number of journals produced in the GLA and all over Europe is a success story. Newspapers are a transnational print product: their often-translated contents are essentially European (only marginally global) and their format, layout, and style are similar throughout Europe (perhaps with the Dutch exception regarding size and the English exception regarding variety). German newspapers were sold and read beyond the GLA, especially in the north and east[27]. The greatest amount of extant seventeenth century copies of German newspapers is

---

23 I. Jentsch, *Zur Geschichte des Zeitungslesens in Deutschland am Ende des 18. Jahrhunderts; mit besonderer Berücksichtigung der gesellschaftlichen Formen des Zeitungslesens*, Leipzig 1937; R. Schenda, *Vom Mund zum Ohr. Bausteine einer Kulturgeschichte volkstümlichen Erzählens in Europa*, Göttingen 1993; A. Würgler, *Unruhen*, pp. 221, 226; A. Messerli, *Lesen und Schreiben 1700 bis 1900. Untersuchung zur Durchsetzung der Literalität in der Schweiz*, Tübingen 2002, pp. 398–410; A. Messerli / R. Chartier (eds.), *Lesen und Schreiben in Europa 1500–1900. Vergleichende Perspektiven*, Basel 2000; P. Albrecht / H. Böning (eds.), *Historische Presse und ihre Leser. Studien zu Zeitungen und Zeitschriften, Intelligenzblättern und Kalendern in Norddeutschland*, Bremen 2005; A. Würgler, *Medien*, pp. 93–99.
24 M. Infelise, *Prima dei giornali. Alle origini della pubblica informazione, secoli XVI e XVII*, Roma / Bari 2002; M. Infelise, *From Merchants' Letters to Handwritten Political Avvisi. Notes on the Origins of Public Information*, in F. Bethencourt et al. (eds.), *Correspondence and Cultural Exchange in Europe 1400–1700* (Cultural Exchange in Early Modern Europe, 3), Cambridge 2007, pp. 33–52; W. Behringer, *Im Zeichen des Merkur. Reichspost und Kommunikationsrevolution in der Frühen Neuzeit*, Göttingen 2003; V. Bauer / H. Böning (eds.), *Die Entstehung*; A. Würgler, *National and Transnational News Distribution 1400–1800*, in Leibniz Institute of European History (ed.), *European History Online (EGO)*, Mainz, URL: http://www.ieg-ego.eu/wuerglera-2012-en URN: urn:nbn:de:0159-2012112605, accessed November 26, 2012.
25 W. Behringer, *Im Zeichen des Merkur*, p. 414. Cf. E. Bogel / E. Blühm, *Die deutschen Zeitungen*.
26 A. Würgler, *News Distribution*.
27 *Ibid.*

stored in Stockholm, London, and St. Petersburg. The Swedish, British, and Russian foreign offices used to read and sometimes translated them carefully[28].

Thanks to the Bremen-based Deutsche Presseforschung, an archive built up in the 1960s with copies of all extant seventeenth century newspapers gathered in libraries and archives across Europe, we know much more about the early modern periodical press. As a result of this great effort, now available in digitalized form, we have free online access to 750 titles (*Zeitungstitel*), 500 enterprises (*Zeitungsunternehmen*), 80,000 issues (*Ausgaben*) with about 375,000 pages. And yet we know only about 15% of all seventeenth century German newspaper production; 85% are missing[29]. For the eighteenth century, we have no central research institution or website (as we have for German newspapers of the seventeenth century or for the seventeenth and eighteenth century periodicals in French[30]), but only the general catalogue *Zeitschriftendatenbank* (*ZDB*) and some local digitalizing projects[31]. The project to establish complete bibliographies of all periodicals (calendars, *Messrelationen*, newspapers, journals, etc.) organized as a series of local bibliographies of printing cities, remains unfinished. The example of Hamburg shows that this method enabled the researchers to discover up to 100% more titles than have been known so far[32].

The decentralized structure of the printing market in the German Language Area invites us to think about the notion "popular" at a local or regional level: images of Saints were very popular in Catholic areas, but quite unpopular or even prohibited in Protestant lands. Illustrated single-leaf prints seem to have been a genre more popular in (southern) Germany than in France, anti-Prussian tracts could be sold in Austria, but not in Prussia – and the like. "Popular" is revealed to be a concept that signals geographic, social, confessional, or political differences.

---

28 E. Bogel / E. Blühm, *Die deutschen Zeitungen*; J. Hillgärtner, *Das Katalogisieren der deutschen Presse des 17. Jahrhunderts im Universal Short Title Catalogue (USTC)*, in "Jahrbuch für Kommunikatonsgeschichte", 16, 2014, pp. 171–185.
29 *Z17*, http://brema.suub.uni-bremen.de/zeitungen17/, accessed January 8, 2018.
30 *Gazettes européennes du 18e siècle*, Université de Lyon 2, http://www.gazettes18e.fr/, accessed January 9, 2018. This site contains the bibliography of all periodicals published in French (in France and outside of France) from 1600 to 1789 (online-version of: J. Sgard [ed.], *Dictionnaire des journaux 1600–1789*, 2 vols., Paris 1991) and provides links to digital copies, if available.
31 *Austrian Newspapers Online*, Österreichische Nationalbibliothek, Wien, http://anno.onb.ac.at/, accessed January 8, 2018; *digiPress – das Zeitungsportal der Bayerischen Staatsbibliothek*, München, https://digipress.digitale-sammlungen.de/, accessed January 8, 2018; *Zefys – Zeitungsinformationssystem*, Staatsbibliothek zu Berlin, http://zefys.staatsbibliothek-berlin.de/, accessed January 8, 2018.
32 H. Böning, *Deutsche Presse*, vol. 1/1, pp. I–XXXII; H. Böning, *Gedanken zu den Möglichkeiten und Erfordernissen einer Statistik des frühneuzeitlichen Pressewesens im deutschen Sprachraum*, in "Jahrbuch für Kommunikatonsgeschichte", 18, 2016, pp. 7–23, here pp. 1 f. For particular *genres* cf. E.-B. Körber, *Biobibliographie der Zeitungsextrakte* (Presse und Geschichte. Neue Beiträge, 47), Bremen 2012; E.-B. Körber, *Messrelationen: Geschichte der deutsch- und lateinischsprachigen "messentlichen" Periodika von 1588 bis 1805* (Presse und Geschichte. Neue Beiträge, 92), Bremen 2016.

5 Consumption

To work on "popular prints" means to integrate a quantifying approach and thus to experience the advantages, the limits, and especially the results of bibliometric research. The problem goes far beyond the incompleteness of any existing bibliography based on extant holdings. Even a comprehensive bibliography of all items ever printed, including the prices at which they were sold, would not explain to us what a "popular print" exactly was. All bibliographies and economic information about prices, channels of distribution, and rates of literacy are therefore interesting, but they do not solve the problem of defining "popular print".

To ask for the impact of print on the everyday life of early modern populations, we may further consider other aspects. We can look at the occasions where large groups of people came into contact with printed products and how they consumed or used printed products in everyday life[33], as the following examples may illustrate. Images of the Saints were possibly the first bestsellers of the printing commerce. The earliest single leaf woodcuts in the GLA appear in the early fifteenth century and show the portraits of the Virgin Mary, St. George, St. Barbara, St. Catherine, St. Francis, and others. St. Christopher was especially popular – in the sense of widely liked – in the fifteenth century. We find big frescos and paintings both in and outside of big and small churches. One reason for St. Christopher's celebrity lies in the popular belief that those who "see" Christopher's image will not die from a *mors mala* (sudden death without receiving the extreme unction) on that particular day. This means that purchasing a woodcut with his image and nailing it to the kitchen wall could spare you the, potentially long, journey to the next church offering this iconic service. Therefore, it might not be by chance that the oldest extant German xylography dated from 1423 shows Saint Christopher[34]. This consumption of print, of course, has nothing to do with text literacy. Illiterate persons could look at images and understand them, though they were not always obvious or easy to understand. "Reading" images was a cultural skill as well as reading texts. But printed illustrations and text legends do not necessarily need to be deciphered to have an impact. Looking and believing could be more important than reading. The woodcuts or engravings could be consumed in different ways; they could be influential without being read. Images of saints have reportedly been used as medicine and therefore were worn as "talismans" or eaten as "pills", so we must acknowledge these uses of printed items as other ways of consuming "popular" prints[35]. In the end, printing might have influenced many people rather

---

[33] J. Raymond, *Introduction*, p. 13.
[34] A. Würgler, *Medien*, pp. 7 f.; M. Melot, *Wesen und Bedeutung der Druckgraphik*, in M. Melot et al. (eds.), *Die Graphik. Entwicklungen, Stilformen, Funktion*, Genf / Stuttgart 1981, pp. 7–131, here pp. 23–25.
[35] A. Hauser, *Was für ein Leben. Schweizer Alltag vom 15. bis 18. Jahrhundert*, Zürich 1987, p. 129; W. Meyer, *Die Schweiz in der Geschichte*, vol. 1, Zürich 1995, p. 213; H. Talkenberger, *Historische Erkenntnis durch Bilder. Zur Methode und Praxis der Historischen Bildkunde*, in H.-J. Goertz (ed.), *Ge-

through the "magic" power of woodcut images displaying the Saints than through the text of the Bible.

Fig. 2: Saint Christophorus, Anonymus, single leaf woodcut, southern Germany, c. 1423, Copyright of The University of Manchester.

If the woodcut bearing the Saint's image was important in life before death, the printed indulgences were important for life after death, which was supposed to be much longer. Gutenberg and his contemporaries profited from this business by using the new typographic technique to print enormous amounts of indulgences – some issues are said to have reached up to 190,000 copies. In any case, more people bought (Gutenberg's) indulgences than (his famous) printed Bibles[36]. And again, the effect of this printed paper did not lie in the reading, but in the signing, paying – and believing.

---

schichte. Ein Grundkurs, Reinbek bei Hamburg 1998, pp. 83–98; M. Janzin / J. Güntner, *Das Buch vom Buch. 5000 Jahre Buchgeschichte*, 3rd ed., Hannover 2007.
36 A. Würgler, *Medien*, p. 11; S. Füssel, *Gutenberg und seine Wirkung*, Frankfurt a.M. 1999, p. 21; F. Fifty, *Thousand Veronicas. Print Runs of Broadsheets in the Fifteenth and Early Sixteenth Centuries*, in A. Pettegree (ed.), *Broadsheets. Single-Sheet Publishing in the First Age of Print* (Library of the Written Word, 60), Leiden / Boston 2017, pp. 76-113.

One of the most famous examples to prove the impact of the printing press on general history is, of course, the German Reformation. Bibliographies tell us that the explosion of printed titles from 1517 to 1525 in favor of the Reformation was unprecedented. This explosion of titles goes along with a structural change of the products, which can be summarized by the elements: from Latin to German, from folio to quarto, from thick books to thin tracts (*Flugschriften*) and from images of Saints to protestant-illustrated single leaf woodcuts[37]. Intensive discussions about the reception of these prints, especially in the 1980s and 1990s, have shown that it is too simple to reduce the impact of these prints to readers only. Their influence was multiplied by preachers translating the Latin and mostly German tracts and illustrated broadsheets into conversations with interested urban and rural audiences[38]. This holds for the political consequences of the Reform as well; the Great German Peasants' War of 1525. This rural revolt is unmatched in its social, geographical, and ideological dimensions. It was only possible because of the printing press: the so-called *Twelve Articles* containing the rebels' program were printed in 25 editions within a few weeks. The area of the diffusion of these *Twelve Articles* and the area touched by the revolt in 1525 overlapped[39].

Events are short-lived, even if they cause fundamental changes such as the Reformation. Consequently, we must look for other, more structural and longer-lasting impacts of print to measure its popularity. One way to do this is to explore a steady bestseller from the fifteenth to the eighteenth centuries: almanacs and calendars. The simple form displayed the months and days in broadsheet size, indicating Easter and the Saints' celebration days, the movements of the stars and, consequently, the days to sew and to harvest, to cure illnesses and so on. Later, the *Schreibkalender* became popular: thin booklets adding moral short stories or summaries of the past year's events, leaving space for personal (daily or monthly) notes in the "agenda" section. A large number of early modern ego-documents were written down on such

---

37 A. Würgler, *Medien*, p. 17.
38 R.W. Scribner, *For the Sake of Simple Folk: Popular Propaganda for the German Reformation*, Cambridge MA 1981; P. Blickle, *Gemeindereformation. Die Menschen des 16. Jahrhunderts auf dem Weg zum Heil. Studienausgabe*, 2nd ed., München 1987 [1985]; M.U. Edwards, *Printing, Propaganda and Martin Luther*, Berkeley CA 1994; A. Pettegree, *The Reformation and the Culture of Persuasion*, Cambridge MA 2005; C. Schnyder, *Reformation*, Stuttgart 2008.
39 P. Blickle, *Die Revolution von 1525. Studienausgabe*, 2nd ed., München 1983 [1975; 4th ed. 2004], pp. 23 f., 90–92 and 96 (map). The *Twelve articles* were, however, not read in all the areas of revolt in the same way. Cf. P. Blickle, *Der Bauernkrieg. Die Revolution des Gemeinen Mannes*, 4th ed., München 2012 [1998]. For the media aspects also A. Würgler, *Medien in Revolten – Revolten in Medien. Zur Medialität frühneuzeitlicher Bauernrevolten und Bauernkriege*, in P. Rauscher / M. Scheutz (eds.), *Die Stimme der ewigen Verlierer? Aufstände, Revolten und Revolutionen in den österreichischen Ländern (ca. 1450–1815)*, (Mitteilungen des Instituts für Österreichische Geschichtsforschung, 121) Wien / München 2013, pp. 273–296, here pp. 282 f.

"writing calendars"[40]. After Gutenberg, printers in almost all printing cities produced at least one type of this annual bestseller, as we know from Switzerland, where 10,000 to 60,000 copies of each city's calendar were produced (eighteenth century)[41]. The so-called *Krakow-Calendar*, printed in Vienna, is said to have been sold in some 250,000 copies. Estimates for the eighteenth century totaled about two million copies every year[42]. After their peak in the nineteenth century, calendars lost their attraction, but one may still find the current edition of the *Hinkender Bote / Messager boiteux / Corrier zoppo* (Limping messenger), in local bookshops[43]. Another way to look at the everyday impact of print is linked to one of the great gaps – up to 80%, as mentioned above – of all known bibliographies and catalogues based in libraries: the so-called "official prints and ordinances". To print edicts and ordinances was probably the major interest of a ruler or government when installing or accepting the installation of a printer's shop. For printers, this genre represented a steady income without the risk of censorship. Such edicts and ordinances were usually pinned to the door of the town hall or the church and read aloud in the streets and during the Sunday service in the church. Given the obligation for every household to have at least one adult member present at each church service, the edicts and ordinances are likely to have been the printing products with the greatest number of listeners. Thus, official printings became popular in the sense of being "widely heard", but not necessarily in the sense of being "widely liked". The making of the modern state by police-ordinances (and direct taxes) was not welcomed by the peoples concerned. This is proved by the numerous late-medieval and early modern anti-fiscal and anti-state revolts in the German territories and in the Swiss Cantons (and elsewhere in Europe)[44]. Nevertheless, "popular" print contributed to the shaping of the early modern state.

---

40 B. von Krusenstjern, *Was sind Selbstzeugnisse? Begriffskritische und quellenkundliche Überlegungen anhand von Beispielen aus dem 17. Jahrhundert*, in "Historische Anthropologie", 3, 1994, pp. 462–471; K. von Greyerz, *Ego-Documents: The Last Word?*, in "German History", 28, 2010, 3, pp. 273–282.
41 T.E. Tschui, *Die Bilderwelt des "Berner hinkenden Boten". Von seinen Anfängen bis zur Blütezeit am Ende des 18. Jahrhunderts*, in "Berner Zeitschrift für Geschiche", 68, 2006, pp. 63–104, here pp. 63, 66: 40 titles in the Swiss Cantons.
42 H. Tersch, *Schreibkalender und Schreibkultur. Zur Rezeptionsgeschichte eines frühen Massenmediums*, Graz – Feldkirch 2008, p. 18; A. Landwehr, *Geburt der Gegenwart: eine Geschichte der Zeit im 17. Jahrhundert*, Frankfurt a.M. 2014, p. 23: 200 titles with 10,000 (estimated) copies each in seventeenth-century Germany.
43 F. de Capitani, *Messager boiteux (Corrier zoppo)*, in M. Jorio (ed.), *Dizionario storico della Svizzera*, electronic version dated May 22, 2008, http://www.hls-dhs-dss.ch/textes/i/I45241.php, accessed January 11, 2018 (also available in German and French); A. Würgler, *Medien*, pp. 49, 102; G. Petrat, *Einem besseren Dasein zu Diensten. Die Spur der Aufklärung im Medium Kalender zwischen 1700 und 1919*, München 1991; A. Landwehr, *Geburt*; H. Tersch, *Schreibkalender*; T.E. Tschui, *Die Bilderwelt*; E. Fischer / W. Haefs / Y.-G. Mix (eds.), *Von Almanach bis Zeitung. Ein Handbuch der Medien in Deutschland 1700–1800*, München 1999.
44 P. Bierbrauer, *Bäuerliche Revolten im Alten Reich. Ein Forschungsbericht*, in P. Blickle (ed.), *Aufruhr und Empörung. Studien zum bäuerlichen Widerstand im Alten Reich*, München 1980, pp. 1–68;

6 Conclusion: Problems and projects

The existing problems around the field "popular print in the GLA" are situated at different levels. First, the key notions are difficult to define: the term "print" in itself is not difficult to describe, but it is often used in the restricted sense of "typography" ("printed text") thus excluding the printed images and maps (xylography and engravings); the term "popular" or "populär" is not familiar in German and there is no precise translation. The term "German" turns out to be difficult to handle if you look at the "German Language Area" which was historically variable and not clear cut (bilingual and mixed zones, enclaves etc.). The second level of problems concern the variety of catalogs and bibliographies existing or being established. They are all useful, and yet (so far) incomplete and often incompatible. The third level of problems concerns the difficulties in gathering data about the perception, uses, and consumption of "popular" printings by the population.

The most important projects improving the infrastructure for scholars working on popular print in the GLA are comprehensive bibliographies: inserting the pamphlets to the online version of *VD16*; completing *VD17* for books, journals, and pamphlets as well as integrating the periodically printed newspapers to the *VD17*; completing *VD18* for books, pamphlets, and – hopefully someday – for newspapers and journals. The same goes for the *USTC* allowing comparative research at the European level. Future research projects need to continue the studies on consumption – in the wider sense of looking, hearing, reading, eating – of printed products ("popular prints"), texts and images. They should include different uses of print in everyday life by the population, but also through the contact that subjects have with state or church authorities[45]. They finally should include the transnational dimensions of the early modern print market, for instance, the transfer of goods and ideas, the translation of news and art, the border-crossing and transcultural processes of diffusion, adaptation, transformation, and perception of material and ideal elements of print culture in Europe.

P. Blickle, *Unruhen in der ständischen Gesellschaft 1300–1800* (Enzyklopädie deutscher Geschichte, 1, München 1988 [4th ed. 2012]); P. Blickle (ed.), *Resistance, Representation, and Community* (The Origins of the Modern State in Europe 13th to 18th Centuries, E), Oxford 1997; A. Würgler, *Soziale Konflikte*, in M. Jorio (ed.), *Historisches Lexikon der Schweiz*, electronic version dated January 8, 2013, http://www.hls-dhs-dss.ch/textes/d/D25757.php, accessed January 9, 2018 (also available in French and Italian).

45 Cf. A. Würgler, *Unruhen*, pp. 133–157, 223–226; D. Zaret, *Petitions and the "Invention" of Public Opinion in the English Revolution*, in "American Journal of Sociology", 101, 1996, pp. 1497–1555; D. Zaret, *Origins of Democratic Culture. Printing, Petitions and the Public Sphere in Early Modern England*, Princeton NJ 2000, pp. 81–99, 217–265; A. Würgler, *Voices from among the 'Silent Masses'. Humble Petitions and Social Conflicts in Early Modern Central Europe*, in "International Review of Social History", 46, 2001, Supplement 9, pp. 11–34.

II. Markets, Prices, and Collections

Francesca Tancini
The Railway Library and Other Literary Rubbish that Travels by the Rail

> Keepers of [railway] bookstalls, as well as of refreshment-rooms, find an advantage in offering their customers something hot and strong, something that may catch the eye of the hurried passenger, and promise temporary excitement to relieve the dullness of a journey[1].

1 Introduction

Around the mid-nineteenth century, a new sort of book appeared on the shelves: books produced for a mass market mainly using mechanical printing processes such as steam-operated printing machines, industrially produced paper, stereotyped and electrotyped printing matrices, and so forth. Of course, this was not the first example of cheap books for a large, uncultivated, mass market. Famous examples are "chap-books" and "penny dreadfuls" in England, the *Bibliothèque Bleue* and the *Imagerie d'Épinal* in France, the Remondini prints in Italy.

In this case, however, both the public and distribution were completely different from those earlier cheap books. These nineteenth-century books blossomed in connection with the development of railway transportation: it was probably the first time the audience had grown so rapidly and probably the first time books were circulated so quickly through new distribution means, such as the railway network, using specific marketing policies to maximize sales. These books were "the most inspired publishing invention of the era"[2].

The absence of specific characteristics regarding their contents, audience, and format makes it hard to define books of this kind. One relevant research goal is therefore to identify common features in their production, material components, distribution and marketing strategies, and to define them. The story of their birth will be traced, to see how this genre installed itself on the market and established its own public through pricing and editorial features, using illustrated front covers as a marketing and selling tool, a tool to widen the audience and reach a more general, popular kind of reader.

---

1 H.L. Mansel, *Sensation Novels*, in "Quarterly Review", 113, April 1863, pp. 483–491, reprinted in H.L. Mansel, *Letters, Lectures, and Reviews*, London, John Murray, 1873, pp. 213–252, here pp. 218–219.
2 R.D. Altick, *The English Common Reader. The Social History of the Mass Reading Public 1800–1900*, Chicago IL 1957, p. 299.

2 Absence of a coeval term

The books that are the topic of this chapter were known in the nineteenth century as "yellow-backs". This term denoted a very specific, at first peculiarly British, editorial format with typical features involving not only the physical and material appearance but also the way it was distributed and commercialized. However, the word "yellow-back" was a vernacular one and was never employed to identify them in contemporary publishers' advertisements or editorial prospectuses. It was probably one of those words used verbally by printers, publishers, and readers for a long time without ever being printed. The Victorian printer Edmund Evans (1826-1905) – who was the true father of this genre, since a very large quantity of yellowbacks were engraved and printed by his firm – first hinted at this term as a long-used label in his posthumous autobiography written in the late 1890s:

> These *yellow-backs* as they were called – though I did an immense number of covers [...] on a grey paper, enamelled, which suited the colours black, red, blue, or green very well, and did not look so common as the yellow enamelled – these *yellow-backs* were very popular, for railway reading books particularly[3].

The illustrator Walter Crane (1845–1915) emphasised their color in his *Reminiscences*, using the synonym "mustard" when recalling his production of "covers of cheap railway novels, which we sometimes called, from their generally yellow hue and sensational character *mustard plaisters*"[4]. James Redding Ware's *Passing English of the Victorian Era* defined them as "cheap two-shilling editions of novels, which were generally bound in a yellow, glazed paper, printed in colours"[5]. But that was in 1909. In fact, these terms – yellow-backs, mustard plaisters – were never used in advertising practice and were never to be found in print, at least not until the late 1880s and early 1890s, when this publishing phenomenon was in its later, waning phase[6].

In the absence of a contemporary term to define them univocally, it was essential for their success and salability that they were recognizable as an editorial genre. Their recognizability banked on the identification of material components rather than on names: the physical substance they were manufactured from, its color and tangible features, these features all served to make the editorial genre stand out, exactly as

---

3 E. Evans, *The Reminiscences of Edmund Evans*, ed. by R. McLean, Oxford 1967, p. 28.
4 W. Crane, *An Artist's Reminiscences*, London 1907, p. 75.
5 J. Redding Ware, *Passing English of the Victorian Era. A Dictionary of Heterodox English, Slang, and Phrase*, London 1909, reprinted in J. Redding Ware, *Ware's Victorian Dictionary of Slang and Phrase*, Oxford 2013, p. 270, *ad vocem*.
6 The term "yellow-back" is documented in 1891 in A. Conan Doyle, *The Boscombe Valley Mystery*, in "The Strand Magazine", October 1891, 2, pp. 401–416. See also P.I.E., *The Vagaries of Book-buyers*, III, in "Book-lore", January 1887, 1, pp. 6–9, here p. 9, and J. Carter / N. Barker (eds.), *ABC for Book-collectors*, London 1952 (2004), p. 233, *ad vocem*.

would happen a century afterwards with the *libri gialli*, the *libri rosa*, or the *noir*, and as had already happened, a century or so before, with the *Bibliothèque bleue*[7].

Its first definition was given by Michael Sadleir, the true pioneer of yellow-back studies:

> *Yellow-back* was the nickname given to the particular type of cheap edition evolved about the middle of last century for display and sale on railway bookstalls. It was usually (but not always) a cheap edition of fiction; it usually (but not always) cost two shillings; its basic colouring was usually (but not always) yellow – to which last characteristic, not surprisingly, it owed its soubriquet[8].

3 By way of definition

In fact, though their name suggested yellow as an identifying factor, the color of the paper used for the cover varied in hue and changed freely from pink to lilac, from blue to red, making that a minor detail to define this kind of editorial item. Their textual content was again not relevant in determining the yellow-back features. The sensational, spectacular, and even shocking features so often highlighted in connection with railway fiction need to be viewed alongside other features that figured massively in railway bookstalls. Yellow-backs might be works of fiction (detective stories, sensation novels) as well as world classics of literature, poetry, wide-ranging manuals (cookery, home management, farming, gardening, etiquette, investment handbooks), travel guides, children's books, or educational works (primers, schoolbooks, alphabets, song books).

Thus, contents and color were not consistent common features in yellow-backs, but their price was: they always sold for less than half-a-crown – their value usually ranging between sixpence and two shillings, that is to say between one tenth and half the price of clothbound one-volume editions, usually sold at no less than a crown[9]. Another consistent characteristic was that they were always bound in pictorial paper covers[10] – either monochrome paper wrappers at the lower end, or varnished paper

---

[7] One notes the strong symbolic value of color, which is never a secondary detail in making an editorial or literary genre recognizable.
[8] M. Sadleir, *Yellow-backs. Origins and Rise to Power of the Yellow-back. Facts and Phases of the Yellow-back Period. Why to Collect Yellow-backs?*, in J. Carter (ed.), *New Paths in Book-collecting. Essays by Various Hands*, London 1934, pp. 127–161, here p. 127.
[9] Note that before 1971 British currency was not decimalized; money was divided into pounds (£), shillings (s.) and pence (d.) – £1 = 20s., 1s. = 12 pennies – and there existed coins of different value such as the half-crown = 2s. 6d., or the crown = 5s.
[10] For a definition of the term "pictorial", see J. Carter / N. Barker (eds.), *ABC for Book-collectors*, p. 167, *ad vocem*.

over boards, in two or more colors, at the upper, in both cases mainly printed from relief blocks (woodblocks or stereotyped metal plates). Invariably, their covers were decorated – either pictorially, with large illustrations commissioned from important artists and painters, or typographically, with editorial cartouches and engraved titles produced by apprentices within the printer's workshop. They were always one-volume editions, because this would secure reader loyalty to the series rather than to the single title. They were ranked in series and were usually issued periodically – though this was not so strictly stated and publishers often switched series and series number. And again, they were always small pocket books, never bigger than an 8vo (Foolscap, Crown, or Post) – but other formats, usually smaller, were produced as well, such as 12mo, 16mo, or 24mo.

To sum up the identifying features of yellow-backs, they were small, one volume editions, ranked in series, bound in illustrated or decorated paper covers, and sold at a price comprised between 6d. and 2s. 6d. As such, they were invariably included in a series of one volume editions as, for example, Chapman and Hall's Select Library of Fiction[11], marketed as "cheap (or cheaper) editions"[12], advertised as "sewed"[13] or "wrapper", or "boards"[14], with the frequent addition of descriptive details such as "fancy covers", "pictorial boards", "illustrated wrapper worked in colour", "picture boards", and varying combinations of these factors.

Another common profile of yellow-backs lies outside their material nature or appearance and pertains to their distribution. Undeniably, yellow-backs were bound up with railway transportation: distributed through the railway network, they directly sprouted from travelers' increasing demand for recreational occupation during long journeys. They were therefore sold, at first, in railway bookstalls and even on railway platforms, when no bookstalls were available, by a "newsboy" or "basket boy". However, their immediate success soon pushed them out of station stands to attract high-street booksellers throughout the United Kingdom.

---

11 For example, see C. Clarke, *Charlie Thornhill*, 5th ed., London, Chapman and Hall [1866], advertised in "The Bookseller", August 31, 1865, p. 680: "Select Library of Fiction. Clarke (C.) Charlie Thornhill, new edit., 12mo 0 2 0 Chapman & Hall".
12 For example, S. Thomson, *Wild Flowers. How to See and How to Gather them*, London, Routledge, Warne, and Routledge, 1859, advertised in "The Athenaeum", May 15, 1858, p. 616: "Wild Flowers. Cheap Edition. Price 2s., boards".
13 For example, R.B. Mansfield, *The Log of the Water Lily*, London, Nathaniel Cooke, 1854, advertised in "The Athenaeum", May 20, 1854, p. 620: "2nd. edit. Cr. 8vo, 1s. swd", where "swd" stands for "sewed", thus implying a cover made of pictorial paper wrappers printed in color.
14 For example, S.W. Hayward, *Eulalie*, London, Henry Lea, 1869, advertised in "The Publishers' Circular", July 15, 1869, p. 421: "Hayward (W. Stephen) – Eulalie; or, the Red and White Roses. Post 8vo. pp. 494, boards, 2s. (Juvenile Library) (Lea) [2337].".

4 More copious literature came in demand

In mid-nineteenth-century England railways developed throughout the country and more and more people travelled by train[15]. At first – from the 1840s on – railways facilitated mainly newspaper distributors, offering the publishing industry a reliable way of sending goods across the nation[16]. Then, as railways began to spread and travelers started to multiply, book kiosks appeared in many stations.

> Sometimes they had been started by the enterprise of local booksellers, who generally combined a display of refreshment for the body with that of food for the mind. [...] Then the railway companies began to find bookstalls a convenient means of providing occupation for men disabled, or for the widows of men killed, in their service. [...] But, as journeys lengthened and travellers multiplied, more copious literature came in demand[17].

Among the cultural and social reasons hiding beneath the birth of the yellow-backs, several factors should be listed. One such was that yellow-backs helped create a "surrogate landscape", to quote the words of historian Wolfgang Schivelbusch. His theory suggests that, to escape the embarrassment of prolonged and at the same time too-brief confinement and enforced proximity with strangers within the same closed compartment, reading became almost obligatory: "the traveller's gaze could then move into an imaginary surrogate landscape, that of his book"[18]. See Figure 1.

That was particularly true for those travelling in second-class carriages, which were compartmentalized, so that reading became not only a way to pass the time but also

> a surrogate for the communication that no longer took place. [...] The perusal of reading matters is an attempt to replace the conversation which is no longer possible. Fixing one's eyes on a book or a newspaper, one is able to avoid the stare of the person sitting across the aisle. The embarrassing nature of this silent situation remains largely unconscious[19].

---

15 On this subject, see part. J.R. Kellett, *The Impact of Railways on Victorian Cities*, London 1969; J.R. Kellett, *Railways and Victorian Cities*, London 1979; M. Freeman, *Railways and the Victorian Imagination*, New Haven CT 1999; N. Daly, *Railway Novels. Sensation Fiction and the Modernization of the Senses*, in "EHL", 66, 1999, 2, pp. 461–480; M. Hammond, *Reading, Publishing and the Formation of Literary Taste in England*, Aldershot 2006; M. Hewitt, *The Dawn of the Cheap Press in Victorian Britain. The End of the 'Taxes on Knowledge', 1849–1869*, London 2015.
16 *The Newspaper Train*, in "The Graphic", May 15, 1875, with a full-page illustration by H. Johnson portraying the different stages in newspaper distribution by train.
17 H. Maxwell, *Life and Times of the Right Honourable William Henry Smith, M.P.*, New Edition, Edinburgh, William Blackwood, 1896, pp. 28–29. See also J.N. Allen, *Railway Reading, With a Few Hints to Travellers*, in "Ainsworth's Magazine", 24, 1853, pp. 483–487.
18 W. Schivelbusch, *The Railway Journey. The Industrialization of Time and Space in the Nineteenth Century*, Berkeley CA 1986, p. 64.
19 *Ibid.*, pp. 68, 75. See also M. Hammond, *Reading, Publishing and the Formation of Literary Taste*.

Fig. 1: Nathaniel Parker Willis, *Pictures of Society and People of Mark*, London, Ward, Lock, and Tyler [1871]. Front cover printed in colours (red, green, black) on yellow paper by Evans after Crane.

Of course, though, yellow-backs were at first specifically meant for railway travelers, a captive audience of many rush-hour commuters seeking for light, inexpensive, and appealing books to read and while away the boredom of the journey. An anonymous article appeared in 1854 in "The Leisure Hour" describing the situation:

> A hundred miles or two will keep [passengers] five or six hours in the carriage, and they must have something to pass away the time. [...] The habit of reading in railways has created new classes of readers, and spread the taste for reading, and awakened so general a desire for the accumulation of books, that myriads of volumes are now sold elsewhere, which, but for railway reading, would not have been sold at all. [...] Looking at this new fact in a moral light, its aspect is not so pleasant as it might be, in as much as no small amount of literary rubbish travels by the rail[20].

---

[20] *A London Railway Station*, in "The Leisure Hour", June 29, 1854, pp. 412–414, here p. 413.

"But", the anonymous journalist continues, "works of the very best class are now to be found on the railway stalls"[21]. These "works of the very best class" were the output of the entrepreneurial vision of William Henry Smith Jr (1825–1891) – that very same W.H. Smith that populates railways and airports nowadays. He was the one who set everything in motion, the one who saw the railway potential for his business and was able to secure exclusive sale rights for railway bookstalls – covering some 1,000 miles of track in 1848. His first railway bookstall was opened at Euston Station in 1848. This was the first of what would become 1,742 bookstalls by 1902.

It should be noted that W.H. Smith, later appointed First Lord of the Admiralty under Disraeli's government (1877), was dubbed by "Punch", the satirical magazine, as "Old Morality": he succeeded in securing a virtual monopoly for his railway bookstalls because he promised to make them respectable, to clean up the stations providing suitable reading for the new public, instead of "cheap French novels of the shadiest class and mischievous trash of every description which no respectable bookseller would offer"[22]. This intent met the more general concern that was the basis of the *Great Education Bill*, approved in 1870 but latently present since the late 1840s.

5. The shape of the butterfly

In this peculiar railway setting, it was the cover that sold the book and not, or at least not largely, its content. See Figure 2. As Henry Longueville Mansel described in an article of 1863, externally these books had the shape

> of the butterfly, with a tawdry cover, ornamented with a highly-coloured picture, hung out like a signboard, to give promise of the entertainment to be had within. The picture, like the book, is generally of the sensation kind, announcing some exciting scene to follow. [...] Written to meet an ephemeral demand, aspiring only to an ephemeral existence, it is natural that they should have recourse to rapid and ephemeral methods of awakening the interest of their readers, striving to act as the dram or the dose, rather than as the solid food, because the effect is more immediately perceptible[23].

This, as described by Mansel, is after all the core of modern marketing strategy. Content-wise, nothing distinguished yellow-backs from books bound in cloth. For example, the first yellow-back ever published – Horace Mayhew's *Letters Left at the Pastrycook's* – was advertised as published either in wrapper (1s.) or in cloth (1s. 6d.)[24]. See Figure 3.

---

[21] *Ibid.*
[22] H. Maxwell, *Life and Times of the Right Honourable William Henry Smith*, pp. 28–29.
[23] H.L. Mansel, *Sensation Novels*, pp. 218–219.
[24] *Letters Left at the Pastrycook's* is conventionally taken as the first real yellow-back ever published. H. Mayhew, *Letters Left at the Pastrycook's, Being the Clandestine Correspondence between Kitty Clover*

Fig. 2: Bret Harte, *Sensation Novels*, Condensed, London, Ward, Lock, and Tyler, [1874]. Front cover printed in colors (red, orange, black) on white paper by Evans after Crane.

In order to maximize sales, the same book would be bound and sold in different trade bindings – bindings that steered the book towards different, diverging publics. And for each binding variant, a different marketing strategy was developed. While those on cloth – usually sold within a "Library or Standard Edition Series" – were bought by a higher class of public that would certainly keep them after reading, yellow-backs – sold as "Cheap or Railway Edition Series" – were generally bought by commuters or lower-class readers who cared nothing about books as aesthetic products and would generally not keep them after reading.

---

at School and her 'Dear, Dear Friend' in Town, London, Ingram, Cooke, and Co., 1852. *Ingram, Cooke & Co.'s List of New Books for December*, in "The Athenaeum", November 27, 1852, p. 1307.

Fig. 3: Horace Mayhew, *Letters Left at the Pastrycook's*, London, Ingram, Cooke, and Co., 1852. Front cover printed in colors (red, blue) on white paper by Evans.

It is clear that the main draw for these books was that the attractive picture on the front cover was printed in color to catch the eye of the hurried passenger off the shelves. "Brightness of colour was always a thing to be desired", recalled Edmund Evans, and indeed it was the main selling tool for yellow-backs[25].

The word "yellow-back" was never used in contemporary advertising practice. The market presented, defined, and distinguished yellow-backs from other books, bound in cloth, using the price and details of binding alone. Price was consequently always clearly marked on the front cover or spine, or used as a name for the series (*Shilling Library, Shilling Series, Sixpenny Volume Library*, etc.).

Price always resulted from the material features of the series the volume was part of. A book bound in paper wrapper could cost up to eighteen pence (1s. 6d.); had it cost more, it would have been bound in boards. The cover could be printed in one

---

25 E. Evans, *The Reminiscences*, p. 28.

color on colored paper[26]; or a color block of the simplest kind might be added to the key block, sometimes for 6d. more[27]; as the years passed, up to three detailed color blocks might be printed, on white or colored paper, for the same price[28]. See Figure 4.

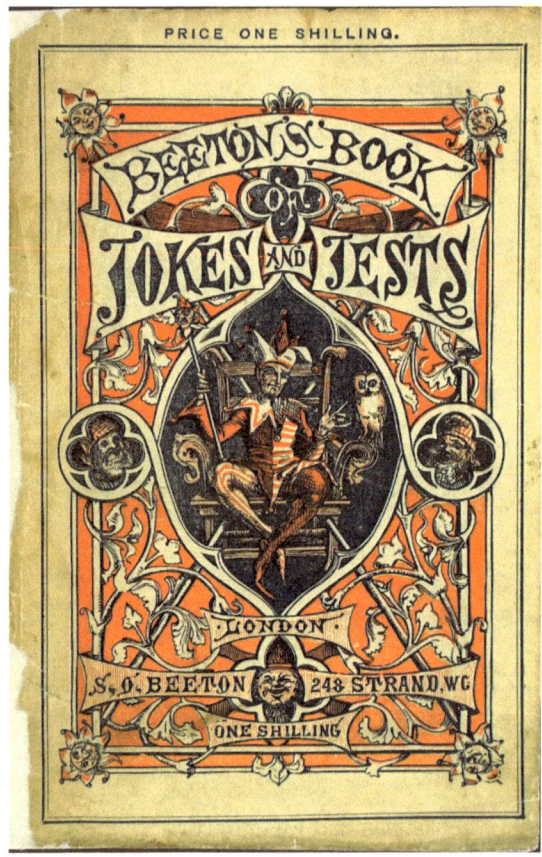

Fig. 4: *Beeton's Book of Jokes and Jests*, London, Frederick Warne & Co., 1866 [but 1865]. Front cover printed in colors (red, black) on white paper by Evans after Crane.

---

26 For example, the *Smith, Elder, & Co.'s Standard Authors* series, which had a front cover printed in only one working (black key on orange paper), cost 1s.; Miss Urquhart, *The Heiress of the Blackburnfoot, A Tale of Rural Scottish Life*, London, Smith, Elder, & Co., 1866.

27 The *Blackwood's London Library* series had for example a front cover printed in two workings (one of which was the black key, with an additional red one for the darker areas on orange paper) and cost 1s. 6d.: G. Ferry, *The Cavaliers and Free-lances of New Spain*, London, J. Blackwood, [1857]. Books included in the *Books to Amuse and Interest* series had a front cover printed in red and black (key) on white paper and cost 1s. (*Beeton's Book of Jokes and Jests*, London, Frederick Warne & Co., 1866 [but 1865, with S.O. Beeton on front cover].

28 For example, books included in the *Chapman & Hall's Standard Authors* series had a front cover printed in red, green and the black key on white paper and cost 1s.: [B. Hemyng], *On the Line, or, Tales of the Royal Mail, by a Railway Guard*, London, David Bryce, [1866], reissue of [1870] by Chapman & Hall.

On the other hand, books bound in paper-over-board covers usually cost no less than two shillings, and sometimes reached half-a-crown; their covers were typically printed in three overprinted colors – variations of red and green, or red and blue, and the key block. The paper might be colored in pulp, varnished, or colored with another simple working, and sometimes ruled or patterned[29]. See Figure 5.

Fig. 5: [B. Hemyng], *On the Line*, London, David Bryce, [1866], reissue of [1870] by Chapman & Hall. Front cover printed in color (red, green, black) on yellow paper by Evans after Crane.

The more complex the cover design, the smaller the number of colors used, with the aim of cutting costs, since the printing charge was diminished by eliminating one or more workings, that is to say overprintings. A book in boards could cost 1s. only if it had an editorial cover repeated identical for the whole series (only varying in title and

---

29 For example, the *New Works for Railway and Home Reading* series, which had a front cover printed in red, green and the black key on orange paper, varnished, cost 2s. 6d.: J. Payn, *Lost Sir Massingberd*, London, Sampson, Low, Son, and Marston, 1865.

author)[30], or if it was of smaller format and printed in no more than two colors[31]. It is important to consider how closely the price of each copy was related to the printing technique and the number of colors used. It was obviously not the engraver's aesthetic choice which determined the quantity of blocks used or the refinement of the engravings. It was the financial agreement between the engraver and the publisher which established whether a cover, or an illustration, had to be printed in two, three, or more overprintings.

6 Printers and artists

In the Routledge and Kegan Paul Archive there is a price list of the printer Edmund Evans's work dated March 24, 1868: for covers in two colors (or workings), the minimum print run was 3,000; for covers in three workings, the minimum was 1,000. In this latter case, a print run of

> 1,000 or 2,000 copies cost 10s. each 1,000 copies
> 3,000 copies cost 7s. each 1,000 copies
> 4,000 copies cost 5s. 6d. each 1,000 copies
> 6,000 copies cost 4s. each 1,000 copies
> 10,000 copies cost 2s. 6d. each 1,000 copies[32].

The best result, in terms of color, came from paper colored in pulp, dyed, or varnished, used both as an additional tint and to prevent paper soiling. At first, they were printed on thick white paper, then the trade required a toned paper so that the covers should not soil too easily, and yellow enameled paper was used. For the same reason, the key block could be colored instead of black, a thing that allowed the publisher to obtain the most from workings. Sometimes the production had to be done so speedily, and the costs had to remain so low, that the publisher did not commission a specific drawing for a yellow-back. Instead, he would recycle woodblocks for black and white illustrations produced for magazines or as frontispieces for clothbound books, as was the case with the full-page illustrations drawn by John Everett Millais and engraved by the Dalziel Brothers for the monthly instalments of Trollope's *Orley Farm*[33], reused

---

30 The *Holiday Library for the Young* series, which had the same design for every title in the series, was advertised in "The Publishers' Circular", (January 15, 1850), p. 33: "Price One Shilling Each, in Illuminated Covers; or 1s. 6d. in Morocco Cloth".
31 For example, J.E. Carpenter, *The National Song Book*, London, Routledge, Warne, & Routledge, 1864, sold in boards at 1s. with two workings (red and black key on yellow paper) and in 24mo.
32 Routledge and Kegan Paul Archive, University College London (now deposited at the National Archives, Kew), RKP.1, f. 318.
33 A. Trollope, *Orley Farm, With Illustrations by J.E. Millais*, London, Chapman and Hall, 1862, vol. 1, p. 18.

on the front cover of yellow-backs which had no relation at all to the original text[34]. However, normally the best artists in town would be hired and were asked to supply drawings especially designed for yellow-back front covers. It is in these cases that the marketing philosophy emerges more prominently. Archival sources give details about the ways specific parts of the text to be illustrated were selected, as in a letter where the engraver asks the illustrator to "make [the drawing] as interesting as possible – even if you exaggerate – the publishers are anxious to have a good cover for this. If you can find a more telling subject do it"[35]. Or in another letter where the engraver asks the illustrator to "Introduce some pretty girls!"[36]. Or, again, one where the engraver asks to select a scene

> to be taken from the play now performing at the Olympic, will you run through the book and then see the play and do a scene from the play that is also in the book. [...] I have to submit a sketch before it is drawn on wood. [...] I will pay you for all this extra[37].

The printer used to involve specific professionals in order to obtain a cover illustration: the artist who produced the drawing, the artisan who traced it on the woodblock, the engraver who specialized in skies, clouds, or waves, the typeface designer who cut titles and authors' names, the decorator who outlined borders and frames, etc. For example, to print *The Bravo* front cover the printer Edmund Evans employed the artist Thomas Henry Nicholson (to drawn the cover), the engraver John Greenaway (to cut the front and back cover blocks) and George Bonner's workshop (to trace the titles)[38].

7 An increasing demand

The production figures are impressive. George Routledge and Sons launched their *Railway Library* in 1848 – the same year W.H. Smith's established his first bookstall at Euston Station – and this series alone listed more than 1,200 titles by 1899. Routledge

---

34 Among many possible examples see the front cover of D.M. Mulock Craik, *The Ogilvies*, London, Chapman and Hall, [1879].
35 Letter from Edmund Evans to Walter Crane, dated June 9, 1864, Manchester, John Rylands University Library, WCA/2/2/2, ff. 1–2.
36 Letter from Edmund Evans to Walter Crane, undated [1868], Manchester, John Rylands University Library, WCA/2/2/2, ff. 2–5, with reference to *Routledge's Handbook of Conjuring*, London, George Routledge and Sons, 1868.
37 Letter from Edmund Evans to Walter Crane, dated October 8, 1866, Manchester, John Rylands University Library, WCA/2/2/1, f. 62, with reference to A.M. Hall, *The Whiteboy*, London, Chapman and Hall, [1866] (reissue of [1884]).
38 J.F. Cooper, *The Bravo*, London, Routledge, 1854, Charles E. Young Research Library, University of Los Angeles (Sadleir 3489 2); for what concerns artists and attributions see Louis Round Wilson Special Collections Library, University of North Carolina at Chapel Hill, Z258 .E82, f. 33r.

had a dozen other series, among them a *Popular Library of Non-fiction Works*, a *Books for the Country Series*, a *Cheap Series*, a *Shilling Novels*. The same goes for Chapman & Hall, with its *Select Library of Fiction*, subsequently acquired by Ward & Lock, which reached 1,000 titles.

The popularity of these books was immediate. Edmund Evans recalled:

> I have known publishers order an illustrated cover for a remnant they had in stock, and not only sell off that remnant, but a reprint would be demanded [...] I have had advanced sheets for three publishers of the same book, each, of course, wanting their own published first[39]!

Each title had a standard print run between 2,000 and 6,000 copies at one time but it could reach and even surpass 20,000[40]. It is difficult to tell how many titles were actually published in each series: some of them had already been published in other series, some series merged into others, only a select list of titles being included in the listing and their numbering continuously changed. It is therefore difficult to determine the exact number of books published, let alone the number of reissues – impressively high – and this opens the field to interesting new methodologies and research avenues, although this is not the place to elaborate on this.

They were usually reprinted without interruption for many years, recycling the same stereotyped text and sometimes changing the cover design or series name or number. For example, *Common Shells of the Sea-Shore* was issued several times by the same publisher with changes only in paper color and this specific detail turns out to be the only evidence for dating one issue: the title was first issued by Warne in 1865, in a cover printed on pink paper[41]; it was then issued again in 1869, on blue paper[42], and then again, in 1873, on yellow paper[43]. See Figures 6, 7, and 8. On the other hand, the same cover was being used for several titles, such as the moonlight landscape first used for *Castle of Ehrenstein*[44] and then again for *Pilgrims of the Rhine*[45]; or, the same cover might be used for the whole series, thus greatly increasing the readers' loyalty[46].

---

39 E. Evans, *The Reminiscences*, p. 28.
40 See documents in the Routledge and Kegan Paul Archive, University College London (now deposited at the National Archives, Kew), RKP.8, f. 381.
41 Rev. J.G. Wood, *The Common Shells of the Sea-Shore*, London, Frederick Warne & Co., 1865.
42 Rev. J.G. Wood, *The Common Shells*, London, Frederick Warne & Co., 1869.
43 Rev. J.G. Wood, *The Common Shells*, London, Frederick Warne & Co., [1873].
44 G. Payne Rainsford, *The Castle of Ehrenstein*, London, George Routledge & Sons, [1864].
45 E. Bulwer Lytton, *The Pilgrims of the Rhine*, London, George Routledge & Sons, 1866.
46 For example, the same cover design – engraved and printed by Edmund Evans after a drawing by John Gilbert now at Manchester City Gallery (1947.286/63b) – was used for many titles of the series, such as the following titles by J.F. Cooper, *The Last of the Mohicans*, London, George Routledge and Co., 1854; *The Pioneers*, London, George Routledge and Co., 1854; *Oak Openings*, London, George Routledge and Co., 1855; *Deer Slayer*, London, George Routledge and Co., 1855; *Satanstoe*, London, George Routledge and Co., 1856.

Fig. 8: J.G. Wood, *The Common Shells of the Sea-Shore*, London, Frederick Warne & Co., [1873]. Front cover printed in color (red, blue, black) on yellow paper by Evans after Crane.

Fig. 7: J.G. Wood, *The Common Shells of the Sea-Shore*, London, Frederick Warne & Co., 1869. Front cover printed in color (red, blue, black) on blue paper by Evans after Crane.

Fig. 6: J.G. Wood, *The Common Shells of the Sea-Shore*, London, Frederick Warne & Co., 1865. Front cover printed in color (red, blue, dark blue) on pink paper by Evans after Crane.

> These covers attracted the public taste so much at that time that publishers frequently gave orders for an illustrated cover for a remnant they had in stock, and not only were they able to sell off the remnant by this means, but often a reprint was demanded[47].

The demand was so high that W.H. Smith had his work cut out to provide enough books for sale in his bookstalls.
Curiously enough,

> it had always been one of Smith's rules not to have the smallest property in any publication [...] [so as] to deal impartially with every publishing house. [...] But a time came when the supply of bookstall literature ran low[48].

As a consequence, Smith's manager and head of the book department, Mr. Jabez Sandifer (1823c.–1887)[49], was commissioned to buy up old copyrights, to buy paper, contracts for printing, to receive designs for covers and

> in short, [to] undertake all necessary steps in setting out on a heavy publishing venture. [...] BUT these books were issued by arrangement with Messrs. Chapman and Hall, whose names, and not that of Smith & Son, appeared on the titles[50].

Smith's advertisements were usually displayed, all the same, on endpapers and pastedowns and his name was sometimes recorded as that of the printer on the last page of the text[51].

8 Hachette's "Bibliothèque des Chemins de Fer"

At the very beginning, this editorial format was uniquely and intrinsically British – a true creation of Victorian times. However, as soon as they were put on sale, such editions became a European phenomenon.

W.H. Smith's first bookstall opened at Euston Station in 1848. In 1851, Louis Hachette (1800–1864) went to London by train to visit the Great Exhibition and found what W.H. Smith had been doing with railway bookstalls. Hachette followed Smith's example and exported it to France. In May 1852, the Compagnie du Nord accepted Hachette's proposal and he received permission to install his own network of book-

---

47 H.M. Cundall, *Birket Foster, R.W.S.*, London 1906, p. 65.
48 H. Maxwell, *Life and Times of the Right Honourable William Henry Smith*, p. 52.
49 *Feb. 15*, "The Bookseller", March 4, 1887, p. 239.
50 *Ibid*.
51 This happened, for example, in Mrs. M. Caldwell, *Emilia Wyndham*, London, Chapman and Hall, [1864] (reissue of 1872).

stores and newspaper-stands in every railway station owned by the company network. Hachette's first bookstall (*kiosque de gare*) opened at the Gare de Lyon in 1852, and the number grew to 1,179 by 1896, all selling his volumes from the brand-new series *Bibliothèque des Chemins de Fer*.

Documents at the Archives Nationales explicitly state that Hachette asked to be allowed to sell "tous les Ouvrages soumis au Colportage"[52]. And so it did.

The *Bibliothèque des Chemins de Fer* had seven different series, each identified with a different color for the paper wrappers: 1re série, *Guides de Voyageurs*, in scarlet red covers; 2e série, *Histoire et voyages*, in green covers; 3e série, *Littérature Francaise*, mustard; 4e série, *Litteratures Anciennes et Étrangères*, yellow; 6e série, *Livres Illustrés pour les Enfants*, also known as the *Bibliothèque Rose*, established in 1856 and aimed at children, with pink covers; 7e série, *Ouvrages Divers*, beige.

All the same, yellow-backs and books from the *Bibliothèque des Chemins de Fer* were radically different: the *Bibliothèque* had plain typographical covers, deeply linked to its national ancestors, such as the *Bibliothèque Charpentier*, while yellow-backs from the very beginning had colored and illustrated covers. Color was what boosted the identity of this brand-new genre.

With Hachette's *Bibliothèque des Chemins de Fer* each color identified the subject and embodied the genre – in the same way as would happen in Italy a century afterwards with the *libri gialli* (an Italian term that became synonymous with detective, mystery, or crime stories). In the yellow-back case, the color identified the editorial genre and distribution channels rather than the literary genre.

At the end of the nineteenth century, the yellow-backs were disappearing from bookstalls, but the symbolic value they embodied was still deeply rooted in late-Victorian and Edwardian society. When Bram Stoker published his *Dracula* in 1897, the gothic novel was deliberately bound in yellow with the one-word title in simple red lettering[53]. The book was bound in cloth and cost 6s.; it was not a cheap book for popular reading at all, but the yellow color was chosen as it was synonymous with the more transgressive elements of Victorian culture.

Despite W.H. Smith's positive efforts at cleaning up stations and giving the new reading public suitable reading material, the yellow color of yellow-backs still remained as a symbol and identified the cheap, sensational, disreputable "literary rubbish that travels by the rail".

---

[52] Paris, Archives Nationales, F 17/2681: *Rapport au Conseil d'Administration du Cercle de la Librairie et de l'Imprimerie, par la Commission nommée pour l'examen de la question concernant l'Établissement de Magasins de Librairie dans les Gares*. More work should be done on this topic, particularly on some archival documents at the Archives Nationales in Paris (*ibid.*, 148 AQ: *Dépôt de la Librairie Hachette*). See E. Parinet, *Les Bibliothèques de Gare, Un Nouveau Réseau pour le Livre*, in "Romantisme", 80, 1993, pp. 95–106; J. Mistier, *La Librairie Hachette, de 1826 à nos jours*, Paris 1964, esp. pp. 122–136, 297–323.

[53] B. Stoker, *Dracula*, London, Archibald Constable and Company, 1897.

Goran Proot
Shifting Price Levels of Books Produced at the Officina Plantiniana in Antwerp, 1580–1655

1 Introduction

The evaluation of the price of a book is complex and requires a good understanding of the context within which this price is fixed. Anyone who regularly walks into a local bookshop has at least an intuitive sense of what a regular novel, non-fiction book, travel guide or comic strip should cost. Customers can differentiate between "cheap" and "expensive" books, both amongst different categories of books and within a specific category. Close observers may also be able to produce reasons why a given work is more expensive than another one. This may have to do with the content of the matter, material features of the commodity, and with marketing as such, or different combinations of those factors. Design books, for example, are often beautifully made, well-executed and set in tasteful typography, with lots of colors and illustrations printed on high-gloss paper, often soundly bound. The target audience of this kind of book may be rather limited, resulting in limited print runs and therefore higher production prices per copy, which, in turn, helps to explain a substantial bill at the counter. Retail prices are factored into the bookseller's cut on top of the wholesale prices fixed by the publisher, whose first concern is where to locate a specific book in the market, production costs being only one factor in the whole story.

Just as today, in early modern society a book's price was one of the key factors in accessing printed information, knowledge, and ideas. Those who could not consult books in a library at a religious institution, a court, or a university, were basically left with the possibility either of borrowing books or of buying them. In this context, the price of books was an important impediment. How much did people have to pay for information, knowledge, opinions, or stories, helping them improve their lives and engage in societal debates? An assessment of the price of books in the early modern period is therefore crucial better to understand this important barrier.

Note: This contribution springs from research founded by the European Research Council (ERC) under the European Union's Horizon 2020 research and innovation programme (Grant Agreement nr. 694476). The author would like to thank the team members of the EmoBookTrade team, especially Professor Angela Nuovo, Francesco Ammanati, Giliola Barbero, Flavia Bruni, Andrea Ottone, and Erika Squassina, as well as Christian Coppens and Giles Mandelbrote, advisors of the project. In the course of the present survey, the author contacted curators and librarians in many different research and heritage libraries and collections based on the European continent and in the United Kingdom as well as in the United States. He would like to thank all of them for their help in identifying editions and providing details. He would also like to express his gratitude to Maurice Whitehead for his help with the English version of the text.

Generally speaking, studies dealing with book prices in the early modern period remain rare, and this observation also holds for the Southern Netherlands. The reasons for this neglect are manifold. An interdisciplinary subject by nature, the study of early modern book prices was often set aside by economic historians on the one hand (as being "too bookish") and by book historians on the other (as involving "too much economics"). In addition, the subject is a methodological minefield, involving economics, statistics, and bibliography. First-hand books have to be distinguished from second-hand books. In the trade, first-hand books often circulated unbound, but customers would often have them bound upon acquisition, either at the book shop or elsewhere. Prices entered in cashbooks kept at the shop usually do not detail the price of the actual book and additional binding costs, the potential range of which is very broad. Moreover, it makes a difference if payments are made in cash or entered in an account, in which case some customers received discounts, for instance, if they were regulars, or when placing substantial orders. In the early modern period, life cycles of books were also much longer than they are today. As a result, a first-hand book is not always a recent publication; it may have been produced several years or even decades earlier, in a completely different economic climate; it may have been published locally or else far away, involving packing, tolls, and shipping. Not only the "age" of a specific edition needs to be known, but also its format and other material features, such as paper, type, language, and illustrations, because they all may have an impact on the price. This involves an understanding of the international trade, networks, and thorough bibliographical knowledge. Last but not least, surveys of economic aspects of the book trade depend heavily on business archives, which, apart from that of the Officina Plantiniana in Antwerp, have received only scant attention[1].

The Plantin-Moretus archives are so overwhelmingly vast that they have overshadowed most others and, at the same time, demoralized many a book historian. A virtual reconstruction of the archives of the Plantin-Moretus Museum published by Christian Coppens in 1998–1999 re-groups the documents according to subject matter[2]. This re-organized inventory clearly indicates how many, and how many different documents related to economic aspects of the Officina Plantiniana have been preserved. To name just a few, the *Journals*, recording daily transactions, run from 1576 to 1865; *Livres de boutiques* (transactions at the shop) from 1556 until 1840; then there are registers recording transactions with booksellers, the trade with Spain and Portugal, a large series of *Carnets de Francfort* recording transactions at the Frankfurt Fairs. In addition, there are series documenting compositors' and printers' wages, purchases of paper, and so on. For the year 1589 alone, the *Journal* records about 7,900 titles, the Lent and September *Carnets de Francfort* for that year about 3,000, and the *Livre de boutique* some 2,300. The amount of information seems to be simply indigest-

---

[1] Recently, a major study about another important Antwerp firm was published by S. van Rossem, *Het gevecht met de boeken. De uitgeversstrategieën van de familie Verdussen (Antwerpen, 1589–1689)*, Antwerpen 2014.

ible, in part explaining why, in 1972, the curator of the Museum Plantin-Moretus, Leon Voet wrote: "Of all aspects relating to the Plantin printing shop the problem of sales has up to now been least dealt with"[3]. Voet cites a handful of studies, most of which pertain to specific kinds of printed products, such as prints, maps, or music books. The curator himself provided several analyses for different business years, but mostly based on subtotals and totals recorded in the documents, and rarely on itemized transactions[4]. Subsequently, the number of economic analyses based on Plantin's book production, or on that of his successors, remained limited, and Voet's remarks were therefore echoed twenty-four years later by Jan Materné[5]. Though Materné himself embarked on a major economic analysis of the trade of the famous Antwerp firm, this undertaking was unfortunately discontinued after a number of contributions[6].

The present contribution resumes the thread in offering a long-term overview of prices of an important part of the book production by the Officina Plantiniana from 1580 until 1655. By doing so, it complements some of Denucé's investigations, corroborates a number of his conclusions, and also extends the period studied by him by fifteen years. I shall also focus more on methodological questions and pay attention to the question of "cheap" books within Plantin's production and that of his successors.

2 Production list M321

The starting point of the present analysis is manuscript M321 at the Museum Plantin-Moretus in Antwerp, beginning with the words "Catalogvs librorvm a Chr Plantino Ann°. M.D.LXXXX. impressorvm" (Catalogue of the books printed by Christopher Plantin in 1580). It is a dynamic production list of titles with prices for the book trade starting in 1580, and was completed year by year, by several hands, down to 1655. Of a total of 165 leaves, 131 are used, listing 2,367 entries of editions and, in a number of cases, different issues of editions.

---

[2] C. Coppens, *The Plantin-Moretus Archives: An Index to Jan Denucé's Inventory of 1926*, in "De Gulden Passer", 76–77, 1998–1999, pp. 334–360.
[3] L. Voet, *The Golden Compasses. A History and Evaluation of the Printing and Publishing Activities of the Officina Plantiniana at Antwerp in Two Volumes*, 2 vols., Amsterdam 1969–1972, here vol. 2, p. 387, no. 1.
[4] L. Voet, *Production and Sales Figures of the Plantin Press in 1566*, in S. van der Woude (ed.), *Studia bibliographica in honorem Herman de la Fontaine Verwey*, 1966, pp. 418–436; L. Voet, *The Golden Compasses*, vol. 2, chap. 16, and appendices 1–6.
[5] J. Materné, *La librairie de la Contre-Réforme: le réseau de l'Officine plantinienne au XVIIe siècle*, in F. Barbier / S. Juratic / D. Varry (eds.), *L'Europe et le livre: réseaux et pratiques du négoce de librairie, 16e–19e siècles*, Paris 1996, pp. 43–59, here p. 44.
[6] For this article, especially the following contribution is important: J. Materné, *The "Officina Plantiniana" and the Dynamics of the Counter-Reformation, 1590–1650*, in S. Cavaciocchi (ed.), *Produzione e commercio della carta e del libro secc. XIII–XVIII*, Firenze 1992, pp. 481–490.

The document's structure remains basically unchanged throughout the entire period. Entries often literally correspond with actual title pages, citing title and author (though sometimes abbreviated), and these are often followed by names of editors and translators. Bibliographical formats are almost always present, and about one in two entries mentions the presence of illustrations; in 15% of the cases, details about paper are given. Although those details sometimes appear in sixteenth-century entries too, the majority of them date from the period 1601–1655. In more than forty cases, entries mention typographical details, such as the use of very small or very large type. Furthermore, almost all entries duly note the number of sheets required for the production of one copy and its price. The former element is a technical one specific to the trade, explaining and justifying the price.

Prices are expressed in *Carolus Gulden* (Carolus guilders), the account money usually used in the Officina Plantiniana for earnings and expenses[7]. One Carolus Gulden consisted of *florijnen* (florins), each one of which was made up of twenty stuivers (stivers)[8].

From comparison with other parts of the bookkeeping, it is clear that the prices mentioned are to be understood as prices on account, to be settled by the buyer at a specific point in the future, usually within six months. Unlike cash, money on account is not susceptible to fluctuation. The prices entered here seem to be fixed in or not much later than the moment of production, and are to be considered as a *prix juste*, a correct and fair price according to what the market considers right[9]. Depending on the situation, discounts could be granted, for so-called *libri nigri* (black books) up to 40%, or, in the case of *libri rubro-nigri* (red and black books, i.e., liturgical books) up to 25%[10].

Not unimportant for this analysis, prices always pertain to first-hand, unbound books, i.e. *in albis*, thus avoiding difficulties connected with bindings and other types of finishing.

The production list is beyond any doubt a very valuable source for the study of prices of first-hand books on offer by the Officina Plantiniana over a period of 76 years. It allows for comparisons of pricing strategies of the last ten years under its founder, Christopher Plantin (c. 1520–1589), and by three successors of his: Jan Moretus I (in charge of the firm from 1589 until 1610), Balthasar Moretus I and Jan Moretus II (active

---

[7] L. Voet, *The Golden Compasses*, vol. 2, p. 445. About Carolus Gulden as account money, see E. Aerts / H. van der Wee, *Les Pays-Bas espagnols et autrichiens*, in J. van Heesch / J.-M. Yante / H. Lowagie (eds.), *Monnaies de compte et monnaies réelles. Pays-Bas méridionaux et principauté de Liège au Moyen Âge et aux Temps modernes*, Louvain-la-Neuve 2016, pp. 163–200, here especially pp. 182–188. There is only one exception in this production list. On fol. 113r the price for a copy of Rembertus Dodoens, *Cruydtboeck* from 1644 is explicitly priced in cash (*parata pecunia*). With thanks to Diederik Lanoye.
[8] L. Voet, *The Golden Compasses*, vol. 2, p. 445, no. 2. In turn, 1 stuiver makes 4 *oorden*, but the latter name never explicitly appears in M321. I will always refer to *florijnen* or *stuivers*.
[9] R. de Roover, *The Concept of the Just Price: Theory and Economic Policy*, in "Journal of Economic History", 18, 1958, 4, pp. 418–434.

1611–1641), and Balthasar Moretus II (1642–1674), for whom M321 documents the first fourteen years of his career.

The sheer number of entries in the document may suggest that it is complete, but that is not the case. Comparison with Leon Voet's bibliography of the works published by Christopher Plantin, covering the period 1555–1589, and with Dirk Imhof's bibliography of his successor, Jan Moretus I, for the years 1589–1610, both show that many – but not all – editions and issues are present in the list[11]. Not listed, for instance, are the numerous *Geboden en uytroepen*, commissioned by the city of Antwerp, besides other publications, but, overall, M321 seems representative for the year 1589–1610. For the following years, comprehensive bibliographies dealing with the production of Jan Moretus I's successors are lacking. Many editions are already present in the *Short Title Catalogue Flanders* (*STCV*), but at this point, this online retrospective bibliography has not yet covered the entire production[12].

3 Assessment of book prices

There are different methods for assessing historical book prices. One can consider either nominal prices paid for copies of editions, or nominal prices per printing sheet. In both cases, price evolution in time has to be factored in, as price levels constantly vary. This can be done in different ways, for example by calculating price indexes for consecutive time-spans, or by comparing book prices with wages.

The calculation of prices per printing sheet requires some explanation. The printing sheet, or simply sheet, is a standard unit in printing shops. Since the time of Gutenberg, books printed with moveable type have been printed on large sheets of paper[13]. Compositors prepare the form with moveable type for one side first, then as

---

10 In the second half of the seventeenth century, the masters of the Officina Plantiniana wanted to sell off their stocks of black books, see K. Selleslach, *Het einde van het zwarte tijdperk. De uitverkoop van de "libri nigri" door de "Officina Plantiniana"*, in "De Gulden Passer", 94, 2016, 2, pp. 263–286.
11 L. Voet, *The Plantin Press. A Bibliography of the Works Printed and Published by Christopher Plantin at Antwerp and Leiden*, 6 vols., Amsterdam 1980–1983; D. Imhof, *Jan Moretus and the Continuation of the Plantin Press. A Bibliography of the Works Published and Printed by Jan Moretus I in Antwerp (1589–1610)*, 2 vols., Leiden 2014. Production list M321 contains only a handful of broadsheets, probably because most works produced in this format did not belong to the category of works for the open market, but had been ordered and paid for by a single party.
12 The *STCV* is freely available online: www.stcv.be. For a discussion of its completeness, see G. Proot, *Survival Factors of Seventeenth-Century Hand-Press Books Published in the Southern Netherlands. The Importance of Sheet Counts, Sammelbände and the Role of Institutional Collections*, in F. Bruni / A. Pettegree (eds.), *Lost Books. Reconstructing the Print World of Pre-industrial Europe*, Leiden 2016, pp. 160–201.
13 Still one of the best introductions is P. Gaskell, *A New Introduction to Bibliography*, 2nd edition, New Castle 2006.

many sheets as needed for the entire print run are printed on one side of the sheets. Then the form for the other side is composed and printed on the back of all the sheets. After drying, sheets are folded and, when needed, tucked into one another to make gatherings, which are then put in the right order to be bound as books when needed. In this process, it does not matter how many pages are printed on one side of a sheet; the number may vary from one page per side to twenty-four, thirty-two, or even more. What really matters for printers is the quantity of printing sheets required to produce one copy of a book, big or small. As a result, a book printed in large folio format consisting of ten printing sheets should cost as much as a book printed in the much smaller octavo format with an equal number of printing sheets. In this example, the first book will comprise 20 leaves or 40 pages, while the second one will have 80 leaves or 160 pages. In both cases, investments in materials (paper, type, ink, …) and labor time are more or less the same. This explains why Plantin's production list, and other documents related to the trade, indicate numbers of sheets per copy, rather than leaves or pages[14].

The production cost for a sheet of a plain book of the most frequent bibliographical formats (folio, quarto, octavo) printed in black ink only in a normal type size remains relatively stable across editions produced at the same period of time. But some features may impact production cost, the most important of which are the use of different colors, of illustrations (in relief or in intaglio), very small formats, special paper, and specific types (very small type or «exotic» ones). To begin with the latter: "exotic" languages such as, for instance, Greek or Hebrew, require compositors and proofreaders with specific language skills, and in addition material investment in special type. Very small formats (duodecimo, and especially twenty-fourmo (24mo), thirty-twomo (32mo) or smaller) are usually set in (very) small type, increasing composition times, while printing times remain more or less equal. The use of extra large sheets can be somewhat slower and sometimes require larger printing presses, but, even when normal presses are involved, whiter, much thicker, much thinner, or other special papers mainly increase material costs, as special paper is more expensive. Sheets in different colors require different inks and complicate the printing process. Each color sheet has to go under the press twice, doubling printing times. One way or another, when printing in black, this type has to be raised, or parts to be printed in red have to be masked or temporarily taken out, and the other way around for the second color, while the final result needs to be registered correctly[15]. The insertion of illustra-

---

14 See for example the printed book seller's catalogue by Chrétien Wechel, *Index librorum omnium, quos suis typis excudit Christianus Wechelus*, Paris, C. Wechel, 1544, 8vo, which does not mention prices but the number of sheets. Cf. G. Guilleminot-Chrétien, *Prostant in nostra taberna: "les catalogues du libraire Chrétien Wechel"*, in S. Hindman et al. (eds.), *Le livre, la photographie, l'image & la lettre. Essays in honor of André Jammes*, Paris 2015, pp. 46–53.

15 For a discussion of different techniques, see A. Stijnman / E. Savage, *Printing Colour 1400–1700. History, Techniques, Functions and Receptions*, Leiden 2015.

tions and specific ornaments in relief is not very complicated, mainly requiring extra investments in designs and their execution by specialized woodcutters. Woodblocks can go under the press in the same forms together with moveable type and do not stretch the printing process. This is different with illustrations and embellishments executed in intaglio. Sheets combining relief and intaglio printing have to go under two different presses, and even Plantin and the Moretuses usually subcontracted the insertion of intaglios to specialized workshops who mastered the roller press[16]. This operation delayed the production and was paid for by piece. Also the design of engraving or etchings had to be paid for, as well as for the execution into copper.

4 Pricing strategy

With this information in mind, the entries in list M321 can be analyzed. A total of 338 records were excluded, because they were incomplete, unclear, or posed other problems. The remaining 2,029 records are distributed over the four generations of masters as follows: 298 entries from the period 1580–1589 were produced under Christopher Plantin, 502 under Jan Moretus I between 1589 and 1610, 961 under Jan Moretus II and Balthasar Moretus I in the period 1610–1641, and 234 under Balthasar Moretus II between 1641 and 1655; 34 entries cannot yet with certainty be attributed to any of the four generations, but could prove useful for a number of calculations[17].

4.1 Price per copy

Table 1 gives an overview of the nominal and relative numbers of editions according to price per copy in stuivers for four generations of master printers at the Officina Plantiniana according to list M321. Price ranges redouble each time. The first category consists of copies priced at less than 1 stuiver, the second category prices between 1 stuivers (inclusive) and 2 stuivers (exclusive), and so on. Figure 1 is based on the same information there presented in relative numbers (percent).

---

[16] A. Griffiths, *The Print before Photography. An Introduction to European Printmaking 1550–1820*, London 2016, p. 44.
[17] This is the case for 9 entries from 1589, 12 from 1610 and 13 from 1641.

Tab. 1: Nominal and relative number (between brackets) of editions listed in M321 grouped according to redoubling price ranges and per generation; prices in stuivers (Carolus Gulden)

	Christopher Plantin		Jan Moretus I		Jan M. II & Balthasar Moretus I		Balthasar Moretus II	
	n.	%	n.	%	n.	%	n.	%
< 1 st	3	(1.0)	11	(2.2)	10	(1.0)	0	–
1 ≤ 2 st	45	(15.1)	24	(4.8)	46	(4.8)	5	(2.1)
2 ≤ 4 st	72	**(24.2)**	53	(10.6)	72	(7.5)	10	(4.3)
4 ≤ 8 st	71	**(23.8)**	105	**(20.9)**	105	(10.9)	24	(10.3)
8 ≤ 16 st	47	(15.8)	116	**(23.1)**	219	**(22.8)**	29	(12.4)
16 ≤ 32 st	31	(10.4)	58	(11.6)	156	**(16.2)**	34	(14.5)
32 ≤ 64 st	14	(4.7)	48	(9.6)	104	(10.8)	24	(10.3)
64 ≤ 128 st	9	(3.0)	51	(10.2)	90	(9.4)	35	**(15)**
128 ≤ 256 st	5	(1.7)	30	(6)	127	(13.2)	40	**(17.1)**
256 ≤ 512 st	1	(0.3)	4	(0.8)	27	(2.8)	27	(11.5)
512 ≤ 1024 st	0	–	2	(0.4)	4	(0.4)	4	(1.7)
≥ 1024 st	0	–	0	–	1	(0.1)	2	(0.9)

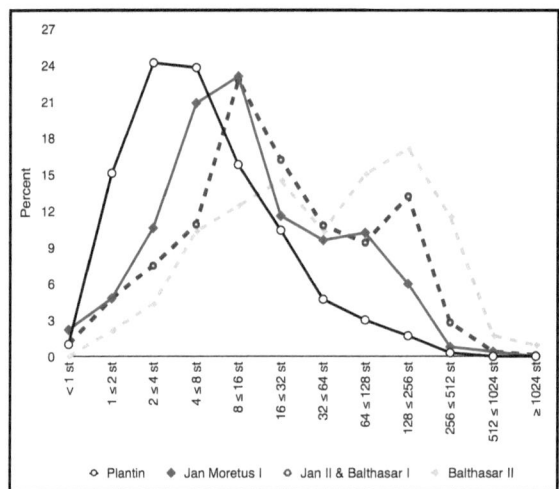

Fig. 1: Relative number of editions listed in M321 according to price per copy.

Both Table 1 and Figure 1 indicate a clear shift towards more expensive books. Between 1580 and 1589, during Plantin's time, the two categories with the highest number of books are those costing between 2 and 4 stuivers per copy (24.2%) and between 4 and 8 stuivers per copy (23.8%). One generation later, under Jan Moretus I (1589–1610), the most populated categories are those between 4 and 8 stuivers per copy (20.9%) and between 8 and 16 stuivers (23.1%). Under Jan II and Balthasar I, this shifts up again one category, to that of books sold at between 8 and 16 stuivers per copy (22.8%) and between 16 and 32 stuivers (16.2%). Finally, under Balthasar Moretus II, the category costing between 128 and 256 stuivers is the one with most books (17.1%), followed by the category between 64 and 128 stuivers per copy (15%)[18]. This shift can also be traced by looking at how many books cost below a specific price over all four generations. For instance, under Plantin, 64.1% of all titles listed in M321 cost 8 stuivers or less, under Jan Moretus I this portion dropped to 38.5% of his editions in M321, while under his successors this diminished further to 24.2%, and under Bathasar Moretus II no more than 16.7% of his editions cost less than 8 stuivers per copy.

In part, this is the result of inflation. Figure 2a shows that wages in this period systematically rose as well, from about 12 stuivers per day to about 20 stuivers for compositors at work at the Officina Plantiniana[19]. In spite of this increase, the number of editions listed year by year in M321 which cost for one copy as much as an average daily compositor's wage, or less, decreases systematically as well (fig. 2b). In the period 1590–1595, 68% of all books listed in M321 cost the equivalent of one day's work of a compositor. Fifty years later, in the period 1641–1645, a compositor's daily wage would give access to 30% of the books published in the same period at the Officina Plantiniana. In other words, book prices went up much more rapidly than wages. In addition, trendlines on both graphs indicate that those changes are systematic and coherent.

4.2 Price per sheet

Because books basically consist of a number of sheets, prices can also be assessed per sheet, making it easier to single out specific elements influencing price levels.

---

18 Compare with J. Materné, *The "Officina Plantiniana"*, p. 486–487 (Table 3). Materné uses a threshold of 10 stuivers instead of average laborer's wages.

19 Average price per day based on weekly wages paid to 63 different compositors at work at the Officina Plantiniana between 1590 and 1655 as listed in C. Verlinden / E. Scholliers (eds.), *Documenten voor de geschiedenis van prijzen en lonen in Vlaanderen en Brabant, Deel II (XIVe–XIXe)*, Brugge 1965, pp. 1062–1227. In order to obtain a more nuanced idea of real wages, wages per week are here each time divided over seven days. The compositors at the Officina Plantiniana were well-remunerated, because unskilled labourers earned after the period 1600–1610 only about 8.4 stuivers per day, see E. Scholliers / C. Vandenbroeke, *Structuren en conjuncturen in de Zuidelijke Nederlanden 1480–1800*, in D.P. Blok et al. (eds.), *Algemene geschiedenis der Nederlanden*, Haarlem 1980, 5, pp. 289–290. Materné cites an increase of wages for pressmen: "Average wages paid to the pressmen per ream consumed rose from 18 stivers in the 1590s to 39 stivers in the 1540", cf. J. Materné, *The "Officina Plantiniana"*, p. 486. Those wages probably pertain to teams of a pressman and an inker, who always worked together.

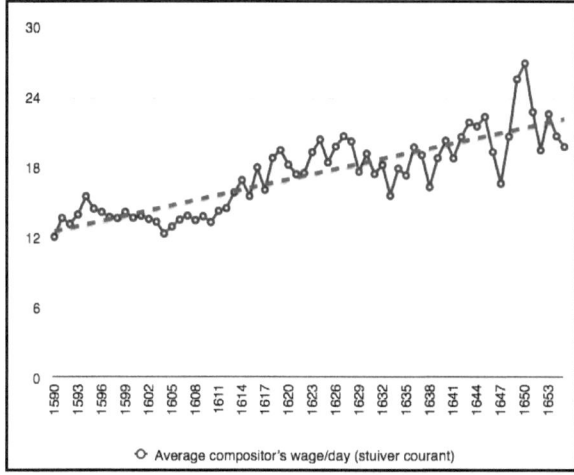

Fig. 2a: Average wage per day in stuivers courant (Carolus Gulden), based on weekly compositors wages paid by the Officina Plantiniana.

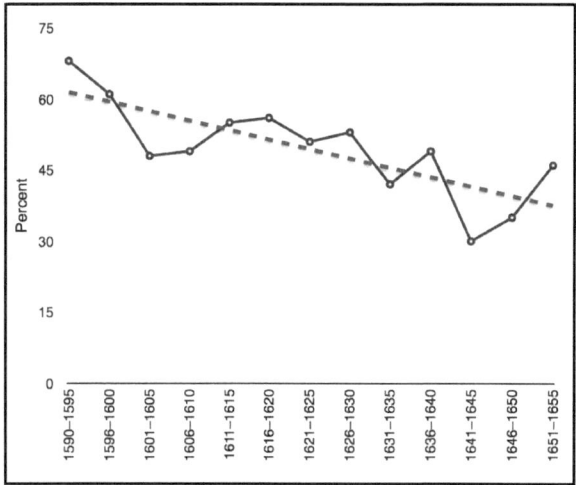

Fig. 2b: Relative number of editions priced equally or less than the average daily wage of compositors at the Officina Plantiniana, 1590–1655.

If the price per copy systematically goes up, this is not necessarily because copies become all the more voluminous. Figure 3 clearly shows that prices calculated per sheet gradually increase as well. Between 1580 and 1655, prices increase 3.5 times, from about 0.39 stuivers per sheet to about 1.40 stuivers[20]. See Figures 3 and 4.

---

20 This is in line with Materné's calculations, which are partly based on different documents, see J. Materné, *The "Officina Plantiniana"*, p. 486: "The average price per sheet printed increased from 0.69 stivers in the 1590s to 1.31 stivers in the 1640s".

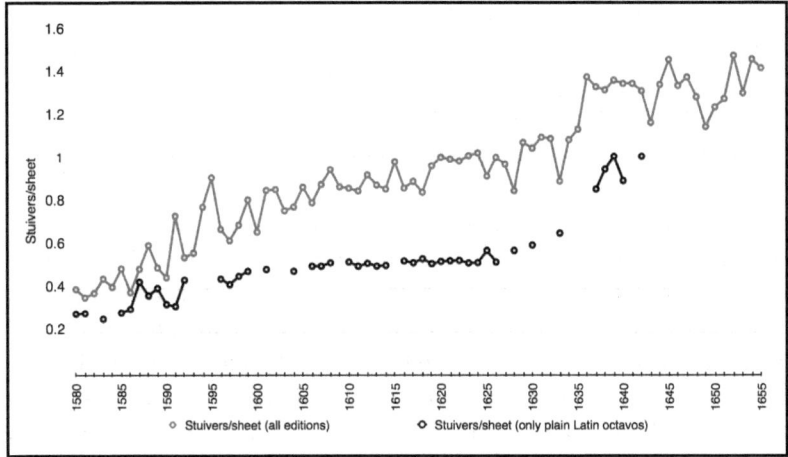

Fig. 3: Average price per sheet in stuivers for the period 1580–1655 as listed in M321 (n = 2,029) compared with the average price per sheet of plain Latin octavos (n = 80).

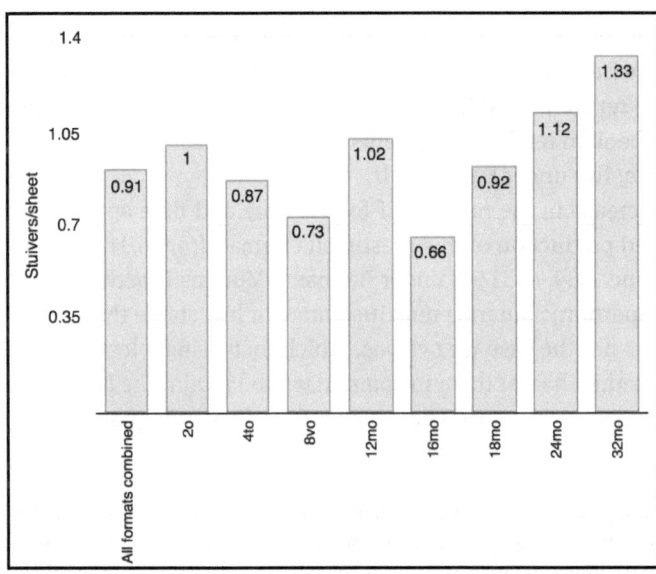

Fig. 4: Average price per sheet according to bibliographical format, 1580–1655, as listed in M321 (n = 1,844).

This price increase can in part be explained by rising wages for compositors, printers, and proof-readers, for supplies (type, paper, ink, inkballs, frisket sheets, ...), and other materials (presses), infrastructure, in addition to other costs. A number of factors having to do with the actual books themselves also weigh on the price per sheet. Figure 4 indicates the impact of the bibliographical format on prices.

Books conceived as 16mo or 8vo are cheapest; quartos are also slightly cheaper than the overall average price per sheet, and 18mos, which are in the dataset very infrequent, are slightly more expensive. Folios cost about 10% more per sheet than average, which is not surprising, but duodecimos turn out to be more or less as expensive. Other small formats, such as 24mo and 32mo, are much more expensive, the latter costing twice as much as a 16mo.

In the course of time, the use of specific bibliographical formats shifts continuously. In the fifteenth century, for instance, books in the Southern Netherlands were predominantly printed as folios or quartos[21]. At the end of the incunable period, octavos became more important, surpassing quartos in quantity around 1520. Around the 1540s, the small 16mo is being used more frequently. This handy format is often used for cheap text editions of the classics and is called "Italian" after the country where it was developed. Booksellers refer to the 16mo with the term "enchiridion", meaning handbook, referring to both its indispensability and practical small size[22]. They easily fit in pockets and therefore are always within reach. Plantin recognizes its virtues and uses it regularly for text editions; under Jan Moretus I, however, this format gradually fell into disuse, disappearing almost completely from the Officina's production lists after 1610. See Table 2.

The opposite happens with books in 12mo: almost never used by the first generation, these became more frequent under Jan Moretus I and his successors. The presence of editions in 24mo remained stable, in contrast to the smallest format, 32mo, which was used for one book in ten by Jan Moretus II and Balthaser Moretus I, and still for one in every twenty-five under Balthasar II.

Remarkable is the increase in the number of folios. Time and time again, each new generation intensified production of this prestigious format, from 6.3% in Plantin's days between 1580 and 1589, to 33.5% under Balthasar Moretus II between 1642 and 1655. Though the proportion of quartos remained more or less stable throughout the entire period, this was not the case for octavos, which increasingly lost ground. Balthasar II produced less than half of them in comparison to Plantin: the latter produced about four books in ten as an octavo against about two in ten for quartos.

---

21 G. Proot, *Metamorfose. Typografische evolutie van het handgedrukte boek in de Zuidelijke Nederlanden, 1473–1541*, Antwerpen 2017, p. 24, graph 2.1. Needham estimates the number of folio incunables in the west at about 8,900 editions, quartos at about 15,700 editions, octavos ca. 3,200 editions, sextodecimos ca. 275. Smaller formats, such as 32mo and 64mo are preserved in some dozens only. Cf. P. Needham, *Format and Paper Size in Fifteenth-Century Printing*, in C. Reske / W. Schmitz (eds.), *Materielle Aspekte in der Inkunabelforschung*, Wiesbaden 2017, pp. 59–107, here p. 71 and p. 99.

22 In his printed booksellers' catalogues with prices, the Paris publisher Robert Estienne I refers regularly to 'enchiridii forma' to indicate 16mos. For an analysis of those catalogues, see G. Proot, *Prices in Robert Estienne's Booksellers' Catalogues (Paris 1541–1552): A Statistical Analysis*, in «JLIS.it» 9, 2018, 2, pp. 193–222, doi:10.4403/jlis.it-12459. See also G. Proot, *Prices in Robert Estienne's Booksellers' Catalogues (Paris 1541–1552): A Statistical Analysis*, in G. Granata / A. Nuovo (eds.), *Selling & Collecting: Printed Book Sale Catalogues and Private Libraries in Early Modern Europe*, Macerata 2018, pp. 177–209.

Tab. 2: Nominal and relative number (between brackets) of editions listed in M321 grouped according to bibliographical format and per generation

	Christopher Plantin		Jan Moretus I[23]		Jan M. II & Balthasar Moretus I		Balthasar Moretus II	
	n.	%	n.	%	n.	%	n.	%
2o	16	(6.3)	48	(11.5)	198	(21.9)	77	(33.5)
4to	57	(22.3)	102	(24.5)	161	(17.8)	45	(19.6)
8vo	113	(44.1)	145	(34.9)	225	(24.9)	43	(18.7)
12mo	4	(1.6)	36	(8.7)	130	(14.4)	25	(10.9)
16mo	40	(15.6)	33	(7.9)	12	(1.3)	5	(2.2)
18mo	2	(0.8)	2	(0.5)	0	(–)	2	(0.9)
24mo	23	(9)	41	(9.9)	88	(9.7)	23	(10)
32mo	1	(0.4)	9	(2.2)	91	(10.1)	10	(4.3)
Total	256		416		905		230	

The change in the course of time can already be perceived under Jan Moretus I. What is perhaps even more striking is that each one of his successors confirm and intensify the changes he made, so that it seems to be fairly evident that they carried out a well-considered business strategy. Intrinsically being the most expensive ones in terms of price per sheet, editions in folio, 12mo, and smaller formats were favored, and cheaper formats such as octavo and 16mo diminished. This transition is directly linked to the policy of subsequent generations increasingly to concentrate on the lucrative business of religious, and especially, liturgical books[24].

To some extent, changes in the distribution of different formats follow more general trends. Between 1601 and 1655, Antwerp printers and publishers decrease the production of octavos by a little more than 10%: from about 41% in the period 1601–1605 to about 28% in the period 1651–1655[25]. Also the relative number of quartos

---

[23] The numbers correspond fairly well with those given by Imhof, who based his on the bibliography of Jan Moretus I, which is more complete than production list M321, cf. D. Imhof, *Jan Moretus*, vol. 2, p. LXIX: broadsheets 9.5%, 2o 9.8%, 4to 25.1%, 8vo 31.5%, 12mo 5.7%, 16mo 8.1%, 18mo 0.6%, 24mo 6.4% and 32mo 2.1%. The percentages in Table 2 are also different because the latter excludes broadsheets.

[24] D. Imhof, *De Plantijnse uitgeverij onder Balthasar II Moretus (1641–1674). Een vergelijking met het uitgeversfonds van zijn grootvader Jan I Moretus (1589–1610)*, in "Jaarboek voor Nederlandse boekgeschiedenis", 16, 2009, pp. 113–129; D. Imhof, *Jan Moretus*, vol. 1, pp. XXXIX–LXXXV.

[25] Statistics derived from the *Short Title Catalogue Flanders* (STCV, www.stcv.be), based on a download from December 31, 2017; with thanks to Susanna de Schepper. About the representativity of the STCV, see G. Proot, *Survival Factors*. The distribution of book production also depends on the printing centre. For Mechelen, which is a peripheral location, trends differ, see D. Lanoye, *De Mechelse drukpers voor 1800*, in "Jaarboek voor Nederlandse boekgeschiedenis", 16, 2009, pp. 131–150, table 1 on p. 42.

decreased, from about one in three at the beginning of the century to about one in four fifty years later. In the same period, folios gain importance, going up from ca. 8% to ca. 12%. The importance of 12mos increased greatly, from about 12% to about 25% in fifty years time. And if 24mos are still rare at the beginning of the seventeenth century, they comprise about 10% of the books fifty years later.

So it seems that the strategic trends observed at the Officina Plantiniana are in line with what happens in Antwerp at large, with this nuance that they seem to appear earlier than elsewhere and that they are also more prominent, indicating that the Moretuses did not merely follow the market, but rather drove it to new directions.

Subsequent generations of master printers at the Officina Plantiniana printed different kinds of works in some of the different bibliographic formats, too. In the period 1580–1589, Plantin reserved the 16mo format, the cheapest of all formats, for religious works on the one hand (18 titles out of 39, or 46.2% of all his 16mos) and for literary works on the other (15 out of 39; 38.5%)[26]. In addition, he also occasionally produced a work in this format dealing with philosophy, language, the arts, or with geography and history. His successor used the 16mo format for religious works or for language and literature only (resp. 19 and 13 editions), and in turn his successors almost only produced religious works in this format, but ever fewer[27].

Octavos follow a similar trend only second to 16mos amongst the cheapest format in terms of price per sheet. Under Plantin, 26.6% of the 8vos belonged to the category of religious works, the rest of the works in this format dealing with philosophy (1.8%), social sciences (6.4%), language (9.2%), natural sciences and mathematics (6.4%), technology and applied sciences (8.3%), geography and history (12.8%), but the majority of the octavos fall in the group of literature and rhetoric (28.4%). During the next generation, the number of religious books in the group of the 8vo format doubled (59.3%), causing a drop of 8vos in all other categories, amongst which that of literature and rhetoric remained the largest one (20.0%). Jan II and Balthasar I reserved 87.8% of all octavos for religious works, while Balthasar II raised this number to 100%.

This trend is also noticeable in more expensive book formats. Plantin, for instance, used folios as a format for religious works in addition to works the categories of natural sciences and mathematics, the arts, literature and rhetoric, and geography and history, while later master printers at the Officina Plantiniana focused increasingly on religious works in this format. In the smallest and most expensive formats the differences are even more pronounced, as they were reserved, after Plantin's death, for religious books only. This had to do with the fact that Plantin's successors increasingly concentrated on religious works, and within this category foremost on *libri rubro-nigri* or liturgical works. This policy was continued also after 1655, the last year recorded in

---

26 This and the following calculations are based upon Dewey Decimal Classification, which I attributed to the entries in M321 used in this survey. Only the main groups were used.

27 Jan Moretus II and Balthasar I have only one 16mo dealing with literature and rhetoric in the M321 list against 11 religious editions, Balthasar II produced only five 16mos, 3 of which were religious.

document M321. In the year Balthasar Moretus II died, virtually all books coming from his presses were religious, the lion's share of which were liturgical[28].

4.3 Illustrations, color, and paper

The subsequent masters of the Officina Plantiniana not only produced fewer cheap formats in favor of more expensive ones: gradually they also increased the use of illustrations, produced more works combining black and red, and provided more and more limited print runs on special paper[29]. Figure 5 reflects the portion of illustrated editions listed in M321; "illustrated" means here illustrated with at least one image.

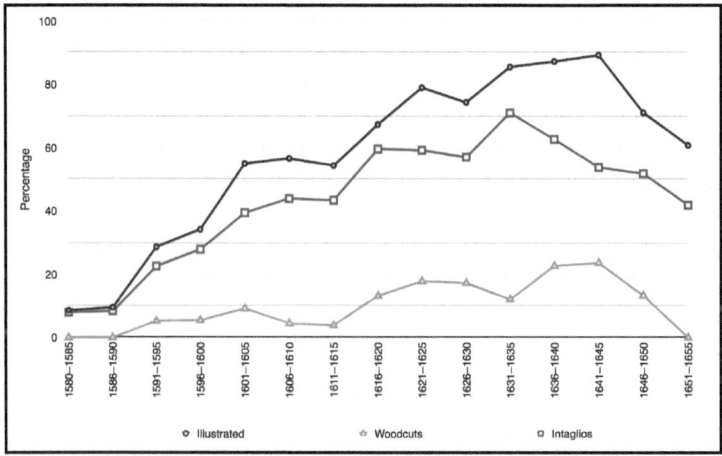

Fig. 5: Relative number of editions listed in M321 mentioning at least one illustration, woodblocks, or intaglios (n = 2,029).

Because the production list does not include the years 1555–1579, this period cannot be evaluated in the same way as the period 1580–1655. The foundations for the policy of illustrating editions increasingly with intaglios were laid by Plantin[30]. According to M321, by the time of his death, about 10% of all editions had at least one illustration – usually on the title page. Afterwards, the proportion of illustrated editions kept growing until the period 1641–1645.

In 166 cases only, the number of illustrations is explicitly stated. In 96 cases, this number varies between one and ten; in 31 cases there are between 11 and 20 illustra-

---

28 D. Imhof, *De Plantijnse uitgeverij*, p. 119 (graph).
29 About the development of intaglio illustrations in Plantin's editions, see L. Bowen / D. Imhof, *Christopher Plantin and Engraved Book Illustrations in Sixteenth-Century Europe*, Cambridge 2008.

tions, and in 38 cases, there are more than 20 images included. Comparisons with actual copies show that this information is in most cases accurate. The decrease of illustrated editions in the period 1646–1655 should be nuanced. In this period, Balthasar Moretus II kept focusing on the production of liturgical editions, which usually include one or more images. Therefore it is likely that the person who completed the production list in those years paid less attention to this aspect.

The commercial importance of editions with illustrations – even if this is limited to one only – should not be underestimated. When a book is illustrated, the price per sheet more or less doubles: an edition which, according to the production list, has no images, cost on average 0.61 stuivers per sheet as opposed to one with illustrations on average 1.13 stuivers; an edition with woodcuts came on average at 0.92 stuivers per sheet, against 1.15 stuivers for intaglios[31].

The difference between the average price per sheet for a so-called "plain" edition and the price per sheet for all editions combined, can be deduced from Figure 3. The black circles reflect average prices per sheet of unillustrated octavo editions in Latin printed with black ink only. Those plain editions can serve as a benchmark. As a result of increasing prices for materials and wages, the average price per sheet of this kind of book follows an upward trend, but there is a great difference with the average price per sheet for all editions combined.

As Dirk Imhof has demonstrated, Plantin's successors increasingly changed the composition of their publisher's list[32]. More than his predecessors, Balthasar Moretus II focused almost exclusively on liturgical editions. Typically, those were printed in red and black, an operation adding to material costs for ink and expanding production times. At present, it is not clear what the impact of these features was on selling prices, but it is known that Plantin maintained lower maximum discounts to whole sellers for liturgical works than for books in black ink only.

Very often, liturgical books were embellished with one or more images. At first, the Moretuses had variant editions on offer, a cheaper one illustrated with woodcuts or a more expensive one with intaglios, but gradually they favored print runs with intaglios[33].

Editions with intaglios had a much greater market value than those with woodcuts. Although production costs for the former are certainly higher, clients would be charged chiefly for their luxurious appearance. This becomes clear when comparing prices and costs of variant editions.

---

30 L. Bowen / D. Imhof, *Christopher Plantin*, pp. 1–16.
31 Average selling prices for the entire period 1580–1655.
32 Compare with n. 24.
33 K.L. Bowen, *Tabellen van illustraties in liturgische werken*, in D. Imhof (ed.), *De boekillustratie ten tijde van de Moretussen*, Antwerpen 1996, pp. 178–181, here table D, p. 181.

Tab. 3: Prices and costs of variant editions of Richard Stanihurst's *Hebdomada Mariana*, 1609[34]

	Woodcut edition	Intaglio edition
No. of sheets	11	11
No. of illustrations	8	8
Print run	1,000 copies	500 copies
List price per copy	7 stuivers	14 stuivers
Price per sheet	0.64 stuivers	1.27 stuivers
Cost for the production of illustrations		
Design	fl. 12 st. 10	–
Cutting/engraving	fl. 9	fl. 53
Reworking of the engravings	–	fl. 5
Printing of the engravings	–	fl. 15
Total costs for the illustrations	fl. 21 st. 10	fl. 73
per copy	0.43 stuivers	2.92 stuivers

The table indicates that copies with intaglios cost twice as much as those with woodcuts, 14 stuivers as opposed to 7 stuivers, the difference in production cost of intaglios amounting to 2.49 stuivers per copy (2.92 stuivers minus 0.43 stuivers for woodcuts). In other words, the extra production cost is generously being compensated for.

This example is not an exception to the rule. In practice, the business managers of the *Golden Compasses* usually doubled prices for editions with intaglios[35]. By doing so, they did not only increase turnover, but more importantly also their profits. Apparently, this did not pose any problem for the market; on the contrary. Luxurious editions kept selling well, especially liturgical books. In some cases, copies of woodcut variants had to be upgraded by pasting over with engravings printed on separate sheets to meet the demand.

In about 15% of all cases, the production list provides details about the paper used for an edition or a part of a print run. Under Plantin this happened fairly seldom, but in the seventeenth century remarks about paper quality become more frequent. Jan Moretus I and his successors used paper increasingly as a simple means to differentiate the books on offer. The only thing the printers needed to do is to vary paper sorts for a specific part of the total print run. Copies on smaller paper or paper of a lesser quality could be priced cheaper and were in reach of broader audiences. Copies on large, special or thicker paper went for sale at higher prices and aimed at men of substance. The number of copies was usually limited, and this exclusiveness justified higher prices.

---

34 Cf. D. Imhof, *Jan Moretus*, p. 44. Not all costs were counted, because Jan Moretus I probably could reutilize a number of woodcuts or engravings from previous projects.

35 Already around 1574, Plantin developed a sophisticated system for pricing editions with intaglios, see L. Bowen / D. Imhof, *Christopher Plantin*, Appendix 2, pp. 359–363. It seems that his successors applied less complicated systems.

The production list does not always specify the existence of print runs on different paper. In some cases, only a very limited number of special copies was produced, serving as presentation copies for authors, backers, or patrons. Since they seem never to have been intended for circulation on the regular market, the fixing of separate prices was redundant[36].

It is not easy to calculate the extra material cost for the production of runs on special paper, because the terminology used in list M321 does not explicitly correspond with that in documents recording deliveries of paper at the Officina Plantiniana. Neither does the inspection of actual copies always help. The paper has aged for about four centuries, wiping out, for instance, the difference between *papier blanc* and *papier commun*. At any rate, examples demonstrate that copies on special paper were very profitable. In 1599, Jan Moretus I produced three variants of a voluminous *Missaal* in folio format, comprising 167 sheets of paper per copy. The edition with intaglio illustrations was priced at 9 florijnen, and a variant of that on better paper at 10 florijnen, i.e. 1 florijn or 20 stuivers extra. From paper deliveries, we know that the difference between the cheapest and the most expensive paper could amount to 100%. In 1610, for instance, Jan Moretus I purchased the former kind at $8\frac{1}{3}$ stuivers per ream, and the latter for twice as much[37]. Reckoning with these numbers, the production cost of a deluxe copy should add about $2\frac{3}{4}$ stuivers at most[38]. But maximizing his profit, Moretus charged 20 stuivers extra.

5 Conclusions

Plantin's successors gradually and systematically oriented the Officina Plantiniana publisher's list towards a high-end market in the realm of religious, and foremost, liturgical books. Not only Jan Moretus I focused more than his father-in-law on more expensive book formats, but the following generations would continue and reinforce this policy. From generation to generation, the Moretuses produced more and more religious editions, especially liturgical books, in various formats, amongst which large numbers of 12mos, 24mos, and 32mos. That such small volumes were relatively speaking fairly expensive seems not to have curbed sales – on the contrary. In his days, Plantin had found ways including intaglio illustrations in his editions rather than using woodcuts. In addition, and perhaps more importantly, he had created a

---

36 This is the case for Carolus Scribani's *Antverpia*. M39 indicates that 25 copies on large paper were produced, ten of which were reserved for the Antwerp Jesuits. Because M321 does not mention this extra run, it is not certain that they were meant for the regular market. See also D. Imhof, *Jan Moretus*, p. 30.
37 Antwerpen, Museum Plantin-Moretus, Arch 126, fol. 216 right. With thanks to Kristof Selleslach.
38 For this calculation, I used prices from 1610, not 1599, so in reality the extra cost was probably even lower.

market for those beautifully illustrated, but more expensive editions. Time and time again, the next generation increased the number of illustrated editions, sometimes in different variants, with woodcuts or intaglios, but, in the course of time, the latter variant would drive out the former one. More often than his father-in-law, Jan Moretus I had variant print runs produced on different kinds of paper, this way serving regular and high-end clients, and his successors would continue to do so.

Large formats as well as the very small ones per sheet cost more than octavos or quartos. Likewise, copies on better paper, with intaglio illustrations and printed in red and black, were more expensive than plain books. Analysis of individual cases clearly demonstrates that the extra charge for special features went much beyond the extra cost for material and labor. The prices Plantin and the Moretuses fixed were in other words not merely based on objective cost criteria, but rather on market prices, i.e., fair prices people would be prepared to pay at a certain place, at a certain time, and for a certain product[39]. The orientation towards ever more luxurious books was very profitable, because profit margins were much higher than on plain books.

The Officina Plantiniana produced ever fewer and fewer ordinary books, and plain editions in cheaper formats such as octavo. As nominal prices per copy constantly rose, fewer books were within the reach of ordinary people. By the time Balthasar Moretus II in 1641 became master printer, the Officina had long abandoned the production of books for the populace. In 1642, the price per sheet of a plain Latin octavo had risen to about 1 stuiver, while illustrated books in red and black went on sale for about 1.3 stuivers per sheet. This was two to three times more than what the Antwerp magistrate in the same year allowed to be charged for chapbooks used in schools[40]. In most cases, those schoolbooks were printed as quartos, and, if they contained any illustrations at all, they were always executed in relief with worn-out woodblocks. The average price per sheet being about 0.44 stuivers, most schoolbooks cost 2 to 4 stuivers per copy. This was a category of books, which the Moretuses by that time had long almost completely abandoned.

The research leading to this publication has received funding fron the European Research Council (ERC) under the European Union's Horizon 2020 research and innovation programme (ERC project EMoBookTrade – Grant Agreement n° 694476)

---

39 This confirms the views described by R. de Roover, *The Concept of the Just Price*.
40 V.A. Dela Montagne, *Schoolboeken te Antwerpen in de 17e eeuw*, in "Tijdschrift voor boek- en bibliotheekwezen", 5, 1907, pp. 1–35.

Flavia Bruni
Faraway, So Close: Frontier Challenges for Inter-National Bibliographies

It is only apparently a paradox that what was once "popular" may have become extremely rare today[1]. Fine volumes of scholarship have found their way in the greatest numbers into the collections of libraries and have survived in large quantity and in good condition. On the contrary, books that circulated widely and on a larger social scale soon met their fate of dispersal and consumption. Such lack of balance is reflected in library catalogues and bibliographies, where we can find several copies of large scholarly books, but only a few survivors of what we recognize as cheap prints. Cheap imprints are often known in unique copies. Otherwise modest items have gained crucial relevance by virtue of their rarity. The search for such items is now acknowledged as essential for a reliable reconstruction of early modern printing. In this article I am going to discuss the dispersal of books across national boundaries as an issue undermining the completeness of national bibliographies. For this purpose, I have selected a few case studies focusing on cheap imprints, which are now only found far away from home[2].

This paper originated from the final report on the survey of editions printed in Italy in the first half of the seventeenth century I drew up for the *Universal Short Title Catalogue* of the University of St Andrews[3]. The *USTC* is, to date, the only bibliography of all books published throughout Europe before 1650. In about twenty years, the project team has worked to create a comprehensive resource on the first two centuries of printing in Europe[4]. Despite a different approach to each country, depending on

---

[1] Despite being well-established in professional literature, the notion of "popular print" is still rather problematic. Other chapters in this volume offer insights in order to suggest a new approach to the idea of "popular print". On this matter, see R.W. Schribner, *Is a History of a Popular Culture Possible?*, in "History of European Ideas", 10, 1989, pp. 175–191, reprinted in the collection of essays by L. Roper (ed.), *Religion and Culture in Germany (1400–1800)*, Leiden 2011, pp. 29–51, especially p. 29. An attempt at defining and measuring the "popularity" of early modern books was Laura Carnelos's project PATRIMONiT. *From Cheap Print to Rare Ephemera: 16th-Century Italian 'Popular' Books at the British Library*, on which see below, n. 16.

[2] I am in debt to Andrew Pettegree and Neil Harris for their revision of this text. On the factors related to the survival and disappearance of early printed books see N. Harris, *La sopravvivenza del libro, ossia appunti per una lista della lavandaia*, in "Ecdotica", 4, 2007, pp. 24–65; and the essays collected in F. Bruni / A. Pettegree (eds.), *Lost Books. Reconstructing the Print World of Pre-Industrial Europe*, Leiden 2016. All online references were accessed on June 30, 2018.

[3] *Universal Short Title Catalogue* (USTC), online: http://www.ustc.ac.uk. I started working for the USTC as a research assistant in 2009 and from 2012 to 2015 was responsible for the survey of Italian production 1601–1650.

[4] A. Pettegree / G. Kemp, *The Universal Short Title Catalogue. Creating and Exploiting a Major Bibliographical Resource*, in "La Bibliofilía", 119, 2017, 1, pp. 159–171.

http://doi.org/10.1515/9783110643541-007

the previous existence of a national bibliography or, on the contrary, the lack of it, some traits emerged as shared by different printing domains. According to Andrew Pettegree, director of the project, around 30% of the corpus of editions printed before 1601 are now known only from a single copy. These unique survivors are often found in a library far distant from the original place of publication, often even outside national borders[5].

As for France, where no attempt to build a national bibliography had been yet undertaken, the data gathered by the *USTC* team demonstrated that over 30% of French vernacular editions are not to be found in any French library. As for the southern Netherlands, where a previous bibliography did exist, the proportion of autochthonous books found only in libraries outside Belgium was even higher, reaching a peak of 40%. Similarly, we are aware from trial studies on Basel and Strasbourg, and on the basis of the exclusion of some linguistic areas, that the coverage of *VD16* and *VD17*, the German national bibliography for the sixteenth and seventeenth centuries respectively, is far from complete[6].

The *USTC* was launched in November 2011 as a free-access online database comprising books published before 1601. From 2012 to 2016, the *USTC* project team worked to extend the coverage to 1650. The fundamental reference for the survey of sixteenth-century books printed in Italy was obviously *EDIT16*, the online bibliography of sixteenth-century Italian books managed by the Central Institute for the Union Catalogue of Italian Libraries and Bibliographic Information (Istituto Centrale per il Catalogo Unico/ICCU), also including books printed outside Italy in the Italian language[7]. In the absence of a specific resource for seventeenth-century Italian production, the basis for the survey of editions printed in Italy in the first half of the seventeenth century was provided by the Italian collective catalogue (*Catalogo*

---

[5] A. Pettegree, *The Legion of the Lost. Recovering the Lost Books of Early Modern Europe*, in F. Bruni / A. Pettegree (eds.), *Lost Books*, pp. 1–27, at p. 2. In an article on *The Late Use of Incunables and the Paths of Book Survival*, in "Wolfenbütteler Notizen zur Buchgeschichte", 29, 2004, pp. 35–59, Paul Needham noticed that "a single copy is by far the commonest survival state for incunable editions" (p. 36).

[6] *Verzeichnis der im deutschen Sprachbereich erschienenen Drucke des 16. Jahrhunderts* (*VD16*), online: http://www.vd16.de; *Verzeichnis der im deutschen Sprachraum erschienenen Drucke des 17. Jahrhunderts* (*VD17*), online: http://www.vd17.de. A. Pettegree, *Lo Universal Short Title Catalogue: verso un censimento globale del libro antico*, in R. Rusconi (ed.), *Il libro antico tra catalogo storico e catalogazione elettronica*, Roma 2012, pp. 95–108, at pp. 100–101. On the scope of *VD16* and *VD17* see also J. Beyer, *How Complete are the German National Bibliographies for the Sixteenth and Seventeenth Centuries (VD16 and VD17)?*, in M. Walsby / G. Kemp (eds.), *The Book Triumphant. Print in Transition in the Sixteenth and Seventeenth Centuries*, Leiden 2011, pp. 57–77.

[7] *Censimento nazionale delle edizioni italiane del XVI secolo* (*EDIT16*), online: http://edit16.iccu.sbn.it. On *EDIT16* and its latest developments see R.M. Servello (ed.), *Il libro italiano del XVI secolo. Conferme e novità in EDIT16*, Roma 2007; and S. Buttò, *EDIT16: dal Censimento alla rete*, in F. Bruni (ed.), *Il libro antico tra perdite e sopravvivenza: rarità, valorizzazione, collezionismo e ricerca*, forthcoming. See also below.

del Servizio Bibliotecario Nazionale/SBN), also managed by the ICCU[8]. A database of bibliographic records extracted from the *SBN* was enriched through the matching and eventual addition of copies and new editions found in other bibliographies and catalogues, including those of private libraries not in the *SBN* such as the Vatican Library, and especially those of foreign countries: France, Germany, Ireland, Spain, Switzerland, the UK, and the US[9].

Tab. 1: Overview of *USTC* master list of Italian editions 1601-1650

Source	Number of editions	%
SBN	35,402	76%
Other sources	7,349	15%
Fieldtrips	1,986	5%
Edizioni Veneziane[10]	1,883	4%
Total	46,620	[100%]
Total not *SBN*	11,218	24%

A closer look at the breakdown of data for the *USTC* master list of Italian editions printed in the first half of the seventeenth century (tab. 1) provides some significant insights on the dissemination of Italian editions in libraries in and outside Italy today. Without any doubt, the *SBN* covers the largest amount of editions accounted for, 76% of a total of 46,620 editions. Still, about one fourth of the corpus resulted from other sources. About 10% of master records (i.e. related to editions) came from catalogues and bibliographies based on Italian collections which are not part of the *SBN* network, first among the others the Vatican Library (tab. 2). But a relevant amount of editions, roughly estimated at 15%, is only to be found in collections outside Italy.

Tab. 2: Overview of *USTC* non-*SBN* master list of Italian editions 1601-1650

Source	Number of editions
Vatican Library	1,498
National Library of Scotland	1,043[11]
Bibliothèque nationale de France	964
British Library	854
Catálogo Colectivo del Patrimonio Bibliográfico Español	776

---

8 *OPAC Servizio Bibliotecario Nazionale*, online: http://opac.sbn.it.
9 Among them: *BnF catalogue général*, online: http://catalogue.bnf.fr; *Catálogo Colectivo del Patrimonio Bibliográfico Español* (*CCPB*), online: http://catalogos.mecd.es/CCPB; Copac, online: https://copac.jisc.ac.uk; *Gemeinsamer Bibliotheksverbund Catalogue* (*GBV*), online: http://gso.gbv.de; SwissBib, online: https://www.swissbib.ch.
10 C. Griffante (ed.), *Le edizioni veneziane del Seicento: censimento* [Venezia], Milano 2003–[2006].
11 This number comprises a collection of broadsheets printed by the Stamperia Camerale in Rome.

Source	Number of editions
Oxford various	441
SwissBib	305
Others	1,339
Total	7,349

Even leaving the Vatican Library aside, as its consideration would need another approach and raise different issues, these figures demonstrate how many discoveries can result from the investigation of libraries outside national borders[12]. Already for the sixteenth century, the *USTC* recorded over 22,000 Italian imprints located in French libraries. About 300 of these are unique copies, previously unknown, meanwhile many others were known to exist in only one or two copies within the confines of Italy[13].

The format of Italian editions printed between 1601 and 1650 found only in libraries outside Italy (tab. 3) seems to confirm that as a general rule larger volumes have been granted a longer life, well preserved on library shelves, whereas smaller books are the rarest ones to find, as they were often intended for regular use, and hence destined to consumption[14].

Tab. 3. Format of Italian editions 1601-1650 found only in libraries outside Italy according to the *USTC*

Format	Number of editions
4o	1,567
Broadsheet (plano)	1,100
8°	1,027
Folio	650
12°	593
16°	112
24°	30
32°	7
Total	5,086

---

12 A. Pettegree, *Lo Universal Short Title Catalogue*, pp. 100–101.
13 See http://ustc.ac.uk/index.php/news/view/new-italian-imprints-discovered-in-french-libraries. Over 5,000 of these items have been inspected and fully described in the survey of Italian books in French libraries undertaken for the *USTC* by Shanti Graheli.
14 For a comprehensive analysis of factors possibly affecting the survival of early printed books see N. Harris, *La sopravvivenza del libro*, pp. 44–46: Dimensioni; and G. Proot, *Survival Factors of Seventeenth-Century Hand-Press Books Published in the Southern Netherlands: The Importance of Sheet Counts, Sammelbände and the Role of Institutional Collections*, in F. Bruni / A. Pettegree (eds.), *Lost Books*, pp. 160–201, especially pp. 182–185: "Bibliographic Format".

In the contemporary information world, a global survey of the book production of each specific printing domain and its dissemination beyond national borders looks more like an obligation rather than an option. The major library catalogues are not only useful for finding and requesting books to read; they increasingly serve as sources of information on the books themselves, and are thus turning into bibliographies. The latest developments of *EDIT16* confirm its evolution from a survey on the holdings of national collections to a comprehensive bibliography of sixteenth-century Italian imprints[15].

In June 2017, the ICCU launched the addition to *EDIT16* of editions and copies found in the British Library. The agreement between the two institutions was the result of a longstanding effort involving librarians was on both sides since 2012[16]. As a result, the British Library was the first foreign library to appear among *EDIT16* localizations, joining over 1,580 libraries in Italy, the Vatican, and San Marino. The code UK0001 marks the localization of more than 9,000 records in a library abroad. The British Library provided the impressive amount of 1,426 images, related to 768 editions; 379 bibliographic records have a digital copy attached provided by the British Library. Even more significantly, 843 records have been created on the basis of unique copies of editions not found in Italian libraries[17]. Similar agreements with more institutions abroad are in the pipeline and will hopefully bring a new flow of copies and editions to *EDIT16* in the next few years[18].

According to my survey for the *USTC*, in the first half of the seventeenth century Italian book production concentrated in a few main printing places (fig. 1). The distribution of production in such centers remained steady in the new findings. I was able to observe some small but significant variations, though, for minor printing centers (tab. 4). Here the loss of copies can cause a modest, occasional printing activity, to be largely or entirely neglected. The ephemeral production of some peripheral towns may well have disappeared altogether.

---

15 S. Buttò, *EDIT16: dal Censimento alla rete*.
16 Among them, Stephen Parkin, Curator of Printed Heritage Collections 1450–1600 at the British Library; and Neil Harris, who actively promoted the survey of foreign collections in *EDIT16*: see N. Harris, *La sopravvivenza del libro*, p. 47, n. 35. This was also made possible thanks to a 2-year Marie Curie Individual Fellowship awarded in February 2015 to Laura Carnelos to research on the project *PATRIMONiT. From Cheap Print to Rare Ephemera: 16th-Century Italian 'Popular' Books at the British Library* under the supervision of Cristina Dondi. See https://www.cerl.org/collaboration/projects/marie_curie and https://www.cerl.org/collaboration/projects/patrimonit.
17 I am grateful to Costanza Messana, director of *EDIT16*, for providing data updated to July 2018. For a first report see P. Lolli, *EDIT16 apre all'estero*, mail sent to aib–cur@list.cineca.it, June 8, 2017. See also http://www.iccu.sbn.it/opencms/opencms/it/archivionovita/2017/novita_0016.html; and S. Buttò, *EDIT16: dal Censimento alla rete*.
18 S. Buttò, *EDIT16: dal Censimento alla rete*.

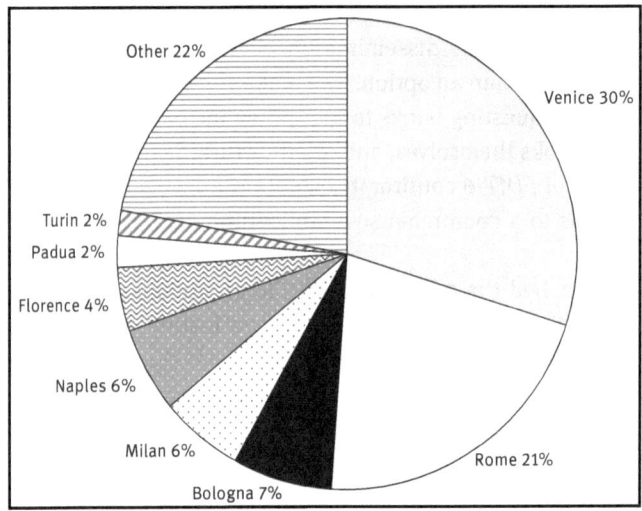

Fig. 1. Printing centers in Italy between 1601 and 1650 as represented in the USTC.

The data provided in column 3, Table 4 relates to Italian editions printed between 1601 and 1650 that today seem to be available only abroad. The selected examples cover Italy in its entirety, including the main islands, and provide a wide range of sizes as for the number of editions and proportion of new findings. The individual history of each state to which these towns belonged can provide some helpful insights to explain the dispersal of books and their resulting current location. On the whole, and more relevantly, this figure shows how a global survey, beyond national collections, can significantly enhance our knowledge especially of minor printing centers and peripheral areas of print.

Tab. 4: Italian editions 1601-1650 not found in Italy (June 2017)

	Editions (total)	Editions not found in Italy	% of editions not found in Italy
Palermo	499	60	12%
Milan	2,714	347	13%
Lucca	126	22	17%
Bergamo	224	53	24%
Cagliari	36	9	25%
Pistoia	51	13	25%
Catania	15	4	27%
Verona	502	159	32%
Como	73	28	38%
Cherasco	3	2	67%
Agrigento	2	2	100%

Milan, for instance, was the fourth Italian printing center at the time, in spite of being represented by only about 6% of the total production (fig. 1). 13% of Milanese editions printed between 1601 and 1650 are known today through copies available only in libraries outside Italy (tab. 4). The rate of dispersal might prove to be even higher by comparing the number of copies, rather than editions, available in Italy and abroad[19].

At the other end of the scale, there is no evidence of any printing activity in the Sicilian town of Agrigento until the beginning of the eighteenth century, except for the short period between 1594 and 1603, when the Spanish bishop Juan de Horozco y Covarrubias set up a press to print his own works. The production of this short-term business seems to be limited to two editions: the *Emblemata moralia*, currently documented by seven known copies, none of which in Italy[20]; and the *Sacra Symbola*, of which three copies in Spain and three in Italy are known[21]. The Italian collective catalogue *SBN* currently registers two copies of the *Sacra Symbola* and none of the *Emblemata moralia*; but, since none of the Italian copies appeared to have been recorded in *SBN* until 2017, both the editions entered the *USTC* thanks to copies preserved in Spain and the US[22].

What books are these, found many miles away from where they were produced? Answering such question is not straightforward. Any kind of imprint could travel, and for several reasons. Large, expensive books, already valued as collectible items by contemporaries, possibly found their way to collections in their home country and beyond. But cheap imprints are inveterate travelers too. Often tiny and handy to carry, chapbooks are the perfect travel mates, appealing across all social or cultural barriers. Not originally intended to sit on library shelves in costly bindings, pamphlets

---

[19] I excluded the Vatican Library from this consideration of foreign libraries to focus solely on books which travelled a long way from the place where they were printed.
[20] Juan de Horozco y Covarrubias, *Emblemata moralia*, Agrigento, 1601, *USTC* 4037497 (copy: Illinois University Library, Urbana, IL) and 5005198 (IB B106125, copy: Cáceres, Real Monasterio de Santa María de Guadalupe); five more copies are in listed in S. López Poza, *Sacra Symbola, de Juan de Horozco Covarrubias*, in Á. Ezama et al. (eds.), *"La razón es aurora". Estudios en homenaje a la profesora Aurora Egido*, Zaragoza 2017, pp. 89–104, at p. 90: Universidad de Zaragoza; Universidad de Murcia; University of Glasgow, Stirling Maxwell Collection; Seminario Menor San Torcuato, Guadix (Granada); Universidad de Granada.
[21] Juan de Horozco y Covarrubias, *Ad sanctissimum dominum N. Clementem VIII. pontif. maxim. Sacra symbola*, Agrigento, 1601, *USTC* 4037498 (copies: Biblioteca Diocesana de Zamora, Biblioteca Histórica de la Universidad de Valencia and Real Academia de la Historia, Madrid) and 5005199 (IB 106126, copy: Biblioteca Diocesana de Zamora); *SBN* FOGE034265 (copies: Lucera, Biblioteca Comunale Ruggero Bonghi and Monreale, Biblioteca Ludovico II De Torres). An additional copy, to be found in the Biblioteca Comunale of Palermo, is listed in S. López Poza, *Sacra Symbola*, at p. 89.
[22] The record FOGE034265 was actually already in *SBN*, but the misspelling of Agrigento in the publication area and the missing link to the relevant authority file caused any search by place of printing to be vain. This reminds us the potential damage of an inaccurate material description, or a small typing error.

have only occasionally been able to avoid destruction to end up in a proper, stable book collection[23]. What makes such books so remarkable, despite their modest features and scant material value, is their rarity. This is especially true when they happen to be rediscovered far from their hometown.

It is not easy to infer the fortunate circumstances that saved some cheap imprints from oblivion, whereas other copies disappeared forever. In his essay on the survival and disappearance of early printed books, Neil Harris persuasively suggests a combination of several factors at the basis of survival[24].

Censorship had an unquestionable and longstanding impact on the rate of survival[25]. Only one copy of a book against the papacy in the Italian vernacular claiming to have been printed in Rome in 1617 is currently known in Italy[26]. Not surprisingly, it seems to have had better fortune abroad: two of the three other copies known are now located in the United Kingdom, one at the British Library and one at the Bodleian Library in Oxford, and an additional one is at the National Library of Spain, in Madrid[27].

In some cases a collection, or even a single miscellaneous volume, acted as a time-capsule: a large number of ephemeral imprints unexpectedly survived many centuries of history only because they had been bound with other items they are often not even related to[28]. This is indeed the case of a peculiar French broadsheet, the only known copy of which is found today in a library in Rome (fig. 2)[29].

---

23 See also A. Pettegree, *The Legion of the Lost*, p. 2: "Unlike the First Folio, which was much prized by contemporaries, many printed works published in the first two centuries of print were never destined for the shelves of libraries. They served their purpose, were read for the information they contained, and then discarded. Many are known now from only a single copy, often grubby and worn"; and N. Harris, *La sopravvivenza del libro*, pp. 48–49: "Genere, materia e destino di biblioteca".
24 N. Harris, *La sopravvivenza del libro*, p. 42.
25 A. Pettegree, *The Legion of the Lost*, pp. 16–19. Censorship might have some unpredictable effects as well: see N. Harris, *La sopravvivenza del libro*, pp. 49–51: "Censura e soppressione".
26 *Scala politica dell'abominatione, e tirannia Papale, di Benvenuto Italiano: a tutti gli prencipi, republiche, stati, e signori, et ad ogn'altro nobil' spirito amatore dell'ortodossa, e christiana fede*, In Roma, alli 20 di maggio 1617 [i.e. Venice, 1617?] *SBN* CFIE053170; *USTC* 4041127. Perhaps printed in Venice according to the *Catalogue of Seventeenth-Century Italian Books in the British Library*, London, The British Library, vol. 1, 1897, p. 95. The only copy currently known to be in Italy is at the Biblioteca nazionale centrale in Florence, shelfmark RARI.Guicc.9.4.14. It appeared on *SBN* in April 2018.
27 London, British Library, shelfmark 698.b.41.2; Oxford, Balliol College Library, Special Collection, shelfmark 915.c.13(3); Madrid, Biblioteca Nacional de España, Sede de Recoletos, shelfmark U/8871 (digital copy available online: http://bdh-rd.bne.es/viewer.vm?id=0000112631&page=1).
28 N. Harris, *La sopravvivenza del libro*, pp. 45 and 61–64. Harris further discussed the case of the miscellany as a time capsule in his paper presented at the "Lost Books Conference", University of St Andrews, June 19, 2014: *A Spanner in the Statistical Machine. The Deplorable Behaviour of the Miscellany*.
29 Rome, Biblioteca Casanatense, ms. 2462. I am grateful for this reference to Rozanne M. Versendaal, who is working on this and some other similar amusing broadsheets for her dissertation, and to Andrea Cappa, at the time at the Biblioteca Casanatense, for his help on the analysis of the volume.

Fig. 2: *Mandement de Quaresme*, Rome, Biblioteca Casanatense [ms. 2462].

The broadsheet is part of the genre of parodic texts, in this case mocking the Church, therefore typologically defined as "amusing"[30]. It is bound in a miscellaneous volume comprising a few imprints and manuscript sheets differently sized, for the most part news and letters in Italian or French[31]. The "amusing" broadsheet is placed just before the final flyleaf, following a few other manuscript sheets in various hands: among them, the most remarkable are a series of reviews on a work to be published (although

---

[30] *Mandement de Quaresme pour mettre ordre a tous friands morceaux, fripponeries, et autres abusions bachiques qui de iour à autre se vont augmentant*, s.l., s.n., s.d. On such so-called "joyful summons" see the project "Uncovering Joyful Culture: Parodic Literature and Practices in and around the Low Countries (13th–17th centuries)" directed by Katell Lavéant, online: https://joycult.hypotheses.org/.
[31] I would infer a date about 1630 for this collection of documents, as they date from the beginning of the century to 1626. A manuscript index at the beginning shows that the material was perhaps bound together shortly after being collected.

it eventually never was), and a manuscript index of the edition of Titus Livius printed in Lyon by Antoine Vicent in 1553. Folding marks provide clear evidence that all these handwritten notes were once kept loosely in the volume, likely folded between the leaves. This is further proved by the absence on the "amusing" broadsheet of any numbering, either the contemporary handwritten number in the right upper corner or the nineteenth-century number stamped in the bottom right corner of each leaf, both to be found all over the volume. A note on the final pastedown reports that the volume was rebound and refurbished in 2008. It was likely at this later stage that the broadsheet, glued to a strip of paper, eventually became part of the volume. It was, indeed, not included in the old manuscript index at the beginning of the volume itself.

No ownership inscription or other material evidence help us fathom how this volume joined the collections of Cardinal Casanate in Rome. Rather than an unknown owner, for this unique survivor we must thank the long-lasting habit of keeping ephemera in notebooks and diaries.

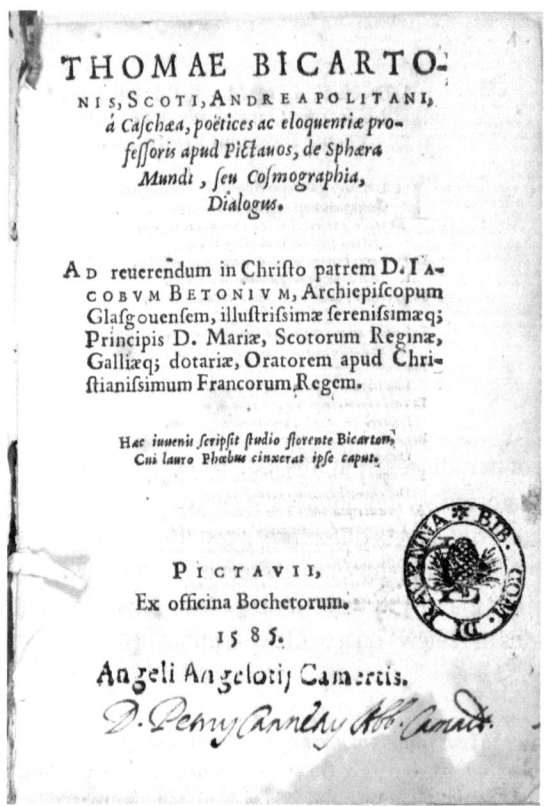

Fig. 3: T. Bicarton, *De sphaera mundi, seu cosmographia, dialogus*, Pictauii, ex officina Bochetorum, 1585, Ravenna, Istituzione Biblioteca Classense [F.A. 026.006.L2 (1)], title page.

Similarly unknown are the reasons that brought another stray survivor from provincial France to Italy. The book in question is a pocketsize volume, now in the Biblioteca

Classense in Ravenna, uniting a few works of Thomas Bicarton[32]. Originally from St Andrews in Scotland, Thomas Bicarton was "poetices ac eloquentiae professor" in Poitiers, as stated on the first title page of this collected volume. His works and their publishing history seem not to have attracted any interest to date and should be investigated further. The *USTC* registers 9 editions under his name, 2 printed in Tours and 7 in Poitiers[33].

The miscellaneous book in Ravenna comprises four imprints. According to the *USTC*, those bound in first and fourth place are complete and unique copies of two editions: the *De sphaera mundi, seu cosmographia, dialogus* printed in Poitiers by the Bouchet brothers in 1585 (fig. 3), and the *De vita diui Thomae Aquinatis panegyricus* also printed in Poitiers by the Bouchet brothers the following year[34] (fig. 4). The two imprints they are bound with look rather like parts of some other editions, as indicated by the lack of imprint on both title pages and, even more clearly, by their incomplete signature statement: 2A⁸ for the *Traduction de l'ode seconde des Epodes d'Horace*, E-G⁸ for the *Somnium de doctoratu D. Bonaventurae Irlandi*. I was not able to identify from where these excerpts have been taken. All we can say about them is they are extremely rare, perhaps even lost editions, whose unique fragmentary copy is now found faraway from its place of origin.

This volume tells us something about its past and former owners. On the title page of the imprint bound first, we can see the stamp of Angelo Angelozzi and an ownership inscription by Petrus Cannetus[35] (fig. 3). Angelo Angelozzi from Camerino lived in Rome around the mid-seventeenth century. His library was dispersed after his death and many books are found around the world with his stamp on the title page[36].

---

[32] Ravenna, Biblioteca Classense, shelfmark F.A. 026.006.L2 (1–4): T. Bicarton, *De sphaera mundi, seu cosmographia, dialogus*, Pictauii, ex officina Bochetorum, 1585 (*SBN* RAVE069067; *USTC* 207090); T. Bicarton, *Traduction de l'ode seconde des Epodes d'Horace, traictant des louanges de la vie rustique*, S.l., s.n., s.d. (*SBN* RAVE069068); T. Bicarton, *Somnium de doctoratu D. Bonaventurae Irlandi pridie quàm doctoris insignibus ornatus est, visum*, S.l., s.n., s.d. (*SBN* RAVE069069); T. Bicarton, *De vita diui Thomae Aquinatis panegyricus*, Pictauii, ex officina Bochetorum, 1586 (*SBN* RAVE069070; *USTC* 207001). I first came across this item when working for the *SBN* survey of sixteenth-century editions located in the libraries of Emilia Romagna. I am grateful to Barbara Gentile of the Biblioteca Classense for sending me the images of the title pages of the first and fourth imprint.
[33] *USTC* 207002, 206574, 206988, 110466, 207090, 207001, 206899, 110473, 356.
[34] See above, n. 32.
[35] "Angeli Angelotij Camertis" and, immediately below, "D. Petrus Cannetus Abb. Camald.".
[36] See, for instance, the provenance database of the Biblioteca Nazionale di Napoli: http://www.bnnonline.it/index.php?it/324/possessori/possessori_508e7ec2a179d/418, and a digitised book of the Biblioteca Alessandrina of Rome carrying his stamp on the title page: https://books.google.it/books?id=i8bUb2DPRb0C&lpg=PP1&ots=M686c7o99r. On Angelo Angelozzi da Camerino and his library see G. Colucci, *Delle antichità picene dell'abate Giuseppe Colucci patrizio camerinese. Tomo XI*, Fermo, dai torchi dell'autore, 1791, p. XXXIII.

Petrus Cannetus (1659–1730) was an abbot of the Camaldulensian monastery of Classe from 1704 to 1714. As an erudite man, he put much effort into transforming what was a modest monastic library into an up-to-date encyclopedic collection, which later became the core of the Biblioteca Classense[37]. Despite such significant evidence of provenance, we still cannot infer much about the reasons why this book travelled the long way from Poitiers to Ravenna and ended up in the hands of Angelo Angelozzi.

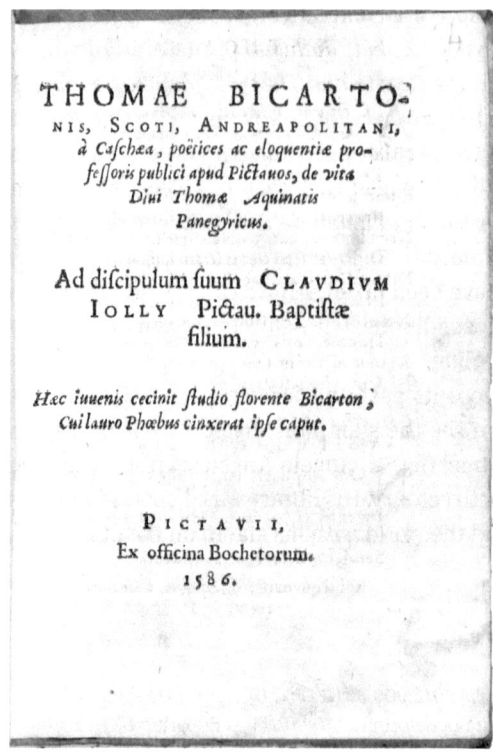

Fig. 4: T. Bicarton, *De vita diui Thomae Aquinatis panegyricus*, Pictauii, ex officina Bochetorum, 1586, Ravenna, Istituzione Biblioteca Classense [F.A. 026.006.L2 (4)], title page.

Peripheral printing was largely ephemeral, relying to a large extent on importation from the major printing centers and being essentially addressed to meet the demands of the local market rather than meant for larger circulation. Books proudly showing the names and devices of famous printers operating in leading printing centers on their title pages had good overall survival chances. Being expensive, they were accordingly treasured as collectibles[38]. On the contrary, the material features of some barely decent imprints were more often dictated by the needs and mundane occasions of a

---

37 A. Petrucci, *Canneti, Pietro*, in *Dizionario Biografico degli Italiani*, vol. 18, 1975, available online: http://www.treccani.it/enciclopedia/pietro-canneti_(Dizionario-Biografico)/.
38 See N. Harris, *La sopravvivenza del libro*, pp. 54–56: "Peso del centro editoriale e prestigio dell'editore", and p. 60: "Prezzo".

community rather than by the tastes of fine collectors. Only a few of them were occasionally able to find shelter on the shelves of a durable collection for the centuries to come. It might be surprising to observe that this is more likely to have happened far from the place of printing[39].

Between 1562 and 1563, Jacob Marcaria printed in Riva del Garda several pamphlets related to the Council of Trent for the editors and booksellers Pietro Antonio Alciati and Giovanni Battista Bozzola[40]. Two of such pamphlets, printed by Marcaria in 1562, contain in 8 unnumbered leaves the conciliar decree on the *communione sub utraque specie*. Both editions, one for Alciati and one for Bozzola, are unknown to both *EDIT16* and *ESTeR*[41]. Their rarity is quite predictable, because such imprints were targeted to a limited audience and possibly a local market. This seems to be proven by the existence of a few more editions of the same work published between 1562 and 1564, most of which known only through a small number of copies. See Table 5.

Tab. 5: Known copies of 1562-1564 Italian editions of the "Doctrina de communione sub utraque specie"

EDIT16 CNCE	USTC	Imprint	Copies in Italy	Copies abroad
12955	860930	Brixiae, [Damiano Turlino] ad instantiam Baptistae Bozolae, 1562	12	10
12972	860965	Patauii, apud Christophorum Gryphium, 1563	9	2
14683	860933	Patauii, apud Laurentium Pasquatium & socios, 1562	4	2
14705	861005	Brixiae, ad instantiam Io. Baptistae Bozolae, 1564	4	1
14684	860932	Venetiis, apud Andream Arriuabenum, 1562	5	-
12958	860945	Patauii, [Cristoforo Griffio?], [not before 1562])	3	1

---

39 Being of little interest outside their *Sprachraum*, such publications escaped consumption by remaining unread: see N. Harris, *La sopravvivenza del libro*, pp. 61–64.
40 On Jacob Marcaria see *Editori e stampatori di Trento e Rovereto* (*ESTeR*), online: http://www.esterbib.it; http://www.esterbib.it/veditipografo.php?ID=21; and *EDIT16* CNCT 10. On Pietro Antonio Alciati see http://www.esterbib.it/veditipografo.php?ID=35 and *EDIT16* CNCT 988. On Giovanni Battista Bozzola see http://www.esterbib.it/veditipografo.php?ID=36 and *EDIT16* CNCT 790.
41 *Doctrina de communione sub utrqvae [sic] specie et paruulorum publicata in sessione quinta sacri oecumenici Concilij Tridentini sub S.D.N. Pio IIII. Pont. Max. die XVI. Iulij. M.D.LXII.*, Ripae, ad instantiam Petri Antonii Alciatis, 1562; *Doctrina de communione sub utraquae specie et paruulorum publicata in sessione quinta sacri oecumenici Concilij Tridentini sub S.D.N. Pio IIII. Pont. Max. die XVI. Iulij. M.D.LXII.*, Ripae, ad instantiam Baptistæ Bozolæ, 1562. Neither of the two editions is recorded in the *Catalogo Bibliografico Trentino*, online: http://www.cbt.biblioteche.provincia.tn.it, or in the *Stampe antiche della Biblioteca comunale di Trento* (*STABAT*) catalogue, online: http://www.stabat.it, either.

EDIT16 CNCE	USTC	Imprint	Copies in Italy	Copies abroad
14682	860931	Bononiae, Ioannes Rubeus excudebat ad instantiam Petri Pisanelli, 1562	1	–
–	–	Ripae, [Jacob Marcaria] ad instantiam Petri Antonii Alciatis, 1562	–	1
–	–	Ripae, [Jacob Marcaria] ad instantiam Baptistæ Bozolæ, 1562	–	1

The two editions of the *Doctrina de communione sub utraque specie* printed by Marcaria in 1562 appear to be preserved only in one copy each, both in foreign libraries: one in the Zentralbibliothek of Zürich, bound in a volume once property of the Swiss reformer Heinrich Bullinger; the other one, also part of a *Sammelband*, is at the Herzog-August-Bibliothek of Wolfenbüttel[42].

Tab. 6: Years of activity and production of Jacob Marcaria according to each source

Source	Years of activity	Number of editions
EDIT16	1562-1563	28
SBN	1558-1563	29
STABAT	1558-1563	44
USTC	1558-1563	48
ESTeR	1557-1563	68

The production of Jacob Marcaria also represents a perfect case study for introducing another threat to the accuracy of our knowledge of the history of printing as a result of sectional bibliographies. The number of editions printed in Riva del Garda by Jacob Marcaria differs considerably from one online resource to another (tab. 6). *EDIT16* records 28 pamphlets, whereas the *ESTeR* database on editors and printers of Trento and Rovereto provides the most complete overview on the production of Marcaria to date by listing 68 imprints. *STABAT*, an online database of books published in Trentino between 1481 and 1700 described through the collections of the municipal library and historical archive of Trento, according to its scope offers digital copies of 44 imprints available in the participating institutions[43]. The *USTC* lists the editions found in *EDIT16* and *STABAT*, which partially overlap, with a few more from addi-

---

42 Zürich, Zentralbibliothek, shelfmark Ms A.84.a, see https://www.swissbib.ch/Record/157415309; Wolfenbüttel, Herzog-August-Bibliothek, shelfmark A: 478.1 Quod. (3), see https://gso.gbv.de/DB=2.1/PPNSET?PPN=355366428. I am grateful to Urs Leu and Sandra Weidmann for sending me digital images of the Zentralbibliothek Zürich copy, and to Valentina Sebastiani for images of the Wolfenbüttel copy. I owe to Matteo Fadini the reference to the Wolfenbüttel copy.
43 *STABAT*, online: http://www.stabat.it.

tional sources[44]. As for *EDIT16* and *SBN*, an apparently close number misleadingly covers up a rather significant discrepancy. Some of the editions recorded in *EDIT16* are not represented in *SBN*, whereas *SBN* describes some Hebrew editions, which are excluded from *EDIT16*[45]. The omission of Hebrew editions from *EDIT16* causes the production and time period of activity of Marcaria to be significantly misrepresented in the Italian national bibliography for the sixteenth century.

The experience of the *Universal Short Title Catalogue* and the examples shown above from other catalogues and bibliographies provide suggestions for the development of both specialized and national bibliographies. An effective mutual effort is essential toward the completion of bibliographies beyond material obstacles and national borders. Books only available in libraries outside their countries of origin, or in foreign languages and alphabets, must be added to the core of national bibliographies and considered as a whole for a thorough reconsideration of printing and the book trade especially in peripheral areas. This is especially crucial for those sides of the book market which would otherwise result completely neglected in bibliographies and catalogues, negatively affecting access to resources and research on them. This is, to a large extent, the case of cheap print[46].

We tend to forget that bibliography is a work in progress. Neil Harris estimated the total production in sixteenth-century Italy as 80.000 editions[47]. We have now found about 85% of this supposed total production (over 68.000 editions)[48]. The results of

---

44 As a result of a partnership with *STABAT* (see http://ustc.ac.uk/index.php/news/view/trent-joins-preserving-the-worlds-rarest-books-programme) and especially thanks to the work of Matteo Fadini, the *USTC* was able to add locations and links to *STABAT* records (including full digital copies) for 2 incunabula, 77 sixteenth-century and 94 seventeenth-century Trentine editions. About a hundred of them were previously unrecorded in the *USTC*, *EDIT16* and *SBN*.

45 Some of the editions listed in *EDIT16* are currently only found in libraries which are not part of the *SBN* network; on the other hand, *EDIT16* does not register editions entirely in other alphabets than Latin.

46 The first nine types of books which Rudolf Hirsch listed as more likely to have disappeared than others in an essay on the circulation of early modern manuscripts all belong to the domain of popular print: "We can state with some confidence that certain types of books are more likely to have disappeared than others: 1) Cheap books, in general; 2) Small books, in general; 3) Household books, like cookbooks, instructions on how to prepare vinegar or brandy etc.; 4) Books classed as pseudo–science, like prescriptions, almanacs, prognostications, dream books, books of secrets; 5) Technological books (so called *Kunstbüchlein* or *Probirbüchlein*) with instructions on how to harden iron, write in invisible ink, etc.; 6) Medical books, like remedies against the plague, herbals for medicinal use; 7) School books, like ABCs, copies of the *Pater Noster* and the *Credo*, broadsides used in teaching, grammars, readers, wordbooks; 8) Vernacular popular literature; 9) Books for private devotion and popular legends"; R. Hirsch, *Printing, Selling and Reading: 1450–1550*, Wiesbaden 1967, p. 11; cited in N. Harris, *La sopravvivenza del libro*, pp. 36–37.

47 N. Harris, *Un ammiraglio, un cane e i Vaticinia*, in R.M. Servello (ed.), *Il libro italiano del XVI secolo*, pp. 43–91, at p. 56.

48 S. Buttò, *EDIT16: dal Censimento alla rete*.

this analysis allows as to infer that what is left out largely comprises cheap books and lost editions. Under a scholarly perspective, the discovery of one cheap imprint previously unknown to bibliography is strikingly more significant than the finding of a book already available in several copies, regardless of the value of its material features[49]. The scope of bibliography and its latest developments push toward a comprehensive survey and description of cheap imprints beyond any frontier.

I gathered the data and examples illustrated above from 2012 to 2017. When I revised this text for publication I was able to notice that a few relevant changes had already occurred in the lapse of time between the first and the second draft of this article: new copies have emerged, in Italy and abroad, joining former unique surviving copies – which are not unique any longer. This reminds us of the urgency to integrate resources whenever we can, along with the need for an accurate description of collections that have not been catalogued to date, in a perspective without frontiers. Until we have scrutinized every imprint, from national libraries to the tiniest and most peripheral collections on national soil and abroad, our knowledge is imperfect, and every estimation provisional. Rather than being a discouraging premise, this should be a challenging target and an impulse toward international partnerships and agreements for cooperation.

---

[49] On the misleading use of the term "rare" to indicate valuable books in the antiquarian book trade, see N. Harris, *La sopravvivenza del libro*, pp. 32–36.

III. Transnational Approaches

Jean-François Botrel and Juan Gomis
"Literatura de cordel" from a Transnational Perspective

New Horizons for an Old Field of Study

1 "Literatura de cordel" as a field of study

In Spain, as in other European countries, the 1960s marked the beginning of studies on popular printed literature. The studies conducted by Robert Mandrou on the *Bibliothèque bleue* and by Victor Neuburg on chapbooks are recognized as pioneering works that laid the foundation for fruitful lines of research on both sides of the English Channel, and in Spain Julio Caro Baroja blazed the trail with the publication in 1969 of his *Ensayo sobre la literatura de cordel*[1]. In addition to contributing decisively to a reassessment of popular printed culture as a field of study and providing a rich interdisciplinary analytical perspective (Caro Baroja was an anthropologist), that book coined the definition "literatura de cordel". The term was used to refer to a heterogeneous mass of printed matter that was short and inexpensive, crude in appearance and widely distributed, which had circulated in Spain since the early days of printing. The term was a modern invention, alluding to the supposed custom of sellers of popular prints of hanging their wares on strings to offer them to the public. Despite being a neologism, not used by contemporary printers, sellers, or readers, the expression "literatura de cordel" has achieved success among scholars of Spanish popular printed culture, mainly because it gives coherence to a corpus of great textual and physical diversity.

In Spain, *pliego suelto* (single sheet) was the name given to the basic unit of paper that was used by all the printers to make books. The *pliego suelto* was the basis of *literatura de cordel*. Works of this kind were published on a single *pliego suelto* folded twice (producing a booklet with eight pages), on half a *pliego*, or on two, three or four *pliegos* joined together. As a result, studies frequently use the term *pliego suelto* or *pliego de cordel* to refer generically to the printed matter of which *literatura de cordel* consisted. With the publication of the first *pliego suelto* in Spain in 1482, this publishing formula began a successful career that lasted over four centuries. Printers very soon realized that the production of *pliegos de cordel*, which could be made quickly and sold immediately, brought them easy income.

---

1 J. Caro Baroja, *Ensayo sobre la literatura de cordel*, Madrid 1969.

Note: This work forms part of the research project PGC2018-097445-A-C22, financed by the Ministry of Science, Innovation and Universities (Spain).

http://doi.org/10.1515/9783110643541-008

From then on, the publishing genre of *literatura de cordel* gradually expanded and diversified over the centuries. The textual and physical diversity of *literatura de cordel* makes it hard to establish definite boundaries for it, or a precise taxonomy. The genre was modelled by the printers, especially those who concentrated on producing popular literature, adapting their range to the demands of their readers, adding and removing titles, enlarging their collections with various kinds of printed material, and combining texts that had a long tradition with newly created work, as we can see in their sales catalogues. It could be said that, basically, printers were the real creators of *literatura de cordel*.

As a result, the typology of the printed material of which the genre consists is very varied[2]. The *romance* must, of course, be singled out, because of its numerical importance. "Romance" is a problematic term in various ways: on the one hand, in an international context it may lead to confusion because it is identical with the English word "romance". In the Spanish context, however, the word *romance* refers to the meter that has been most popular since medieval times, consisting of octosyllabic lines of verse with assonant rhymes in even lines. Because of the prominence of *romance* verse in *literatura de cordel* as a whole, many *pliegos sueltos* with texts that used this rhyme system were called "romances". Thus the term was used to define the printed material.

The *romances* that were printed as *pliegos sueltos* over the centuries were diverse. In the first half of the sixteenth century, they were traditional *romances*, epic, historical or chivalric, which had been transmitted orally since medieval times. From 1550, *romances* began to incorporate matters that eventually predominated in *literatura de cordel* as a whole: news about crimes ("casos horribles y espantosos" horrible, dreadful cases), miracles, natural disasters, wars, political events (coronations, royal marriages, births of princes and princesses), or stories of captives (Christians captured by the Turks). In Spain, compositions of this kind whose main aim was informative (about real or fictitious happenings) were called "relaciones de sucesos" (accounts of events)[3]. Fiction also had a place in *romances*. Mostly in the form of amorous adventures in which the lovers experience a series of incidents in their attempts to overcome the obstacles that are placed between them. Another subject that is very much present in *romances* is religion, with texts for the teaching of the Catholic doctrine, for devotion to the Virgin Mary or the saints, or for moral reflection. Finally, another important group consisted of burlesque or satirical *romances*, which aimed to entertain the reader with their jokes.

---

2 See a general approach to literatura de cordel in J.-F. Botrel, *Literatura de cordel*, in *Diccionario Español de Términos Literarios*, forthcoming, and *El género de cordel*, in L. Díaz G. Viana (ed.), *Palabras para el pueblo*, vol. 1: *Aproximación general a la literatura de cordel*, Madrid 2001, pp. 41–69.

3 The Sociedad Internacional para el Estudio de las Relaciones de Sucesos (SIERS) has been doing extraordinary work on news accounts for decades.

In addition to poetic *pliegos sueltos*, *literatura de cordel* also includes a group of texts written in prose. On the one hand, we find calendars, forecasts and almanacs, one of the typologies most widely disseminated in Europe[4]. Calendars showed the days of the week, the months and the Christian festivals, almanacs offered astrological events in the coming year, eclipses, conjunctions, and movable feasts, and forecasts predicted the most outstanding events of the year. On the other hand, a second type of *pliego suelto* written in prose was the so-called "historia". Physically, *historias* were longer than *romances*, consisting of several *pliegos* sewn together (between three and eight, giving from 24 to 64 pages). The first titles were those of the so-called *historias caballerescas breves* (short tales of chivalry)[5]. They corresponded to twenty novels of medieval origin that were published as *pliegos de cordel* between 1480 and 1530. A few more titles were added to them as the centuries went by, until these traditional stories were prohibited in 1757 and replaced with a new collection of 40 *historias* published in Madrid (and later in many other cities) by the printer Manuel Martín[6]. During the nineteenth century, the repertoire of *historias* experienced a spectacular boom and over 200 new titles were published. The stories were generally taken from European novelistic literature (Chateaubriand, Dumas, Hugo, etc.) and from contemporary history. Thus, with the passing of the centuries, a group of stories that at the beginning of the *cordel* genre barely constituted a tiny part of the total assortment gradually grew in volume until it became a considerable part of *literatura de cordel*.

In addition to prose and poetry, a very numerous group of *pliegos sueltos* that was characteristic of Spanish printed popular literature consisted of titles derived from the theater. These *pliegos* proliferated especially during the eighteenth century, with the publication of complete plays or parts of plays that mostly came from the Spanish Golden Age. In the first place, individual comedies were published: single plays that generally consisted of no more than 40 pages. Short works, such as *sainetes*, *entremeses*, and *loas*, which were performed in theaters in the intervals of performances of plays, were also published as *pliegos de cordel*. Together with these plays that were printed in their entirety there were theatrical *pliegos sueltos* of another kind, known as *relaciones de comedias* (extracts from plays). They were well-known fragments of plays, consisting of lines spoken by single characters who told the stories of their lives, and they were extracted from the original work and printed as *pliegos sueltos*.

---

4 H.-J. Lüsebrink / Y.-G. Mix / J.-Y. Mollier / P. Sorel (eds.), *Les lectures du peuple en Europe et dans les Amériques du XVIIe au XXe siècle*, Brussels 2003.
5 V. Infantes, *La narración caballeresca breve*, and N. Baranda, *Compendio bibliográfico sobre la narrativa caballeresca breve*, both in M.E. Lacarra (ed.), *Evolución narrativa e ideológica de la literatura caballeresca*, Bilbao 1991, pp. 165–181 and 183–191.
6 J. Gomis, *Echoes from the Middle Ages: Tales of Chivalry, Romances, and Nation-building in Spain (1750–1850)*, in "Studies in Medievalism", 24, 2015, pp. 93–113.

Relaciones de comedias enjoyed great success in the eighteenth century and formed an outstanding typology in the *cordel* genre. They were very well-known and widely disseminated, as is shown by the fact that printers published "relaciones satíricas o burlescas" (satirical or burlesque extracts), which parodied a *relación de comedia* line by line, altering a few words or phrases and assuming that readers would recognize the original work and the wittiness of the changes that had been made. Finally, another kind of *pliego suelto* derived from the theatre was the type that offered summaries of complete plays or recreated the lives of well-known characters who appeared in comedies from the Golden Age.

The *romances, historias, relaciones de comedias*, and other *pliegos de cordel* mentioned so far are publications in which text predominates over pictures. However, *literatura de cordel* included works in which images had greater, if not absolute, importance: first, *estampas*, folio or quarto sheets printed on only one side, bearing a picture of a saint. *Estampas* were of a religious nature and fulfilled a devotional, thaumaturgical, and doctrinal function; secondly, *gozos*, leaflets with hymns corresponding to a particular religious appellation, which is represented in a picture of greater or smaller size; thirdly, *aleluyas*, sheets with 48 images printed on one side, similar to the Dutch penny prints, the English catchpenny prints, the German *Bilderbogen* or the French *images d'Épinal*. The term *aleluya* is misleading, because they are not religious prints, and the explanation for it is the dual origin of this typology. On the one hand, in Castile *aleluya* was the name given to sheets of paper with various pictures of saints, which were cut up and thrown in the air in the Easter and Corpus Christi processions.

At the same time, in Catalonia *auques* was the name given to sheets of paper with various rows of images printed on them, which were used in a game of chance and represented things such as the sun and moon, occupations, animals, the world upside down, etc. *Auques* were introduced in Madrid in the middle of the nineteenth century by the Catalan printer José María Marés y Roca. As a result of the formal similarity between *auques* and *aleluyas*, the latter term was applied, first in Madrid and then in the rest of Spain, to printed matter that had nothing to do with religious festivities. The second half of the nineteenth century was the period of greatest popularity for *aleluyas*, which represented many different themes: adaptations of novels, biographies of personalities, episodes of Spanish history, education, city guides, moral instruction, etc.

Thus the physical and textual diversity of the printed material that constitutes *literatura de cordel* is considerable, and this has presented difficulties for research. Since the publication of Julio Caro Baroja's book, three lines of work have been explored in research on *pliegos de cordel*. First, a systematic process has been developed for seeking, cataloguing, and critically examining material dispersed in libraries, archives and private collections. In this respect, special mention must be made of the great work done by Antonio Rodríguez-Moñino, the precursor of many later studies, whose principal contribution in the field of *literatura de cordel* was his *Diccio-*

nario bibliográfico de pliegos sueltos poéticos (siglo XVI)[7]. Following in his wake, many researchers have pursued the traces of *pliegos de cordel*, attempting to make at least a partial reconstruction of a publishing panorama that will always remain incomplete, given the ephemeral nature of these publications, which were for immediate consumption and deteriorated easily.

Secondly, another important group of investigations has concentrated on studying the contents disseminated in *pliegos sueltos*, establishing thematic classifications, analyzing the structure of their content, tracking intertextual relationships between different items and between *pliegos sueltos* and other kinds of printed matter, or linking the cultural representations disseminated by means of *literatura de cordel* with the historical context in which this material appeared. Among the many publications that have taken this approach, particular mention must be made of the studies published by Joaquín Marco and of María Cruz García de Enterría, which are now considered classic works among the studies on *literatura de cordel*[8].

Finally, a third line of research has focused on the cultural practices that led to the appearance of *pliegos sueltos*: the processes of creation and production of the printed material, the paths of distribution, the agents who sold them, the advertising strategies, the performance associated with reading them, or the diversity of the audiences at which *pliegos de cordel* were aimed. The early works of Jean-François Botrel were pioneers in this field[9]. However, the study of these practices calls for the consultation of archival sources that are difficult to locate, which explains why the volume of work published in this third line of research is perceptibly smaller than in the other two.

2 "Literatura de cordel" from a transnational perspective

Literatura de cordel in Spain, therefore, is now a recognized field of study with a long tradition of research and one that nevertheless continues to arouse interest among philologists, historians, and anthropologists. However, there is one aspect that research on *pliegos de cordel* has neglected until now and that is fundamental if one

---

[7] A. Rodríguez-Moñino, *Nuevo diccionario bibliográfico de pliegos sueltos poéticos (siglo XVI)*, Madrid 1970.
[8] J. Marco, *Literatura popular en España en los siglos XVIII y XIX. (Una aproximación a los pliegos de cordel)*, Madrid 1977; M.C. García de Enterría, *Sociedad y poesía de cordel en el Barroco*, Madrid 1973.
[9] J.-F. Botrel, *Les aveugles, colporteurs d'imprimés en Espagne*, I: *La confrérie des aveugles de Madrid et la vente des imprimés, du monopole à la liberté du commerce (1581–1836)*, in "Mélanges de la Casa de Velázquez", 9, 1973, pp. 417–482; *Les aveugles, colporteurs d'imprimés en Espagne*, II: *Des aveugles considérés comme mass-media*, in "Mélanges de la Casa de Velázquez", 10, 1974, pp. 233–271; *Aspects de la littérature de colportage en Espagne sous la Restauration*, in *L'infra-littérature en Espagne aux XIXe et XXe siècles. Du roman feuilleton au romancero de la guerre d'Espagne*, Grenoble 1977, pp. 103–121.

wishes to obtain a more complete understanding of the genre. It is the insertion of this cultural phenomenon in a broader context than that of Spain, which would permit the development of a transnational perspective that could be used to establish connections between corpuses of publishing material that are disparate but share certain features that allow us to speak of a European culture of popular publications. It is a fact that the study of popular literature has traditionally been conducted within a national focus, although the isolation of this field of investigation may possibly have been more pronounced in Spain than in other European countries. Apart from a very few exceptions, there are no studies that have proposed an interpretation of *literatura de cordel* from a European viewpoint[10].

In Europe, in recent years, a new impulse has been given to the transnational perspective in the field of studies of popular printed literature, of which the present volume is a good example. Among the causes that explain this rebirth are, of course, the research policies promoted by the European Union, but also the gradual development of the digital humanities, which permit access to an ever greater volume of digitalized printed material, and also, possibly, a desire on the part of the research community to adopt new focuses for an object of study that has been worked on extensively in the framework of national frontiers. In the following pages we will refer to the benefits that a comparative perspective may bring to the study of *literatura de cordel* and, by extension, of popular printed culture in Europe. For this purpose, we will concentrate on three examples that have to do with contents, production strategies and the paths used for the circulation of *pliegos sueltos*.

2.1 Contents: Spanish gallows literature

In a seminal study, Hans-Jürgen Lüsebrink used the expression "gallows literature" to refer to two kinds of French printed matter that, between the seventeenth and nineteenth centuries, disseminated texts about people who were sentenced to death: the "complainte criminelle" and the "relation"[11]. In the last few decades, there have been various publications about the development of gallows literature in several European countries, in relation to the study of the death penalty in general[12] and to certain

---

10 J.-F. Botrel, *Une bibliothèque bleue espagnole? Les historias de cordel (XVIIIe–XXe siècle)*, in T. Delcourt / E. Parinet (eds.), *La Bibliothèque Bleue et les littératures de colportage*, Paris / Troyes 2000, pp. 193–209; R. Chartier / C. Espejo (eds.), *La aparición del periodismo en Europa: comunicación y propaganda en el Barroco*, Madrid 2012.
11 H.-J. Lüsebrink, *La letteratura del patibolo. Continuità e trasformazioni tra '600 e '800*, in "Quaderni Storici", 49, 1982, pp. 285–301.
12 V. Gatrell, *The Hanging Tree. Execution and the English People, 1770–1868*, Oxford 1996, pp. 109–221; A. Prosperi, *Delitto e perdono. La pena di morte nell'orizzonte mentale dell'Europa cristiana, XIV–XVIII secolo*, Torino 2013, pp. 503–536.

groups of printed material[13]. Pascal Bastien has recently made an innovative analysis of gallows literature published in France and England: taking Lüsebrink as his starting point, he differentiates between the *complaintes* or "execution ballads" and the *relations*, but inserts them into a much broader publishing context, which includes various printed materials connected with executions[14].

In the case of *pliegos de cordel*, as Gomis emphasised in a recent article[15], there have been no studies specifically on Spanish gallows literature. Until now, historians and literary scholars have presented Spanish execution ballads[16] mixed with a variegated collection of accounts of accidents and crimes described merely as crime reports, without classifying them in the framework of the ritual of punishment. On the basis of all the studies on *pliegos sueltos*, one might think that there was no gallows literature in Spain. However, knowledge of the existence of this printed material in other European countries highlights this assumed absence as an anomaly. The early development of the modern state system in Spain, with all its mechanisms of coercion, and the establishment of a publishing industry in the early days of printing are two factors that make it hard to explain why the Spanish monarchy should not have used execution ballads as an instrument to strengthen its power.

In fact, if we search in the catalogues and lists of *pliegos sueltos* it is not hard to detect titles that speak of the crimes and subsequent punishment of a criminal and therefore, a priori, justify identifying those publications as gallows literature: *Criminoso y fiero caso: sucedido día de San Francisco del año mil quinientos nouenta y dos. Que trata de la diabólica inuención que ciertos vaqueros hizieron para robar el ventero de la venta la Torre, quatro leguas de Gibraltar, y de la justicia que dellos se hizo* (Terrible criminal case: that occurred on the day of Saint Francis in the year fifteen hundred and ninety-two. Which tells of the diabolical deceit perpetrated by some cowherds to rob the landlord of the La Torre inn, four leagues from Gibraltar, and of the justice that was done to them) (1593); *Nueva y verdadera relación, de un lastimoso caso, que*

---

[13] J.A. Sharpe, *Last Dying Speeches: Religion, Ideology and Public Execution in Seventeenth-Century England*, in "Past & Present", 107, 1985, pp. 144–167; M.-Y. Crépin, *Le chant du cygne du condamné: les testaments de mort en Bretagne au XVIIIe siècle*, in "Revue historique du droit français et étranger", 70, 1992, pp. 491–509; E. Gogniat, *Avouer au seuil du gibet. Enjeu social et judiciaire du testament de mort d'un brigand pendu à Genève en 1787*, in "Crime, Histoire et Sociétés", 8, 2004, pp. 63–84; U. McIlvenna, *The Power of Music: The Significance of Contrafactum in Execution Ballads*, in "Past & Present", 229, 2015, 1, pp. 47–89; R. Salzberg / M. Rospocher, *Murder Ballads: Singing, Hearing, Writing and Reading about Murder in Renaissance Italy*, in K.J.P. Lowe / T. Dean (eds.), *Murder in Renaissance Italy*, Cambridge 2017, pp. 164–185.
[14] P. Bastien, *L'exécution publique à Paris au XVIIIe siècle. Une histoire des rituels judiciaires*, Seyssel 2006; *Une histoire de la peine de mort. Bourreaux et supplices, 1500–1800*, Paris 2011.
[15] J. Gomis, *Los rostros del criminal: una aproximación a la literatura de patíbulo en España*, in "Cuadernos de la Ilustración y Romanticismo", 22, 2016, pp. 9–33.
[16] We use the term "execution ballads" to refer to ballads that told the story of the crimes and punishment of delinquents, in the knowledge that there were physical differences between English broadside ballads and Spanish pliegos sueltos.

sucedió a ocho días deste presente mes de Noviembre y año de mil y seiscientos y diez y seis, en la ciudad de Écija, donde se declara el grande estrago y muertes que hizo en casa del Doctor Bermudo, médico, un esclauo suyo, martes al amanecer, y la justicia que del se hizo (New and true account of a pitiful case that happened on the eighth day of this present month of November in the year sixteen hundred and sixteen, in the city of Écija, which tells of the great devastation and murders committed in the house of Doctor Bermudo, medical practitioner, by a slave of his, on Tuesday at dawn, and the justice that was done to him) (1616); *Nuevo romance, en que se refieren, los valerosos hechos, muertes, y atrocidades del valiente Manuel del Castillo, natural de la Ciudad de Toledo, y ajusticiado en Valladolid* (New romance which describes the valorous deeds, murders and atrocities of the valiant Manuel del Castillo, native of the City of Toledo and executed in Valladolid) (1720); *Nuevo y curioso romance. Para que sepan hombres, niños y mugeres el horroroso caso ejecutado en el pueblo de Monterrubio de la Sierra, el día 2 de setiembre de 1841, por Lorenzo Malmierca, castigado a pena de la vida el día 14 de noviembre del año 42* (New and curious ballad. So that men, women and children may know the horrendous case perpetrated in the town of Monterrubio de la Sierra, on September 2, 1841, by Lorenzo Malmierca, sentenced to the penalty of death on November 14, in the year 42).

The criticisms of execution ballads that numerous intellectuals made in the eighteenth and nineteenth centuries also highlight the existence of this sub-genre in Spain. For example, the Count of Campomanes declared that "romances de ajusticiados" (execution ballads) should not be read in schools because they produced "in coarse people the seed of committing offences, and of becoming braggarts, depicting as glorious acts the murders, robberies, and other crimes that led them to execution"; Juan Meléndez Valdés severely criticised the subject matter disseminated in these *pliegos sueltos* ("acts of bravado and the ill-fashioned lives of outlaws and robbers, with outrageous resistance to justice and its ministers, acts of violence and abductions of maidens, cruel murders, disrespect of temples, and other such misdeeds"); and José Marchena drew on his memories to verify the existence of this custom of putting the life and work of those who were condemned to death into verse: "I myself, though not very old, remember that after they hanged a famous thief called Antonio Gómez, a benevolent poet straightaway celebrated his exploits in a ballad that the young children immediately learned and sang"[17]. In fact, in 1767 King Carlos III issued a decree forbidding the printing of forecasts, almanacs, "romances de ciegos" (blind singers' ballads) and, specifically, "coplas de ajusticiados" (execution ballads). The reason for the prohibition was that these texts produced "impresiones perjudiciales

---

17 P. Rodríguez, Conde de Campomanes, *El fomento de la industria popular. La educación popular de los artesanos*, with a foreword by G. Anes, Oviedo 1991, p. 176; J. Meléndez Valdés, *Obras completas*, edited by A. Astorgano, Madrid 2004, p. 1095; J. Marchena, *Filosofía moral y elocuencia; o Colección de los trozos más selectos de poesía, elocuencia, historia, religión y filosofía moral y política, de los mejores autores castellanos*, vol. 1, Bordeaux, Imprenta de Don Pedro Beaume, 1820, p. XLI.

en el público, además de ser una lectura vana y de ninguna utilidad a la pública instrucción" (harmful impressions upon the public, as well as being vain reading of no utility for public instruction). This was one of the legal measures against *pliegos de cordel* that had most impact in the eighteenth century, and it is significant that it included gallows literature among the sub-genres that were forbidden, which proves the existence and importance of this kind of printed material in Spain.

Finally, we must add another fact that not only confirms the presence of gallows literature in Spain but also provides information about some peculiarities that, as far as we know, have no equivalent in other European countries. In 1748, King Fernando VI granted the blind brotherhood in Madrid a monopoly on the sale of *relaciones de los reos ajusticiados en esta Corte* (accounts of prisoners executed in this court)[18]. We shall refer later to the relationship that existed in Spain between blind people and *pliegos de cordel*. What it is important to highlight here is that between 1748 and 1767 the blind in Madrid were responsible for composing, printing, and selling ballads about the crimes and execution of those who were sentenced to death: for this purpose, each time that a death sentence was pronounced the brotherhood asked the authorities for a summary of the sentence so that they could prepare an account of it in verse. A petition that they made in 1751 was expressed as follows: "Please instruct the court clerk for this case to provide us with details of the crimes subject to the proceedings taken against the aforesaid prisoners, in order to prepare an account in verse so that it may serve as a warning, as has been the usage and custom"[19]. The monopoly on gallows literature enjoyed by the blind in Madrid indicates an attempt by the political authorities to achieve control of the preparation and dissemination of these publications. However, the idea that these "relaciones de reos" (stories of offenders) were a mere propaganda instrument in the hands of the authorities must be qualified by the constant criticisms that the intellectual elites made against these publications, and especially by the previously mentioned prohibition issued by Carlos III in 1767. It seems that Spanish gallows literature was not such a docile instrument of ideology as one might at first suppose.

The above-mentioned indications enable us to say that gallows literature did indeed exist in Spain, and that specialized studies are needed to determine the distinguishing features of this corpus, to analyze the texts and establish relationships with other sources about criminal cases (legal proceedings, press reports, sermons), and to include the "stories of offenders" in the dynamics of execution, as a further part (prior, simultaneous, or subsequent) of the ritual of punishment[20]. At any rate, what it

---

18 J.-F. Botrel, *Les aveugles, colporteurs d'imprimés en Espagne*, I, pp. 440–442.
19 Madrid, Archivo Histórico Nacional, Consejos, Libro 1338, fol. 133 "Se sirva mandar al relator de esta causa nos dé los asuntos de los delitos, arreglados a los autos seguidos contra dichos reos, para hacer relación en verso, para que sirva de escarmiento como ha sido uso y costumbre".
20 In the line marked out by J.-F. Botrel, *Crime et châtiment de Teresa Guix (1816–1839): du fait-divers à la rédemption par la littérature*, in A. Molinié / M.-C. Zimmermann / M. Ralle (eds.), *Hommage à*

is important to emphasize here is that it is the transnational comparative perspective that has enabled us to highlight this absence in the studies on *literatura de cordel*, encouraging research in an area that had previously been neglected.

2.2 Production: Agustín Laborda and Cluer Dicey

The transnational focus also proves very useful for studying the strategies for the production of popular printed literature. Establishing comparisons between the publishing activities of printers who lived at the same time in different countries makes it possible to cast light on aspects that, either because they are too obvious or because they are too remote, remain in the shadow in studies that keep to familiar ground, restricted to national boundaries.

This can be illustrated with a specific example: Agustín Laborda and Cluer Dicey were printers in Valencia and London in the eighteenth century and their lives ran almost in parallel (1714–1776 in the case of Laborda, 1715–1775 in Dicey's case)[21]. They were two of the most important printers of *pliegos sueltos* and chapbooks in Spain and England in the eighteenth century[22]. An analysis of their careers highlights the contrasts between the two cases. The ways in which they came to be directors of printing businesses were divergent. Cluer belonged to a family of printers and he was put in charge of the print shop in Bow Churchyard by his father, whereas Agustín entered the printing world at the bottom, as an apprentice, and became the owner of a print shop in Calle Bolsería as a result of his marriage to his master's daughter. The size of the two businesses was also different: the Diceys not only possessed two print shops in London, at Bow Churchyard and (from 1754) at Aldermary Churchyard, but were also proprietors of the "Northampton Mercury" and of a lucrative patent medicine business; Laborda, on the other hand, devoted himself exclusively to managing his small workshop, which had only two presses, and he specialised in the production of *pliegos sueltos*. The socioeconomic levels of the two printers were, again, diverse: Cluer's purchase of Claybrooke Hall, a sumptuous mansion near Northampton, as a holiday home in 1765 contrasts with Agustín's purchase the same year of a modest property in Valencia, which he used both as a home and as a workshop. However, this must not obscure the fact that, as several studies have shown, Laborda's socio-economic rise

---

Carlos Serrano, vol. 2: *Cultures et écritures*, Paris 2005, pp. 42–54; or by L. Domergue, *Un bandolero frente a la justicia, la literatura y el arte*, in *Actas del seminario de Ilustración aragonesa*, Zaragoza 1987, pp. 170–194.
21 J. Gomis / A. Serrano, *Una aproximación comparada a la imprenta popular del siglo XVIII en España e Inglaterra: Agustín Laborda y Cluer Dicey*, in "Cuadernos de Ilustracion y Romanticismo", 24, 2018.
22 J. Gomis, *Menudencias de imprenta. Producción y circulación de la literatura popular (Valencia, siglo XVIII)*, Valencia 2015; V. Neuburg, *Popular Literature. A History and Guide. From the Beginning of Printing to the Year 1897*, Harmondsworth 1977.

was very remarkable: his declared assets in 1743 amounted to 500 pounds, but by the end of his life, in 1776, he had accumulated a fortune of nearly 10,000 pounds.

Despite these disparate origins and situations, Dicey and Laborda shared a similar publishing strategy, concentrating on material that reached a wide audience and basing their strategy on three key factors: mass production, the constant introduction of new material and an expanding distribution network. This strategy is reflected in the catalogues that the two printers produced to publicize their material: a catalogue is a valuable source for the history of a printing business and a useful tool for establishing comparisons of the production of popular printed material in different countries.

On the one hand, in the mid-1760s Agustín published a *Memoria de los Romances, Relaciones, Historias, Entremeses, Estampas, Libros, y otras menudencias, que se hallan en Valencia en la Imprenta de Agustín Laborda y Campo*[23]. On the other hand, in 1764 Cluer Dicey and his partner, Richard Marshall, published *A catalogue of maps, prints, copy-books, drawing-books, histories, old ballads, patters, collections, &c. Printed and sold by Cluer Dicey and Richard Marshall, at the Printing Office, in Aldermary Church-Yard, London*[24]. A comparison between the two catalogues underlines some characteristic features of the publications produced by Laborda and Dicey and of popular printed literature in Spain and England. First, even the appearance of the catalogues is very different: Laborda's catalogue consists of 8 pages and reveals an evident endeavor on the part of the typographer to make the most of the space on the page (with titles closely squeezed together), whereas Dicey-Marshall's extends to 104 pages, with a very generous use of space (complete titles, large section headings, numerous explanations of titles and sections). Secondly, the fact that 80% of the London catalogue is devoted to the maps and prints section establishes another clear distinction between the items produced by Cluer and by Agustín: for the former, these printed images were one of his main publishing lines, as can be gathered from the quantity of them (over 1500) and their position in the catalogue (the title begins with "maps" and "prints"). Laborda also included images in his publications, but they were far fewer and less varied: in his catalogue he announced 122 prints, all on religious themes, whereas the thematic diversity of Dicey's prints was much greater.

If we go on to analyze the printed texts, in quantitative terms Dicey's output is only slightly higher than Laborda's: the former's 153 histories, 105 patters, and 286 ballads compare with the latter's 317 *romances*, 87 *relaciones de comedias*, and 44 *entremeses*. The numbers are similar, amounting to around 500 titles.

---

[23] The catalogue, reproduced by Jaime Moll, can be consulted in the Biblioteca Virtual Miguel de Cervantes at http://www.cervantesvirtual.com/obra/un-catalogo-de-pliegos-sueltos-de-la-imprenta-de-agustin-laborda-y-campo/, accessed June 15, 2018.
[24] It can be consulted online at http://diceyandmarshall.bodleian.ox.ac.uk/refframe.htm, accessed June 15, 2018.

One of the clearest differences between English and Spanish popular printed literature is the almost absolute predominance of verse in the latter, compared with the powerful presence of prose in English chapbooks. This disparity can be seen distinctly if we analyze the form of expression in the categories that we have just mentioned: *romances, relaciones de comedias*, and *entremeses* are all verse compositions, whereas in the English publications there is a balance between prose and verse (258 histories and patters compared with 286 ballads). This difference between street literature and *literatura de cordel* is an indication of the different levels of literacy in English and Spanish society in the eighteenth century, which is also reflected in the physical appearance of the printed material: *romances* were printed on 4 pages, which sometimes extended to 8 if the publication included a second part, and their metrical and narrative systems facilitated reading (often oral), whereas chapbooks offered longer texts (generally between 8 and 24 pages) and their prose required greater reading ability.

Apart from these differences, the catalogues produced by Agustín Laborda and Cluer Dicey both show publishing strategies that concentrate on absorbing the greatest possible number of popular printed materials in order to satisfy the varied nature of the demand and thus cater to a wider range of customers (with regard to age, reading skills or financial situation). This was one of the key factors in their success as printers, and it can be highlighted by a comparative perspective.

2.3 Distribution: the blind brotherhoods and the sale of "pliegos sueltos"

Studies on the distribution of printed matter in Europe have considered the role of the pedlar or colporteur from various points of view, recently from a transnational perspective[25]. In the case of *literatura de cordel*, one of the most characteristic features of its dissemination was the participation of the blind in the sale of printed material.

Although we know of individual cases of blind poets and sellers of *pliegos de cordel* in the sixteenth century[26], it was not until the second half of the seventeenth century that the blind took a collective interest in popular printed literature. Starting in the Late Middle Ages, a series of blind brotherhoods had been founded in various

---

25 L. Fontaine, *Histoire du colportage en Europe, XVe–XIXe siècle*, Paris 1993; J. Salman, *Pedlars and the Popular Press: Itinerant Distribution Networks in England and the Netherlands, 1600–1850*, Boston MA / Leiden 2014; R. Harms / J. Raymond / J. Salman (eds.), *Not Dead Things. The Dissemination of Popular Print in England and Wales, Italy and the Low Countries, 1500–1820*, Boston MA / Leiden 2013.
26 A. Rodríguez-Moñino, *Cristóbal Bravo, ruiseñor popular del siglo XVI (intento bibliográfico, 1572–1963)*, in A. Rodríguez-Moñino, *La transmisión de la poesía española en los siglos de oro*, Barcelona 1976, pp. 253–283; P.M. Cátedra, *Invención, difusión y recepción de la literatura popular impresa (siglo XVI)*, Mérida 2002.

cities in Spain. Their initial objectives were mutual aid among their members and the performance of prayers in the streets[27]. In 1680, in Madrid, the brotherhoods of Our Lady of the Visitation and Souls in Purgatory embarked on a series of lawsuits against various booksellers and printers because of the sale of *pliegos de cordel*[28]. This legal confrontation continued during the early decades of the eighteenth century until, in 1727, King Felipe V signed a Royal Resolution that nobody except the blind and their widows should be allowed to sell "gacetas y otros papeles curiosos" (gazettes and other curious papers). In 1739, the printed matter that came under the monopoly of the Madrid brotherhood was specified: items that did not exceed four pages, in other words, a *pliego suelto*. And, as we have mentioned, in 1748 the privilege was extended to the "relaciones de los reos ajusticiados" (accounts of prisoners executed).

Until recent years, the case of the blind brotherhood in Madrid and their monopoly on the sale of *pliegos de cordel* was the only one that we knew of in Spain. A similar privilege that King Fernando VI granted in 1749 to the brotherhoods of the True Cross in Valencia has recently been studied. Between that year and 1770, when the privilege was ended, the Valencian brotherhood jealously defended the prerogative concerning the sale of printed matter that had been given to them, with a series of complaints against anyone who did not respect their monopoly: printers, booksellers, pedlars and even "falsos pobres y estropeados" (false poor and cripples)[29]. There are indications that the brotherhoods in Málaga, Granada, Córdoba, Cádiz, and Murcia were able to enjoy similar monopolies during the second half of the eighteenth century.

There were two reasons why the state granted these privileges to the blind brotherhoods. On the one hand, it is evident that it was an attempt to offer a means of subsistence to a social group especially exposed to indigence and begging. On the other hand, through these monopolies the State tried to control the circulation of potentially dangerous printed matter. By reducing the number of sellers to the blind who belonged to a particular brotherhood, the authorities provided themselves with an effective means for keeping watch over printers, sellers, and readers of literature that, because of its low cost and quick production, had proved recalcitrant to the control of the censor for centuries. From this point of view, the blind were, as Botrel said, "colaboradores objetivos del poder" (objective collaborators with the authorities)[30].

The comparative perspective can cast light on our interpretation of the blind brotherhoods in Spain and the sale of *pliegos de cordel* in various ways. First, it allows us to contextualize the supposed exceptionality of the phenomenon of blind brotherhoods, often understood as a Spanish peculiarity. On the contrary, the tendency of the blind to organize themselves in brotherhoods was common in Europe, and,

---

27 J. Gomis, *Pious Voices. Blind Spanish Prayer Singers*, in "Renaissance Studies", 33, 2019, 1, pp. 42-63.
28 C. Espejo, *Pleito entre ciegos e impresores (1680–1755)*, in "Revista de la Biblioteca, Archivo y Museo", 2, 1925, pp. 206–236.
29 J. Gomis, *Menudencias de imprenta*.
30 J.-F. Botrel, *Les aveugles, colporteurs d'imprimés en Espagne*, I, p. 428.

although this is a field in which little work has been done, we know of their existence in a considerable number of cities. For example, in Paris, from the middle of the thirteenth century, there was the Quinze-Vingts hospice, a community of blind people that functioned in a way that, according to Zina Weygand, is reminiscent of the mendicant orders. Another hospice, inspired by the Quinze-Vingts, was founded in Chartres in 1291 by Renaud Barbou (the elder)[31]. In Sarrant, a town in Gascony, there was a brotherhood of the blind that bore the name of Our Lady of the Visitation[32]. In the German context, Irina Metzler has located a corporation of the blind in Strasburg, founded in 1411, another brotherhood for "poor people who live from prayers, such as cripples, the blind and other people", founded in Zülpich in 1454, and another brotherhood of the blind and deaf in Tréveris, the founding of which dates back to 1437[33]. A considerable number of blind brotherhoods were concentrated in Italy. We find them in Genoa (1299), Venice (1315), Florence (1324), Padua (1358), Milan (1471), Bologna (1566), Rome (1613), Siena (1624), and Palermo (1661)[34]. Finally, Portugal also had a blind brotherhood, the Sociedade do Menino Jesus dos Homens Cegos, founded in Lisbon in 1749[35].

Secondly, the international perspective allows us to identify the possession of a monopoly on the sale of popular printed matter that was enjoyed by some Spanish blind brotherhoods in the eighteenth century as a genuinely Spanish singularity. Only the brotherhood in Lisbon had a similar privilege, and it is possible that it was founded for that purpose, taking as a model the brotherhoods in Madrid and Valencia, which had already obtained their respective monopolies. As far as we know, the brotherhoods of the blind in the rest of Europe did not have any connection with the sale of printed matter, nor did any of the numerous Italian brotherhoods, which in the fifteenth and sixteenth centuries, in common with the Spanish brotherhoods, practiced the occupation of reciting prayers. Therefore, the importance that the blind

---

[31] Z. Weygand, *Vivre sans voir. Les aveugles dans la société française, du Moyen Age au siècle de Louis Braille*, Paris 2003.
[32] C. Gilard-Fito, *La confrérie des musiciens de Sarrant aux 16 et 17 siècles*, in "Bulletin de la Société Archéologique, Historique, Littéraire & Scientifique du Gers", 3, 2002, pp. 304–338.
[33] I. Metzler, *A Social History of Disability in the Middle Ages: Cultural Considerations of Physical Impairment*, New York / Abingdon 2013, pp. 179–181.
[34] L. Carnelos, *Street Voices. The Role of Blind Performers in Early Modern Italy*, in "Italian Studies", 71, 2016, pp. 184–196; R. Cessi, *La Fraglia dei ciechi in Padova*, in "Bollettino del Museo Civico di Padova", 8, 1905, pp. 105–114; L. Cajani, *Gli statuti della compagnia dei ciechi, zoppi e stroppiati della Visitazione (1698)*, in "Ricerche per la storia religiosa di Roma", 3, 1979, pp. 281–313; *Compagnia di Santa Maria del Giglio detta dei Ciechi*, in L. Artusi / A. Patruno (eds.), *Deo gratias. Storia, tradizioni, culti e personaggi delle antiche confraternite fiorentine*, Roma 1994, pp. 250–253; D. Zardin, *La mendicità tollerata. La 'scola' milanese dei ciechi di S. Cristoforo e le sue regole (sec. XVI–XVIII)*, in F. Ruggeri (ed.), *Studi in onore di mons. Angelo Majo*, Milano 1996, pp. 355–380.
[35] F. Guedes, *Os Livreiros em Portugal e as suas associações desde o século XV até aos nossos dias*, Lisboa 2005, p. 28.

brotherhoods officially acquired in the sale of *pliegos de cordel* is a special feature in the history of the peddling of printed matter in Europe.

Thirdly, with regard to this last point, the fact that it is an exceptional feature does not, of course, mean that this phenomenon cannot be studied in a European framework. On the contrary, connecting the Spanish situation with those of other countries makes it possible to articulate an interpretation that extends beyond national boundaries. The granting of monopolies to the blind brotherhoods can be understood, as we have noted, as an attempt by the State to control the dissemination of *pliegos sueltos*. This kind of censorship would not focus on the printed material but on the intermediary who transported and distributed it. Similar attempts, aimed at pedlars or colporteurs, can be identified in other countries like England, with increasing regulation stemming from the introduction of the *Act for licensing Hawkers and Pedlars* in 1697, the Netherlands, with legislation that was progressively more hostile towards peddlers from 1660[36], France, with tight control on peddling in the middle of the nineteenth century, a measure that was accompanied by a renewed impulse in terms of preventive censorship, or Italy, where religious and civic authorities increasingly attempted to regulate the book trade[37]. Thus, the case of the blind brotherhoods in Spain could be situated within a broader dynamic in which the distribution of books and printed matter became an objective for the civil authorities, who in this way tried to increase their control over printed matter.

3 Conclusions

Like the corpuses of popular printed matter in other European countries, *literatura de cordel* has a research history that goes back half a century. The location, cataloguing and reproduction of *pliegos sueltos*, and research on their contents, their production and dissemination processes, and their readership have helped to shape a dynamic and established field of study. However, it is a field of study that is still being presented now in isolation from the European context, without creating connections with other popular forms of printed literature. In our view, this transnational perspective could provide a new approach to research on *literatura de cordel*. The examples suggested in these pages, concerning the contents, production and dissemination of *pliegos sueltos*, show how greatly a comparative focus can enrich our understanding of this cultural phenomenon. With regard to gallows literature, the transnational focus has made it possible to distinguish a sub-genre that had previously been ignored in Spain. In the area of production, the comparison between the publishing activities of

---

36 J. Salman, *Pedlars and the Popular Press*.
37 J.-J. Darmon, *Le colportage de librairie en France sous le Second Empire. Grands colporteurs et culture populaire*, Paris 1972.

Agustín Laborda and Cluer Dicey emphasises the diversity of the strategies of printers who specialised in popular literature and it highlights aspects of *literatura de cordel* that would remain neglected if they were not contrasted with other European corpuses. Finally, placing the importance of the blind brotherhoods in the dissemination of *pliegos sueltos* in relation with the roles of the pedlar or colporteur beyond the boundaries of Spain makes it possible to enrich our understanding of the circulation of popular printed matter throughout the length and breadth of Europe. Thus the benefits of the transnational perspective are twofold: an improvement in our knowledge of *literatura de cordel* (or the popular corpus in any other country) and of European popular printed culture in general.

Alice Colombo
The Translational Dimension of Street Literature

The Nineteenth-Century Italian Repertoire

1 Translation and street literature: preliminary thoughts

Over the past five decades, book historians have paid increasing attention to cheap ephemeral publications, contributing to the realization that street literature in the chapbook and broadside format has a strong international character. A number of national-scale studies have revealed that between the seventeenth and nineteenth centuries chapbooks and broadsides were enjoyed by broad audiences in many European countries[1]. It has also become clear that national repertoires of chapbooks and broadsides share conspicuous similarities in terms of genres, themes, titles, and characters. Such affinities have occasionally been attributed to the fact that national repertoires interact with and influence each other by means of transnational relations[2]. Nevertheless, we are still far from having a clear and comprehensive idea of what this transnationalism involves and how it is achieved. Peddlers have been identified as a key factor in the distribution and dissemination of cheap print across national borders[3]. Other categories of travelers, including missionaries and tourists, also appear to have contributed to the movements of printed materials[4]. The physical transplantation of texts from their context of origin to a new cultural setting, however, does not suffice to justify how different national heritages of chapbook and broad-

---

[1] R. Chartier / H. Lüsebrink (eds.), *Colportage et lecture populaire. Imprimé de large circulation en Europe XVIe–XIXe siècles*, Paris 1996; H. Lüsebrink / Y. Mix / J. Mollier / P. Sorel (eds.), *Les Lectures du Peuple en Europe et dans les Ameriques du XVIIe au XXe Siècle*, Bruxelles 2003; J. Salman / J. Raymond / R. Harms (eds.), *Not Dead Things. The Dissemination of Popular Print in England and Wales, Italy, and the Low Countries, 1500–1820*, Boston MA / Leiden 2013; J. Salman, *Pedlars and the Popular Press, Itinerant Distribution Networks in England and the Netherlands 1600–1850*, Boston MA / Leiden 2014.
[2] See in particular H. Lüsebrink, *Littératures populaires et imprimés de large circulation en Europe. Perspectives d'analyse comparatistes et interculturelles*, in "Dix-huitième Siècle", 30, 1998, pp. 143–153; N.Ó CiosÁin, *Bibliothèque Bleue, Verte Erin, Some Aspects of Popular Printed Literature in France and Ireland in the 18th and 19th Centuries*, in "Lisa", 3 2005, 1, pp. 55–69.
[3] J. Salman / J. Raymond / R. Harms, *Not Dead Things*. See in particular A. Milano, *Selling Prints for the Remondini. Italian Pedlars Travelling through Europe during the Eighteenth Century*, ibid., pp. 75–96.
[4] See for example W. Jones, *The Jubilee Memorial of the Religious Tract Society*, London, The Religious Tract Society, 1850, especially p. 369; G. Spini, *Risorgimento e Protestanti*, Napoli 1956, p. 58.

side literature came to develop common features. Such correspondences are rather the result of more or less conscious translational processes whereby chapbooks and broadsides were made intelligible in the new linguistic and cultural setting before some of their traits became refracted and embedded in local traditions. The idea that the transnational and translational dimensions of cheap print are inextricably interconnected was initially put forward by Hans-Jürgen Lüsebrink[5]. Furthering Peter Burke's call for more comparative and intercultural approaches to popular literature, Lüsebrink indicated translation as a possible angle from which to investigate how chapbook and broadside narratives have transited from one cultural area to another and became known internationally[6]. So far, Lüsebrink's proposed approach has received little consideration, both among print historians and translation scholars, who have not engaged with ephemeral print yet. As a result, our understanding of the translational – and therefore transnational – life of chapbook and broadside literature remains significantly limited.

The reluctance of book historians of cheap print to focus on translations can be attributed, at least in part, to practical reasons. Researching non-translated cheap ephemeral publications is already very problematic. First, chapbooks and broadsides often lack bibliographical details, which makes it hard to establish when and where these were published. Secondly, these materials are often uncatalogued and hence difficult to be found and accessed. Thirdly, due to their fragile constitution and the fact that they were intended to have an ephemeral existence, many chapbooks and broadsides are likely to have gone lost, leaving us wonder about the representativeness and relevance of the samples that have survived.

These uncertainties inevitably accentuate when translations become involved, that is when the attention is no longer exclusively on a certain chapbook or broadside but also on the connection that this has with its transnational variants. Lack of bibliographical records can make it extremely challenging to determine whether the text of a chapbook or a broadside has been translated from another language or/and has inspired translations in another linguistic and cultural area[7]. In addition, the difficulty of locating and accessing the publications and the scarce chance of survival of ephemera prevent us from establishing the exact extent to which chapbook and broadside literature was being translated. There are also encouraging indications, however, suggesting that the translational dimension of cheap print "can" be explored and that it is therefore possible to achieve a deeper understanding of the transnational life of

---

[5] H. Lüsebrink, *Littératures populaires*; H. Lüsebrink, *Traduire l'almanach populaire, essai de typologie et mise en perspective socio-culturelle*, in H. Lüsebrink / Y. Mix / J. Mollier / P. Sorel (eds.), *Les Lectures du Peuple*, pp. 145–155.
[6] P. Burke, *The 'Bibliotheque Bleue' in comparative perspective*, in "Quaderni del Seicento Francese", 4, 1981, pp. 59–66, especially p. 62. H. Lüsebrink, *Littératures populaires*; H. Lüsebrink, *Traduire l'almanach populaire*.
[7] H. Lüsebrink, *Littératures populaires*, pp. 149–150.

these materials. The increasing scholarly interest received by street literature has led to a growing awareness of the historical, cultural, and social relevance of chapbooks and broadsides. This, in turn, has resulted in a greater sensitivity to conserving and preserving such fragile publications. More and more libraries are cataloguing chapbooks and broadsides as part of their special collections, some of which are being made available electronically[8]. The greater accessibility to primary sources granted by these developments creates the ideal conditions for comparative translational studies of national chapbook and broadside repertoires to thrive. Further encouragement to explore the translational trajectories of street literature comes from the publications themselves. As mentioned above, the lack of bibliographical details characteristic of ephemeral publications is considered a major obstacle to research translated street literature. However, it is important to stress that not all chapbooks and broadsides are devoid of such information and that, in fact, when present, this can provide valuable insights into their translational nature. Useful in this regard are also the indications that emerge when we extend our attention to the textual and typographical component of chapbooks and broadsides. This chapter illustrates some examples of how cheap ephemeral print can manifest its translational nature and shows how these manifestations can help us achieve a better understanding of how chapbooks and broadsides carry genres, themes, titles, and characters across languages and cultures. The examples are taken from the nineteenth-century Italian repertoire. It is hoped that their discussion will encourage more research into the translational dimension of street literature. The definition of translation adopted in this analysis is the one elaborated by translation scholar Gideon Toury.

A major exponent of the descriptive branch of translation studies, Toury approaches translation from a target-oriented perspective[9]. He stresses that translations are "facts of the culture that [...] host them" and that, as such, they are to be studied in

---

[8] See for example the Bodleian Libraries' *Broadside Ballads Online* (http://ballads.bodleian.ox.ac.uk), the McGill Library's *Chapbook Collection* (https://digital.library.mcgill.ca/chapbooks/), the *Scottish Chapbooks Project* (http://scottishchapbooks.org/) and the Biblioteca Universitaria di Napoli's online repository of chapbooks (http://www.bibliotecauniversitarianapoli.beniculturali.it/index.php?it/203/libretti-popolari).

[9] Descriptive translation studies (DTS) emerged in the 1970s as a reaction against the prescriptivism that characterized previous paradigms of translation. Such prescriptivism was grounded in "the idea that the study of translation should be geared primarily to formulating rules, norms and guidelines for the practice and evaluation of translation or to developing didactic instruments for translator training" (T. Hermans, *Translation in Systems. Descriptive and Systemic Approaches Explained*, Manchester 1999, p. 7). The descriptivist alternative discarded this approach in favor of an empirical study of the "observable aspects of translation" based on the assumption that "the investigation of translation may well start with the thing itself and its immediate environment; i.e. with translations and their contexts rather than with source texts" (*ibid.*). Descriptive translation studies have marked an important step forward in the study of translation and continues to influence current appreciations of translation as a cultural and social practice.

close relation to the context in which they came into being[10]. Toury refuses to regard a certain text as a translation on the sole premise that such text is relatable to an identified source. For him, translation is

> any target culture text for which there are reasons to tentatively posit the existence of another text, in another culture/language, from which it was presumably derived by transfer operations and to which it is now tied by a set of relationships based on shared features[11].

Toury terms such text "assumed translation" in that its translational status is determined on the assumption – not the certainty – that it was derived from a pre-existing text[12]. An assumed translation can change its status to "genuine translation" or to "pseudotranslation". The shift from assumed to genuine translation occurs when a text that was tentatively identified as a translation turns out to have an actual source text. An assumed translation acquires the status of pseudotranslation when there is reason to posit that a genuine source text has never existed. Toury emphasizes that pseudotranslations have no less cultural relevance than assumed and genuine translations. In fact, he explains, pseudotranslations "often prove highly revealing for the understanding of cultures or cultural sectors and processes of changes in them, and especially the role played therein by translations at large"[13]. In addition, pseudotrasnlations can "give a fairly good picture of notions shared by the members of a community, not only as to the status of translated texts, but also as to their salient characteristics"[14].

The inclusiveness of Toury's characterization of translation offers a suitable terminological and theoretical framework to reflect on the variety of textual and translational situations encompassed by cheap ephemeral publishing. By situating the study of the translational dimension of street literature at the interface between translation studies and print history, the analysis conducted in this chapter encourages the two disciplines to fruitfully interact towards informed appreciations of how translation impacts on the transnationalization of chapbooks and broadsides.

---

10 G. Toury, *Descriptive Translation Studies – and Beyond* (Benjamins Translation Library, 100), rev. ed., Amsterdam 2012, pp. 17–34.
11 *Ibid.*, p. 31.
12 *Ibid.*, p. 29.
13 *Ibid.*, p. 48.
14 *Ibid.*, p. 54.

2 Possible translations of street literature and how to identify them

Cheap ephemeral publications can contain important clues about their translational nature. The ways in which these clues are presented are various and similar to those pertaining to other literary traditions in the more durable book format. Some chapbooks and broadsides are typographically designed to encourage the side-by-side reading of two or more versions of the same text. In *Atti di fede, speranza, carità e contrizione* (Acts of faith, hope, charity, and contrition), a nineteenth-century 10-page chapbook published in Milan by Giovanni Silvestri, the German and Italian versions of four prayers are displayed respectively on the verso and recto pages[15]. Although they are visually different – the German version is set in the blackletter type and the Italian in the roman type – the two texts are bound to each other by a close translational relationship which makes them very similar in content. We do not know whether the source language is German or Italian and none of the paratextual and bibliographical information helps solve this doubt. Curiously, the title of the chapbook is in Italian but the information provided in the colophon is in German – "Mailand, bei Johann Silvestri". The facts that the texts belong to linguistic and cultural traditions in which writing and reading are performed from left to right and source texts are conventionally displayed before their translations cannot be taken as a parameter for establishing the directionality of the translational flow either. Indeed, there are cases of parallel texts in which the usual visual order of source and target text is inverted[16]. The left and right columns of a political broadside published by the Palermitan Vittorio Giliberti in the 1880s contain respectively an Italian translation and a French transcription of a version of the *Marseillaise*[17]. The Italian version differs from the French text mainly for variations aimed at preserving the rhythm, rhyming scheme, and purpose of the French text. All references to France are omitted and new references to Italy are introduced[18]. As a result, the call to raise and fight for freedom originally addressed to French patriots has become directed to the Italian people. Other inconsistencies between the two texts are determined by the absence of the French sixth stanza in the

---

15 The chapbook is held at the Biblioteca Braidense in Milan (Stampe pop. O207). The exact date of publication of the booklet is unknown and difficult to establish for the publishing business of Giuseppe Silvestri was operative throughout the whole century.
16 In the context of this essay, "parallel texts" are exclusively to be intended as texts placed alongside their translation(s).
17 The broadside is part of the Biblioteca Braidense's collection of *Stampe popolari* (Stampe pop. Letteratura Popolare Straniera, 21). The date of publication of the broadside is not indicated but bibliographical records suggest that Giliberti was active during those years.
18 Examples of references to Italy can be found in the opening line "Su coraggio, bella Italia" (Rise up, beautiful Italy) and in one of the choruses "All'armi fratelli! / Legioni formate / L'Italia inondate, / Di sangue stranier!". (To arms brothers! / Set up legions; / Let Italy be flooded / With foreign blood).

Italian version and by the fact that their choruses have different lengths. The French version has one chorus of seven lines[19]. This is presented in full only the first time and then abbreviated into the first verse followed by "ecc" at the end of each stanza. In the Italian text, two choruses of four lines alternate each other and are repeated in full after each stanza[20].

Parallel texts do not constitute the only occasions on which street literature openly manifests its translational nature. The title page of different nineteenth-century chapbook editions of *La Catalana Punita* (The punished Catalan woman), include the specification "tradotto dallo Spagnolo in Italiano" (translated from Spanish into Italian). The name of the alleged translator is also revealed – Fulgenzio Bozzolini[21]. A series of Italian moral and religious tracts in the chapbook format from the late 1820s are explicitly labelled as translations from English[22]. The clause "traduzione dall'inglese" follows the tracts' titles on both their respective title pages as well as in the publications that advertise them[23]. Some of the tracts' title pages display the initials of the translators. For instance, *La Viola Mammola* (The violet), *Le Due Agnelline* (The two lambs), and *Il Naufragio* (The shipwreck) are said to have been translated by C.D.H, R. R. di B., and H.[24]. In *Le Cinque Vedove di Waterside* (The five widows of Waterside) the translator is made known through the pseudonym Simonide[25]. Despite having been issued by different publishers – Audin, Batelli, and Molini in Florence, the Insegna della Lupa in Siena, the Società Tipografica in Rome, Trani in Naples, Nobili in Bologna, and Silvestri in Milan – the tracts share conspicuous similarities on the typographical level. Most of the chapbooks are in 32mo, contain between 20

---

19 The chorus reads "Aux armes, citoyens! Formez vos bataillons! / Marchons, marchons, / Qu'un sang impur abreuve nos sillons! / Marchons ca ira, / Marchons ca ira, / La République / En France elle regnera".

20 The other chorus in the Italian version recites "Giuriam, giuriam vendetta, / Per tante crudeltà! / Giuriam per te, patria diletta, / O morte, o libertà!" (We vow, we vow revenge, / For many cruelties / We vow for you, dear homelad / death or liberty).

21 The editions to which I am referring are held at the British Library. Three of them were published in Lucca [071.c.19.(6.); 1071.c.22.(20.); 11429.b.57.(14)] and one in Naples [1072.b.20.(1.)]. The dates of publication of the four editions, respectively 1815, 1820, 1825, and 1825, are estimated (they are all followed by a question mark). Two eighteenth century British Library copies [11426.b.74.(21.) and 1071.c.24.(13.)] suggest that the story of *La Catalana Punita* was already circulating as a chapbook and identified as a translation from Spanish in previous years. The copies are assumed to have appeared in Todi in 1795 and in Naples in1798.

22 So far, I have tracked down 24 of these such tracts.

23 See for example *Il Nuovo Ricoglitore* of June 1829, p. 480.

24 The tracts were published in different editions by different publishers. The editions of *La Viola Mammola* and *Le Due Agnelline* that I have examined are those published in 1827 by respectively Audin in Florence and at the Insegna della Lupa in Siena; that of *il Naufragio* was published in 1828 by the Milanese Silvestri. The three chapbooks are all held at the British Library [899.f.1.(2.); 4414.df.76.(1.) and 4399.aa.32.(4.)].

25 The edition that I have considered is at Trinity College Library Dublin (OLS B-4-111 no.7).

and 32 pages and have titles and texts that are set in the same type and arranged on the page following the same layout. Texts do not need to be forthrightly presented as translations or be displayed alongside their transnational variants to raise the suspicion that they might be the result of translational processes. "Translationese" – namely the language that makes a translation read awkward due to its excessive closeness to the source text – and exoticisms – such as foreign words – can be important indicators in this regard. The four-page chapbook *Relazione d'una orrenda vendetta eseguita contro un indiano per aver ucciso a tradimento il constabile* (Account of a horrible revenge taken against an Indian for having treacherously killed the constable), published by the Venetian Giuseppe Molinari in 1837, contains examples of both[26]. The word "constabile", on the title page and throughout the text is a clear calque of the English "constable"[27]. When we turn the page, we learn that the anecdote related by the pamphlet took place in Saint-Louis, Missouri, and that it was originally reported by "I fogli di Boston" (The Boston papers). As we read on, we come across other exoticisms that confirm the foreignness of the setting, starting from the name and title of the constable killed – "il Sig. Hummont luogotenente dello sceriffo" (Mr. Hummont, Deputy Sheriff). The crowd that witnessed the murder calls for "giustizia alla Linch" (justice à la Linch), a clear reference to "Lynch's Law", from which "lynching" was derived. The words "yellow fellow" and "slow fire" put in brackets after respectively "indiano" (Indian) and "fuoco lento" (slow fire) further contribute to the text's foreign feel. The 16-page chapbook published in Bergamo by Natali and titled *Esquimaux, massacro de' missionari in Groelandia* [sic] (Esquimaux, massacre of the missionaries in Greenland) contains some foreign words, starting from the Gallicism "esquimaux" in the title[28]. In the body

---

[26] The chapbook is held at the Biblioteca Braidense (Stampe pop. P118).
[27] In translation studies a calque is commonly defined as a word or expression that reads unidiomatic due to its being distinctly modelled on a source language lexical item (see for example M. Shttleworth / M. Cowie, *Dictionary of Translation Studies*, Abington / New York 2014, pp. 17–18; S. Hervey / I. Higgins / S. Cragie / P. Gambarotta, *Thinking Italian Translation*, London / New York 2000, p. 27).
[28] The chapbook is held at the Biblioteca Braidense (Stampe pop. Q13). The year of publication of the chapbook is not indicated. Bibliographical records suggest that the publisher was active throughout the whole century. The title of the chapbook is misleading in that it reflects the booklet's actual content only very partially. The chapbook is composed of three different parts. The first part (pp. 3–5) provides a very brief and biased introduction to Greenland and its inhabitants. On p. 3 Greenland is depicted as a land "abborrita" (sic) (loathed), "inospitale" (inhospitable), and "consacrata al genio del male" (consecrated to the genius of evil) and the Eskimos as savages. The second section (pp. 6–9) reiterates some of the information contained in the first part, reinforcing, on p. 6, the perception of the Eskimos as "brutal[i]" (brutal), "ignorant[i]" (ignorant), and "feroc[i]" (fierce). A 21-line passage reports the fact to which the title presumably refers. This is said to have occurred in 1834, when a party of about 150 Eskimos allegedly killed and devoured a group of missionaries. Another anecdote follows concerning the rescue made by a certain Captain Hugon of a shipwrecked French woman who was kept captive by the Eskimos. The third section, which takes up most of the chapbook (pp. 9–16), is completely unrelated to what precedes it. It consists of eight parts, each devoted to the description of a different species of animals – rattlesnakes, boas, crocodiles, harlequin snakes, hyenas, porcupines, parrots, and vultures.

of the text, the chief of one of the Eskimo tribes is called with the English name "Hair-by". Interestingly, two illustrations have captions in French. The first illustration (fig. 1), adjacent to the paragraph describing the "Serpente Sonagli" (rattlesnake), is accompanied by the caption "Serpent à sonnetes" [sic]. The second illustration (fig. 2), inscribed in a frame with floral patterns on the chapbook's back cover, represents a woman holding an enormous snake and a man standing next to a shorter and seemingly younger person. The woman and the couple are respectively identified with the captions "Serpent Boa" and "Africain". The captions suggest that the illustrations were originally published in a French publication, thus adding to the suspicion that the Italian chapbook is the transnational version of a pre-existing source.

Fig. 1: *Serpent à sonnetes*, Esquimaux, p. 9, Biblioteca Braidense, Stampe Pop., Q13.

Fig. 2: *Serpent Boa/Africain*, Esquimaux, p. 16, Biblioteca Braidense, Stampe Pop., Q13.

This section pinpointed some typographic, textual, and paratextual features, which might identify the chapbooks and broadsides that contain them as potential, or, as Toury would put it, "assumed" translations. The detection of such features constitutes a first important step in researching the translational dimension of these publications. In what follows, we shall look into whether and how the three situations just delineated – parallel texts, texts explicitly presented as translations, and texts which read as translations – can help us progress in the study of the transnationalization of street print and its cultural relevance. Toury's definition of translation will be used as a reference throughout the investigation.

3 Further into researching possible translations

According to Toury,

> Once a particular text in a language other than TL [target language] has tentatively been marked as the corresponding source of an assumed translation, the next step is to map the assumed translation onto its assumed counterpart, in an attempt to determine the (uni-directional, irreversible) relations that obtain between the pairs of texts and hold them together[29].

The identification of the assumed source text constitutes the condition necessary for comparative analysis to take place and, hence, for tracing the stages that mark the trajectory of the text in question across linguistic and cultural boundaries. Indeed, the comparison between assumed source and target text makes it possible to observe the similarities and differences in content that result from the assumed translation process. By focusing on the features shared by the assumed source and target text, we can gain a concrete idea of how translation contributes to the formation of shared repertoires of literature – chapbooks and broadsides, in our case. The examination of how the two texts differ from each other in close connection with the sociocultural and historical environment in which the assumed translation originated, can offer important insights on the role of translation in making the same narrative available and meaningful in new linguistic and cultural settings, ensuring its continuous existence.

As highlighted by Toury, however, the retrieval of the assumed source text can be "a very tricky process"[30]. Of the three situations outlined in the previous section, parallel texts seem to pose less of a problem in this regard, at least on the surface level.

3.1 Parallel texts

Parallel texts are usually intended to facilitate the direct comparison between a given source and its translation, thus apparently constituting a prime example of what Toury would identify as a "genuine" translation. The direct proximity of the German and Italian versions of the four prayers in *Atti di fede, speranza, carità e contrizione* made it immediately obvious that such versions are closely related to each other and that the nature of their relationship is translational. The already mentioned impossibility of establishing the source language and, therefore, to tell source text from translation, however, calls for an extension of Toury's acceptation of genuineness in translation. As we have seen, according to Toury, a translation can be said to be genuine when its source text has been ascertained to exist. Inherent to this defini-

---

29 G. Toury, *Descriptive Translation Studies*, p. 32.
30 *Ibid.*, p. 32.

tion is the expectation that the source and the translation are bound to each other through a uni-directional relationship which sees the translation as a derivation of the source. This unidirectionality has direct implications on the process of comparative analysis, which will customarily entail the mapping of the translation against the source. In *Atti di fede, speranza, carità e contrizione* the German and the Italian versions of the prayers can be seen as being both the source and genuine translations of each other. Therefore, the comparative analysis will have a bi-directional orientation. The comparison of the Italian and French versions of the *Marseillaise*, which Giliberti juxtaposed in his broadside, raises other issues that further stretch Toury's definition. The common knowledge that the *Marseillaise* originated in France leaves no doubt as to which of the two texts is the translation. However, the variations that distinguish the Italian from the French version (i.e. the shifts implemented by the translator to preserve the rhythm, rhyming scheme, and purpose of the French anthem, as well as the different choruses) might lead us to wonder whether the French text published by Giliberti is the actual source of the Italian translation. Since its debut on April 24, 1792, the *Marseillaise* has existed in many variants, most of which maintain the original rhythm and overall patriotic feeling that also permeates the Italian version[31]. Any of these editions might potentially have been used as a source by the author of the Italian version. The difficulty of determining on which source text the Italian *Marseillaise* was based does not preclude that the source actually existed, nor does it prevent us from considering and researching the Italian version as a genuine translation – of the French text next to which Giliberti places it or any other version of the French anthem.

Despite defying traditional theorizations of translational relationships, the pairs of texts in *Atti di fede, speranza, carità e contrizione* and Giliberti's broadside are transnational variants of each other and intended to be read as such. The analysis of the link between the German and Italian versions of the four prayers and of the Italian *Marseillaise* against the French version selected by Giliberti constitutes a useful point of departure to speculate on the translational and transnational life of street literature as well as on the cultural and social importance of translations of this kind of materials. We might want, for instance, to consider whether the adoption of a different translation approach – literal for the prayers in *Atti di fede, speranza, carità e contrizione* and free in the *Marseillaise* case – reflects the attribution of a different function to the two publications. We might then look further into such function by relating it to the question of whether the texts contained by the two publications are intended to be read from a comparative perspective or as a uniform whole. The fact that the German

---

[31] For more information about the origins and the history of the *Marseillaise* see H. Hudde, *Un air et mille couplets. La Marseillaise et "les Marseillaises" pendant la Révolution*, in D. Rieger (ed.), *La chanson française et son histoire*, Tübingen 1987, pp. 75–87; L. Mason, *Songs, Mixing Media*, in R. Darnton / D. Roche (eds.), *Revolution in Print, The Press in France, 1775–1800*, Berkeley / London 1989, pp. 252–269.

and the Italian prayers closely reproduce each other might, for example, suggest an underlying invitation to comparative reading, often intrinsic to parallel texts, aimed at improving the reader's skills in one of the two languages[32]. Such aim seems not to be the main concern of Giliberti, whose side-by-side positioning of an Italian and French version of the *Marseillaise* might be interpreted as a symbolic attempt to bridge France's and Italy's revolutionary pasts in a celebratory commemoration of the two countries' proletarian fight for equality and freedom[33]. Considerations of this kind can provide a solid basis for broader reflections on the role of translation in shaping the international repertoire of chapbook and broadside literature. More interesting insights into possible ways of researching translations of street print and into how these can help us reflect on the cross-lingual and cross-cultural life of these materials arise when we focus on situations where it is not possible to immediately compare two transnational correspondents.

3.2 Texts presented as translations

The fact that a certain text is declared to be a translation suggests that a source is likely to exist (or to have existed) to which the text in question bears a translational relationship. Such a source, however, might be impossible to locate. Toury identifies three possible causes for this impossibility. The first is that a source text might have vanished[34]. This hypothesis seems to be particularly relevant to street literature, which, as already mentioned, has low chances of survival. The second hypothesis is that there might never been a single source text[35]. This might also be the case of many translated chapbooks and broadsides. Indeed, it is important to bear in mind that, when dealing with these materials, we might often be dealing with texts that result from the protracted reworkings of centuries-old written and oral cultural traditions. The third possible scenario is one in which a source text has never existed, or one in which we are in the presence of a pseudotranslation[36]. It is difficult to estimate whether and which of these scenarios applies to *La Catalana Punita*, for which I have not been able to track down any transnational correspondent so far. Indeed, as Toury points out, "there is really no way [...] to distinguish between texts whose sources have simply vanished and texts which never had a single-text source"[37]. Despite this diffi-

---

32 See for example V. Leonardi, *The Role of Pedagogical Translation in Second Language Acquisition. From Theory to Practice*, Bern / Oxford 2010, p. 97.
33 I have discussed this point further in A. Colombo, *Translation, Book History and the Transnational Life of Street Literature*, in "Translation Studies", 2018. DOI: 10.1080/14781700.2018.1534699.
34 G. Toury, *Descriptive Translation Studies*, p. 48.
35 *Ibid.*, p. 29.
36 *Ibid.*
37 *Ibid.*, p. 48.

culty, it is still possible for us to draw interesting inferences on the translational life of cheap ephemeral print. Toury observed that for a text to pass off as a translation, certain features need to be incorporated into it that have come to be "associated [in the target culture] with translation and more often than not with the translation of texts of a particular type and/or from a particular source language and textual tradition"[38]. The declaration that *La Catalana Punita* was translated from Spanish into Italian and that the translation was carried out by Fulgenzio Bozzolini can be seen as examples of such features. The assumption that they would prompt the reader to associate the chapbook in question with other (genuinely) translated chapbooks might suggest that the practice of translating chapbook literature was far from uncommon. Further confirmation of this can be found in the fact that street literature was characterized by "familiarity, repetition and continuity" and that its audience expected to come across themes, genres, paratextual components (e.g. titles and illustrations) with which it was already well accustomed[39]. It seems unlikely, therefore, that the publisher of *La Catalana Punita* would introduce elements extraneous to this tradition, especially in a position as prominent as the title page.

Unlike in the case of *La Catalana Punita*, the claims that identify *La Viola Mammola*, *Le Due Agnelline* and *Il Naufragio* as translations from English turned out to be verifiable as well as authentic. The three chapbooks are the genuine translations of respectively *The Simple Flower* by Charlotte Elizabeth, *The Two Lambs* by Lucy Cameron and the anonymous *Sea Boy's Grave*[40]. The identification of the source texts was mainly made possible by tentatively searching close English translations of segments of the Italian texts in Google as well as the close English translations of the Italian titles across online library catalogues and digitised collections of chapbooks (see, for example, the links in footnote 40). When present, non-translated proper nouns of places and people such as "Il Signor Shelby" in *La Viola Mammola* and "Roberto Reikes di Gloster" and "Enrico Williams" in *Il Naufragio*, acted as very effective keywords. A Google search of their most direct English equivalents, respectively "Mr. Shelby", "Robert of Gloucester" and "Henry Williams", made it possible to retrieve the digitized or partially digitized source texts[41]. These are all evangeli-

---

[38] *Ibid.*, p. 53

[39] A. O'Malley, *Poaching on Crusoe's Island. Popular Reading and Chapbook Editions of Robinson Crusoe*, in "Eighteenth-Century Life", 35, 2011, 2, pp. 18–38, especially p. 27.

[40] Like the translations, the source texts were published in various editions by different publishers. The edition of *The Simple Flower* that I examined was published in Dublin by Philip Dixon Hardy & Sons in 1854 and is held at Trinity College Library Dublin (OLS POL 6319 no.7); that of *The Two Lambs* was published in London by Houlston & Sons in 1824 and is available at http://hockliffe.dmu.ac.uk/items/0213F.html. The edition of *The Sea Boy's Grave* under consideration was issued in by J. Groom in 1850. It can be accessed at http://ufdc.ufl.edu/UF00057811/00001.

[41] The fact that no clues of this kind are present in the text of *La Catalana Punita* contributes to the difficulty of finding the chapbook's potential source.

cal tracts published on behalf of religious tract societies, mainly the Religious Tract Society of London. This was founded in 1799 in connection to the rise of the Evangelical movement in Britain with the aim to spread evangelical values among children and the poor at home as well as abroad[42]. Tracts contained a strong Protestant message, which was often conveyed through quotes from the Protestant Scriptures. It is clear that this kind of literature would constitute a threat to the traditional Catholic values on which nineteenth-century Italy was solidly grounded. The very fact that the Italian tracts are presented as translations and that the translators' identity is hidden behind initials and pseudonyms might be read as an indication of the extent to which such publications were considered dangerous. Achille De Rubertis informs us that some representatives of the Catholic Church expressed their concern about the widespread circulation and free distribution of translations of booklets written by "mani eterodosse" (heterodox hands) and demanded that such translations be withdrawn from the market[43]. It would seem that, based on the premise that restrictions and prohibitions would call more attention to the translations, no preventing measures were taken except for one – the addition of the warning on the title page of some of the translated tracts "Ad uso dell'educazione dei fanciulli inglesi o protestanti" (For the use of English or Protestant children)[44]. The specification "traduzione dall'inglese" might be seen as further stressing the foreign and heterodox origins of the publications. Clearly, further research into translated tracts and their impact on the Italian context, together with the analysis of the translational shifts that made the tracts accessible to an Italian readership, would contribute important insights into the transnational circulation of cheap print.

3.3 Texts that read as translations

As suggested by the non-translated proper names in the tracts, exoticisms can greatly help to identify an assumed translation's source. Among the exoticisms found in the text of *Relazione d'una orrenda vendetta* were the calque "constabile" and the English expressions "yellow fellow" and "slow fire". A combined search of these three elements authenticated the claim, made in the chapbook, that the anecdote was originally reported in the Boston papers. The text of the pamphlet is clearly derived from a

---

[42] V.E. Neuburg, *Popular Literature. A History and Guide*, London 1977, pp. 249–264; S. Pedersen, *Hannah More Meets Simple Simon. Tracts, Chapbooks and Popular Culture in Late Eighteenth-Century England*, in "Journal of British Studies", 25, 1987, pp. 84–113; R.D. Altick, *The English Common Reader. A Social History of the Mass Reading Public, 1800–1900*, 2nd ed., Columbus OH 1998, pp. 75–77 and 99–108; W. Jones, *The Jubilee Memorial*, pp. 368–370.
[43] A. de Rubertis, *Una scrittrice irlandese censurata in Toscana*, in "Bullettino Senese di Storia Patria", 12, 1941, 1, pp. 45–51, p. 45.
[44] *Ibid.*, p. 49.

letter published in the "Boston Liberator" of May 21, 1836, and in the "Boston Evening Gazette"[45]. The Italian version abridges the original letter through the omission of small details and passages, especially those capturing the gruesomeness and violence of the execution of the constable's murderer. It is difficult to tell whether the Italian translation draws directly on the text of the letter as published in one of the Boston papers or whether it is a direct translation of an already available abridgment in the chapbook format or an intralingual reworking of an Italian unabridged translation of the letter[46].

What is certain, and definitely more important, is that the text of *Relazione d'una orrenda vendetta* can be seen as being translationally bound to its primary source (the letter in the Boston papers) and that the analysis of such a bond can shed new light on the role of translated street print. Besides re-encoding the content of the original into a new linguistic and cultural context, the genuine translation in question adapted a piece of allegedly authentic news to meet the requirements of an audience that was much broader than that of the newspapers for which it was originally intended. Compressed into the four-page chapbook, the original text became attuned to the sensational tales which creatively blended facts and fiction in descriptions of executions, tortures, and murders and which recurred in the street literature of Italy and other countries[47].

In other words, we are in the presence of what Bettina Lerner identified as "translation from high to low", that is a translation that brings "upper-class culture down to the level of the masses"[48]. This suggests that translation can potentially carry the same text not only across linguistic and cultural boundaries but also – and simultaneously – across social classes as well as genres and formats. Research into the extent of this potential would provide more depth to understanding the role of translation in shaping the international repertoire of street print.

The sixth and last publication considered in this study, *Esquimaux, massacro de' missionari in Groelandia*, raises similar points to those made in relation to *La Catalana*

---

[45] The issue of the "Boston Liberator" in question can openly be accessed at http://fair-use.org/the-liberator/1836/05/21/the-liberator-06-21.pdf. A transcription of the letter as published in the "Boston Evening Gazette" is contained in P. Reuben / J. Timbs, *Blessings of American Law*, in "The Mirror of Literature, Amusement and Instruction», 2, 1845, 6, pp. 90–92, p. 90. Reuber and Timbs inform us that the letter was written on April 28, 1836, but do not provide the date of the issue of the newspaper in which it was published. Research across online historical newspapers databases shows that the letter had circulated very widely in the British and Irish press.
[46] I have not come across any Italian unabridged version of the letter.
[47] See in particular A. Natale, *Il sensazionale e il prodigioso nella letteratura di consumo (Secoli XVII–XVIII)*, Roma 2008; M. Rospocher / R. Salzberg, *Murder Ballads. Singing, Hearing, Writing and Reading about Murder in Renaissance Italy*, in T. Dean / K. Lowe (eds.), *Murder in Renaissance Italy*, Cambridge 2017, pp. 164–185.
[48] B. Lerner, *A French Lazarillo, Translation and Popular Literature in nineteenth-century France*, in "Nineteenth-Century French Studies", 38, 2009, 1/2, pp. 9–23.

Punita. The fact that it has so far been impossible to locate a potential source text prevents us from identifying the chapbook in question as a genuine translation. As already stressed, however, this does not undermine the possibility of considering this publication interesting evidence of the translational life of street print.

4 Conclusions

The points raised in this chapter showed that researching the translational dimension of street literature is not only possible but also fruitful. Chapbooks and broadsides can be rather explicit about the translational nature of their texts and, like books, they can act as the carrier of assumed translations, genuine translations and pseudo-translations. The analysis of a text that meets any of these translational conditions can raise important questions and open up new research avenues towards better conceptualizations of the interdependence of the translational and transnational dimensions of cheap print. It is hoped that translation studies and book history will increasingly be engaged in pursuing such avenues.

 This project has received funding from the European Union's Horizon 2020 research and innovation programme under the Marie Sklodowska-Curie grant agreement No 660143

Jordi Sánchez-Martí
The Printed Popularization of the Iberian Books of Chivalry across Sixteenth-Century Europe

1 Introduction

As the curate and the barber bring the hapless and delusional Don Quijote back home, they encounter a canon from Toledo who directs severe criticism against the genre of the *libros de caballerías*, i.e. the prose chivalric romances that were composed and printed in the Iberian Peninsula starting in the 1490s. Blamed for the titular hero's insanity, these books are found to be morally and stylistically objectionable by the canon, who is deeply concerned that it is to the "desvanecido vulgo, a quien por la mayor parte toca leer semejantes libros"[1]. The canon's notion that chivalric romances circulated widely among the lower echelons of society is consonant with the following observation made by Don Quijote himself: "con gusto general [the *libros de caballerías*] son leídos y celebrados de los grandes y de los chicos, de los pobres y de los ricos, de los letrados e ignorantes, de los plebeyos y caballeros …, finalmente, de todo género de personas de cualquier estado y condición que sean"[2].

These two quotations convey the impression that at the turn of the seventeenth century, when the first part of *Don Quijote* was published, the *libros de caballerías* had achieved widespread popularity. Besides, as this literary corpus was printed and distributed beyond the Pyrenees during the sixteenth century, it also succeeded in captivating large numbers of European readers from diverse social backgrounds. While the earliest printed instantiations of the genre targeted customers belonging to the elite, as time went by the same romance texts were marketed to more popular readers, attaining large circulation among social strata that were clearly below the level of the elite on social, cultural, and economic grounds[3].

---

[1] Miguel de Cervantes, *Don Quijote de la Mancha*, edited by F. Rico, Barcelona 2001, I.xlviii.551: "the shallow rabble, who are the main readers of this kind of books". Subsequent quotations from *Don Quijote* are cited from this edition with reference to part, chapter, and page number. All translations in this chapter are my own.
[2] I.l.568: "the books of chivalry are read with general delight and praised by great and small, rich and poor, the learned and the ignorant, plebeians and gentlemen …, in conclusion, by people from all social backgrounds".
[3] See T. Harris, *Popular, Plebeian, Culture: Historical Definitions*, in J. Raymond (ed.), *The Oxford History of Popular Print Culture*, vol. 1: *Cheap Print in Britain and Ireland to 1660*, Oxford 2011, pp. 50–58; Harris argues that "popular culture include[s] elite forms that had become popularized, and thus beliefs, practices, and artefacts that were widely disseminated, widely accessible, and widely accessed, even if not produced or generated by the people" (p. 52); I take the same viewpoint; for a different

This chapter examines the various processes and decisions adopted by European printers and publishers that contributed to the popularization of the genre across the continent during the sixteenth century. I start by considering the printed distribution of the books of chivalry on the Iberian Peninsula and then follow the genre's dissemination abroad in chronological order as they were printed first in Italy, followed by France and England[4].

2 Spain

The Castilian books of chivalry started to appear in print probably in 1496, when the now lost *editio princeps* of Garci Rodríguez de Montalvo's *Amadís de Gaula* (books I–IV) seems to have been published[5]. With more than 200 separate editions printed throughout the sixteenth century[6], the genre became a best-selling phenomenon in Spain and was well represented in Don Quijote's fictitious library, which comprised "más de cien cuerpos de libros grandes" (I.vi.76: "more than a hundred large books"). These editions were actually recognizable by their large size ("libros grandes"), since they were all printed in folio format. In addition, there were other visual markers that made the genre easily identifiable to potential customers: the title page was illus-

---

view, see K. Whinnom, *The Problem of the "Best-seller" in Spanish Golden-Age Literature*, in "Bulletin of Hispanic Studies", 57, 1980, pp. 189–198, who considers that "construing 'popular' simply as 'widely diffused', and not as implying something produced by or for the populace [is] a distinction which is [...] in this period of somewhat dubious validity" (p. 189).

4 Owing to space limitations, this chapter contains no discussion of the printed distribution of the Iberian books of chivalry in Dutch and German; see B. van Selm, *De "Amadis van Gaule"-romans: Productie, verspreiding en receptie van een bestseller in de vroegmoderne tijd in de Nederlanden, met een bibliografie van de Nederlands vertalingen*, Leiden 2001; and H. Schaffert, *Der Amadisroman: Serielles Erzählen in der Frühen Neuzeit*, Berlin 2015.

5 See R. Ramos, *Para la fecha del "Amadís de Gaula": "Esta sancta guerra que contra los infieles començada tienen"*, in "Boletín de la Real Academia Española", 74, 1994, pp. 503–521. The earliest extant copy belongs to the 1508 edition printed in Saragossa; see A.S. Wilkinson (ed.), *Iberian Books: Books Pubished in Spanish of Portuguese or in the Iberian Peninsula before 1601* (hereafter *IB*), Leiden 2010, no. 16414. See also G. West, *La historia de un ejemplar único: British Library: C.20.e.6.*, in J.M. Lucía Megías (ed.), *Amadís de Gaula, 1508: Quinientos años de libros de caballerías*, Madrid, Biblioteca Nacional de España, 2008, pp. 159–161. For Montalvo, see G. Anes (ed.), *Diccionario Biográfico Español* (hereafter *DBE*), 50 vols., Madrid 2009–2013, vol. 44, pp. 45–47.

6 This information comes from the editions listed in J.M. Lucía Megías, *Imprenta y libros de caballerías*, Madrid 2000, pp. 597–608. For a different selection of works, see D. Eisenberg / M.C. Marín Pina (eds.), *Bibliografía de los libros de caballerías castellanos*, Zaragoza 2000. For an overview of the entire literary corpus, see H. Thomas, *Spanish and Portuguese Romances of Chivalry: The Revival of the Romance of Chivalry in the Spanish Peninsula, and its Extension and Influence Abroad*, Cambridge 1920.

trated with a woodcut representing a knight riding a horse and the text was printed in two columns primarily using gothic typefaces[7].

The bibliographic presentation of the Iberian books of chivalry has been associated with an upper-class readership. Based on the conventional idea that folio-sized volumes were attractive but costly, Daniel Eisenberg has suggested, "the romances were read by the upper or noble class, and perhaps by a few particularly well-to-do members of the bourgeoisie. Certainly they were not read by, nor to, the peasants"[8]. In fact, since Spanish printers continued to publish this literary corpus without changing its typical physical appearance throughout the sixteenth century, it would appear that they pursued only this line of business, impervious to the demands and needs of customers of more modest means. These traditional notions, however, may sometimes be misleading and point to the wrong conclusion. In order to assess to what extent printers cared about the needs of clients below the level of the elite, the issue is not whether they chose to maintain the genre's standard visual codification, but instead whether they could offer the same product at a price that was affordable to this class of readers.

The cost of printing books in the sixteenth century depended to a large extent on the amount of paper used, since this ingredient represented about 75% of the total financial outlay, and thus a significant reduction in the cost of paper could bring down a book's selling price[9]. Printers had two ways of reducing their expenditure on paper: either by making typographical changes to fit more text per page, thus decreasing the amount of paper used, or by using low-grade paper that was substantially cheaper. It seems that during the second half of the sixteenth century printers were willing to explore these avenues to expand their client base, reaching a more popular public[10]. A case in point is the 1580 edition of *Amadís de Gaula* printed in Alcalá de Henares by Querino Gerardo. See Figure 1.

This book contains 236 folios with the text printed in roman in two columns of 57 lines of letterpress each, despite the type-page measuring only 230 x 146 mm[11].

---

[7] For a discussion of this generic morphology, see J.M. Lucía Megías, *Imprenta*, esp. pp. 431–447. In the second half of the century printers started using roman typefaces, although the gothic ones did not disappear entirely; cf. the edition of *Palmerín de Olivia* printed in Toledo as late as 1580 (IB 16751); for a description, see E. García Dini, *Per una bibliografia dei romanzi di cavalleria: Edizioni del ciclo dei "Palmerines"*, in *Studi sul Palmerín de Olivia*, vol. 3: *Saggi e ricerche*, Pisa 1966, pp. 18–20. The use of rotunda gothic typefaces was traditional in sixteenth-century Spain; for a description, see P. Gaskell, *A New Introduction to Bibliography*, Oxford 1972, p. 18.
[8] D. Eisenberg, *Who Read the Romances of Chivalry?*, in "Kentucky Romance Quarterly", 20, 1973, pp. 209–233, at p. 223.
[9] P. Gaskell, *Introduction*, p. 177.
[10] See J.M. Lucía Megías, *Imprenta*, p. 48; cf. L. Binotti, *Humanistic Audiences: "Novela sentimental" and "libros de caballerías" in Cinquecento Italy*, in "La Corónica", 39, 2010, pp. 67–113, at p. 109.
[11] IB 16481; D. Eisenberg / M.C. Marín Pina (eds.), *Bibliografía*, no. 652. For a description, see J. Martín Abad, *La imprenta en Alcalá de Henares (1502–1600)*, Madrid, Arco, 1991, no. 887; see also J.M. Lucía

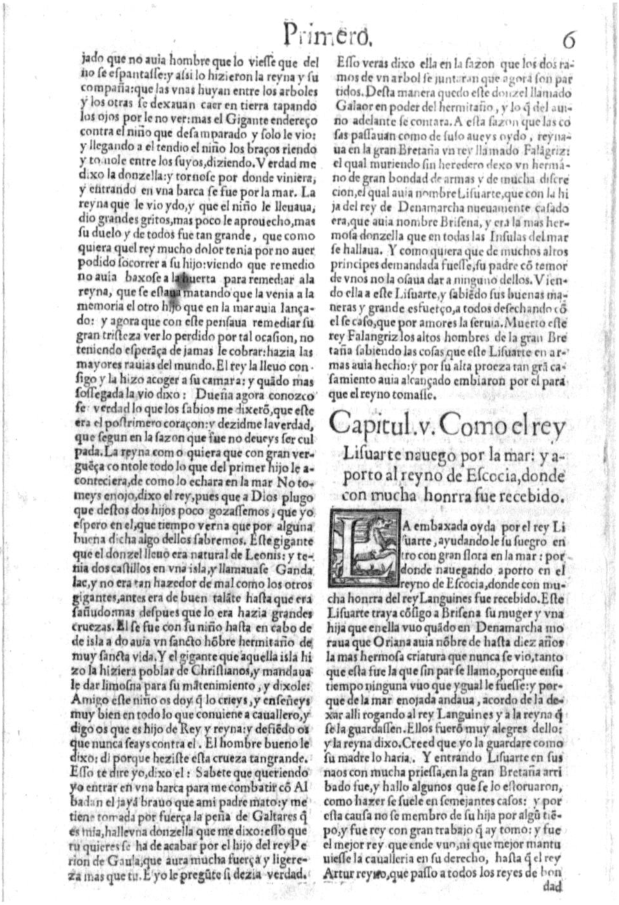
Primero. 6

Capitul.v. Como el rey Lisuarte nauegó por la mar: y aporto al reyno de Escocia, donde con mucha honrra fue recebido.

Fig. 1: *Amadís de Gaula*, Alcalá de Henares, Q. Gerardo, 1580, 6r (Valladolid, Universidad de Valladolid, U/Bc 03820).

By contrast, the earliest extant edition of *Amadís*, printed in 1508 by Jorge Coci using rotunda type, contains 302 folios, with two columns of only 46 lines of letterpress each on a more generous type-page measuring 238 x 156 mm[12]. Not only did the 1580 edition require much less paper than the one dated 1508 (33 sheets less per copy), but it was also printed on low-grade paper, thus cutting the overall paper expenditure

Megías, *Libros de caballerías castellanos en las Bibliotecas Públicas de París: Catálogo descriptivo*, Pisa 1999, no. 9; and J.M. Lucía Megías, *Imprenta*, p. 449. Querino Gerardo was active in Alcalá between 1579 and 1584; see J. Delgado Casado, *Diccionario de impresores españoles (Siglos XV–XVII)*, Madrid 1996, no. 331.

12 *IB* 16414; D. Eisenberg / M.C. Marín Pina (eds.), *Bibliografía*, no. 635. For a description, see F.J. Norton, *A Descriptive Catalogue of Printing in Spain and Portugal, 1501–1520*, Cambridge 1978, no. 625; and J. Martín Abad, *Post-incunables ibéricos*, Madrid 2001, no. 42. For Coci, see *DBE*, vol. 14, pp. 25 f.

significantly. These typographical and material choices combined to lower the price tag carried by a copy of the 1580 edition, which despite being printed in folio cannot be characterized as a deluxe edition, as Lucía Megías suggests[13]. In fact, it should be described as "a folio of economy"[14].

There was an alternative method to mark down chivalric books: instead of selling them complete in a single bibliographic unit, publishers broke them up in smaller divisions that could be sold for a fraction of the price. By dividing the original work and reducing the paper expenditure, publishers contrived to make these separate fascicles affordable to large segments of society. For instance, an edition of *Palmerín de Olivia*, printed in Toledo in 1555, divided the work in four parts[15], as did another edition printed in Medina del Campo in 1562 by Francisco del Canto[16]. Although the chapters in each part of the latter are numbered in separate sequences, the continuous foliation of the two parts together with the presence of a colophon at the end of part two suggests that these formed a bibliographic unit probably meant to be sold together as one item. See Figure 2.

Spanish printers and stationers strived to popularize the books of chivalry by cutting production costs while keeping the folio format. The implementation of this strategy coincided with the expansion of education in Castile at a time when printed books were produced more cheaply and in large quantities[17]. As a result, the Iberian books of chivalry reached a wide and socially diverse public inclusive of "farmers, small-town merchants of Jewish descent and shopkeepers", as the archival work conducted by Sara Nalle has confirmed[18].

---

13 J.M. Lucía Megías, *Imprenta*, p. 449.
14 See S. Galbraith, *English Literary Folios 1593–1623: Studying Shifts in Format*, in J.N. King (ed.), *Tudor Books and Readers: Materiality and the Construction of Meaning*, Cambridge 2010, pp. 46–67, at p. 48.
15 *IB* 16749; D. Eisenberg / M.C. Marín Pina (eds.), *Bibliografía*, no. 1881. Only one copy of part two survives; for a description, see J.M. Lucía Megías, *Catálogo descriptivo de libros de caballerías hispánicos. VII. Un "Palmerín de Olivia" recuperado: Toledo, ¿Juan Ferrer?, 1555 (Biblioteca del Palacio Real: I.C.91)*, in "Voz y Letra", 6, 1995, pp. 41–57. See also C. Pérez Pastor, *La imprenta en Toledo*, Madrid 1887, no. 277.
16 *IB* 16750; D. Eisenberg / M.C. Marín Pina (eds.), *Bibliografía*, no. 1882. The only extant copy is held at the Biblioteca de Catalunya (shelfmark Bon. 9–III–11) and preserves only the first two parts; for a discussion, see J.M. Lucía Megías, *Imprenta*, pp. 41–43, with a facsimile reproduction of the title page on p. 42. See also C. Pérez Pastor, *La imprenta en Medina del Campo*, Madrid 1896, no. 136.
17 As Maravall states, "no one, no matter how tight one's budget, found it necessary to do without any book", J.A. Maravall, *Culture of the Baroque: Analysis of a Historical Structure* (Theory and History of Literature, 25), Minneapolis MN 1986, p. 85. At the beginning of the seventeenth century, Cristóbal Suárez de Figueroa reflected on this issue: "los libros antes raros, y de gran precio, se han buelto [sic] mas comunes", *Varias noticias importantes a la humana comunicación*, Madrid, 1621, fol. 232r ("books that once were rare and costly have become more common").
18 S. Nalle, *Literacy and Culture in Early Modern Castile*, in "Past and Present", 125, 1989, pp. 65–96, at p. 88. Her research shows that the second-hand book market and the oral transmission of these

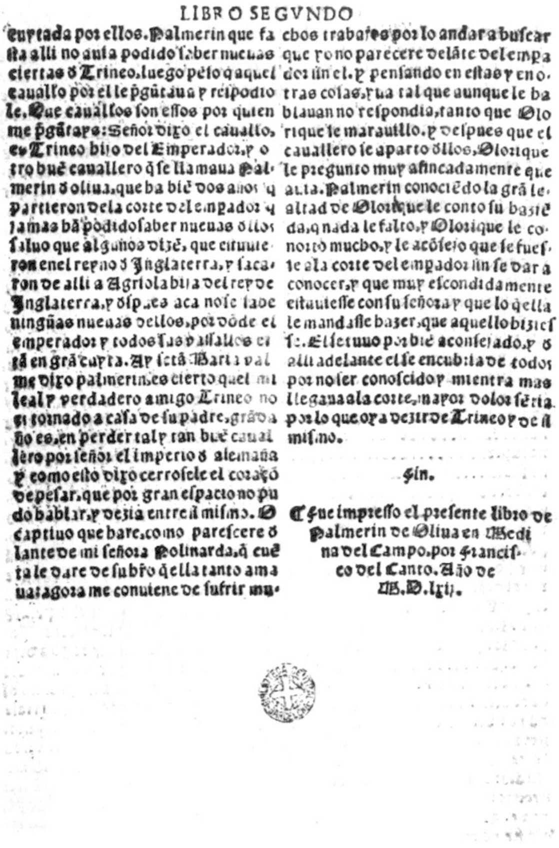
LIBRO SEGVNDO

Fin.

¶ Fue impresso el presente libro de Palmerin de Oliua en Medina del Campo, por Francisco del Canto. Año de M.D.lxii.

Fig. 2: *Palmerín de Olivia*, Medina del Campo, F. del Canto, 1562, 96v (Barcelona, Biblioteca de Catalunya, shelfmark Bon. 9-III-11).

3 Italy

The fame achieved by the Iberian books of chivalry soon crossed borders and spread outside the Iberian Peninsula, awakening the interest of other printers in opening new markets for this literary corpus. In 1519, Antonio Martínez, a printer based in Rome though originally from Salamanca, published an edition of *Amadís de Gaula* in Spanish[19]. Not only did Antonio retain the language of the original, but also the

works also contributed to the popularization of the genre; cf. L.P. Harvey, *Oral Composition and the Performance of Novels of Chivalry in Spain*, in J.J. Duggan (ed.), *Oral Literature: Seven Essays*, Edinburgh 1975, pp. 84–110.

19 *IB* 16421; D. Eisenberg / M.C. Marín Pina (eds.), *Bibliografía*, no. 637. For Antonio Martínez, see M.C. Misiti, *Antonio Salamanca: qualche chiarimento biografico alla luce di un'indagine sulla presenza spagnola a Roma nel '500*, in M. Santoro (ed.), *La stampa in Italia nel Cinquecento*, Roma 1992, vol. 1, pp. 545–563.

genre's conventionalized format – folio size, in gothic typeface, in two columns[20] – since the book was aimed primarily at the same kind of elite readership made up by both Spaniards living in Italy and Italians with some knowledge of Spanish[21].

In sixteenth-century Italy, Spanish books were perceived as a symbol of social prestige, a circumstance that in part explains why the chivalric romances could be printed there in the original Castilian[22]. As the printing business gradually gravitated from Rome to Venice, a center with a more competitive and dynamic business environment, Venetian printers rethought the marketing strategy followed for printing chivalric literature.

First, they offered their Spanish editions of romances as a means to improve the linguistic competence of their Italian customers. The prologue to the 1526 edition of *Palmerín de Olivia* is dedicated to the bishop Cesare Trivulzio (d. 1548) and presented as an instrument for him to perfect his knowledge of Spanish[23]. The same approach was used to market the Castilian editions of *Amadís*, of 1533[24], and *Primaleón*, of 1534, each of which opens with a prologue by Francisco Delicado underscoring the romances' value for learning the language[25].

---

20 For a description, see J.M. Lucía Megías, *Libros de caballerías en París*, no. 1. See also F.J. Norton, *Italian Printers, 1501–1520: An Annotated List, with an Introduction*, London 1958, pp. 101 f.; M.C. Misiti, *Alcune rare edizioni spagnole pubblicate a Roma da Antonio Martínez de Salamanca*, in M.L. López-Vidriero / P.M. Cátedra (eds.), *El libro antiguo español. Actas del segundo Coloquio Internacional (Madrid)*, Salamanca 1992, pp. 307–323; and S. Neri, *Il romanzo cavalleresco spagnolo in Italia*, in A. Bognolo / G. Cara / S. Neri, *Repertorio delle continuazioni italiane ai romanzi cavallereschi spagnoli: Ciclo di "Amadis di Gaula"*, Roma 2013, pp. 91–93, with a facsimile of the title page on p. 92. For the type, see F. Issac, *An Index to Early Printed Books in the British Museum*, pt. II, MDI-MDXX, section II: *Italy*, London 1938, no. 12311. A printed page from this edition is reproduced in J.M. Lucía Megías (ed.), *Amadís 1508*, p. 69. Note that Antonio Martínez used the same format for his 1525 edition of *Sergas de Esplandián* (IB 16427; D. Eisenberg / M.C. Marín Pina (eds.), *Bibliografía* no. 1280); for a description, see R. Mortimer, *Harvard College Library Department of Printing and Graphic Arts Catalogue of Books and Manuscripts*, vol. 2: *Italian 16th Century Books*, Cambridge MA 1974, no. 172. See also H. Thomas, *Antonio [Martínez] de Salamanca, Printer of "La Celestina"*, Rome, c. 1525, in "The Library", 5, 1953, 8, pp. 45–50.
21 For the perceived status of Spanish in Italy, see M. Lefèvre, *Il potere della parola: il castigliano nel Cinquecento tra Italia e Spagna: Grammatica, ideologia, traduzione*, Manziana 2012. See also A. Pallotta, *Venetian Printers and Spanish Literature in Sixteenth-Century Italy*, in "Comparative Literature", 43, 1991, pp. 20–42, where he argues, however, that the publication of Spanish editions "rested on ethnic considerations and was meant for Spaniards living in Italy" (p. 33).
22 See A. Bognolo, *El libro español en Venecia en el siglo XVI*, in P. Botta (ed.), *Rumbos del hispanismo en el umbral del Cincuentenario de la AIH*, vol. 3, Roma 2012, pp. 243–258, at p. 246.
23 D. Eisenberg / M.C. Marín Pina (eds.), *Bibliografía*, no. 1875; not in *IB*. For the text of the prologue, see *El libro del famoso e muy esforçado cavallero Palmerín de Olivia*, in G. di Stefano (ed.), *Studi sul Palmerín de Olivia*, vol. 1, Pisa 1966, p. 779.
24 IB 16436; D. Eisenberg / M.C. Marín Pina (eds.), *Bibliografía*, no. 642. See S. Neri, *Il romanzo cavalleresco spagnolo*, pp. 94–96.
25 IB 16780; D. Eisenberg / M.C. Marín Pina (eds.), *Bibliografía*, no. 1956. For Delicado, see *DBE*, vol. 15, pp. 762–765. For his view that these editions could provide a model for foreign language learn-

Next, Venetian printers also experimented with the visual presentation of these works. While the 1526 edition of *Palmerín de Olivia* maintained the morphology conventionalized by Spanish printers[26], Antonio Nicolini da Sabbio printed the 1533 edition of *Amadís* and the 1534 edition of *Primaleón* using roman typefaces in a single column[27]. Aware that these choices represented a departure from convention, Delicado explains that his edition of *Primaleón* is printed "en buena letra y clara y puntada y pausada que a ojos abiertos lo leerán los que no son ciegos" (sig. Z2v)[28], which they chose to use with no abbreviations ("ninguna abreviadura", *ibid.*) to further increase the text's legibility. Besides contributing to redesigning the visual appearance of the chivalric romances, Delicado also edited the actual text by modifying passages, adding new sections and interpolations. Most significantly, he promoted the division of *Primaleón* into three parts, making clear that he was not simply upgrading the aesthetic appearance of these works. Instead, as Lucia Binotti contends, Delicado's overhaul of the publication of Iberian romances was "intended for his editions to assume the institutional physiognomy of canonical texts, offering them in a package similar to the one that in Italy was being adopted for ancient and newer classics alike"[29]. Delicado imposed upon these works, which originated in the Spanish publishing tradition, the printing conventions that were becoming standard in Venice. In their new textual and printed instantiation, these works became luxury objects aimed at the elites living in Italy as well as in Spain[30].

---

ers, see J.M. Lucía Megías, *Francisco Delicado: un precursor de la enseñanza del español en Italia en el siglo XVI*, in "Cuadernos Cervantes", 9, 1996, pp. 7–17. Note that even Juan de Valdés encouraged Italian readers to peruse *Palmerín* and *Primaleón*; see J.E. Laplana (ed.), *Diálogo de la lengua* (Clásicos y Modernos, 32), Barcelona 2010, pp. 255 and 262–263.

26 For a bibliographical description, see E. García Dini, *Per una bibliografia dei romanzi di cavalleria*, pp. 10–12; and J.M. Lucía Megías, *Libros de caballerías en París*, nos. 30 f.

27 See A. Bognolo, *Entre "Celestinas", novela sentimental y libros de caballerías: La empresa editorial de los Nicolini da Sabbio y Juan Bautista Pederzano en Venecia alrededor de 1530*, in *Serenísima palabra. Actas del X Congreso de la Asociación Internacional Siglo de Oro* (Biblioteca di Rassegna iberistica, 5), Venezia 2017, pp. 727–738. For bibliographical descriptions, see J.M. Lucía Megías, *Libros de caballerías en París*, nos. 3 and 35, respectively; see also L.E.F. de Orduna, *Hallazgo de un ejemplar más de "Amadís de Gaula" (Venecia, Juan Antonio de Sabia, 1533): Biblioteca Jorge Furt. "Los Talas", Luján (Buenos Aires), Argentina, 1–7*, in I.P. Sarno (ed.), *Dialogo: Studi in onore di Lore Terracini*, Roma 1990, vol. 2, pp. 451–469; E. García Dini, *Per una bibliografia dei romanzi di cavalleria*, pp. 27–29; and R. Mortimer, *Harvard Catalogue of Books: Italian 16th Century Books*, no. 19. For the reproduction of pages from the Venetian editions of *Amadís* and *Primaleón*, see L. Binotti, *Humanistic Audiences*, figs. 3–8. For information on the Nicolini da Sabbio, see M. Santoro (ed.), *Dizionario degli editori, tipografi, librai itineranti in Italia tra Quattrocento e Seicento* (hereafter *DETLI*), 3 vols., Pisa / Roma, 2014, no. 423 and *Dizionario Biografico degli Italiani* (hereafter *DBI*), 90 vols., Roma 1960–2017, vol. 78, pp. 495–498.

28 Francisco Delicado, *Prólogo al "Primaleón"*, in C. Perugini (ed.), *La Lozana andaluza*, Sevilla, Fundación José Manuel Lara, 2004, p. 451: "in a good fount of type that is clear [i.e. roman], with punctuation and marking of pauses, that those who are not blind will read it with great ease".

29 L. Binotti, *Humanistic Audiences*, pp. 86 f.

30 *Ibid.*, pp. 104, 108.

The process of bibliographic revision of the genre culminated with the publication of a new edition of *Palmerín de Olivia* printed in Venice in August 1534. This edition, which marked the end of the publication in Italy of the Iberian books of chivalry in the original Spanish, was printed in octavo, probably "with ease of transport in mind"[31], but also with the purpose of expanding the genre's client base. Of this edition Anna Bognolo has said that it was intended for a new public and a new use[32], although she describes neither the new public nor the new use of the 1534 *Palmerín*. Nonetheless, it becomes apparent that Venetian printers and editors strived to make these works more attractive and accessible to more socially diverse customers. The printers' aspirations for commercial success, however, were restricted by the use of a foreign language. Still, their efforts were not in vain, but laid the foundations for "la predisposizione di una buona parte degli stessi lettori ad acquistare, di lì a dieci anni, le più comode edizioni in traduzione", as Neri argues[33].

From the mid-1540s these same works, which up until that moment had been published for a limited audience, started to become available to a wider reading public, not only because they appeared in Italian translation, but also because they were disseminated in a format intended for a less exclusive readership. In 1544, an edition of Mambrino Roseo da Fabriano's Italian translation of *Palmerín de Olivia* came off the press of the Venetian printer Michele Tramezzino[34]. Following the example of the 1534 edition, Tramezzino printed it also in quarto, though instead of the gothic typefaces of the former or the roman typefaces of Delicado's editions, Tramezzino preferred the italic typefaces that were becoming fashionable among Venetian printers for the publication of early modern vernacular texts, influenced by the work of Aldus Manutius[35]. See Figure 3.

---

31 *Ibid.*, pp. 97; *IB* 16744; D. Eisenberg / M.C. Marín Pina (eds.), *Bibliografía*, no. 1876. It exists in two variant states described by E. García Dini, *Per una bibliografia dei romanzi di cavalleria*, pp. 12–14; and J.M. Lucía Megías, *Libros de caballerías en París*, no. 32. The variant title pages are reproduced in S. Neri, *Il romanzo cavalleresco spagnolo*, p. 98, fig. 10.
32 A. Bognolo, *Los Palmerines italianos: una primera aproximación*, in A. González et al. (eds.), *Palmerín y sus libros: 500 años*, México 2013, pp. 255–284, at p. 258.
33 S. Neri *Il romanzo cavalleresco spagnolo*, p. 100.
34 *Censimento nazionale delle edizioni italiani del XVI secolo*, http://edit16.iccu.sbn.it, no. 55981. For a description, see G. Melzi, *Bibliografia dei romanzi di cavalleria in versi e in prosa italiani*, rev. P.A. Tosi, Milano 1865, p. 216; A. Tinto, *Annali tipografici dei Tramezzino*, Venezia 1968, no. 51; and E. Toda y Güell, *Bibiografia espanyola d'Itàlia: dels orígens de la imprempta fins a l'any 1900*, 5 vols., Castell de Sant Miguel d'Escornalbou, 1927–1931, no. 3717. For information on Mambrino Roseo, see A. Bognolo, *Mambrino Roseo da Fabriano: vita provvisoria di uno scrittore*, in A. Bognolo / G. Cara / S. Neri, *Repertorio*, pp. 25–68; and *DBI*, vol. 88, pp. 465–468. For Michele Tramezzino, see *DETLI*, no. 565b.
35 See P.F. Grendler, *Form and Function in Italian Renaissance Popular Books*, in "Renaissance Quarterly", 46, 1993, pp. 451–485, at p. 476.

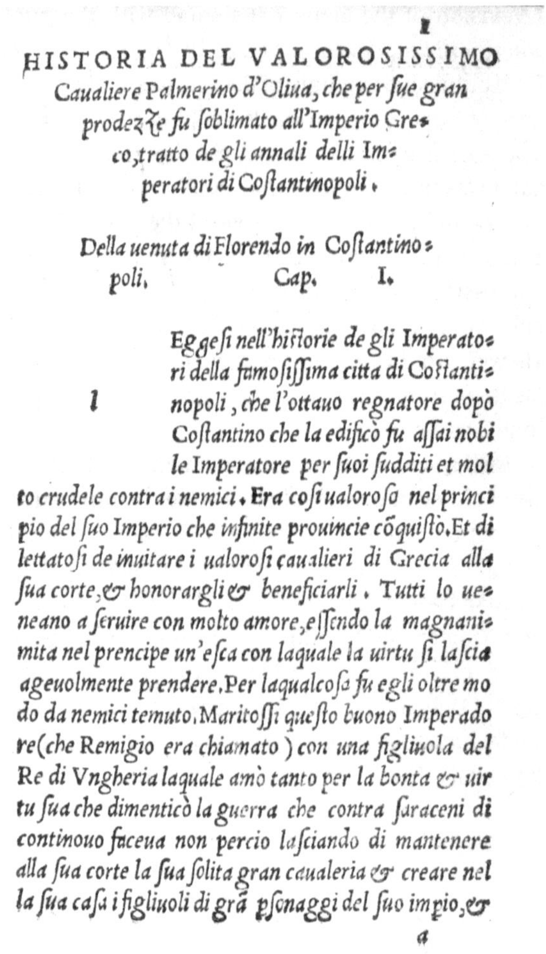

HISTORIA DEL VALOROSISSIMO

Caualiere Palmerino d'Oliua, che per sue gran
prodezze fu soblimato all'Imperio Gre‑
co, tratto de gli annali delli Im‑
peratori di Costantinopoli.

Della uenuta di Florendo in Costantino‑
poli.   Cap.   I.

Eggesi nell'historie de gli Imperato‑
ri della famosissima citta di Costanti‑
nopoli, che l'ottauo regnatore dopò
Costantino che la edificò fu assai nobi
le Imperatore per suoi sudditi et mol
to crudele contra i nemici. Era cosi ualoroso nel princi
pio del suo Imperio che infinite prouincie cōquistò. Et di
lettatosi de inuitare i ualorosi caualieri di Grecia alla
sua corte, & honorargli & beneficiarli. Tutti lo ue‑
neano a seruire con molto amore, essendo la magnani‑
mita nel prencipe un'esca con laquale la uirtu si lascia
ageuolmente prendere. Per laqualcosa fu egli oltre mo
do da nemici temuto. Maritossi questo buono Imperado
re (che Remigio era chiamato) con una figliuola del
Re di Vngheria laquale amò tanto per la bonta & uir
tu sua che dimenticò la guerra che contra saraceni di
continouo faceua non percio lasciando di mantenere
alla sua corte la sua solita gran caualeria & creare nel
la sua casa i figliuoli di grā psonaggi del suo impio, &
a

Fig. 3: *Palmerino d'Oliva*, Venice, M. Tramezzino, 1544, a1r (Barcelona, Biblioteca de Catalunya, shelfmark Toda 4-II-6).

Tramezzino's choices set the norm for the publication of the Italian translations of the *libros de caballerías*, resulting in a product that was more affordable and could reach a larger, more popular audience than Delicado's monumental editions[36]. In order to entice middlebrow readers, Tramezzino adjusted not only these texts' material presentation, but intervened in their literary aspect too. When Mambrino Roseo translated the Iberian romances, he was not instructed to render his source faithfully, but instead was allowed simply to abridge the narrative plot in a linguistic register his popular audience could identify with. The relatively easy reading and handling of these books was a catalyst for the commercial success the genre enjoyed in Italy

---

36 Cf. A. Pallotta, *Venetian Printers and Spanish Literature*, p. 34.

during the rest of the sixteenth century. So high must have been the demand for this kind of literature that, having completed the translation of the original cycles of *Amadís* and *Palmerín*, Mambrino Roseo felt compelled to create new sequels, which were well received too. With approximately 200 editions of works belonging to the cycles of *Amadís* and *Palmerín* – including the Italian continuations – printed up until 1630, there can be little doubt that this literary corpus achieved tremendous success and popularity in Italy[37].

4 France

France is the next country outside the Iberian Peninsula that saw the printed circulation of the *libros de caballerías*. It started with Nicholas de Herberay des Essarts's translation of *Amadís*, book I, printed in 1540 by the publishing syndicate formed by the Parisian stationers Denis Janot, Jean Longis, and Vincent Sertenas[38]. Up until this moment chivalric literature appeared in France in an old-fashioned format, with works printed as folio volumes with gothic typefaces, two columns, and rudimentary woodcuts, much like the Spanish editions of romances[39]. The French publishers of *Amadis*, however, revamped the romance's textual presentation, printing it in folio, in text lined across the page using roman typefaces together with elaborate, purpose-made woodcut illustrations inside of elegant woodcut frames, all with generous margins. The resulting visual effect betrays the publishers' intention to package this

---

[37] I take this figure from S. Neri, in A. Bognolo / G. Cara / S. Neri, *Repertorio*, p. 195, table 11. For a descriptive list of editions from the *Amadís* cycle, see S. Neri, *Censimento bibliografico del ciclo italiano di "Amadis di Gaula"*, in A. Bognolo / G. Cara / S. Neri, *Repertorio*, pp. 199–257. For the cycle of *Palmerín*, see A. Bognolo, *Los Palmerines italianos: una primera aproximación*, pp. 255–284. This state of affairs enables A. Pallotta, *Venetian Printers and Spanish Literature*, to state: "the readership of the [Iberian] romances extended beyond the upper and middle classes" (p. 34).

[38] A. Pettegree et al. (eds.), *French Vernacular Books: Books Published in the French Language before 1601* (hereafter *FB*), 2 vols., Leiden 2007, nos. 651–654. Two editions were printed in 1540, which exist in various states, for which see S. Rawles, *The Earliest Editions of Nicolas de Herberay's Translations of "Amadis de Gaule"*, in "The Library", 6, 1981, 3, pp. 91–108, at p. 105; and S. Rawles, *Denis Janot (fl. 1529–1544), Parisian Printer and Bookseller: A Bibliography*, Leiden 2017, nos. 109, 110. See also A. Pettegree, *The French Book and the European Book World*, Leiden 2007, pp. 206–209; *Inventaire chronologique des éditions parisiennes du XVIe siècle*, Paris 2004, vol. 5, nos. 1550–1551; and H. Vaganay, *Amadis en français: essai de bibliographie*, in "La Bibliofilía", 5, 1903, pp. 65–79. On Herberay, see M. Bideaux (ed.) / N. Herberay des Essarts (trans.), *Amadis de Gaule*, bk. I (Textes de la Renaissance, 116), Paris 2006, pp. 56–65. For the publishers, see P. Renouard, *Répertoire des imprimeurs parisiens, libraires, fondeurs de caractères et correcteurs d'imprimerie: depuis l'introduction de l'imprimerie à Paris (1470) jusqu'à la fin du seizième siècle*, Paris 1965, pp. 216–217, 284, and 396 respectively.

[39] See R. Cooper, *"Nostre histoire renouvelée": The Reception of the Romances of Chivalry in Renaissance France*, in S. Anglo (ed.), *Chivalry in the Renaissance*, Woodbridge / Rochester NY 1990, pp. 175–238, at p. 177.

vernacular text in a more dignified and refined fashion, similar to that of contemporaneous humanist works[40]. Inspired by notions comparable to those of Delicado a decade before in Venice, the Parisian publishers seem to have made sensible decisions that soon were perceived as archetypal for the publication of Iberian chivalric books in France.

Moreover, these editions' typographic and visual elegance was a good match for the stylized prose of Herberay, whose translation exhibited the inherent capacity of French to reach the expressive and rhetoric levels typically associated with classical languages[41]. Herberay's skillful command of French merited him the epithet "vray Cicero François"[42], as his prose became a model for other writers. He could earn this reputation, in part, because he deviated from "la commune superstition des translateurs"[43], who would have endorsed a word-for-word rendering of the Castilian original, and instead conceived his role as that of a literary mediator who adapted his source to the tastes and mores of his target audience, as Herberay proclaims in the prologue:

> Et si vous appercevez en quelque endroict que je ne me soye assubjecty à le [i.e. the Spanish original] rendre de mot à mot: je vous supplye croyre que je l'ay fait [...] pource qu'il m'a semblé beaucoup de choses estre mal seantes aux personnes introduictes, eu regard es meurs et façons du jourd'huy[44].

With this approach, Herberay transformed the original romance, whose narrative and generic paradigms originated within a medieval frame of reference, into an early modern work whose narrative and thematic development pointed to the emergence of the novel[45].

The publishers of Herberay's translation envisaged the printed volume as a deluxe product aimed at the premium end of the market formed by customers willing to pay a

---

[40] Cf. S. Rawles, *Earliest Editions of "Amadis"*, p. 93. For a discussion of the illustrations of the French *Amadis*, see J.-M. Chatelain, *L'illustration d'"Amadis de Gaule" dans les éditions françaises*, in *Les Amadis en France au XVIe siècle*, Paris 2000, pp. 41–52; see also M. Bideaux (ed.), *Amadis de Gaule*, bk. I, pp. 74–84.
[41] See L. Wilson, *The Publication of Iberian Romance in Early Modern Europe*, in J.M. Pérez Fernández / E. Wilson-Lee (eds.), *Translation and the Book Trade in Early Modern Europe*, Cambridge 2014, pp. 201–216, here p. 205.
[42] Jean Martin expressed this opinion in the reader address to *Hypnerotomachie ou discours du songe de Poliphile* (1546; FB 13712–13/sig. A3r). See F. Colonna, *Le Songe de Poliphile*, edited by G. Polizzi, Paris 1994, p. 412, n. 3 to p. 9.
[43] M. Bideaux (ed.), *Amadis de Gaule*, bk. I, p. 168: "the superstition common among translators".
[44] *Ibid.*, p. 168: "And if you notice at any point that I have forced myself to render the Spanish original word for word, I beseech you to believe that I have done so because it has seemed to me that many things were unseemly for the people mentioned with respect to the mores and fashions of today".
[45] See N. Cazauran, *"Amadis de Gaule" en 1540: un nouveau "roman de chevalerie"?*, in *Les Amadis en France au XVIe siècle*, pp. 21–39.

high price for it[46]. With this target audience in mind and maintaining their publishing template, the three Parisian stationers continued to print Herberay's translations of books I–VIII of the *Amadis* cycle until 1548, with numerous reprints[47]. While in Spain the first four books of *Amadis* were normally published as a single volume, in France each one of the books of the cycle was issued separately. This strategy proved to be effective, since the separate publication of each individual book enabled publishers to raise the price of each bibliographic unit, thus increasing their profit margins. Had books I–IV been sold as an indivisible volume, the combined price tag would probably have seemed exorbitant even to some wealthy customers.

In 1548, while the same consortium of Parisian stationers – with Étienne Groulleau as a replacement for the late Janot – was publishing the first edition of book VIII of *Amadis*[48], and a reprint of book I[49], both in folio, they also started to explore the octavo size, cheaper to produce and hence affordable to more potential readers. That year they published octavo editions of books I–VII in order to "démocratiser" the romance, as Vaganay stated, who was critical of the text's crammed layout, with 39 lines per page[50]. Aware that this new format made the romance accessible to new readers, a prefatory poem praising the format's versatility and its convenience for female readers was added:

> Or avez vous, Dames de cueur humain,
> Vostre Amadis en si petit volume,
> Que le pourrez porter dedans la main
> Plus aysement beaucoup que de coustume[51].

---

46 A copy of a single book of *Amadis* was worth between 7 and 10 solz; see S. Rawles, *Earliest Editions of "Amadis"*, p. 96.
47 FB 655–702, 706–713. For a comprehensive list of the sixteenth-century French editions of *Amadis*, see R. Cooper, *Romances of Chivalry in France*, pp. 225–234.
48 FB 706–713; see H. Vaganay, *Amadis en français: essai de bibliographie* (VI), in "La Bibliofilía", 6, 1904, pp. 214–231. For Groulleau, see P. Renouard, *Répertoire*, p. 185.
49 FB 717–720.
50 Each one of the books of *Amadis* survives in the following octavo editions: bk. I (FB 714–716), bk. II (FB 724–725, 727), bk. III (FB 737–738), bk. IV (FB 721–723), bk. V (FB 703–705), bk. VI (732–734), bk. VII (FB 729–731); see H. Vaganay, *Les éditions in-octavo de l'Amadis en français*, in "Revue hispanique", 85, 1929, pp. 1–53, at p. 4. Note that Vaganay's knowledge of the printed tradition of *Amadis* was incomplete, since he was unaware of the existence of a copy of the octavo edition of book III published in 1548 (p. 4). M. Bideaux (ed.), *Amadis de Gaule*, bk. I, p. 69, suggests that the Parisian publishers chose this format in order to reach "une clientèle moins fortunée" [a less prosperous clientele].
51 M. Bideaux (ed.), *Amadis de Gaule*, bk. I, p. 163, n. 1: "Ladies of human heart, now you have your Amadis in such a small volume that you can hold it in your hand with much more comfort than normal". This poem was composed by Jean Maugin, whose translation of *Palmerín de Olivia* appeared in 1546 in the wake of Herberay's translations.

This "democratizing" initiative must have produced the desired effect, since in 1550 the same consortium reissued books I–VIII in octavo, although for this reprint they improved the visual presentation of the text and contrived to recreate the same feeling of typographic and iconographic elegance, legibility, and proportionality characteristic of the folio editions. They achieved this optimal result, among other things, by reusing the same woodcuts – though without their decorative frames – and by printing only 32 lines per page on high-quality paper[52]. New octavo editions of the *Amadis* cycle were printed in 1555, 1557, and 1560, when a complete set of books I–XII in octavo was published[53]. In view of the success they enjoyed with this market-oriented strategy, the Parisian consortium chose to intensify the marketability of the Amadisian books by producing even cheaper editions and creating an "économique" textual object, borrowing Vaganay's adjective[54]. Thus, in 1557 they launched a complete edition of books I–VIII in sextodecimo, containing no illustrations[55]. See Figure 4.

The Parisian stationers Groulleau, Longis, and Sertenas took decisive steps toward the popularization of the Iberian romances. The strategic decision to make this literary corpus accessible to readers from less privileged social backgrounds was not prompted by a sudden downturn in the sales of the more expensive folio editions. In fact, folio continued to be the preferred format for the publication of the *editio princeps* of new books from the *Amadis* cycle until 1556[56], while deluxe reprints continued to be issued in folio after 1548, when those same texts were already available in smaller and cheaper volumes[57].

---

[52] The following editions of each book exist: bk. I (*FB* 749–751), bk. II (*FB* 754–756), bk. III (*FB* 765–766), bk. IV (*FB* 752–753), bk. V (*FB* 739–740), bk. VI (*FB* 764), bk. VII (*FB* 761–762), bk. VIII (*FB* 744–748). For a discussion and description of some of these editions with facsimile reproductions, see H. Vaganay, *L'Amadis in-octavo*, pp. 9–22.

[53] Octavo editions printed in 1555: bk. I (*FB* 792–794), bk. II (*FB* 802–804), bk. III (*FB* 811–812), bk. IV (*FB* 797, 799–800), bk. V (*FB* 782–783), bk. VI (*FB* 808–810), bk. VII (*FB* 805–807), bk. VIII (*FB* 789–790), bk. X (*FB* 787); in 1557: bk. IX (*FB* 825–827), bk. X (*FB* 821–822); in 1560: bk. I (*FB* 866–868), bk. II (*FB* 872–873), bk. III (*FB* 883–885), bk. IV (*FB* 869–871), bk. V (*FB* 856–858), bk. VI (*FB* 875–877), bk. VII (*FB* 874), bk. VIII (*FB* 862–865), bk. XI (*FB* 886–888), bk. XII (*FB* 859–861); see H. Vaganay, *L'Amadis in-octavo*, pp. 22–36, 38–51.

[54] See H. Vaganay, *L'Amadis in-octavo*, pp. 36–38, at p. 38.

[55] The following editions were printed in 16º: bk. I (*FB* 828–830), bk. II (*FB* 834–836), bk. III (*FB* 846–848), bk. IV (*FB* 831–833), bk. V (*FB* 818–820), bk. VI (*FB* 840, 843, 845), bk. VII (*FB* 837–839), bk. VIII (*FB* 823–824); S. Rawles, *Earliest Editions of "Amadis"*, p. 102, shows how a copy of the sextodecimo edition of book I required twenty-two sheets, whereas each copy of the folio edition needed seventy-eight sheets. This represents a massive reduction in production costs.

[56] Folio editions since 1548: bk. VIII (1548, *FB* 706–713), bk. IX (1551, *FB* 768–770), bk. X (1552, *FB* 771–773), bk. XI (1554, *FB* 778–781), bk. XII (1556, *FB* 813–816).

[57] Folio editions reissued between 1548 and 1560: bk. I (1548, *FB* 717–720), bk. II (1548, *FB* 726–727; 1550, *FB* 757–760), bk. III (1548, *FB* 735–736), bk. IV (1555, *FB* 795–796, 798, 801), bk. V (1550, *FB* 741–743), bk. VI (1550, *FB* 763; 1557, *FB* 841–842, 844), bk. VII (1548, *FB* 728), bk. IX (1553, *FB* 774–777), bk. X (1555, *FB* 784–786), bk. XI (1559, *FB* 853–855).

Fig. 4: *Le premier livre d'Amadis de Gaule*, Paris, E. Groulleau, 1557, A7v [London, British Library, shelfmark 1075.a.6.(1.)], © The British Library Board.

When printing the *libros de caballerías*, therefore, the Parisian stationers put in place a dual publication program, with one product line – the folio editions – aimed at the elite market, and another range of products – 8° and 16° editions – marketed to customers of more modest means.

This product diversification, however, was interrupted after 1560, when the Parisian syndicate was dissolved and, as a result, the publication of the *Amadis* series was abandoned altogether during the 1560s, with the only exception of the Plantinian edition of books I–XII in quarto[58]. The *Amadis* cycle reemerged in 1571, but the folio

---

58 See L. Voet, *The Plantin Press (1555–1589): A Bibliography of the Works Printed and Published by Christopher Plantin at Antwerp and Leiden*, Amsterdam 1980, vol. 1, pp. 58–71. See also C. de Buzon, *Notes sur la circulation d' "Amadis de Gaule" en Europe de l'ouest: Gabriel Chappuys, traducteur lui-même traduit*, in "Réforme, Humanisme, Renaissance", 87, 2018, 2, pp. 199–232, at pp. 215–217.

format was never to be reused. During the 1570s books XIII–XV were printed in sextodecimo[59], and books XVI–XXI only in this format[60].

Only eight years after the first publication of Herberay's translation of book I of *Amadis*, the same text was being printed in octavo and started to circulate among readers below the level of the elite, including women[61]. When in 1557 the same work was published in sextodecimo, presumably it became accessible to an even wider and more socially diverse class of readers. During the 1570s sextodecimo actually became the standard format for the printed dissemination of the Iberian books of chivalry in France. The large number of editions existing in this format together with their affordability suggests that French printers penetrated the popular book market and, eventually, the Iberian romances became a staple reading matter for French children, as Michel de Montaigne stated in 1588 when including the *Amadis* cycle among the "fatras de livres, à quoy l'enfance s'amuse"[62].

5 England

The printed distribution of the Iberian romances in English translation did not start until the end of the 1570s[63]. These texts' circulation occurred belatedly probably because the Middle English chivalric romances had enjoyed commercial success in print until the end of the 1560s[64]. While the early English printers published both verse and prose romances, the former seem to have been more favorably received during the 1550s and 1560s by the public, which was composed mainly by members of the urban middle classes that could afford to buy these textual artifacts. Not only did the

---

59 Bk. XIII (1571, *FB* 937–939), bk. XIV (1574, *FB* 978, 980), bk. XV (1577, *FB* 1016–1018).
60 Bk. XVI (1577, *FB* 1021–1023), bk. XVII (1578, *FB* 1031–1032), bk. XVIII (1579, *FB* 1039), bk. XIX (1581, *FB* 1042), bk. XX (1581, *FB* 1043–1044), bk. XXI (1581, *FB* 1046). A sextodecimo edition of books I–XXI was printed in Lyon by various printers between 1575 and 1581; see J. Baudrier, *Bibliographie lyonnaise: recherches sur les imprimeurs, libraires, relieurs et fondeurs de lettres de Lyon au XVI siècle*, Lyon 1897, vol. 3, pp. 320–323, 329–330, 336, 345; 1899, vol. 4, pp. 53, 59–60, 86–91, 92; 1913, vol. 10. pp. 288–289.
61 On female readers, see M. Rothstein, *Reading in the Renaissance: "Amadis de Gaule" and the Lessons of Memory*, Newark NJ 1999, pp. 116 f.
62 M. de Montaigne, *Les Essais*, I.xxv, ed. by J. Balsamo et al., Paris 2007, p. 182: "the jumble of books that children find entertaining". Cf. M. Rothstein, *Reading in the Renaissance*, pp. 121–123.
63 The first work to appear in print was M. Tyler, *Mirror of Princely Deeds and Knighthood*, published ca. 1578; A.W. Pollard / G.R. Redgrave (eds.), *A Short-Title Catalogue of Books Printed in England, Scotland, and Ireland, and of English Books printed abroad* (*STC*), 2nd ed. rev. by W.A. Jackson, F.S. Ferguson, and K.F. Pantzer, 3 vols., London 1976–1991, no. 18859. Owing to space considerations, this section centers on the cycles of *Amadis* and *Palmerin*.
64 See J. Sánchez-Martí, *The Publication of English Medieval Romances after the Death of Wynkyn de Worde, 1536–1569*, in E. de Bruijn / B. Besamusca / F. Willaert (eds.), *Western European Narrative Literature in the Early Period of Print*, Berlin forthcoming.

long-lasting printed transmission of the Middle English romances delay the publication of the Iberian books of chivalry, but also determined the way in which these continental narratives were packaged for the English market. Printed in quarto and using black letter (fig. 5) – two visual markers that were typical of the printed verse romances – the English translations of the Iberian chivalric books could be easily recognized by the traditional buyers of English romances.

Nevertheless, if printers wanted to coax these same clients into buying the Iberian narratives, they still had to find ways to minimize the length discrepancy existing between the continental and the insular chivalric texts. Since the former are considerably longer than the latter, they chose to break up the original narratives and print them in smaller bibliographic units, which could also sell for a price comparable to that of the English metrical romances.

❧ The firſt parte of the auncient and honorable *Hiſtorie*, of the valiant Prince *Palmerin D'Oliua*, Emperor of *Conſtantinople*, Sonne to the King *Florendos* of *Macedon*, and the fayre *Griana*, Daughter to *Remicius*, Emperour of *Conſtantinople* : a Hiſtory full of ſinguler and Courtlie recreation &c.

(·.·)

CHAP. I.

Of the ſecrete loue which the Prince Tariſius *bare to the yong Princeſſe* Griana : *and the arriuall of the Prince* Florendos *at Conſtantinople.*

He auncient Hiſtories, of the famous Emperours of *Conſtantinople* doo record, that the eight Emperor ſuccéeding Conſtantine, the founder of that auncient and famous Cittie, was named Remicius, who gouerned ſo iuſtlie, and with ſuch excéeding honour : as not onelie his Subiectes intirelie looued him, but of the kingdoms about him he was ſo feared and reuerenced, that his Empire increaſed moze large then in the time of his Predeceſſors. This Remicius was of ſuch a princely and munificent minde, that no Knight whatſoeuer

A.j. came

Fig. 5: *Palmerin d'Oliva*, part 1, London, J. Charlewood, 1588, A1r (Washington D.C., Folger Shakespeare Library, call no. STC 19157).
By permission of the Folger Shakespeare Library.

In the preface to his *Palmerin d'Oliva*, printed in two parts in 1588, Anthony Munday admits that "some (perhaps) will make exceptions against me, that being but one Booke in other languages, I now deuide it twaine"[65]. Unlike *Amadis de Gaule*, which originally contained separate parts, *Palmerín de Olivia* was composed as a unified narrative and initially printed as one volume. Since the French and Italian versions that Munday used for his translation were also published as one volume, he felt compelled to explain the rationale for dividing it up for the English market[66]. It is worth quoting the justification Munday provides, since it is revealing of the type of audience intended for this edition:

> a Booke growing too bigge in quantitie, is profitable neither to the minde nor the pursse: for that men are now so wise, and the world so hard, as they looue not to buie pleasure at vnreasonable price. And yet the first parte will entice them to haue the second, when (it may bee alleaged) the cost is as great, as though it had come altogether: yet I am of the minde, that a man grutcheth not so much at a little mony, payd at seuerall times, as he doth at once. (sig. *3r).

The circumstances that prompted Munday and Charlewood to break up the text were twofold. Munday argued, first, that the romance's considerable length could prove an obstacle "to the minde" of readers accustomed to shorter and less complex narrative works. Second, a copy of the entire work would have to sell for an "vnreasonable" price, which by contrast became acceptable when halved. This form of textual segmentation was applied to Munday's translations of *Palmerin d'Oliva*[67], *Palmerin of England*[68], and *Primaleon of Greece*[69].

---

[65] *STC* 19157, sig. *3r; *exception* here means, "an objection, adverse criticism, complaint", q.v. *Oxford English Dictionary*, 2nd ed., prepared by J.A. Simpson and E.S.C. Weiner, 20 vols., Oxford 1989, n. 6. For information on Munday, see H.C.G. Matthew / B. Harrison (eds.), *Oxford Dictionary of National Biography* (*ODNB*), 60 vols., Oxford 2004, vol. 39, pp. 739–746. On Munday's paratexts, see L. Wilson, *Playful Paratexts: The Front Matter of Anthony Munday's Iberian Romance Translations*, in H. Smith / L. Wilson (eds.), *Renaissance Paratexts*, Cambridge 2011, pp. 121–132.

[66] For the publication of Jean Maugin's French translation, see A. Freer, *"Palmerín de Olivia" in Francia*, in *Studi sul Palmerín de Olivia*, vol. 3: *Saggi e ricerche*, pp. 177–237. For Munday's use of Mambrino Roseo's Italian translation, see G. Galigani, *La versione inglese del "Palmerín de Olivia"*, in *Studi sul Palmerín de Olivia*, vol. 3, pp. 239–288, at pp. 252–254. It seems odd that Munday and his printer John Charlewood decided to justify this arbitrary division the second time they broke up a romance, since previously they had printed *Palmerin of England* in two parts; cf. J. Sánchez-Martí, *The Publication History of Anthony Munday's "Palmerin d'Oliva"*, in "Gutenberg-Jahrbuch", 89, 2014, pp. 190–207, at p. 192. It may be that some readers expressed disagreement with the division of *Palmerin of England*, an edition Munday mentions in this same preface.

[67] This work was printed in 1588 and reprinted in 1597 (*STC* 19158); see J. Sánchez-Martí, *The Publication of "Palmerin d'Oliva"*.

[68] The first edition of ca. 1581 has not survived; it was reprinted in two parts in 1596 (*STC* 19162), and a third one was added in 1602 (*STC* 19165).

[69] The text of *Primaleon* had already been published in three parts by Delicado (see section 3 above), a division that was retained in the French editions; see S. Neri, *Cuadro de la difusión europea del ciclo*

Munday's paratext further enables us to surmise that the English editions of Iberian romances targeted a diverse clientele that was not restricted to the elite, but included other customers of more limited resources that were used to reading relatively short texts[70]. In addition, his paratexts also contain information about the social circles Munday wanted his translations to be associated with. Initially he dedicated them to members of the nobility – such as Edward de Vere, 17th Earl of Oxford, and Robert Devereux, 2nd earl of Essex[71] – and also to figures with great social prestige – such as Sir Francis Drake[72]. When his translations of *Palmerin of England* and *Palmerin d'Oliva* were reprinted by Thomas Creede in 1596/97, however, Munday rewrote his prefaces, replacing all the prominent dedicatees with the unknown Francis Young of Brent Pelham and his wife Susan[73]. This change seems to signal a readjustment by which the social condition of the Iberian romances' "intended audience" resembled that of their "implied audience"[74].

In addition to defining the material presentation of the romances, the English printers and publishers made other choices with consequences for these texts' literary arrangement. When publishing the *Palmerin* romances, they had no qualms about ignoring the narrative sequence of the cycle's constituent parts. The storyline of

---

palmeriniano (siglos XVI–XVII), in *Palmerín y sus libros*, pp. 285–313, at pp. 294–300. A further division was added in England, since the first thirty-two chapters of part 1 were published separately as *Palmendos* (1589, STC 18064; cf. STC 4910); see J. Sánchez-Martí, *The Publication of "Palmerin d'Oliva"*, p. 199, n. 37. The remainder of Primaleon bk. I was published in 1595 (STC 20366), bk. II in 1596 (*STC* 20366a), and bk. III in 1619 (STC 20367); but cf n. 73. The other romances Munday translated were divided prior to his translation, e.g. *Amadis de Gaule* (bk. I, 1590?; STC 541), or alternatively were relatively short, like *Palladine of England* (1588; STC 5541). For an overview of his translations of Iberian romances, see G.R. Hayes, *Anthony Munday's Romances of Chivalry*, in "The Library", 4, 1925, 6, pp. 57–81.

70 H. Hackett, *Women and Romance Fiction in the English Renaissance*, Cambridge 2000, argues that it was "an audience less aristocratic than that addressed by the French translations or by recent original English romances like *Arcadia*" (p. 65); in the case of the French translations, Hackett must be referring to the early folio editions.

71 Munday dedicated *Palladine of England* (1588) to Devereux (d. 1601) and *Palmerin d'Oliva* (1588) to de Vere (d. 1604); for biographical information, see *ODNB*, vol. 15, pp. 945–960, and vol. 56, pp. 286–289, respectively.

72 He dedicated *Palmendos* (1589) to Drake (d. 1596); see *ODNB*, vol. 16, pp. 858–870.

73 See G.R. Hayes, *Munday's Romances of Chivalry*, pp. 63 and 78 f. Note that Young was also the dedicatee of the second book of *Primaleon* (1596) and probably of a now lost edition of bk. III (1596?); see G.R. Hayes, *Anthony Munday's Romances: A Postscript*, in "The Library", 4, 1926, 7, pp. 31–38. For information on Creede, see A. Yamada, *Thomas Creede: Printer to Shakespeare and His Contemporaries*, Tokyo 1994.

74 "Intended audience" refers to the audience for which a literary work has been created or undertaken and in this case can be identified with the dedicatee; "implied audience" refers to the features an author anticipates for his primary or immediate public; cf. P. Strohm, *Chaucer's Audience(s): Fictional, Implied, Intended, Actual*, in "Chaucer Review", 18, 1983, pp. 137–164.

Palmerín de Olivia, first printed in 1511[75], marks the beginning of the cycle and is continued in this romance's sequels, namely, in *Primaleón*, printed in 1512[76], and in *Palmeirim de Inglaterra*, composed by the Portuguese Francisco de Moraes ca. 1543/44[77]. By contrast, the cycle's printed dissemination in England started with the publication, first, of *Palmerin of England* (ca. 1581), followed by *Palmerin d'Oliva* (1588), *Palmendos* (1589), and *Primaleon of Greece*, books I and II (1595/96). In later paratexts, Munday admitted that *Palmerin d'Oliva* "should haue bin translated before this [i.e. *Palmerin of England*]"[78] and wished that, when these two romances were reprinted, "they will come to a iust order"[79].

The decision to change the cycle's original narrative order was not based on aesthetic considerations, but on commercial ones instead. It seems that Charlewood encouraged Munday to use the Englishness of *Palmerin of England*'s hero as a selling point. In the preface to *Palmerin of England*, book II, Munday appealed to his readers' national sentiment when stating that this romance contributed "to the honour of our countrey of England, and [was] deuised by strangers, to honor it the more"; for this reason Munday hoped to "moue you [i.e. his readers] to allow it [i.e. the romance] the better acceptation"[80].

This national appropriation of the hero's adventures for commercial purposes parallels Herberay's stance in his prologue to *Amadis*, book I, where he highlighted the hero's Frenchness and revealed that his translation's purpose was "exalter la Gaule"[81]. If Amadis's identification with France was vital to this cycle's success in French, it seems reasonable that Munday complied with his printer's wish to replicate the same strategy for England. The commercial utilization of the romances' Englishness probably explains the early translation of a minor, non-cyclic work like *Palladine of England* (1588), "which the French haue published in the honor of England"[82], but also resulted in the initial marginalization of *Amadis* in English, of which only books I and II appeared in the sixteenth century.

English printers and publishers made commercially correct decisions that enhanced the saleability and profitability of the *libros de caballerías* in English trans-

---

75 *IB* 16737; see F.J. Norton, *Descriptive Catalogue*, no. 496.
76 *IB* 16740; see F.J. Norton, *Descriptive Catalogue*, no. 500.
77 See W.E. Purser, *Palmerin of England: Some Remarks on this Romance and on the Controversy concerning its Authorship*, Dublin 1904, pp. 105–117.
78 *Palmerin of England*, bk. II (1616), sig. Ff6r.
79 *Palmerin d'Oliva*, bk. I (1615/16), sig. A3r. See J. Sánchez-Martí, "Zelauto"'s Polinarda and the "Palmerin" Romances, in "Cahiers Élisabéthains: A Journal of English Renaissance Studies", 89, 2016, pp. 74–82, at p. 79.
80 *Palmerin of England*, bk. II (1616), sig. Ff6r.
81 M. Bideaux (ed.), *Amadis de Gaule*, bk. I, p. 167: "to exalt Gaul". See J.H.M. Taylor, *Rewriting Arthurian Romance in Renaissance France: From Manuscript to Printed Book* (Gallica, 33), Cambridge 2014, pp. 163–167.
82 *Palladine of England*, sig. Aa4v.

lation, which continued to appear in print throughout the seventeenth century. If, however, we make a quantitative comparison between the editions of individual titles published in England and those published in other countries, it may appear that the English translations failed to achieve a similar degree of popularity. By contrast, if we observe this literary phenomenon as whole, the English editions and reprints of the different romances produce a cumulative effect that is indicative of widespread distribution and collective popularity[83].

6 Conclusions

The Iberian books of chivalry form a literary corpus originally conceived for an upper-class public, to whom the genre's earliest printed instantiations were addressed. The transnational flux of early-modern Europe's book culture encouraged the printed distribution of the genre outside the Iberian Peninsula, first in Italy and next in France[84]. Taking as a model the Spanish editions, at first the French and Italian printers fashioned their publications as exclusive, high-end products. But soon they realized that expanding the social composition of their clientele could also bring them considerable financial gains. Consequently, printers took steps to reduce production costs, thus making their editions of romances affordable to readers of limited means. While in Spain printers chose to cut down on paper by reducing its quality and quantity without sacrificing the romances' conventionalized folio format, in France and Italy they adopted smaller and cheaper formats, such as octavo and sextodecimo. By contrast, English printers, who inherited the codes used for printing medieval chivalric literature, kept the selling price of their editions low mainly by breaking up the original works into smaller bibliographic units. The commercial strategy printers adopted in their efforts to democratize this literary corpus was ultimately determined by the cultural practices of their separate national book markets. Notwithstanding their different decisions, sixteenth-century printers contrived to create a popular market for the once elitist Iberian chivalric romances. During the second half of the sixteenth century the Iberian books of chivalry crossed borders and crossed different book cultures, while printers and publishers took effective measures so that this corpus crossed social divides too, thus achieving printed popularization across Western Europe[85].

---

83 See L. Wilson, *Serial Publication and Romance*, in A. Kesson / E. Smith (eds.), *The Elizabethan Top Ten: Defining Print Popularity in Early Modern England*, Farnham 2013, pp. 213–221.
84 For the creation of a pan-European book market, see A. Pettegree, *The Book in the Renaissance*, New Haven CT 2010, pp. 65–90.
85 Research for this chapter was funded in part by the Spanish Ministry of Economy and Competitiveness (ref. FFI2015–70101–P), whose support is hereby gratefully acknowledged.

Julia Martins
The Afterlife of Italian Secrets: Translating Medical Recipes in Early Modern Europe

I

In 1529, a book called *Opera nuova intitolata Dificio di ricette* (House of recipes), was published in Venice. It was a small, cheaply printed octavo compilation of recipes in Italian, also called "secrets". The *Dificio* contained hundreds of recipes pertaining to everyday domestic life, from simple remedies to cosmetics and veterinary formulas. Recipe compilations were nothing new; they had circulated in Europe in manuscript form since late antiquity. However, the *Dificio di Ricette* was the first printed recipe book that we know of, and it became an instant bestseller. It was reprinted several times in Italy, and it was translated into other vernaculars, becoming particularly successful in France, where it was reprinted until well into the nineteenth century, as part of the "Bibliothèque bleue", a collection of cheaply printed books sold all over the country[1]. Printed books of secrets, therefore, were a genre that originated in Italy, with the publication of the *Dificio di ricette*. However, they quickly became a European phenomenon, since most of these recipe compilations were translated into European vernaculars as well as into Latin.

These books were composed of practical, usually easy, and straightforward recipes, aiming at solving myriad everyday domestic problems. Therefore, "how to treat the plague" coexisted with "how to make a candle burn underwater", "how to make the skin pale", and "how to make the philosopher's stone". Books of secrets can be read as "how-to" books, since their main goal is utilitarian, and the knowledge they offer the reader is of a practical nature[2]. Although they promise to reveal the "secrets of nature", these books are characterized by the "maker's knowledge"; the recipes are said to have been tested and perfected by artisans, medical practitioners, as well as the compilers themselves[3]. The authors of these books, who compiled recipes and diffused this kind of knowledge, became known as "professors of secrets", since they professed their knowledge to the public[4].

---
[1] *Le Bâtiment Des Recettes: Présentation et Annotation de l'édition Jean Ruelle, 1560*, edited by G. Deblock, Rennes 2015.
[2] W. Eamon, *How to Read a Book of Secrets*, in E. Leong / A. Rankin (eds.), *Secrets and Knowledge in Medicine and Science. 1500–1800*, Farnham 2011, p. 35.
[3] A. Perez-Ramos, *Francis Bacon's Idea of Science and the Maker's Knowledge Tradition*, Oxford 1989, pp. 48–62.
[4] The term was first coined in T. Garzoni, *La Piazza Universale di Tutte le Professioni del Mondo*, Venezia, Giovanni Battista Somasco, 1589; see also W. Eamon, *Science and the Secrets of Nature. Books of Secrets in Medieval and Early Modern Culture*, Princeton NJ 1994.

There were two main ways in which early modern Italian books of secrets became a commercial success through the action of printers and translators. The first aspect of this phenomenon is how individual books were adapted to their new readerships through the activity of publishers and translators. In the first section, I will analyze the cases of four translated books of secrets, showing how printers and translators tried to adapt the recipes to their new audience, not only in terms of language, but also in terms of the cultural peculiarities assumed by them. Vernacularization changed the content of books of secrets, as did the opposite process, of rendering vernacular recipes into Latin. These vertical translations (from a language with higher status to one with a lower status, for instance) coexisted with horizontal ones, between two vernaculars. While editorial and translating strategies may vary, the intent of dissemination of knowledge adapted to new readers becomes clear in all of them. The second way in which printers turned books of secrets into a commercial success outside of Italy has to do with assimilating them to other groups of texts that were already widely read. In France, for instance, books of secrets are integrated into the corpus of the *Bibliothèque bleue* books, a bestselling series of cheaply printed books of different genres characterized by their blue cover. In German-speaking areas, on the other hand, translators and printers assimilate books of secrets into the genre of technical manuals (*Kunstbücher*), which included popular distillation and goldsmiths' manuals. By analyzing translated recipes, I intend to show how translation and assimilation reshaped and transformed not only individual recipes, but the genre of books of secrets as a whole, which also had to be "translated" for new audiences.

II

Several books of secrets were translated from Italian into Latin, which allowed them to circulate in different areas, such as Eastern Europe, and made them more attractive to a more sophisticated readership, such as physicians, by increasing their status as "learned books"[5]. The one that seems to have been the most commercially successful, given its frequent reprints, is *Secreti del Reverendo Donno Alessio Piemontese* (Secrets of Don Alessio Piemontese) a traveler who allegedly had spent 57 years compiling recipes from all origins, and the most popular of the "professors of secrets"[6]. Originally published in Italian in Venice in 1555, it was printed in Latin in Basel in 1560, reprinted in Antwerp that same year, and printed again in Basel in 1561, 1563,

---

5 P. Burke, *Cultures of Translation in Early Modern Europe*, in P. Burke / R. Po-chia Hsia (eds.), *Cultural Translation in Early Modern Europe*, Cambridge 2007, pp. 7–38.
6 Alessio Piemontese is currently thought to be a pseudonym, an idea already signaled by J. Ferguson, *Bibliographical Notes on Histories of Inventions and Books of Secrets*, 2 vols., London 1959; J. Ferguson, *The Secrets of Alexis: A Sixteenth Century Collection of Medical and Technical Receipts*, in "Journal of the Royal Society of Medecine", 1978.

1568, and 1603[7]. It was translated by Johann Jacob Wecker (1528–1586), a Swiss physician who had written several works on medicine and alchemy published in French, German, and Latin. He is responsible for the German translation of Alessio Piemontese's secrets as well, which was also published in Basel[8]. It was not rare for the same translator to produce two translations; besides Wecker's German and Latin versions of *Alessio*, Christophe Plantin also published two versions of the Piemontese's secrets, translated into French and Dutch. Wecker's Latin translation had several changes with respect to the original. The Latin version of the secrets was more sophisticated and complex, including structural changes as well as vocabulary. Furthermore, it was printed along with other Latin compilations of recipes aimed at a more educated readership than the original. A new version of the book, printed in Basel in 1563, combined the 1560 Latin translation with two compilations of secrets written by the translator himself[9]. It was common for translators of medical recipes, usually medical practitioners themselves, to have their recipes added to their translations, as it also happened with John Hester's translation of the Bolognese empiric Leonardo Fioravanti, another famous "professor of secrets"[10]. By looking closely at some translated books of secrets, it is possible to see how printers and translators transformed recipe literature and adapted it to the audience they expected would be interested in these books, their "readers", following different editorial strategies.

In his Latin translation, Wecker tells the reader how the work is structured, and how the recipes are useful for everyday life. Wecker's Latin translation is mindful of the original text. However, the printer transformed the dedication, as well as the format of the book, such as the pagination, the table of contents (it becomes alphabetical instead of organized thematically); it is also stated that the extra compilations had been added for the reader's benefit. The main modification in the Latin version of the text, however, is how it is organized. For instance, in the Latin text, there is a list of the ingredients to be employed as well as their quantities after each recipe, like in a modern cookbook. This is an important change compared to vernacular books of

---

7 A. Piemontese, *Secreti Del Reverendo Donno Alessio Piemontese*, Venice, Sigismondo Bordogna, 1555; A. Piemontese, *De Secretis Libri, Miraquadam Rerum Varietate Utilitateq; Referti; Longe Castigatiores et Ampliores Quam Priore Editione*, Basel 1560; A. Piemontese, *De Secretis Libri Sex Mira Quadam Rerum Varietate Referti Ex Italico in Latinum Sermonem Nunc Primum Translati*, Antwerp, Ioannis Latij, 1560.
8 A. Piemontese, *Kunstbuch Des Wolerfarnen Herren Alexii Pedemontani, von Mancherleyen Nutzlichen Unnd Bewerten Secreten Oder Künsten, Jetzt Newlich Auß Welscher Und Lateinischer Sprach in Teutsch Gebracht, Durch Doctor Hanß Jacob Wecker*, Basel, König, 1616.
9 A. Piemontese, *De Secretis Libri Septem, a Ioan Iacobo Veckero Doctore Medico, Ex Italico Sermone in Latinum Conversi, & Multis Bonis Secretis Aucti. Accessit Hae Editione Eiusdem Weckeri Opera, Octavus de Artificiosis Vinis Liber*, Basel, Petrum Pernam, 1563.
10 L. Fioravanti, *A Short Discours of the Excellent Doctour and Knight, Maister Leonardo Phioravanti Bolognese upon Chirurgerie. With a Declaration of Many Things, Necessarie to Be Knowne, Never Written before in This Order: Wherunto Is Added a Number of Notable Secrets*, London, Thomas East, 1580.

secrets, which rarely contain ingredient lists and quantities are not often mentioned. It is usually assumed the reader will be familiar with the herbs and other ingredients and therefore know how much to use. It is also possible, however, that in vernacular books the readership is thought to be less sophisticated, and therefore less rigorous with quantities in a recipe.

These are small modifications, but it seems the publisher (or maybe the translator himself) imagined a more attentive reader for the Latin version, whose reading was thought to be more thorough and sophisticated. It might have also been expected that these readers were more likely to put the recipes into practice, since the description of the recipes is more detailed, more precise, and "didactic". However, in the Latin version that was reprinted more often, the table of contents is still organized thematically, not adopting the alphabetical order used in other Latin texts, such as the collection of secrets compiled by Giambattista Della Porta, a Neapolitan intellectual who founded his own "academy of secrets" to test recipes[11]. This could indicate that, although Wecker's imagined readers might be more sophisticated than vernacular readers, they would still be used to a thematic organization of knowledge[12]. Although there are no drastic modifications in this translation from Italian into Latin, the adaptations indicate that the imagined new readers would be more learned, read the text more attentively, and arguably put the recipes into practice more than their vernacular counterparts. Since the two versions are both in octavo and cheaply printed, and contain no woodcuts let alone metal engravings, it does not seem to have been anticipated that the Latin version would necessarily be purchased by wealthier readers, though that might sometimes have been the case. Rather, it seems the new reader is merely more instructed than the vernacular audience. Finally, the addition of the new recipes, especially those by the translator himself, indicates a wish to mutually legitimize the authority of the "professor of secrets" as well as that of his translator in their medical and linguistic expertise, while adding a new element to an already well-known book, therefore "updating" it, and maybe rendering it desirable even for people who posessed had the original vernacular version.

The opposite phenomenon, translations from Latin into the vernacular, can be observed with secrets published in Latin and translated into Italian. While Alessio Piemontese's reader is expected to be more educated, the Neapolitain Giambattista Della Porta's imagined vernacular reader is less sophisticated than the original readership of the Latin book. However, the main interest of this case concerns the "omissions". When Della Porta's collection of recipes is translated from Latin into Italian, many recipes are suppressed from the translation, and the, keeping them indeed

---

[11] L. Balbiani, *La Magia Naturalis Di Giovan Battista Della Porta: Lingua, Cultura e Scienza in Europa all'inizio dell'età Moderna*, Milano 1999.

[12] For the different ways of classifying knowledge in tables of contents, see A.M. Blair, *Too Much to Know: Managing Scholarly Information before the Modern Age*, New Haven CT / London 2010.

"secret": so as not to allow people to do "evil deeds", recipes concerning poisons or abortifacients are suppressed, for instance. Giambattista Della Porta's went through a double process of diffusion in both its original Latin and in the vernacular languages it was translated into, such as Italian[13]. The first Latin edition was published in 1558, and its Italian translation, in 1560. It comprised four books and was reprinted seventeen times in Italy, Germany, France, and the Netherlands. In 1589, however, a second Latin edition was published, more than doubling the secrets contained in the original version and composed of twenty books[14]. From 1558 to 1700, the Latin editions were reprinted twenty-four times, six of which following the amplified version after its publication in 1589. The 1560 Italian translation published by Ludovico Avanzi was published ten times until 1612, when the first German translation is published, meaning that it continued to be commercially successful even after the 1589 publication of the second Latin edition of the *Magia Naturalis*, which contained twenty books instead of the original four. To the twenty-six early modern Latin versions twenty Italian editions/reprints were added, as well as thirteen French ones, two English ones, as well as one German and one Dutch version[15]. Confronting these editions, there are almost no modifications in the text, even though printers add their own frontispieces and dedicate the text to different people, besides sometimes altering the pagination and the typographic style. In the 1560 Italian translation, however, there are considerable changes. While speaking of the fidelity of a translation is a dated approach, it is worth stressing how very distant this Italian translation is from the original text, much more than the usual modifications we find in translated recipes[16]. Indeed, the translator "purified" the book of all polemic recipes, in some instances even explaining to the reader why he had decided to do so.

The *Magia Naturalis* was originally addressed to an educated readership; however, thanks to its translations, it reached a wide and diversified audience. The Italian translation of 1560, published in Venice by the printer Ludovico Avanzi[17], is one of the most striking cases of how books of secrets were altered in the translation process because of the new readership they addressed, going beyond the usual adaptations to new readers. The identity of the translator, unfortunately, is still unknown. The possibility that Della Porta himself would be responsible for the translation has been suggested, but the many mistakes due to the translator's incomprehension render that hypothesis very unlikely[18]. Indeed, the unknown translator seems to

---
13 G. Della Porta, *Magiae Naturalis, Siue de Miraculis Rerum Naturalium*, Napoli, Matthias Cancer, 1558.
14 *Ibid.*; *Magia naturalis*, Napoli, Horatium Saluianum, 1589.
15 L. Balbiani, *La Magia Naturalis di Giovan Battista Della Porta. Lingua, Cultura e Scienza in Europa all'inizio dell'Età Moderna*, Milano 1999.
16 L. Venuti, *The Translator's Invisibility: A History of Translation*, London 2008.
17 Ludovico Avanzi was personally interested in books of secrets, and published Leonardo Fioravanti's *Secreti Medicinali* and *Capricci Medicinali* in 1561 and 1565, respectively.
18 G. Gabriele, *Contributi Alla Storia dell'Accademia Dei Lincei*, vol. 1, Roma 1989, p. 705.

have had a mediocre understanding of Latin as well as of natural magic and medicine, since some of the recipes are rendered virtually nonsensical in Italian. Together with the printer, however, the translator changed the original text in many respects. For instance, a new table of contents was added to the alphabetical one, organized according to the order of appearance of the recipes in the book, indicating a concern that the book would be easy to consult by readers familiar with different forms of classification[19].

Furthermore, the long chapters, such as the ones in the second book, were divided into shorter sections, as often happened when Latin works were translated into the vernacular. Again, it seems the reader imagined by the printer and the translator would be more comfortable with shorter texts, maybe reading the chapters in small portions at a time. However, the most significant modifications are the omissions of recipes, which were considered by the translator to be "dangerous" or "immoral". In the second book of the *Magia*, for instance, several recipes are suppressed without any explanation being offered to the reader. This happens to chapter 15 (23 in the Italian version), in which the recipes concerning the female body disappear, such as "How to restore virginity to a woman who may have lost it"[20]. In the following chapter, the entire first Latin part is missing, which contained recipes for enhancing the female libido, as well as some abortifacient recipes. The following section, on "How to diminish women's luxurious appetites", however, is still present in the translation. Other important omissions include chapter 19 of the Latin edition (28 of the Italian one) about poisons. While the recipes concerning the female body had been utterly suppressed with no explanation, in this case the translator tells the reader why he chose not to include them. The translator states that a recipe such as "How to turn a man into a leper" "should not be written, since evil people could take it and do evil deeds". All recipes threatening human life are therefore suppressed; this is the case of poisons as well as the emmenagogue and abortifacient recipes, amounting to several pages from the original text being omitted[21].

Another significant omission in this translation has to do with hallucinogenic plants, such as the "ointment of witches", the most famous and polemic of Della Porta's secrets. In this case, the translator also explains to the reader how he knowingly omitted this recipe in order not to stimulate the curiosity of people who could do evil:

> It is from that [recipe] that are born the ointments made by witches, in which they add many superstitions, and which have the effect of making it seem as though they fly by the air and have dreams, as well as hear singing and see beautiful youths thanks to their natural virtue. But, so

---

19 A.M. Moss, *Too Much to Know: Managing Scholarly Information before the Modern Age*, New Haven CT 2010.
20 G. Della Porta, *Magia Naturale*, Venezia, Ludovico Avanzi, 1560.
21 *Ibid.*

as not to entice the curiosity of impious people who can do evil, we shall stay silent on these compositions which can also be used by evil women, instigated by the devil and who can follow their impulses[22].

This recipe, which was at the origin of the problems Della Porta had with the Inquisition, is therefore omitted from the translation[23]. Maybe publishing it in Latin was "safer", since fewer people would have access to it, and therefore it would be less dangerous than the vernacular version. We can say that the Italian text was "purified" of everything immoral and heterodox that might shock the reader: recipes about the female body, about "dark magic", and about ways to harm others, be it to make people ill, to poison them, or to abort unborn babies, meaning things that would oppose Catholic doctrine. It is possible to suppose that the ecclesiastical control might have been more important in Italy than in other places, since the German translation of the *Magia*, published in 1612 in Magdeburg, contains the original text in its entirety. In this case, the identity of the translator is also unknown; he is referred to only as a "besondern Liebhaber der Philosophiae", someone especially fond of philosophy. We should be wary, though, to equate Protestant regions with more freedom to publish this kind of recipes. It is more likely that, because Della Porta had already had problems with the Roman Inquisition, a book by him might have made the Italian translator more careful. The translator and the printer, therefore, would protect themselves by "purging" the book of any problematic recipes[24].

The third example of how books of secrets were adapted concerns an Italian book of secrets and the untranslatability of some recipes into English. The *Secrets* of Leonardo Fioravanti, a Bolognese empiric practitioner often denounced as a charlatan, were published several times in England, along with other compilations of recipes[25]. He had written about surgery, his own life, and many medical recipes, which had been very successful. While he did not hold a medical degree until well into his fifties, Fioravanti presented himself as a "doctor in surgery and medicine", and argued how it was only through experience that one could unveil the secrets of nature, mocking

---

22 "Di qua nasce l'origine di quelli unguenti i qualli fanno le streghe, nelle quali benche vi mettino molte, superstitioni, nondimeno fanno quegli effetti di fargli parere esser portate, per aria, et sentire suoni, canti, giovani bellissimi per virtu di cose naturali; ma per non fomentare la curiosità degli huomini, et de gli empij, che adoperarebbono queste cose in mala parte, taceremo quelle compositioni, che simili malvagie feminele, instigate dal demonio et da sfrenate voglie adoperano", in G. Della Porta, *Magia Naturale*.
23 M. Valente, *Della Porta e l'Inquisizione. Nuovo documenti dell'Archivio del Sant'Uffizio*, in "Bruniana & Campanelliana", 5, 1999, pp. 415–435.
24 About vernacular translations and censorship, see S. Munari, *Translation, Re-Writing and Censorship during the Counter-Reformation*, in J.M. Pérez Fernández / E. Wilson-Lee (eds.), *Translation and the Book Trade in Early Modern Europe*, Cambridge 2014, pp. 185–200.
25 L. Fioravanti, *A Treatise of Chirurgery Published with Many Excellent Experiments and Secrets*, London, Thomas Wight, 1652.

the Galenic university physicians who gave too much importance to book-learning[26]. However, the most intriguing aspect of this translation are the "untranslatable" words and how the English version dealt with them. Even though Fioravanti was less famous than Alessio, the most well-known professor of secrets at the time, he was also a very well-known author[27]. He had written several books about surgery, medicinal recipes, and even about his own life, most of which had been translated. As Alessio with Johan Jacob Wecker, Fioravanti's secrets also found a translator interested in medicine and the "secrets of nature", the apothecary and distiller John Hester (d. 1592), who had also published on natural philosophy and medicine[28].

A Treatise of Chirurgery Published with Many Excellent Experiments and Secrets, printed in London in 1652, was published together with the *Phioravants Secrets* as well as the *Chyrurgery*, other works by him already successful in Italy, and *The Iewell of Practice*, a work by John Hester[29]. In a letter to the reader that served as an introduction, Hester explains how he decided to publish these works again, since they "had been sold out and people could not find them". It is unclear whether he meant the Italian or English markets, since I could not find an English edition prior to his own. He tells how "ingenious practitioners in physic" were longing for it, especially those of the interested in the chemical "arcana". Once again, an Italian book of secrets is compiled with other similar works of the genre, including one by the translator himself, as it happened in Alessio's case and the translation made by Wecker. Not only were these books associated because of their subject, but it was also a way to publish works by the translator associating his name to a famous "professor of secrets" as well as legitimizing the translation, showing how the translator is an expert in the same matters as the author of the book he translated.

Furthermore in Fioravanti's case, the secrets seem to be addressed to a specialized readership, students of medicine, and members of the College of Physicians, which was not usually the case with Italian books of secrets, aimed at a wide readership. While that may reveal this translation as "less popular", it is still characterized by a discourse aimed at a general audience, and the materiality of the book is consistent with the style books of secrets usually had, such as low quality paper and small format, characterizing it as "cheap print"[30]. Books of secrets were indeed a fluid

---

26 L. Fioravanti, *Il Tesoro Della Vita Humana, Dell'Eccell. Dottore & Cavaliere M. Leonardo Fioravanti Bolognese*, Venezia, Heredi di *Melchior Sessa*, 1570.
27 P. Camporesi, *Camminare il Mondo: Vita e Avventure di Leonardo Fioravanti Medico del Cinquecento*, Milano 2007.
28 J. Hester, *The First Part of the Key of Philosophie*, London, Richard Day, 1580.
29 For a more comprehensive study of John Hester's translations of Leonardo Fioravanti, see I. Pantin, *John Hester's Translations of Leonardo Fioravanti: The Literary Career of a London Distiller*, in A. Pettegree / S.K. Barker / B.M. Hosington (eds.), *Renaissance Cultural Crossroads: Translation, Print and Culture in Britain, 1473–1640*, Leiden / Boston MA 2013, pp. 159–183.
30 About the classification of books of secrets and recipe compilations in general as "popular print", see R. Mandrou, *De La Culture Populaire Aux 17e et 18e Siècles. La Bibliothèque Bleue de Troyes*,

genre, being produced, sold, and read mostly – but not exclusively – by urban middle classes[31]. The line between "elite" and "popular" readers, however, was often blurred where books of secrets were concerned, reminding us that the levels of literacy varied more than these binaries suggest, and that "learned" readers and less sophisticated readers often had access to the same materials[32].

In the translations from Italian into English, as in Fioravanti's case, the complexity of the genre of secrets can easily be perceived. The problem of "untranslatable words", such as Italian expressions with no English equivalent or unknown to the translator, was a frequent one. Several herbs and even some diseases and symptoms fall into that category. In John Hester's case, as most other early modern translators, he tends to keep the unknown expressions in their original Italian, in Romanic characters to differ them from the main text in gothic type. In a recipe about *pellarella* (the modern pellagra) this can easily be seen. Even the title keeps the illness in its original Italian: *Of Pellarella that causeth the hair to fall off*. Furthermore, the translator keeps key elements of the recipe in Italian, such as the symptoms, *carvoli* or sores, typical of the illness, as well as the treatment (*olio magistrale* among others). The names of the medicines suggested to treat the ailment are in Italian, and the recipes to produce them at home are contained in different works by Fioravanti, not published in England, or printed separately. Indeed, this translation by Hester does not correspond to a version of a single book by Fioravanti, consisting indeed of a compilation of extracts made by the translator.

In the Italian context, however, the reader would have had easy access to these formulas and would also have had the possibility of buying some of them directly at Venetian pharmacies[33]. We can question whether an English reader would have been able to use a recipe like that. The illness is in Italian, making it hard for the readers to identify it, symptoms and treatments are also presented in Italian and virtually unavailable to them, since the books in which their formulas appear were not available in England, and it is highly unlikely that English pharmacists would have Fioravanti's remedies on stock. However, these recipes could be of value to English readers in other ways, such as part of a collection, having an "encyclopedic" function, legiti-

---

Paris 1999; L. Andries / G. Bollème, *La Bibliothèque Bleue: Littérature de Colportage*, Paris 2003; W. Eamon, *Science and the Secrets of Nature: Books of Secrets in Medieval and Early Modern Culture*, Princeton NJ 1994. For a criticism of the assimilation of the genre into "popular culture", see R. Chartier, *Culture as Appropriation: Popular Cultural Uses in Early Modern France*, in S.L. Kaplan, *Understanding Popular Culture: Europe from the Middle Ages to the Nineteenth Century*, Berlin 1984, pp. 229–253. While the concept of "popular" has been problematized, however, recipe books are still usually treated as "popular print", especially due to their cheap nature, such as in R. Chartier, *France and Spain*, in J. Raymond (ed.), *The Oxford History of Popular Print Culture: Cheap Print in Britain and Ireland to 1660*, vol. 1, Oxford 2011, pp. 175–186.

31 A. Kavey, *Books of Secrets: Natural Philosophy in England, 1550–1600*, Chicago IL 2007.
32 A. Wear, *Knowledge and Practice in English Medicine, 1550–1680*, Cambridge 2000.
33 W. Eamon, *Science and the Secrets of Nature*.

mizing the other recipes the reader might use. In that case, it would not be a problem if the reader was not able to follow one particular recipe, as it would serve to enhance the status of the collection as a whole even if it could not be used. Books of secrets could have served as a kit of "tools" for the reader to choose from and create his or her own experiments, as suggested by David Gentilcore recently[34]. The new ways a recipe could be used is another result of the translation process, since translators resignify the recipes and add new meanings to books of secrets.

While some translations are poorly done, others achieve a high status in early modern Europe, when the translator and/or the printing workshop are respected. It was the case of Christophe Plantin's French translation of Alessio Piemontese's secrets, published in Antwerp[35]. Although the translator is not named (it could even be Christophe Plantin himself), this translation was highly regarded by contemporaries, which can be seen by the notes other printers added when they published this version, stating its worth, since it came from Plantin's workshop. Plantin was known as a respectable and successful publisher of Latin, French, and Dutch works (and he was also responsible for the Dutch version of Alessio's secrets)[36]. In any case, this edition was considered of such quality that when the *Secrets* were translated in England, the printer chose to have them translated from the French version instead of the original Italian one, creating one of the rare cases of indirect translations of books of secrets.

Although indirect translations are not an unusual phenomenon in early modern Europe, this is one of the few cases I have found of books of secrets being translated from another translation. It seems that, because of the very positive reputation Plantin and his workshop had, the English printer decided to associate his name to the famous Belgian printer, lending further authority to Alessio's book[37]. Of course, it could also have been a choice motivated by the abilities of translators available, who might have known more French than Italian. As with books from other genres, sometimes indirect translations were the only way to reprint a book whose success was highly likely, such as the *Secrets* of Alessio. Not having access to the Italian original or to the Latin translation (or not having someone who could translate those languages),

---

[34] D. Gentilcore, *Food and Health in Early Modern Europe. Diet, Medicine and Society, 1450–1800*, London 2015.

[35] A. Piemontese, *Les Secrets du Seigneur Alexis Piemontois*, Antwerpen, Christophe Plantin, 1557; H.-J. Martin, *Christophe Plantin à Anvers (Annexe)*, in R. Chartier / H.-J. Martin (eds.), *Histoire de l'édition Française*, Paris 1989, pp. 404–435.

[36] Christophe Plantin had obtained privileges for both translations, indicating he was confident of their commercial success. A. Piemontese, *De Secreten van Den Eerweerdigen Heere Alexis Piemontois: Inhoudende Seer Excellente Ende Wel Gheapproboeerde Remedien, Teghen Veel-Derhande Cranckheden, Wonden, Ende Andere Accidenten: Met de Maniere van Te Distilleren, Perfumeren*, Antwerpen, Christophe Plantin, 1561; W. Eamon, *Science and the Secrets of Nature*, p. 139.

[37] See Chapter 1: "Christophe Plantin, a Prince of Printers", in L. Voet, *The Golden Compasses: The History of the House of Plantin-Moretus*, London 1969, pp. 3–135.

and maybe wanting to associate his name as well as Alessio's to the Plantin workshop, the English printer Thomas Wight decided to publish this book as a translation of the acclaimed French version. Indeed, the English translator, the famous physician William Ward (1534–1609), also lent further prestige to the work.

In terms of the work itself, there are very little changes in the recipes. The English translation closely reproduces the French one, which was already quite faithful to the Italian original. However, if the text does not change much, the printer's typographic character choices can tell us something about the universe of secrets. Most of the text is printed using gothic characters, which also happens when books of secrets are translated into German, but the printer is careful about keeping everything "continental" or foreign in Roman type. Citations in Latin are always in these characters, as we would use italics today. Whenever continental cities are mentioned (Antwerp, Athens, Rome), or when the name of someone who is not British is mentioned, such as Christophe Plantin and Alessio himself, Thomas Wight uses Roman type. This strategy used by Wight, as well as other printers at the time, may have marked a certain distance between the world of the reader and the mysterious universe from which the secrets of Alessio came[38]. In this sense, the use of these characters is comparable to our use of italics to mark words from other languages in a text. The "foreignness" of Alessio's secrets is introduced to the reader in a text published in the vernacular and in characters the reader would have recognized; however, the distance between the two worlds is marked by the simple choice of which typographic characters to use in which sections of the book. It could even be a way for the mysterious aura around the name of Alessio to be enhanced.

There was no general idea of the inferiority of indirect translations compared to direct ones in early modern Europe, as there is today. This is demonstrated by the fact that in the title itself it is stated that it is a translation of the French version of the Italian text. This translation is also typical of the period due to the addition of new recipes to the original compilation, and the few corrections made to the text are announced to the reader as positive changes. In fact, in the dedication to Lord Francis Russell of Bedford, a counsellor to Queen Elizabeth I, the worth of the translation is underscored, since it had been made from Christophe Plantin's version, a great printer as well as an important intellectual. Besides emphasizing the traditional qualities of books of secrets (how useful they were to all readers, how morally correct it was to share knowledge with the "people"), the dedication to Lord Russel tells the reader how it is important to disseminate these secrets in people's "natural tongue", since even the less instructed have a natural desire to know and learn. Thanks to this translation, they can do it, since the knowledge is now in their vernacular:

---

[38] About the evolution of gothic and romanic types as well as their use, see S.H. Steinberg, *Five Hundred Years of Printing*, Middlesex 1979.

> I have taken in hand to translate this noble and excellent worke called The secrets of the reverend father Maister *Alexis of Piemont*, first written in the Italian tongue, and after turned into French, and of date into Dutch and now last of all into English, because that as well English men, as Italians, French man or Dutch man, may lucke knowledge and profite heereof, being a worke come out of the hands of so famous a man as *Alexis* is[39].

The translation and diffusion of Italian books of secrets had a clear commercial aim. However, printers and translators seem to have had a perception that their work was for the "common good", and that their translation activity was necessary not only to render the text legible to new readers, but to adapt it in ways these new readers might find useful, which makes us remember how "domestication" (bringing the text to the reader's universe) and "foreignization" (taking the reader to the text's world) are often too narrow models for the historian[40]. There were several strategies that printers and translators could use in the process, to render a book more appealing to a new readership, but the translations were not immune to serious problems, such as untranslatable words or some translators' will to "purify" the recipes from immoral aspects. On the other hand, it is also possible that the words kept in the original language might contribute to create a certain mystery about the book and its "secrets". Regardless of these alterations, it is important to stress how modifications were often presented as neutral, if not positive, and were not generally considered to diminish the value of the book nor to change its "spirit"; keeping the ethos of the original text was something translators were particularly careful to do, while enhancing their own status and legitimizing the "professors of secrets" in the process.

III

Books of secrets became a pan-European phenomenon in the sixteenth century thanks to translation. While in the previous section I aimed to show how individual books were adapted to their new readers, in this section I analyze two strategies to translate books of secrets as a genre, by a clever "rebranding" of the genre to associate it to other texts, which were already best-selling in the areas where printers expected to sell books of secrets. Books of secrets continued to be printed until well

---

[39] W. Ward, *To the Right Honorable Francis, Lord Russel Earl of Bedford One of the Queenes Maiesties Privy Counsell, and Knight of the Most Honorable Order of the Garter*, in The Secrets of the Reverend Maister Alexis of Piemont Containing Excellent Remedies against Diverse Diseases, Wounds, and Other Accidents, with the Maner to Make Distillations, Parfumes, Confitures, Dying, Colours, Fusions, and Meltings, Newly Corrected, London, John Kingstone for Nicolas Inglande, 1558.

[40] W. Boutcher, *From Cultural Translation to Cultures of Translation? Early Modern Readers, Sellers and Patrons*, in T. Demetriou / R. Tomlinson (eds.), The Culture of Translation in Early Modern England and France (1500–1660), Basingstoke 2015, pp. 22–40; L. Venuti, *The Translator's Invisibility*.

into the nineteenth century partly because of these strategies, continuing to have a wide readership after their original success in the sixteenth century[41]. In this section, I discuss these commercial strategies by examining how books of secrets were sold in French and German areas.

At the beginning of the seventeenth century, the Oudot family, printers from Troyes, began to publish several titles of books aimed at a broad readership[42]. Almanacs, hagiographic poems, ballads, and recipe books were printed on cheap paper and in octavo format, and often sold by itinerant peddlers in the countryside as well as in the towns. These books were all in the vernacular, and although some of them had a French origin, many of them were French translations of Italian books, like *Dificio di ricette*. These books were read by a varied readership in terms of literacy, social class, and gender; the ways of reading were also not uniform, as Roger Chartier reminds us about individual silent reading and the more common collective reading aloud[43]. Therefore, we need to be careful with too sharp oppositions between elite and popular readers, people who could and could not read, regional ways of speaking and the standard Tuscan or French from Île-de-France, cities and countryside, expensive and cheap books[44].

Without entering too deeply into this debate, I want to emphasize the importance of Italian books of secrets having been inserted into the *Bibliothèque bleue* to their continued success, regardless of their content having only been slightly modified and further compilations of recipes having been added. From the sixteenth to the nineteenth century, the books from the *Bibliothèque bleue* circulated in virtually all of France[45]. From Troyes, where they were published, they were sent to other important cities, such as Lyon, Rouen, and Paris, and sold in the countryside by itinerant peddlers. They were also traded at fairs, such as the Champagne fair. Although many Italian books of secrets were translated and sold outside the *Bibliothèque bleue* corpus, becoming successful on their own, the insertion of translated books of secrets into the *Bibliothèque bleue* allowed them to profit from an already existing network of printers, bookshops, and peddlers, and the translations of Italian books of secrets became an important part of the books that composed the *Bibliothèque bleue*. Thanks to their blue cover, they were sold virtually everywhere, from the large metropolitan

---

[41] R. Mandrou, *De la Culture Populaire*.
[42] L. Morin, *Les Oudot: Imprimeurs et Libraires à Troyes, à Paris, à Sens et à Tours Bulletin Du Bibliophile*, Bulletin Du Bibliophile, Paris 1901; A. Assier, *La Bibliothèque Bleue Depuis Jean Oudot 1er Jusqu'à M. Baudot 1600–1863*, Paris, Champion, 1874.
[43] R. Chartier, *Loisir et Sociabilité: Lire à Haute Voix Dans l'Europe Moderne*, in "Littératures Classiques", 12, 1980, pp. 127–147.
[44] R. Chartier, *Culture as Appropriation: Popular Cultural Uses in Early Modern France*, in S.L. Kaplan (ed.), *Understanding Popular Culture: Europe from the Middle Ages to the 19th Century*, New York 1984, pp. 229–253; R. Chartier, *Lectures et Lecteurs dans la France d'Ancien Régime*, Paris 1987.
[45] L. Fontaine, *Histoire du Colportage en Europe: XVe–XIXe Siècle*, Paris 1993.

areas to the small countryside villages, where "colporteurs" sold them[46]. Of course, we could also argue that books of secrets were partly responsible for the editorial success of the *Bibliothèque bleue*, since their popularity in Italy attests how avid readers were to gain access to the "secrets of nature". Indeed, books of secrets were an important part of the *Bibliothèque bleue*, and, as Robert Mandrou and other scholars have shown, bestsellers within the corpus[47]. Since books of secrets had become successful in Italy, printers from other countries started seeing them as potential bestsellers when translated. In the French case, these books were translated and published in two ways: as single recipe compilations and as part of the *Bibliothèque bleue* corpus, following different editorial strategies[48]. As a part of the Bibliothèque, they attained a broader circulation and became even more successful in France. Not only were books of secrets associated with an already best-selling group of texts, but their circulation was facilitated by the structure of distribution of the *Bibliothèque bleue*.

The second example of the "rebranding" of Italian secrets concerns their German translations. In German-speacking areas, from Basel to Frankfurt and Hamburg, books of secrets also became bestsellers. While in France they were not associated to a specific genre, but to the heterogenic corpus of the *Bibliothèque bleue*, when books of secrets were translated into German, they were connected to technical manuals. For instance, in German Alessio Piemontese's secrets are usually entitled *Book of the art (Kunstbuch) of the Experienced Mr. Alexis Piedmontese, about Many Useful and Valuable Secrets or Arts*[49]. This is often also the way in which these books were translated into English, suggesting again a link to technical manuals[50]. *Kunstbücher* (books of the arts) were a genre of technical manuals containing domestic recipes as well as complex technical procedures, such as distillation[51]. While in Italy "secrets" were usually understood as a synonym of "recipes", in German-speaking areas as well as in England, "secrets" became synonymous with "arts".

Although we should be careful not to assimilate different genres, at the same time it is important to keep in mind that books of secrets were translated as books of

---

46 P. Brochon, *Le Livre de Colportage en France depuis le XVIe Siècle: Sa Littérature, Ses Lecteurs*, Paris 1954.
47 Although works of piety were the most successful books of the collection, recipe books were the most reprinted ones after the religious genre, p. 45.
48 R. Chartier, *Stratégies Éditoriales et Lectures Populaires, 1530–1660*, in R. Chartier / H.-J. Martin (eds.), *Histoire de l'édition Française*, vol. 1: *Le Livre Conquérant, Du Moyen Age au Milieu du XVIIe Siècle*, Paris 1989, pp. 698–721.
49 A. Piemontese, *Kunstbuch Des Wolerfarnen Herren Alexii Pedemontani, von Mancherleyen Nutzlichen Unnd Bewerten Secreten Oder Künsten, Jetzt Newlich Auß Welscher Und Lateinischer Sprach in Teutsch Gebracht, Durch Doctor Hanß Jacob Wecker*.
50 L. Kassell, *Secrets Revealed: Alchemical Books in Early Modern England*, in "History of Science", 2011, pp. 61–87.
51 P.H. Smith, *What Is a Secret? Secrets and Craft Knowledge in Early Modern Europe*, in E. Leong / A. Rankin (eds.), *Secrets and Knowledge in Medicine and Science 1500–1800*, Farnham 2011, pp. 47–66.

the arts for a reason, since not only are texts translated, but also genres as a whole. Associating them with technical manuals, with which readers were already familiar, helped to introduce them into a new market. Printers had a commercial interest in books of secrets, and therefore tried to find strategies to sell as many copies as possible. In Germanic areas, a possible strategy does not concern a specific corpus of texts, as in the French case, but rather a genre of books. Assimilating secrets into the manuals tradition helped the genre of secrets to become successful in German and English-speaking areas, where there was already a readership interested in recipes from different crafts. Secrets and arts became intimately connected, and the genre of books of secrets became almost a sub-category of *Kunstbücher*[52]. As in the French case, where books of secrets fitted well with other utilitarian texts present in the *Bibliothèque bleue*, the association between books of secrets and technical manuals was a clever editorial strategy. Books of secrets, as *Kunstbücher*, had a utilitarian goal. Both addressed everyday domestic problems and contained practical "how-to" knowledge. Readers already familiar with technical manuals would be more open to new translations from Italy if they saw these books as a part of a tradition such as books of the arts.

In both these cases, it is important to stress the role of the publishers and their editorial work in the modern sense. Both these strategies were clever ways of adapting Italian books to their new French or German-speaking readerships and to the books they were already used to reading[53]. Where books of secrets are concerned, be they transformed into *Kunstbücher* or integrated into the *Bibliothèque bleue* corpus, they still follow a similar editorial formula. From a material point of view, these were books printed in small format, usually in octavo, on cheap and low-quality paper, often with the blue cover characteristic of the *Bibliothèque bleue*, containing few illustrations (although there are some woodcuts on the frontispiece and showing the ovens and vessels appropriate to particular recipes). Furthermore, they are usually in the vernacular, and, since they are cheaply printed, there are often mistakes in pagination and the table of contents. The distribution of these books in the countryside was dependent on itinerant peddlers, who also sold their books in the cities, along with the bookshops and printers workshops. Because they were not expensive, books of secrets were sold in great quantities[54]. These characteristics, which were typical of Italian books of secrets, remain valid for most of the translations, although there are some exceptions. Books of secrets were, however, "rebranded" with the blue cover, which indicated to their reader a fun or useful book, or with the label of "art" and all the success craft tradition had in German-speaking areas.

---

52 P.O. Long, *Openness, Secrecy, Authorship: Technical Arts and the Culture of Knowledge from Antiquity to the Renaissance*, Baltimore MD 2001.
53 P. Burke, *Languages and Communities in Early Modern Europe*, Cambridge 2004.
54 About a comparison of books of secrets' prices, see A. Kavey, *Books of Secrets*.

Printers and translators, if they did not substantially change the editorial formula of books of secrets, did however try to adapt these Italian books to their new readership, in a growing process of vernacularization[55]. Printed books of secrets are already very different from earlier manuscript compilations of recipes. Italian printers adapted their recipes to the readership they imagined these books would have: unsophisticated readers, who only knew the vernacular, who were not familiar with overly technical terms, and who would consult these books in a practical and domestic context. In books of secrets, sentences are usually short, the reader is instructed through informal imperatives (often using the second person), paragraphs are short, and there are often sub-divisions to facilitate the reading. While medieval recipe compilations frequently contain abbreviations, this is hardly ever the case in printed books of secrets, which can indicate how the printers did not expect the reader to be familiar with them. When these Italian books of secrets are translated into other languages, another set of adaptations is necessary, often from a linguistic point of view. Translators often explain terms that they imagine the readers will not be familiar with, following a practice already common in Italian books of secrets, in which we find lists of words (*dichiarazioni*) explained, often originated in the Veneto, in Naples, and in Tuscany.

However, there are also translations where the incompetence of the translator is clear, and the recipes become virtually incomprehensible. The lists of difficult words, however, show us how the opposite trend also existed, with thorough translators worried about the recipes being comprehensible and useful to their new readers. It is not the case of the English translation of Leonardo Fioravanti's secrets, and the recipe called *Of Pellarella that causeth the hair to fall off*. This is an example of a very poor translation, which was often the case in such cheaply printed books, despite the fact that the translator, John Hester, was an apothecary himself. However, it does not seem that the "untranslatable" words were a problem; underlining the possibility that recipe collections formed less a prescriptive medical model to the reader, but rather a "kit" from which the readers could choose their "tools" and create their own medical universe.

Italian books of secrets go through several changes from a linguistic point of view as well as from an editorial perspective, being associated with other genres and integrated into existing groups of texts such as the *Bibliothèque bleue*. But they are also published with other books, including other compilations of recipes, and printed in the same volume with other texts. That is the case of the German translation of Alessio Piemontese's *Secrets*, in which Johann Jacob Wecker's secrets, the physician responsible for the translation, are printed in the same volume. Wecker also translated Alessio's book into Latin and his secrets were printed along Piemontese's. Print-

---

55 S. Fransen, *Introduction: Translators and Translations of Early Modern Science*, in S. Fransen / N. Hodson / K.A.E. Enenkel (eds.), *Translating Early Modern Science*, Leiden 2017, pp. 1–14.

ers often added and suppressed recipes within the translated book without telling the reader. They also often added whole new books to the same volume, which was frequently advertised as a positive thing, since more secrets are offered to the reader. In any case, a famous name, such as Alessio Piemontese's, became associated with texts not originally published together.

Sometimes this is advertised to the reader. In Christophe Plantin's famous translation of Alessio's *Secrets*, the printer combines the first and the second parts of the secrets, which had been published separately in Italy, in one single volume, adding also a new collection of recipes to it: *Les secrets du S. Alexis Piemontois divisez en six livres. Ausquels avons adjoint autres secrets de nouveau adjoustez par iceluy, qu'aucuns ont appellé, le second volume: et les receptes de divers auteurs toutes bien experimentées, et approuvées* (The secrets of Mr. Alexis of Piedmont divided in six books. To which we have added other secrets also by him, which some have called the second volume: and the recipes of several authors, all tried and approved). In the *avertissement*, Plantin addresses the "friendly reader", explaining how the book had been thoroughly revised by "gens bien scavants en Langue Italienne & Françoise, & très experimentés en la Medecine" (learned people, experts in the Italian and French languages, and very knowledgeable in medicine).

This edition also shows us how some printers not only compiled different texts in one single book, but also considered it important (at least to tell the reader) how the book had been expertly translated by people who had both linguistic capabilities and medical knowledge. Plantin also denounces the practice of other printers, who would often "recycle" old recipes, publishing them as new, and affirms that it is not his case. He underscores how these recipes were new, which is not always the case of "gens épris par la malice" (malicious people) and "pris par le désir de gain" (dominated by greed), who would write secrets "indignes d'être lus" (unworthy of being read). As for his new compilation or recipes, Plantin tells the reader how they had been tested by "gens de bon jugement en médecine et en autres sciences exquises" (people who know medicine and other exquisite sciences). This advertisement to the reader is interesting because not only does Plantin tell us about the difficulties in a printer's life, but he also tries to add value to his own workshop, underlining the care with which the texts were edited, translated, corrected, and revised by "experts".

IV

Books of secrets continued to be printed in Italy, Germany, and England until the end of the eighteenth century. In France, although after the French Revolution their popularity diminished, they continued to be reprinted until the nineteenth century. Even though from the end of the seventeenth century these books are reprinted less frequently, they continue to circulate, especially as a part of the *Bibliothèque bleue*.

In conclusion, books of secrets were successful all over Europe for several reasons. They answered readers' curiosity about the miracles of nature and the secrets of crafts; they offered practical solutions to everyday problems, especially complementing domestic medical practices, but also offering ludic recipes to amuse the reader. Printers and translators were the main actors in the process of rendering these Italian secrets available to readers from other areas, making changes on a micro-level, adapting each book to its imagined readership, and on a macro-level, associating the genre of books of secrets as a whole to technical manuals in German areas or to the corpus of the *Bibliothèque bleue* in France. They became bestsellers in their own right, but one of the reasons why they continued to attract interest throughout the centuries, were the strategies publishers and translators adopted. In France's case, they were added to the already existing and successful *Bibliothèque bleue*, being circulated through the network of connections used by the Troyes printers, including peddlers who would sell the books in the countryside. In German-speaking areas, books of secrets were often assimilated into the already successful genre of technical manuals and distillation books. Because books of secrets were flexible, containing different types of recipes and a variety of knowledge, they could easily be integrated into other groups of texts.

Besides associating books of secrets to other genres and integrating them in a corpus such as the *Bibliothèque bleue*, printers also created strategies to adapt the individual Italian books to their new audiences, reshaping their meaning by several changes. The title of the author was often adapted – Leonardo Fioravanti went from Sir to Knight and honorable etc. – and printers were concerned with language and cultural differences. Titles were adapted, and "declarations" were added to explain particularly difficult words. Readers were told that the book had been translated and revised by experts in languages and in medicine. The already polysemic "secret" became associated not only with recipes, but with arts as well. Being malleable texts, books of secrets could transform into different styles to better suit their new readerships, connected to local traditions. Publishers and translators had a central role in this process, making professors of secrets' recipes available to new readers. Furthermore, they often used an already famous name to publish other texts, in a combined volume. Recipes were added, suppressed, and "corrected" in a process that deeply transformed books of secrets while making these Venetian recipe compilations true pan-European texts. While it was thanks to translation that books of secrets reached this success, the process of translation was by no means neutral; the translated books of secrets outgrew the originals, often becoming something else entirely. The autonomy translators had in reshaping the texts they translated often made them almost "co-authors" of the text; the addition of new material was often perceived as positive, as well as the "correcting" of recipes: texts were often "updated" and "upgraded" in translation. As an active process, translations kept the genre of secrets alive while transforming it. It was this process of adaptation, or cultural translation, that allowed the continuing success of recipe literature in early modern Europe.

Niall Ó Ciosáin
Popular Print in Unofficial Languages
Ireland, Scotland, Wales, and Brittany

1 Introduction

One striking feature of scholarship on the history of popular literature, as of that on popular culture as a whole, is an uncertainty or a looseness of definition of the object of study. What qualified something as popular literature, and how should the historian judge what to include and to exclude? This question has been present since the beginning of modern studies of the subject. Robert Mandrou, in his foundational 1964 work *De la Culture Populaire au 17e et 18e siècles*, identified French popular literature, and indeed rural popular culture as a whole, with one particular format and place of production. His book discussed the *Bibliothèque bleue*, which consisted of unbound books covered in blue paper, printed in the town of Troyes in Champagne, and it based its analysis essentially on the holdings of the municipal library there[1].

While there is some discussion of what constituted popular print in this book, Mandrou offered a much more explicit definition in an article that he published the same year, a definition that emphasized above all the modes of distribution and sale. Popular literature consisted of books that were sold by peddlers and that were suitable for this – small, cheap, and simple:

> Everybody knows what a peddlers' book was in the 17th and 18th centuries: a small 12mo or 16mo, sometimes even a 32mo, between 8 and 120 pages, which the peddler carried through town and country, at the bottom of his bag, mixed with household articles and clothes that he sold from door to door[2].

The other pioneer in the study of popular literature in France, Geneviève Bollème, also emphasized the form of distribution, the small size, and the poor quality of paper and type as its defining elements. The books she studied were between 14 x 7 cm and 21 x 15 cm, sold for 1 or 2 sols and were poorly finished both in print and paper[3]. In England, the principal survey of the subject, Margaret Spufford's *Small Books and Pleasant Histories*, published in 1981, also began with the mode of distribution and with specific publishers. A group of printers, all in London, specialized

---

[1] R. Mandrou, *De la Culture Populaire au 17e et 18e Siècles. La Bibliothèque Bleue de Troyes*, Paris 1964.
[2] R. Mandrou, *Littérature de colportage et mentalités paysannes, XVIIe–XVIIIe siècles*, in "Études Rurales", 15, 1964, pp. 72–85, here p. 73.
[3] G. Bollème, *La Bibliothèque Bleue. La Littérature Populaire en France du XVIIe au XIXe Siècles*, Paris 1971, pp. 7 f.

in small books, known as "chapbooks", that they explicitly produced for peddlers or "chapmen" who formed a network of distribution that covered all of England and south Wales[4].

These initial definitions and descriptions of a popular literature were soon challenged, however. In 1980, Jean-Luc Marais pointed out the problems of identifying specific producers and distributors with popular literature. Small books and peddlers' books were not the same thing, and in rural areas peddlers often sold larger and more expensive books. Similarly, Marais pointed out that the printers of the *Bibliothèque bleue* usually had larger and more expensive books in their catalogues[5].

A related critique was made by Roger Chartier, who showed that a clear distinction could not be made between elite and popular content within peddlers' books. Some titles in the *Bibliothèque bleue* were from learned culture and had been reprinted in a cheaper format as soon as their privilege had expired. What characterized popular texts, according to Chartier, was a style of reading which was episodic, and printers edited them to suit – they were "chopped up into smaller units", abridged and simplified[6].

There was one dimension of the popular that did not feature much in these discussions, and that was the issue of language. The texts in question were always in French or in English, and moreover in the metropolitan versions of those languages. Whatever pejorative views learned observers may have had of the books, they were written in the official language of the state, and in the dialect of Paris or London rather than the linguistic variety or dialect of most of the readers. This distinction becomes completely binary when the readers spoke an entirely different language to that of the state and the printing trade – Breton or Basque, Irish or Scottish Gaelic, Welsh.

This is not to say that these scholars completely ignored printing in non-official or regional languages, simply that their focus was understandably on texts in French and English. Indeed Mandrou suggested that the geographical spread of the *Bibliothèque bleue* was limited precisely by language, and that it circulated essentially north of the Loire. He refers in passing to printer-translators in Toulouse and Quimper who produced texts from the *Bibliothèque bleue* in Oc and in Breton, but the tone is slightly dismissive – the South-West was "handicapped" by the lack of French, while Brittany was "en retard". Similarly, Spufford mentions Welsh-language printing in a footnote. However, their focus is on English and French, and their respective corpuses are library holdings published entirely in Troyes and entirely in London[7].

---

[4] M. Spufford, *Small Books and Pleasant Histories. Popular Fiction and its Readership in Seventeenth-Century England*, Cambridge 1981.
[5] J.L. Marais, *Litterature et culture "populaires" aux XVIIe et XVIIIe siècles. Réponses et questions*, in "Annales de Bretagne et des Pays de l'Ouest", 87, 1980, pp. 65–105.
[6] R. Chartier, *Livres Bleus et Lectures Populaires*, in R. Chartier / H.-J. Martin (eds.), *Histoire de l'Édition Française*, vol. 2: *Le Livre Triomphant 1660–1830*, Paris 1984, pp. 498–511.
[7] R. Mandrou, *De la Culture Populaire*, pp. 30, 39; M. Spufford, *Small Books*, p. 76, n. 5.

It is fair to suggest, however, that printing and publishing in non-official languages is by virtue of that very fact "popular". These languages were not languages of the state, having few official uses or none at all, nor were they languages of the market, in the sense that they were not used for paper money or for documents such as contracts or bills. They had a certain status in the domain of religion, as they were used for catechesis and preaching, but above a certain level in all churches, the languages used were English, French, and Latin. Non-official languages were therefore subordinate, in the sense used by sociolinguists, languages "restricted to domains from which power in general societal terms is absent"[8].

Even a substantial printed book in a nonofficial language can be regarded as in a sense "popular". In practice, the majority of printing, as with the official languages, was in smaller and cheaper genres, and can therefore be characterized as popular twice over. In this paper I propose to survey briefly the smaller and cheaper printed productions in the four main Celtic languages in the eighteenth and nineteenth centuries – Breton, Welsh, Scottish Gaelic, and Irish Gaelic. (For brevity I will refer to the last two as "Gaelic" and "Irish" respectively, following normal present-day usage.)

A few rough numbers can serve as context for the different languages. In 1800, the language communities were roughly this size:
- Irish: over 2.5 million
- Breton: 1 million
- Welsh: 400,000
- Gaelic: 250,000

In terms of printed production, the languages are ranked very differently. There are no figures for total output, but if we take books published entirely in those languages, we get the following rough amounts for the nineteenth century[9]:
- Welsh: 10,000
- Breton: 1,200
- Gaelic: 1,200
- Irish: 150

Similar proportions apply in the second half of the eighteenth century (again these are rough amounts):
- Welsh: 1,900
- Breton: 90
- Gaelic: 60
- Irish: 20

---

8 R. Grillo, *Dominant Languages. Language and Hierarchy in Britain and France*, Cambridge 1989, p. 4.
9 For the basis of these calculations, see N. Ó Ciosáin, *Publishing and Reading in the Celtic Languages, 1700–1900: An Overview*, in "Cultural and Social History", 10, 2013, pp. 347–367.

These are massive differences, and are explained, initially at least, by the success of different churches in fostering a vernacular literacy for pastoral and educational purposes. Literacy and a print culture in a language that is not the language of the state or the market requires a predominantly religious foundation. Of course, a religious foundation for literacy and print is well acknowledged for all western European languages, in particular as regards reading ability, with a new emphasis in all churches on devotional reading of texts such as catechisms from the sixteenth century onwards[10]. Moreover, while the role of religion is particularly crucial for non-official languages, a reading literacy, once established on a religious base, can later on be applied to non-religious texts, and a market for secular literature developed to differing degrees in the different languages.

In brief, a small market for printed books in Welsh, such as small-format Bibles, developed in the seventeenth century, following the initial state-sponsored translation of the Bible in 1588. This became a mass market during the eighteenth century, when printing and reading in Welsh were central to a major religious revival that resulted in a series of religious denominations leaving the state church, and this mass market continued to exist well into the twentieth century. Print literacy in Breton was largely created during periods of Catholic missionary activity in the seventeenth century, notably during the Jesuit missions of the 1680s, when small books and hymns were printed and circulated on a large scale. The market stagnated somewhat during the eighteenth century, despite the publication of a handful of books that became classics, and then developed on a large scale during the nineteenth century. Popular print in Gaelic began with influential translations of the Psalms in 1659 and was reinforced by a translation of the New Testament in 1767, reaching its apogee in the later nineteenth century. In Ireland, by contrast, the Catholic Church, to which the vast majority of Irish speakers belonged, perhaps due to its semi-clandestine existence in the seventeenth and eighteenth centuries, did not produce a substantial devotional print literature in Irish, and almost no secular texts were printed before the twentieth century. These four cases represent different levels of engagement by religious institutions with vernacular languages, and go a long way to explaining the different levels of printed production in the long term.

When considering this printed production, and particularly the smaller, cheaper genres of text, an obvious place to start would be the catechism, the essential religious popular text and the most universally owned text in all languages. Given the vast production of catechisms in all four languages, however, it is too large a topic for this article to enter into in any detail. Moreover, there are no easily accessible estimates of the amounts and varieties produced in the different languages.

---

10 For France, F. Furet / J. Ozouf, *Reading and Writing. Literacy in France from Calvin to Jules Ferry*, Cambridge 1982, pp. 166–191; for England, T. Laqueur, *The Cultural Origins of Popular Literacy in England 1500–1850*, in "Oxford Review of Education", 2, 1976, pp. 255–275.

Things are a little easier in the case of the other universal text, this time a secular one. Along with catechisms, the most frequently printed text in early Modern Europe was the annual almanac, a genre that has been well explored by scholars in the principal languages of Europe. In Welsh, almanacs are found in large quantities throughout the eighteenth and nineteenth centuries. The earliest were printed in London by Thomas Jones, who was granted a royal patent for printing almanacs in Welsh, beginning in the year 1679. With the ending of the London monopoly on printing in 1695, Jones became a printer in Shrewsbury, an English town close to the Welsh border that was the main center of printing in Welsh in the eighteenth century, and continued to publish his almanac there. By the early 1700s, numerous competing almanacs had appeared, despite Jones' patent and his copyrighting of a Welsh almanac, and by the nineteenth century there were dozens, printed all over Wales each year, and with substantial print runs. One 16-page almanac in 1877 had a print run of 70,000. Like almanacs everywhere, they had an adaptable format, and many Welsh almanacs included verse submitted by readers[11].

Breton almanacs were produced in substantial numbers from the 1820 to the 1850s by two competing printers, Lédan in Morlaix and Lefournier in Brest, with print runs or 1,000 or 2,000. Moreover, Lédan alleged in 1826 that his almanac was being pirated by a third printer, Guyon in St. Brieuc. Alexandre Lédan, who was the principal printer of Breton in the early nineteenth century and also a writer of Breton, described his almanac as having been translated by himself, presumably from French[12].

Some almanacs in Gaelic were produced from the 1870s onwards, but they were a different production and for a different type of audience to those of the Welsh and Breton books. The title pages, all advertisements, along with a significant part of the text, were in English, and their intended audience was as much affluent anglophone cultural nationalists as the population of the Gaelic-speaking area. An 1875 almanac contains, for example, the usual useful list of markets and fairs, in Gaelic, some even dated in the "Seann-Chunntas" (Old Style or Julian calendar), but also an English-language advertisement for expensive-looking "Highland Costume, in a superior style"[13].

---

11 G.H. Jenkins, *"The sweating astrologer": Thomas Jones the Almanacer*, in R.R. Davies (ed.), Welsh Society and Nationhood. Historical Essays Presented to Glanmor Williams, Cardiff 1984, pp. 161–177; E. Rees / G. Morgan, Welsh Almanacs 1680–1835: Problems of Piracy, in "The Library", 6, 1979, 1, pp. 144–163; for the circulation figure see P.H. Jones, *Printing and Publishing in the Welsh Language 1800–1914* in G.H. Jenkins (ed.), The Welsh Language and its Social Domains 1801–1911, Cardiff 2000, pp. 317–348, at p. 320. A selection of eighteenth-century almanacs can be seen on the website of the National Library of Wales, https://www.llgc.org.uk/en/discover/digital-gallery/printed-material/the-welsh-almanac-collection.

12 G. Bailloud, *L'Imprimerie Lédan à Morlaix (1805–1880) et ses Impressions en Langue Bretonne*, Saint-Brieuc 1999, pp. 44 f. An almanac by Lefournier for 1832 is listed in *Bibliographie de la France, ou Journal Général de l'Imprimerie et de la Librairie*, January 7, 1832, no. 110.

13 *Am Feillre. The Gael Almanac and Highland Directory for 1875*, Edinburgh, MacLachlan and Stewart, 1875.

Finally, no printed almanac was ever produced for sale in Irish, despite the intense commercialization of the economy after 1760 that would have made a list of markets, for example, very useful.

Turning to another of the major categories of cheap popular print, the small songbook, or single sheet ballad, the same proportions of overall production again apply. In Welsh, there was substantial printing of small songbooks already in the eighteenth century. These were generally eight pages long. A bibliography of these collections was published in 1911, which counted some 700 examples, most of them surviving in libraries. Most of these are religious, but there is a significant amount of songs about current issues. More than 60 deal with events in Wales, such as the landing by troops from Revolutionary France in Fishguard, in the south-west of Wales, in 1797, which is the subject of six songs, or the county defense militias, on which there are 15 songs. Events outside Wales, such as wars or epidemics, feature in more than 50 songs[14].

Production was vast in the nineteenth century, when the favored format was the 4-page booklet, and the website of the National Library of Wales contains digital versions of nearly such 4,000 booklets[15]. As well as being in a smaller format, the nineteenth-century examples have another difference from the eighteenth-century booklets that is significant for the overall explanation of the volumes of printed production. The eighteenth-century items were mostly printed in the English towns of Shrewsbury (189 examples) and Chester (72), or in towns in the north of Wales, particularly Trefriw (181) and Wrexham (24), and contained texts of north Welsh origin, although there is a significant representation of Carmarthen (72) and Brecon (13) in the south. The nineteenth-century booklets, by contrast, are overwhelmingly southern, many from the new industrial towns of Merthyr Tydfil and Tredegar, as well as the older industrial town of Swansea.

The Welsh language was a major beneficiary of the industrial revolution, and Welsh the only one of the Celtic languages to see the development of large industrial towns and cities within its language zone. This meant that the number of Welsh speakers more than doubled over the nineteenth century, and large concentrations of urban speakers provided a readership for dozens of periodicals and newspapers[16]. The main industrial cities of Ireland and Scotland, Belfast and Glasgow, were outside the Irish- and Gaelic-speaking areas, and although there was substantial migration into them from those areas, the dominant language of those cities was never anything

---

14 J.H. Davies, *A Bibliography of Welsh Ballads printed in the Eighteenth Century*, London, The Honourable Society of Cymmrodorion, 1911, p. XIV; F.M. Jones, *Welsh Ballads and Literacy*, in D. Atkinson / S. Roud (eds.), *Street Ballads in Nineteenth-Century Britain, Ireland and North America*, Farnham 2014, pp. 106–126.

15 https://www.llgc.org.uk/index.php?id=6839. This database includes some eighteenth-century ballads and some in English, but the vast majority are in Welsh and from the nineteenth century.

16 B. Thomas, *A Cauldron of Rebirth: Population and the Welsh Language in the Nineteenth Century*, in "Welsh Historical Review", 13, 1987, pp. 418–437.

other than English. In the Irish case, moreover, the emigration to industrial cities outside Ireland altogether was greater still – to Liverpool, Glasgow, and Boston.

The production of ballad books and broadsheets in Breton was also significant, even if less than in Welsh. There do not seem to be any surviving examples from the eighteenth century, but the most complete catalogue of nineteenth- and early twentieth-century productions, compiled by Joseph Ollivier in the 1930s, lists over a thousand items, ranging from single sheets to 16-page booklets. As with almanacs, the Morlaix printer Lédan was prominent in this market, even composing some of the songs himself. He also printed the songs of a famous blind travelling singer, Yann Ar Gwenn, who, as was normal in most areas, dictated his songs to Lédan who then produced printed sheets for ar Gwenn to sell[17].

Like cheap ballads in Welsh and elsewhere, those in Breton acted as forms of news, featuring current events such as executions and murder, or catastrophes such as storms and epidemics. The cholera epidemic that swept through western Europe in 1832, for example, was the subject of a ballad in Welsh, while Yann Ar Gwenn lamented its effects in Brittany. Lédan also wrote and printed a ballad sheet that was a translation into Breton verse of official instructions and advice on cholera[18].

In absolute terms, the amount of small-format songs and ballads printed in Irish was modest, but they made up a significant proportion of the overall output. A few dozen single-sheet ballads survive from the early nineteenth century, mostly printed in Cork in southern Ireland, often on larger sheets that contained a mixture of English-language and Irish-language songs. Similarly, in the eighteenth century, songs in Irish were printed along with songs in English in 8-page ballad books, also in the cities of the south such as Cork and Limerick. This mixing of languages was occasionally visible within the songs themselves, in the form of macaronic songs, alternating verses or lines in Irish with verses or lines in English[19].

Another type of linguistic or cultural mixing found in these Irish ballads was the frequent use of a phonetic English-language orthography to represent the sound of texts in Irish, rather than using the original or "correct" spelling. This was probably due, in part if not entirely, to the fact that the printers in question knew little or no Irish, and had possibly taken down the texts from the dictation of travelling

---

17 J. Ollivier, *Catalogue Bibliographique de la Chanson Populaire Bretonne sur Feuilles Volantes*, Quimper 1942; D. Giraudon, *Chansons Populaires de Basse-Bretagne sur Feuilles Volantes*, Morlaix 1985. Ollivier's catalogue was originally published as a series of articles in "Annales de Bretagne" and deals with the northern and western parts of Brittany – Léon, Cornuaille, and Tréguier – omitting the southern district around Vannes, where the dialect of Breton was very different.
18 D. Giraudon, *Chansons Populaires*, p. 79; J. Ollivier, *Catalogue Bibliographique*, no. 547.
19 A. Mac Lochlainn, *Broadside Ballads in Irish*, in "Éigse", 12, 1967/68, pp. 115–122; H. Shields, *Nineteenth-century Irish Song Chapbooks and Ballad Sheets*, in P. Fox (ed.), *Treasures of the Library*, Dublin, Trinity College, 1986, pp. 197–204. Many macaronic songs are reproduced in D.Ó Muirithe, *An t-Amhrán Macarónach*, Dublin 1980.

singers, to print sheets for those singers to sell, as was the practice in all language areas. This points to another weakness of print culture in Irish, the fact that very few printers understood it or could write it conventionally. This offers a contrast to Wales and Brittany. There were, it is true, some eighteenth-century printers of Welsh who seem not to have understood it – Jones points to Durston in Shrewsbury and Adams in Chester – but these were the exception rather than the rule, and by the nineteenth century Welsh and Breton printers were fluent or competent in their languages. Alexandre Lédan, as we saw, composed and printed many ballads and songs himself in the first half of the nineteenth century[20].

In Scottish Gaelic, finally, the printed ballad or small songbook seems not to have been a genre. There are 10 surviving 8-page songbooks, probably printed between 1810 and 1835, but they differ from the material in other languages in such a way as to suggest that they are a different type of production. Most strikingly, the songs and poems in them were not newly composed, but came from various periods as far back as the sixteenth century, and most can be found in eighteenth-century manuscript or print collections of Gaelic verse. By contrast, the songs in the other languages, in common with ballads in the main European languages, were always keen to stress their novelty: *Chanson nevez* (new song) in Breton, *Can newydd* (new song) in Welsh, or *Dwy o gerddi newyddion* (two new poems) for a song booklet in Welsh. This suggests that the Gaelic booklets were produced outside of the normal commercial channels since, as Ollivier put it in his introduction to his Breton catalogue, "the travelling singer had no chance of selling over-familiar old traditional songs". Naomi Harvey agrees, and suggests that the books were published as part of a self-conscious cultural nationalist enterprise, not surprising in the wake of the Ossianic controversy of previous decades[21].

Given the close relationship between literacy in an unofficial language and religious practice, it is not surprising that the devotional song, the hymn or canticle, was one of the dominant genres in all four languages. In Welsh there was an enormous production of hymns in all formats in the eighteenth and more particularly in the nineteenth century. As one illustration, we can take the best-known writer of hymns of the period, William Williams (1717–1791), known as Pantycelyn after his home, who is regarded as a central figure in Welsh literary history. Williams was one of the early

---

20 A. Carpenter, *Garbling and Jumbling: Printing from Dictation in Eighteenth-century Limerick*, in M. Caball / A. Carpenter (eds.), *Oral and Print Cultures in Ireland, 1600–1900*, Dublin 2010, pp. 32–46; F.M. Jones, *Welsh Ballads and Literacy*, p. 107.

21 J. Ollivier, *Catalogue Bibliographique*, p. 1; N.E. Harvey, *Gaelic Chapbooks*, in E.J. Cowan / M. Paterson (eds.), *Folk in Print. Scotland's Chapbook Heritage 1750–1850*, Edinburgh 2007, pp. 323–330. In Irish, however, there was a widespread and intensive manuscript transmission of seventeenth and eighteenth-century poetry and song continued until the middle of the nineteenth century among schoolteachers, farmers and merchants, suggesting that there could well have been a demand for similar Gaelic material in print. A comparative history of manuscript culture in the four languages would of course fill out this comparative history of print.

leaders of Methodism in Wales. His hymns were an element in the religious revival of the eighteenth century and have continued to be sung since. He published his work in both small and larger formats. *Rhai hymnau newyddion ar fesurau newyddion* (some new songs on new melodies), a 12-page booklet of 18 hymns, was printed in 1781 and reprinted twice that year, and another 12-page booklet with the same title but different hymns was published and reprinted the following year. Both booklets were printed by the same printer, Evans, in Brecon, south Wales. At the other end of the scale, Williams' *Caniadau, y rhai sydd ar y mor o wydr* (Songs of those on the sea of glass), a 168-page book of 87 hymns, appeared in 1762, was reprinted in each of the following two years, and reached a fifth edition in 1795. During the nineteenth century, small collections of Williams' hymns were frequently published, such as *Yr Udgorn Arian* (The silver trumpet), a 32-page booklet of 28 hymns, which was in its sixth edition in 1872.

In Breton, the equivalent was the cantique or canticle, a type of hymn that has been an emblematic part of Breton culture since they were printed and sung during the Jesuit missions in the seventeenth century. Some of the earliest and most enduring examples were composed by Julien Maunoir, the most prominent figure in these missions, but later examples tended to be presented as anonymous, with no mentioned author. Their centrality can be measured in the bibliography of the Breton publications of Alexandre Lédan, covering most of the nineteenth century. Out of some 420 titles that are known, about 70 are cantiques, and these are among the titles that had the largest number of editions. There are 3 titles in the Lédan catalogue with 8 editions or more, and 2 of these are cantiques, or to look at it more broadly, of the 39 titles with 4 editions or more, 10 are cantiques (this understates the proportion a little, since there are also 4 long versified saints' lives, with suggested melodies, which are very close to being cantiques)[22].

These cantiques differ from the hymns of Williams Pantycelyn particularly in their length. Typically, a cantique would take up an entire 8-page or even a 16-page duodecimo booklet, whereas Williams' 12-page booklets, as we saw, contained nearly 20 hymns. The classic occasion for the community singing of cantiques was the parish mission, a series of sermons and rituals lasting a week, and in the nineteenth-century Catholic Church, dioceses published collections of cantiques specifically for the missions of a diocese.

The printed literatures of Irish in the nineteenth century, and in Gaelic in the eighteenth and nineteenth centuries, were dominated by collections of individual authors' hymns, two in Scotland and one in Ireland[23]. These were a good deal larger than the 8-page or 16-page Breton collections, but also much smaller than Williams'

---

22 I have compiled these figures from G. Bailloud, *L'Imprimerie Lédan à Morlaix*.
23 There is an extended comparison of these three collections in N. Ó Ciosáin, *Pious Miscellanies and Spiritual Songs: Devotional Publishing and Reading in Irish and Scottish Gaelic, 1760–1900*, in J. Kelly / C. MacMurchaidh (eds.), *Linguistic and Cultural Frontiers: English and Irish, 1650–1850*, Dublin 2012, pp. 267–282.

168-page volume. The earliest of these was *Laoidhe Spioradail* (Spiritual lays) by Dugald Buchanan, which first appeared as a 50-page book in Edinburgh in 1767. It had 9 editions by 1800, and a further 31 editions during the nineteenth century. It contains eight poems, songs, or hymns, on subjects such as death and the last judgement. Buchanan was for many years a schoolmaster with the Scottish Society for the Promotion of Christian Knowledge, an agency engaged in education and publishing, and he oversaw the translation and publication of the first Gaelic New Testament which appeared in 1767, the same year as the *Laoidhe Spioradail*.

Half a century later came Peter Grant, whose *Dain Spioradail* (Spiritual songs) was first printed in Inverness in 1815 and had 22 editions during the nineteenth century. Grant was an itinerant Baptist missionary who became the pastor of a congregation in Spey, south of Inverness, in 1826. Grant followed the progress of his work in print, and he added new songs and new prefaces to later editions. The 1815 edition had 13 songs in 52 pages, the 1820 and 1827 editions had expanded to 18 songs in 96 pages, while editions after 1835 contained 39 hymns or songs in 152 pages or more.

In Irish, the equivalent to Grant and Buchanan, and to Williams and other Welsh hymn writers, was a southern poet, Tadhg Gaelach Ó Súilleabháin (Timothy O'Sullivan). His *Pious Miscellany* was first published in Clonmel, Co. Tipperary, in 1802 and there are 16 surviving editions from before 1860, as well as several other editions that have disappeared, making it by far the most frequently printed book in Irish before the twentieth century. There were a handful of editions after 1860, but they show an abrupt change in the style of presentation. Pre-1860 editions were published in provincial towns, aimed at Irish-speaking devotional readers, using simple roman typeface and were devoid of any explanations in English. After 1860, they were printed in Dublin for a mainly English-speaking readership inspired by cultural nationalism, using a more archaic Celtic typeface and including glossaries of many words in English. This break in print culture reflects a sudden collapse of many Irish-speaking communities in the decades after the Great Famine of 1845–1850, in which the million people who died were predominantly Irish speakers. By contrast, the collections of Buchanan and Grant in Scotland, along with Welsh and Breton hymns, continued to be published into the twentieth century. Indeed, the use of stereotype in later nineteenth-century editions of Grant and Buchanan suggests that this was their period of greatest circulation, and the production figures for cantiques in Breton are similar, with a peak in the period from 1880 onwards[24].

---

[24] There is a graph of cantique production since 1850 in M. Lagrée, *La Littérature Religieuse dans la Production Bretonne Imprimée: Aspects Quantitatifs*, in M. Lagrée (ed.), *Les Parlers de la Foi: Religion et Langues Régionales*, Rennes 1995, pp. 85–94, here p. 90.

2 Popular readers

The larger formats of Williams' *Caniadau* and the later editions of Grant's *Dain Spioradail*, 168 and 152 pages respectively, are a long way from the 8-page booklets of Breton cantiques and from the similar small formats of secular songs discussed earlier. They return us to the question raised at the beginning of this article, of whether popular reading material can be identified exclusively, or even principally, with smaller, cheaper formats. As noted earlier as well, the trend in more recent studies has been to identify a popular style of reading embodied in simpler and more episodic texts. There is another possibility again, however, one that is suggested by the fact that O'Sullivan's *Pious Miscellany* was originally published in 1802 by subscription, with all the names of the 279 subscribers printed in the first edition. We can therefore identify a large group who bought – and presumably read – the book. The addresses of the subscribers – that is, the name of a town, village, or parish – are given for the vast majority. The Catholic clergy, with 39 names, are prominent but do not by any means dominate the list. It would need a great deal of minute investigation to identify most of the people, but in an area of highly commercialized agriculture during the boom of the revolutionary and Napoleonic wars, it is probably safe to assume that they were merchants and prosperous farmers, along with teachers and scribes.

Similar lists, with more detail and usually far more names, are found in Wales and Scotland, in books of a genre that we have not discussed, the secular poetic collection or miscellany. These were published in substantial numbers from the middle of the eighteenth century onwards, and often contained 200 pages or more. They were of two kinds: collections of the work of a single poet or of a small group of poets, published by themselves, and anthologies of songs, collected orally or from manuscripts. We can take two examples from among many, one each from Wales and Scotland.

The first is *Corph Y Gainc, neu, Ddifyrwch Teulaidd* (The body of the branch, or poetic diversions), published in Dolgellau in north-west Wales in 1810. The poetry in *Corph Y Gainc* is mostly by its editor, David Thomas (who used the bardic pseudonym Dafydd Ddu Eryri), but it also contains poems by acquaintances and pupils of his, making it an anthology of verse from north-west Wales, particularly Caernarvonshire. Nearly all the poets lived and worked in an area contained within a circle of 20 km radius, centered south of Caernarvon, on the north-west coast of Wales, while the first five poems are by Goronwy Owen (1723–1769), an earlier writer who was one of the major poets of eighteenth-century Wales and who came from Anglesea, very close by. The subscribers list contains 781 names, together with their addresses and sometimes their occupations. Like the poets, they were concentrated in north-west Wales, making this a highly localised book in both production and reception. See figure 1.

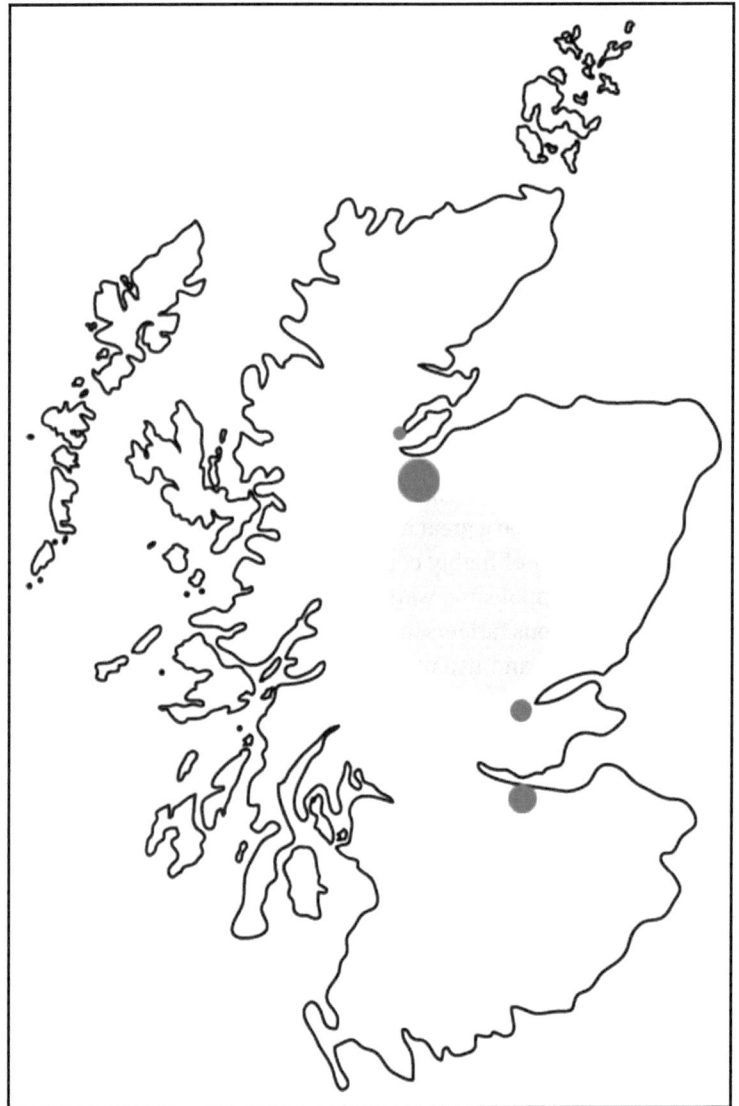

Fig. 1: Subscribers as printed in *Corph Y Gainc*, 1810, by county.

The Gaelic book is *Orain Ghaidhealach agus Bearla ar na Eadar-theangacha* (Gaelic songs and translations from English) by Coinneach MacCoinnich (Kenneth McKenzie), published in Edinburgh in 1792, a collection of original verse and song by McKenzie himself, whose list of subscribers contains 980 names. The bulk of the subscribers were located in the eastern Highlands, in the rural area between Perth and Inverness, in the districts of Atholl, Badenoch, Strathspey, and Rannoch. See figure 2.

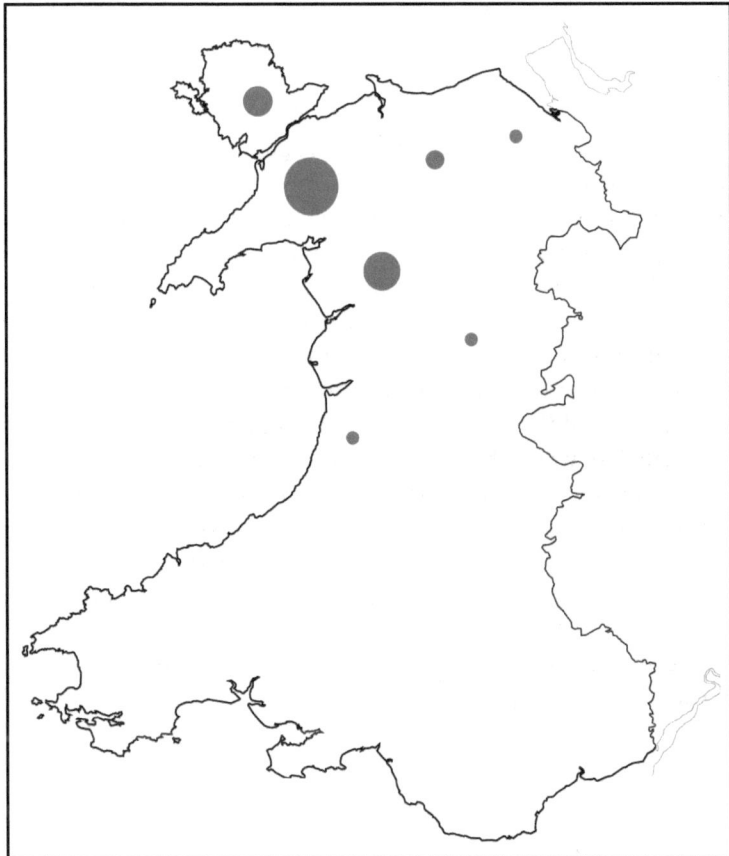

Fig. 2: Subscribers to *Orain Ghaidhealach*, 1792.

Two striking features emerge from these lists. The first is the overwhelmingly rural location of the subscribers. This is remarkable because, while Gaelic speakers mostly lived in rural areas and Welsh-speakers in north-west Wales likewise, literacy and book-owning everywhere in Europe were much more frequent among town populations. Out of 980 names in the McKenzie book, 79 were in Inverness, 36 in Edinburgh, 26 in Perth and 11 in Dingwall. There was only one in Glasgow (Daniel McMartin, a gardener), and four in London (3 sadlers and a watchmaker). In all, 150 of the subscribers were in towns, about 15% of the total.

The urban proportion of the subscribers to *Corph Y Gainc* was substantially higher, at about 30%. However, given the geography and demography of north-west Wales, some of these were very small towns indeed. The largest clusters of readers were in Dolgellau, where the book was printed, with 69 subscribers (9%), and Caernarvon, 44 subscribers or (5.5%). The census of 1811 gives the populations of these towns as about 3,000 and 4,000 respectively. Bangor, with a population of only 2,400, had 33 subscribers (4%), and Llandwrog had a population of 1,600 and 26 subscribers (3.5%). These were much smaller than the largest towns on McKenzie's list, Edinburgh (over 100,000 in 1811), Perth (16,000), and Inverness (10,700), and would not have been very different from their rural surroundings. Two-thirds of the population of Llandwrog in 1811 were employed in agriculture, for example.

The second striking feature of the subscribers is their range of social backgrounds. Here we are on slightly less secure ground than with the spatial distribution, since occupations are given for less than half of the names whereas location is given for almost all. (I have included nobility as an occupation in both cases.) On the Mackenzie list, occupations are specified for 437 people, 45% of the total, and in the Thomas collection, 327 or 42%. The largest grouping in the Mackenzie list can be described as "skilled artisan", about 40% of those where the occupations are given. The biggest single category is "wright", of which there were 50, and to which can be added three wheelwrights and two cartwrights, altogether 12% of those whose occupations are given. There were also 21 shoemakers (5%), 16 weavers (3.5%), 13 smiths and 13 tailors (3% each), as well as five shepherds, three pipers, one dancing-master, and more. Commerce (merchants, shopkeepers, etc.) represented about 14%. Other large groups were the 26 Reverends (6%), 47 soldiers (i.e. names with a military rank specified, making 11%). Only seven were titled nobility (this includes those described as "hon.") along with 18 (4%) described as "esq."

```
Mefirs. Duncan Gow, wright Kincraigie
        Donald Gow, wright Dalguife Atholl
        William Geddes, coachman Culduthell
        Charles Gow, tailor Preffmucharach
        Alexander Gowie, grieve Moyhall
        Alexander Gordon, fadler London
        James Gordon, Inverdruie Strathfpey
        Donald Gordon, weaver Acherneck
        David Gordon, wright Caftle-dunie
        Patrick Gellan, cooper Urray
```

Fig. 3: An extract from the list of subscribers printed in *Orain Ghaidhealach*, 1792.

Skilled artisans were also the biggest group in the Welsh list, coming to about a third of the total whose occupations are given. No one group dominated, and the largest was the 10 smiths (3%), followed by 7 carpenters, 7 tailors, and 6 shoemakers (2% each). North Wales had one of the world's largest slate industries at the time, and the list contains 7 quarry men (2%) and 4 slaters (1%). Commercial occupations, dominated by 15 grocers, came to 10% of the total. Clergy were much more prominent in this list, representing 20% of those whose occupations were specified, reflecting the much closer connection between churches and print culture in Wales, and the same is true of "esquires", who number 60 (18%)[25].

John Griffith, Weaver Tre'r Gof, Caernarvon.
John R. Griffith, Joiner, ditto
Evan Griffith, Nannau Mer.
John Griffith, Gwynwy Bach, Trefdraeth, A.
Ellis Griffith, Skinner, Dolgelley, Mer.
Ellis Griffith, Greuor, Llanrûg, C.
Erasmus Griffith, Tyddyn Parkle, Llanwnda, C.
Griffith, Tremadog, C.
Mrs. Griffiths, Union, Caernarvon.
Mr. Daniel Griffiths, Cilgwyn Llandwrog, C.
John Griffith, Tyddyn y Pwll, Pentir, C.
Llywelyn Griffith, Cooper, Dolgelley, Mer.
Humphrey Griffith, Clock maker. ditto

Fig. 4: An extract from the List of subscribers to *Corph Y Gaingc*, 1810

Most of the remaining names, over half of each list, had addresses that were often highly localized, and it is reasonable to assume that they were for the most part farmers and other agricultural workers. Moreover, in the Scottish list, many of the places listed are now uninhabited or have disappeared altogether, which suggests that those subscribers were smallholders who emigrated or were removed during the Highland clearances of the period[26]. These songbooks, and others like them, constitute a printed literature that is popular by virtue of its readership rather than its format or price. *Corph Y Gainc* contained nearly 300 pages and sold for three shillings and sixpence (forty-two pence), both many times greater than almanacs and ballad books, which usually cost only a few pence each.

3. Conclusions

There existed in the Celtic languages, therefore, a print culture that was popular according to more than one definition, and one that had quite specific characteristics. It coexisted with much larger and more pervasive print cultures in official languages, in English and French, and it remains to map out the relationships with those languages, and the interactions between them, in more detail and over a timespan of

---

25 On the involvement of the clergy in Welsh-language publishing, see I.G. Jones, *The Nineteenth Century*, in P.H. Jones / E. Rees (eds.), *A Nation and its Books: A History of the Book in Wales*, Aberystwyth 1998, pp. 157–171, esp. pp. 164 f.
26 See the comments in R. Black, *The Gaelic Book*, in S.W. Brown / W. MacDougall (eds.), *The Edinburgh History of the Book in Scotland*, vol. 2: *Enlightenment and Expansion 1707–1800*, Edinburgh 2011, pp. 177–187.

a few centuries. It would also be instructive to map the printed production in other non-official languages in Europe, such as Basque, Occitan, Provencal, or Catalan, both for comparative purposes and in order to integrate them into a fully European history of popular print.

IV. Genres and European Bestsellers

Claudia Demattè
The Spanish Romances about Chivalry

A Renaissance Editorial Phenomenon on Which "The Sun Never Set"

The Spanish romances of chivalry from the sixteenth century, the so-called *libros de caballerías*, are, generally identified in the minds of readers as the primary reason for the madness of the most famous errant knight in world literature: Don Quixote. As a matter of fact, Don Quixote not only sells his own properties in order to buy these precious books about the marvelous adventures of knights and ladies, but also "and what with little sleep and much reading his brains got so dry that he lost his wits"[1], to the point of believing that all that was told in these books was true, as "that to him no history in the world had more reality in it"[2].

Cervantes declared that his aim was to put an end to a genre that most critics of the time condemned because it was believed to represent a primary source of "distraction" from good behavior, not just for noble gentlemen and ladies but also for the general public. As a matter of fact, the first modern novel is a perfect representation, even in its excess and parody, of readers from very different social classes. As such, it recalls the romances about chivalry from the previous century[3].

In Spain the diffusion of the genre was rapid and widespread thanks to an invention and a new event in world history, namely: the incunabulum of the *Amadís* primitive[4]. Both the invention of the printing press and the discovery of the New World aided the diffusion of the *libros de caballerías*. While the printed book provided the medium, the chronicles of discovering the Americas gave force and reliability to the amazing tales of the romances and chivalry that helped reach a wide public. While Cromberger, one of the most famous printers in Seville, was publishing Amadís' adventures, Hernán Cortés was conquering Mexico and Pizarro was exploring the Amazon River, a name that recalls the female warriors described in the *Sergas de Esplandián*, one of the continuations of *Amadís de Gaula*. As a matter of fact, the *con-*

---

1 M. de Cervantes, *Don Qujxote*, I, 1: "del poco dormir y del mucho leer se le secó el celebro, de manera que vino a perder el juicio".
2 *Ibid.*, "para él no había otra historia más cierta en el mundo".
3 For the social aspect of the reader in Spanish romances of chivalry, see M. Chevalier, *Sur le public des romans de chevalerie*, Bordeaux 1968.
4 See J.B. Avalle-Arce, *"Amadís de Gaula": el primitivo y el de Montalvo*, n.p. 1990; D. Eisenberg / M.C. Marín Pina, *Bibliografía de los libros de caballerías castellanos*, Zaragoza 2000.

Note: The quotation is from King Philip II who inherited from his father, Emperor Charles V, an empire never seen before or since in terms of vastness.

quistador Bernal Díaz del Castillo describes his wonder with respect to Mexican civilization comparing it to "deeds of enchantments that are written in *Amadís*' book"[5].

Before proceeding, let us first review a few numbers in order to describe the label "best seller of the sixteenth century" for the Spanish romances about chivalry, "one of the most important genres in the sustaining of the Spanish printing industry"[6]. If we consider the 1508 edition of *Amadís de Gaula* by Garcí Rodríguez de Montalvo (Zaragoza, Jorge Coci) as starting point, the number of books published every year up to 1623 numbers from one to twelve new books annually. The most interesting years for our research span from 1525-1555, when an average of ten new books were published each year. At first glance, over 80 books about chivalry were published[7]. Moreover, in order to fully understand this phenomenon, one should also acknowledge the re-editions of the majority of these texts. This is summarized below:
- 114 editions between 1525-1550 (more than 50% of the total amount of the century);
- more than 30 between 1575-1590 (15% of the total); and
- Cromberger's *taller de imprenta*: 50 editions of 21 different titles up to 1550[8].

During the second half of the sixteenth century, again history and print played a determining role in the diffusion of the Spanish romances about chivalry across Europe. It is well known that the sun never set on the Spanish Empire, and the influence of both Charles V, who spent most of his life in central Europe, and Philip II was political, economic, and cultural. This occurred alongside the exponential diffusion of the printed book, which worked as the second ally to the Spanish romances about chivalry in the battle to become the "best seller of the sixteenth century"[9]. "Spanish romances, like Spanish soldiers and viceroys, invaded Italy"[10], said Grendler, and, I would further add, invaded Europe (as we will see in the conclusions drawn below)[11]. As Anna Bognolo states:

---

[5] "[C]osas de encantamiento que cuentan en el libro de Amadís", R. Schevill, *La novela histórica, las crónicas de Indias y los libros de caballerías*, in "Revista de las Indias", 19, 1944, pp. 173–196, here p. 186.
[6] "[U]no de los géneros trascendentales en el mantenimiento de la industria editorial hispánica", J.M. Lucía Megías, *Imprenta y libros de caballerías*, Madrid 2000, p. 69.
[7] For a detailed study of the different printings, see M.R. Aguilar Perdomo / J.M. Lucía Megías (eds.), *Antología de libros de caballerías españoles*, Bogotá 2008, pp. 17–21. When the original edition is missing, the very first conserved edition is considered.
[8] J. García López, *Caballeros, Celestinas y pastores*, in J. García López / E. Fosalla / G. Pontón *La conquista del clasicismo, 1500–1598* (Historia de la literatura española, 2), Barcelona 2013, pp. 287–288.
[9] See H. Thomas, *The Golden Age: the Spanish Empire of Charles V*, London 2010.
[10] P.F. Grendler, *Chivalric Romances in Italian Renaissance*, in "Studies in Medieval and Renaissance History", 10, 1988, pp. 59–102, here p. 81. See also E. Body Morera / V. Foti, *Edizioni italiane dei libros de caballerías nella Biblioteca Nacional de Madrid. Ciclo di Amadís de Gaula*, in "Cuadernos de Filología Italiana", 14, 2007, pp. 259–274.
[11] The very first print in the New World was in México in 1533; while the sale of chivalric romances on the other side of the ocean was prohibited by Spanish authorities, we have proof of their presence there.

> We have to keep in mind that when the printing age started, a good part of Italy was of Spanish dominion. In the Italian peninsula the cohabitation between Spanish and Italian people was common: in the aragonese Naples, in the Rome of the Borgia and in the duchies of Ferrara, Mantova, and Milan the potential readers in Spanish were enormous[12].

And, as a matter of fact, between 1550 and 1610, the Spanish romances about chivalry surpassed every other genre in Italy in terms of popularity[13]. Again, the numbers help paint a clear picture: 80 editions were printed between 1551 and 1570, and approximately 300 by 1630[14].

Between 1539 and 1582, Michele Tramezzino, a well-known printer in Venice and Rome, together with his brother Francesco, came to a new understanding. They understood that the typographic characteristics of the large and voluminous Spanish books of the Amadises, Palmerines, and other heroes would not satisfy Italian readers' tastes nor gain economic advantage. With in-folio, xylographic images, gothic characters, and around 300 folios per book[15], such volumes were mainly conceived for a rich and elite Spanish public[16]. This did not suit the economy or the speediness of the Venetian publishing market, which was based on high-density printing and direct distribution to a large public (also known as "the pocket edition, easy to read and accessible in price"[17]). Thus the novels about chivalry first published by Tramezzino, and subsequently by all other printers, were small in size (in octavo, in duodecimo or twelvemo)[18],

---

12 "[H]ay que tener en cuenta que en el momento de la eclosión de la imprenta buena parte de Italia era española. En la península italiana la convivencia de españoles e italianos era habitual: en la Nápoles aragonesa, en la Roma de los Borja y en los ducados de Ferrara, Mantua y Milán los lectores potenciales en castellano eran innumerables", A. Bognolo, *El libro español en Venecia*, in P. Botta / M.L. Cerrón Puga (eds.), *Rumbos del hispanismo en el umbral del Cincuecentenario de la AIH*, vol. 3, Roma 2012, pp. 243–258, here p. 244. Antonio de Salamanca published in Rome *Amadís de Gaula* (1519), *La Celestina* (1520), *Esplandián* (1525).
13 Ibid., p. 252. See also B. Richardson, *Printing, Writers, and Readers in Renaissance Italy*, Cambridge 1999.
14 "Estas novelas se difundieron con mecanismos parecidos al fenómeno de los *best selling books*, iniciando una especie de moda literaria que condicionará no sólo las costumbres de lectura de la época, sino también algunos hábitos sociales. See S. Neri, *La literatura caballeresca en Italia*, in "Revista Digital Universitaria de la UNAM", 16, 2015, 8. For Palmerín's diffusion, see table 2 in S. Neri, *Cuadro de la difusión europea del ciclo palmeriniano*, in A. González et al. (eds.), *Palmerín y sus libros, 500 años*, México D.F. 2013, pp. 285–314, here pp. 312–313.
15 On Spanish printing and books of chivalry see J.M. Lucía Megías, *Imprenta y libros de caballerías*, Madrid 2000.
16 See J.M. Lucía Megías / Mª C. Marín Pina, *Lectores de libros de caballerías*, in *Amadís de Gaula, 1508: quinientos años de libros de caballerías*, Madrid 2008, pp. 289–311.
17 "[N]ovelas 'de bolsillo', de fácil lectura y de precio asequible", A. Bognolo, *Libros de caballerías en Italia*, in *Amadís de Gaula, 1508: quinientos años de libros de caballerías*, ed. José Manuel Lucía Megías, Madrid 2008, pp. 333–342, here p. 336.
18 The format 12º is used for some books printed by Pietro Bosello, i.e. *Valeriano* (1558) and *Baldus* (1555). For *Valeriano*, see C. Demattè, *Pietro Lauro traductor y autor de libros de caballerías en Venecia:*

they contained no pictures, not even on the front cover, and used cursive typography. All these features were conceived with less exigent readers in mind and were intended for a wide number of readers[19].

Michele Tramezzino embarked on an undertaking that found an excellent partner in Mambrino Roseo de Fabriano[20], an enthusiastic and prolific writer who devoted his entire life to translating the majority of the Spanish romances about chivalry. Together they also started a new fashion in Italy, namely: the composition of new books representing the Italian continuations of the adventures of the two most famous knights, Amadís and Palmerín[21].

> Regarding dedication, Mambrino Roseo exceeds any other European writer. Surprisingly, he didn't live in Venice but in Rome, where the Tramezzino brothers had their important bookshop, a center of commercial and intellectual relationships. He was in touch with the poets' circle of Pope Paul III and Cardinal Alessandro Farnese[22].

Tramezzino's activity as a translator and writer of romances about chivalry triggered a literary fashion in Italy that rapidly spread across Europe and quickly became an editorial phenomenon.

The very first translation of a Spanish romance about chivalry in Italy was the *Historia del valorosissimo cavalliere Palmerino de Olivia* (1544). The translations of its two sequels, *Primaleone* and *Platir* in 1548, translated by Mambrino and published by

---

digresión y censura en el Valeriano d'Ongaria (1558), in M.R. Aguilar Perdomo (ed.), *Imaginarios, usos y representaciones de los libros de caballerías españoles*, forthcoming.
19 E. Pace, *Aspetti tipografico-editoriali di un 'best-seller' del secolo XVI: l'Orlando furioso*, in "Schifanoia", 3, 1987, pp. 103–114; M. Beer, *Romanzi di cavalleria. Il Furioso e il romanzo italiano del primo Cinquecento*, Roma 1987.
20 The role of this author born in Fabriano, near Ancona, is the reason for the title of the "Progetto Mambrino" for a research group from the Università degli Studi di Verona under the direction of Anna Bognolo. See A. Bognolo / S. Neri / G. Cara (eds.), *Repertorio delle continuazioni italiane ai romanzi cavallereschi spagnoli*, vol. 1: *Amadís de Gaula*, Roma 2017. For Mambrino Roseo's life, see A. Bognolo, *Vida y obra de Mambrino Roseo da Fabriano, autor de libros de caballerías*, in "eHumanista", 16, 2010, pp. 77–98 and the bibliography quoted there.
21 In order to consider the amplitude of the phenomena, we do not only consider translations from the Spanish original books, but also the number of Italian original continuations that were added to the different chivalric cycles without forgetting the independent books. For a complete survey on this matter, see A. Bognolo, *La prima continuazione italiana dell'Amadís; l'Aggiunta al Quarto Libro di Mambrino Roseo da Fabriano (Venezia 1563)*, in *Literatura caballeresca entre España e Italia (Del "Orlando" al "Quijote")*, Salamanca 2004, pp. 429–441; A. Bognolo, *Libros de caballerías*, pp. 333–342 and the bibliography cited there.
22 "[D]edicación supera la de cualquier otro escritor europeo. Sorprendentemente, no vivió en Venecia sino en Roma, donde los hermanos Tramezzino tenían su importante librería, centro de relaciones comerciales e intelectuales. Tuvo relaciones con los círculos de los poetas de la corte de Paolo III y del cardenal Alessandro Farnese", A. Bognolo, *El libro español en Venecia*, p. 252 n.

Tramezzino, soon appeared[23]. See Figure 1. Between 1546 and 1551, owing to the collaboration between the two, the translation of the entire original Spanish, twelve book saga except for two volumes (the eighth book, which narrated the death of Amadís, and the eleventh, *Rogel de Grecia*, were published very late in Spain) of *Amadís de Gaula*[24].

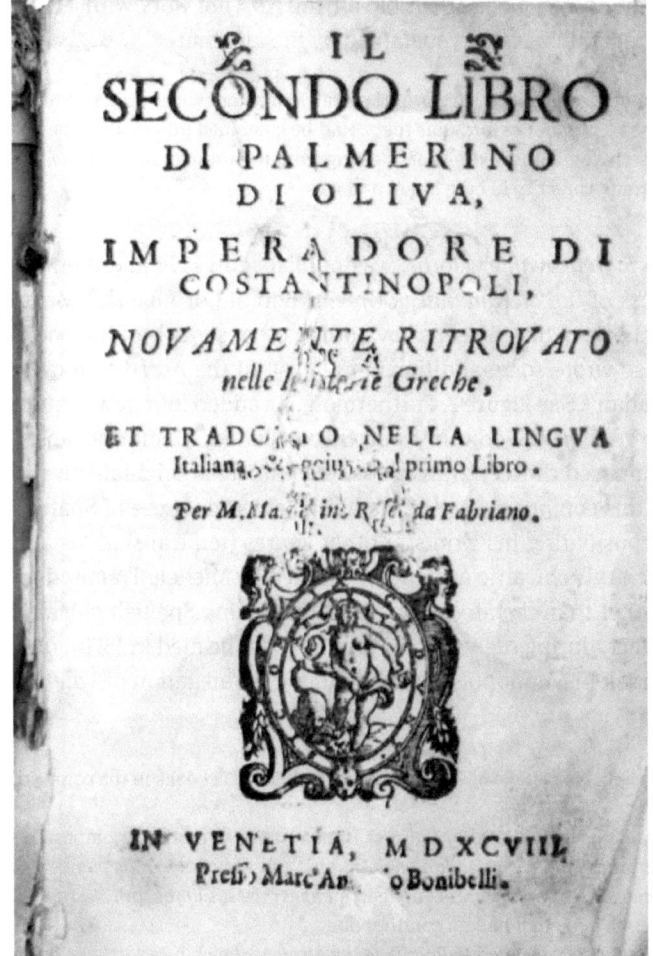

Fig. 1: *Il secondo libro di Palmerino d'Oliva*, Venezia, Marcantonio Bonibelli, 1597.

---

23 Following the important essays by Marín Pina, the last book of essays on the cycle is *Platir*. See the volume A. González et al. (eds.), *Palmerín y sus libros: 500 años*, México D.F. 2013, where we find a recompilation of data about the Italian and European diffusion of the Palmerín cycle (Bognolo and Neri).

24 S. Neri, *El Progetto Mambrino. Estado de la cuestión*, in A. Dotras Bravo (ed.), *Tus obras los rincones de la tierra descubren. Actas del VI Congreso Internacional de la Asociación de Cervantistas*, Alcalá de Henares 2008, pp. 577–590.

Thus, in less than ten years, Tramezzino exploited all the Spanish originals of the most important cycles in order to satisfy the Italian readers' thirst for these stories. Without a doubt, a new idea took shape based on Roseo's ease in writing (at this point he had translated 2,500 folios of chivalric adventures)[25] and Tramezzino's editorial genius (writing chivalric novels *ex novo* in order to present these deeds to the Italian public as if they were part of the original cycle). This would have seemed an almost impossible commitment for Roseo who, as Bognolo affirms, did not work with a team of collaborators. Roseo's individual work is sustained by the fact that

> his experience as translator gave him a huge store of narrative memory, an enormous mental encyclopedia that included a number of formulas that could be combined differently, repeated and imitated, building 'serial prefabricated pieces' starting from the traditional repertory, following a largely used narrative practice in both Spain and Italy[26].

The first sequel, *La historia del cavallier Flortir*, was published in 1554 and then followed by six original parts of the *Sferamundi di Grecia* (Book 13 of *Amadís*). Meanwhile, Mambrino Roseo chose to "fill the gaps" by adding other sequels of the books already published. He also wrote some additions to almost all the Amadisian cycle already translated into Italian[27]. See Figure 2. Furthermore, he added four new sequels to the *Palmerines*' cycle[28]. When his editorial output concluded, Mambrino Roseo could boast of having composed thirteen translations and nineteen original chivalry novels. As Neri remarks, this comprises 74% of the Italian chivalric prose of Spanish inspiration, all without considering his works in other genres (ten translations and five original texts)[29]. During this chivalric avalanche[30] caused by Michele Tramezzino, there were few printers other than the aforementioned publishing Spanish chivalric literature. As a matter of fact, during the Venetian printer's life (he died in 1578), only Pietro Bosello dared to break his monopoly by publishing the translation of *Valerián*

---

[25] The hypothesis is calculated on an average of 200 leaves per book, with 12 books in the course of his life.
[26] A. Bognolo, *Libros de caballerías en Italia*, p. 340 (transl. mine). About Mambrino's composition technique, see A. Bognolo, *La prima traducción italiana del Amadís*, and A. Bognolo, *Los palmerines italianos: una primera aproximación*, in A. González et al. (eds.), *Palmerín y sus libros*, pp. 262 ff.
[27] With the exception of the sixth book that had no continuation.
[28] As Bognolo points out, Roseo also translated *Palmerín de Inglaterra* to which he added two original continuations published by Portonotaris (*Il Progetto Mambrino. Per una esplorazione delle traduzioni e continuazioni italiane dei libros de caballerías*, in "Rivista di Filologia e Letterature Ispaniche", 6, 2003, p. 195). Bognolo focuses his analysis on Roseo's five books but not on Pietro Lauro and his original work *Polendo* (*Los palmerines italianos*, p. 262), analyzed by M. Bombardini, *El Polendo de Pietro Lauro: un heredero italiano de Palmerín*, in "Historias fingidas", 2, 2014, p. 175; C. Demattè, *Pietro Lauro traductor*.
[29] S. Neri, *El Progetto Mambrino. Estado de la cuestión*, p. 580.
[30] The label *avalancha* is used by A. Bognolo, *Libros de caballerías*, p. 334, and S. Neri, *El Progetto Mambrino. Estado de la cuestión*, p. 580.

de Hungría in 1558 in Venice. This chivalric novel by Dionis Clemente had met with limited success in Spain[31], but was published in two volumes over two consecutive years.

Fig. 2: *Aggiunta di Amadis di Grecia*, Venezia, M. Tramezzino, 1592

On the other hand, Portonotaris presented Roseo's translations of *Palmerín de Inglaterra* in 1554 and its continuation, *Il terzo libro de i valorosi cavallieri Palmerino d'Inghilterra et Floriano suo fratello*, five years later in 1559. After Tramezzino's death, Orazio Rinaldi translated the first part of *Belianís de Grecia*, which was published in Ferrara in 1586 by the printer Vittorio Baldini. The second part appeared in a

---

31 D. Clemente, *Valerián de Hungría*, ed. J. Duce García, Alcalá de Henares 2010; J. Duce García, *Estudio y edición del "Valerián de Hungría" de Dionís Clemente*, tesis doctoral, Universidad de Zaragoza, 2009; C. Demattè, *Pietro Lauro traductor*.

translation by Orazio Rinaldi one year later in Verona and was printed by Sebastiano dalle Donne. In 1587, this same printer also published the translation of *Félix Magno*, by Camillo Camilli[32]. The very last case of printers who entered into the business are the heirs of Altobello Salicato. In 1601, they published the *Specchio de' prencipi e cavallieri*[33]. Lucio Spineda drew on Tramezzino's heritage at the beginning of the seventeenth century when he promoted a second renaissance of the Spanish chivalric genre in Italy. Spineda chose to bet once more on the *spagnole romanzerie*, but this is part of another story[34].

The map of the genre's diffusion throughout Europe has been widely investigated and reveals a complicated situation comprised of: translations of the Spanish originals into many languages; the Italian, French and German continuations; and the translation of these European sequels into Spanish and other languages[35]. This picture allows us to conclude that during the second half of the sixteenth century, romances about chivalry became fashionable across Europe (and the New World). Considering that almost 200 editions of just the Palmerín cycle came out between 1511 and 1620 in six languages[36], it can be considered one the very first examples of the international bestseller genre.

In order to paint a more vivid picture about the Spanish chivalric genre's development in Europe, I will briefly discuss the case of France and Holland as far as the *Amadís* saga is concerned. In my opinion, these two countries represent significant examples.

France, together with Italy, is the *viaticum* to the success of these books making it into other languages since, after the publications of the French translations, these

---

32 C. Demattè, *Dal Félix Magno al Felice Magno: note sulla traduzione italiana di un libro di cavalleria cinquecentesco spagnolo*, in "Il Confronto Letterario", 35, 2001, pp. 33–50.
33 D. Gagliardi, *"Quid puellae cum armis?" Aproximación a doña Beatriz de Bernal y a su Cristalián de España*, Barcelona 2003, pp. 168 ff.
34 The Italian humanists used this despective label for books of chivalry (E. Sarmati, *Le critiche ai libri di cavalleria nel Cinquecento spagnolo (con uno sguardo sul Seicento). Un'analisi testuale*, Pisa 1996; S. Neri, *La literatura caballeresca en Italia*. On Spineda see D. Gagliardi, *Quid puellae cum armis?*.
35 For the chivalric books' reception in Europe, see the essays collected in *Amadís de Gaula, 1508: quinientos años*. For the translations into Italian, see S. Neri, *Note sulla prima edizione conservata de 'I quattro libri di Amadis di Gaula' (Venezia, 1547) nell'esemplare unico della Bancroft Library (University of California)*, in "Tirant", 13, 2010, pp. 51–72; http://parnaseo.uv.es/Tirant/Butlleti.13/05_Neri.pdf; S. Neri, *Cuadro de la difusión europea del ciclo del* Amadís de Gaula *(siglos XVI–XVII)*, in J.M. Lucía Megías / M.C. Marín Pina / A.C. Bueno (eds.), *Amadís de Gaula: quinientos años después. Estudios en homenaje a Juan Manuel Cacho Blecua*, Alcalá de Henares 2008, pp. 565–591; C. Demattè, *Dal Félix Magno al Felice Magno*.
36 Neri identifies 191 editions, 52 of which are without existing copies (*Cuadro de la difusión europea del ciclo palmeriniano*, pp. 312–313). As to the five Italian translations and seven Italian continuations, the numbers are incredible: almost eighty editions in less than a century. See table 1 by Neri for the very first four books and book 9 (1530) of *Amadís* (S. Neri, *Cuadro de la difusión europea del ciclo del* Amadís de Gaula, *siglos XVI–XVII*).

were used (not the originals in Spanish) to produce issues in The Netherlands, Germany, and England. In France from 1546-1574, and thanks to the enthusiasm of King Francis I, the first of the twelve books of the *Amadís* were published from translations of the original Spanish romances[37]. Afterwards, a new French romance about chivalry appeared in 1577, while the translation of the Italian supplements expanded in circulation and seven more translated books of the *Amadís* saga appeared before 1581[38]. In order to stress the variety and change of the public in France, it is interesting to note that one

> of the most important characteristic[s] of the French cycle is the variety of formats and the presence of simultaneous translations of the very same books: the translators were as a matter of fact frequently competing among themselves[39].

When it comes to Holland, we have to point out that the 62 editions underline the importance of the genre in Flemish translation. The editorial promoter was Marten Nuyts (Martín Nucio in Spanish), who, thanks to long periods spent in Spain and especially in Seville (where he would eventually come to know the Cromberger). It is thanks to this that he accumulated enough knowledge and experience to start his own printing house in Antwerp, which was dedicated to the publication of Spanish books. It is Nuyts we can thank for the introduction of the *Amadís* cycle in Flemish, and he most likely translated the first two books that come directly from Spanish. The third and fourth books were also translated from Spanish and printed by another printer, Daniel Vervliet, who spent six years in Spain. We have to keep in mind that all the translations are anonymous, and that all subsequent books are translated from the French translations and respect their numeration, additions, and omissions. Nevertheless, in the words of María del Rosario Aguilar Perdomo, in Holland the

> presence of the first four books of Amadís, all printed in 1598, and book XII, can doubtlessly be explained with the series having become a true bestseller before the end of the sixteenth century[40].

---

37 Three books are missing from the French saga, which changes the books' numbers: [6] (Florisando), [8] (Lisuarte de Grecia de Juan Díaz), and [11.2] (Florisel de Niquea, parte IV). For more details, see *ibid.*, pp. 565–591.
38 The seven Italian books translated were book XII and the six parts of *Sferamundi* (S. Neri, *Cuadro de la difusión europea del ciclo palmeriniano*, pp. 312–313).
39 "una de las características fundamentales del ciclo amadisiano francés es la oscilación de los formatos [...] y la presencia de traducciones paralelas y contemporáneas de los mismos libros, cuyos traductores compiten a menudo entre sí", *ibid.*, p. 313.
40 "la presencia de los cuatro primeros libros del Amadís, todos impresos en 1598, más el libro XII se explica sin duda, por la condición de auténtico bestseller que distinguía la serie ya para finales del siglo XVI", M.R. Aguilar Perdomo, *Por los caminos de Flandes: las ediciones holandesas del Amadís de Gaula*, in "Historias fingidas", 5, 2017, forthcoming: http://historiasfingidas.dlls.univr.it/index.php/hf/index (transl. mine). See this article for an updated overview of the question and bibliography about Holland's books of chivalry.

If today's pervasiveness of digital books causes us to consider whether digital libraries allow for quick and widespread access, but do not necessarily provide deeper knowledge, then it is interesting to compare this current situation to the editorial phenomenon described here. Specifically the one that occurred in Italy, and especially in Venice, just a century after the invention of the printing press, which marked an important shift in reading habits away from an elitist activity to a common practice[41]. Michele Tramezzino was, without any doubt, one of the most important editors in Venice in the sixteenth century. This is demonstrated by his brilliant intuition by betting on the fact that the Spanish romances about chivalry could become an incredible business and cultural adventure that would create a European literary fashion never before imagined.

---

[41] Bognolo spoke about chivalric literature "de consumo" (A. Bognolo, *Libros de caballerías en Italia*, p. 336).

Elisa Marazzi
Crossing Genres: A Newcomer in the Transnational History of Almanacs

1 Barbanera and the historiography on almanacs and cheap print

Despite the vast historiography on Italian almanacs, historians have neglected a whole family of publications, issued from at least 1762 under the name of the fictional astronomer Barbanera[1]. No mention of Barbanera can be detected in the numerous studies issued in Italy in the wake of Cuaz and Braida's preliminary works from the 1980's[2], which were, in turn, triggered by French historiography. The latter had in fact driven attention towards the circulation of almanacs among lower classes in eighteenth-century France, especially thanks to Geneviève Bollème[3]. In the 1980's a new generation of historians revealed that there was a greater interest in the circulation of such ephemeral printed products across social and cultural boundaries, fostering a new wave of studies that also flourished in Italy[4]. Nonetheless, either difficulty in tracing copies of such diverse and ephemeral publications or the apparent immutability of the Barbanera almanacs that remained loyal to the first editions' outline for over three centuries, might have resulted in the little interest expressed towards the publication.

The establishment of a dedicated foundation and research center (Fondazione Barbanera 1762)[5], has recently made it possible to overcome such difficulties and

---

[1] For practical reasons the name of the fictional editor is used to identify all of the different editions, whose titles, mentioned when necessary, are diverse and ununiform. Since it is not a title, the term "Barbanera" will not be identified as such by the means of typographical conventions.
[2] M. Cuaz, *Almanacchi e "cultura media" nell'Italia del Settecento*, in "Studi storici", 25, 1984, 2, pp. 353–361, and L. Braida, *Le guide del tempo. Produzione, contenuti e forme degli almanacchi piemontesi nel Settecento*, Torino 1989.
[3] G. Bollème, *Les Almanachs populaires aux XVIIe et XVIIIe siècle. Essai d'histoire sociale*, Paris 1969. An interest in the history of astrology has conversely fostered the study of almanacs in the English-speaking world after the work of B. Capp, *Astrology and the Popular Press. English Almanacs: 1500–1800*, London 1979.
[4] For an account of such studies see M. Formica, *Gli almanacchi romani del XVIII e del XIX secolo*, in "Studi settecenteschi", 15, 1995, pp. 115–162. More recent works worth mentioning at an international level are J. Salman / G. Verhoeven, *The Comptoir-Almanacs of Gilles Joosten Saeghman. Research into Seventeenth-Century Almanacs in the Dutch Republic*, in "Quaerendo", 23, 1993, 2, pp. 93–114, and M. Perkins, *Visions of the Future. Almanacs, Time, and Cultural Change 1775–1870*, Oxford 1996.
[5] Located in Spello, in the province of Perugia, the Fondazione Barbanera 1762 (FB) preserves more than 8,000 almanacs, published both in Italy and abroad, and especially the ones ascribed to the astronomer called Barbanera. These were frequently issued in Foligno, the birthplace of the longer selling edition, which is still published nowadays.

account for what will be called throughout this article, "a family of almanacs" in light of the more recent issues related to the historiography on cheap print[6].

How can Barbanera be of interest to an international audience of scholars when Barbanera almanacs have been characterized by their national circulation, at least prior to the late nineteenth century? Unlike other almanacs – the most famous being *Der Hinkende Bote/Le Messager Boiteux* – Barbanera almanacs were not printed in a border area and did not undergo any translation or adaptation[7]. On the contrary, it was not until the end of the nineteenth century that Barbanera almanacs traveled overseas, following the paths of Italian immigrants, both in North America and South America[8]. Despite this, Barbanera almanacs represent an interesting case study from a transnational perspective. These are outlined below.

First, alongside the history of the publication of Barbanera almanacs, we can also retrace different phenomena that are likely to enrich the international state of the art. There may have been a reduction in interest in the field of almanacs in recent years, as the field appears to have been fully explored by a huge number of scholarly works[9]. However, this research deserves to be kept alive through a transnational perspective, as was argued during the international conference held in 1999 in Versailles St. Quentin-en-Yvelines[10].

Second, the aforementioned body of research has led to the assumption that the cross-cultural circulation of cheap print does not only need to be read in a geo-cultural perspective, but also from a socio-cultural point of view[11]. This article focuses on the second option, and retraces in the Barbanera almanac a transnational phenom-

---

[6] Some of the following considerations have been already published in Italian in E. Marazzi, *Sotto il segno di Barbanera. Continuità e trasformazioni di un almanacco tra XVIII e XXI secolo*, Milano 2017, issued from the research on FB's collections and other local archives.

[7] The Italian *Gran pescatore di Chiaravalle* also ought to be mentioned in a brief account of "transnational almanacs", since it was translated into Spanish; not to mention the manifold European editions of Franklin's *Poor Richard Almanac*. On almanacs in translation cf. H.-J. Lüsebrink / Y.-G. Mix / J.-Y. Mollier / P. Sorel (eds.), *Les lectures du peuple en Europe et dans les Amériques (XVIIe–XXe siècles)*, Bruxelles 2003.

[8] We have evidence, in 1917, 1932, 1938, and in 1960 of at least three different editions deliberately issued for an audience of emigrants. A 1938 item is part of an edition printed in Naples and distributed in the USA, whereas the ones printed in 1917 and 1932 were printed on behalf of two credit institute based respectively in Massachusetts and in Argentina. In the 1960's, a Barbanera co. publishing enterprise based in New York issued an edition that was manifestly inspired to the ones printed in Foligno (see further). The reference items can be found in FB, call numbers: BN 1/12.1917; BN 1/15.1938; BN 1.Misc(1); BN 1/16.1960–1968.

[9] For an exhaustive bibliography of the Italian research on almanacs see M. Formica, *Gli almanacchi romani del XVIII e del XIX secolo*, in "Studi settecenteschi", 15, 1995, pp. 115–162.

[10] Proceedings edited by H.-J. Lüsebrink / Y.-G. Mix / J.-Y. Mollier / P. Sorel (eds.), *Les lectures du peuple*.

[11] Cf. R. Chartier / H.-J. Lüsebrink (eds.), *Colportage et lecture populaire. Imprimés de large circulation en Europe XVIe–XIXe siècles*, Paris 1996; for the Italian reflection on such themes see L. Braida / M. Infelise (eds.), *Libri per tutti. I generi editoriali di larga circolazione tra antico regime ed età contem-

enon, by exploring: What can be defined as the "porosity" of popular publishing? It can be argued that in addition to including in its pages some excerpts inspired by the most successful publishing genres of the time for over three centuries, Barbanera represents a relevant example of the now renowned mobility and mutability of almanacs and of their multifarious reception across the social ladder.

2 Barbanera's history in a transnational perspective

2.1 A reassuringly fixed structure

As often happens in the history of almanacs, Barbanera is not a proper title. Rather, it is the name of an astronomer to which a wide range of publications that prophesized the future were attributed. Although Barbanera almanacs were printed in a range of different areas, they were predominantly printed in central Italy, especially in Foligno, which was at the time situated in the Papal States. Nowadays it is located in the region of Umbria. The astronomer's first attested mention dates back to 1753 and is actually related to a Bolognese almanac. Nevertheless, Barbanera was to earn greater success in Foligno, where the oldest mention can be traced back to a one-sheet calendar from 1762, entitled *Discorso generale del famoso Barbanera per l'anno 1762* (General discourse by the famous Barbanera for the year 1762)[12]. See Figure 1.

Barbanera's family produced both one-sheet calendars, especially in the eighteenth century, and almanacs in the form of booklets. The oldest booklet printed in Foligno has been recently discovered in the Sächsische Landesbibliothek of Dresden and was originally issued in 1768. See Figure 2. The name Barbanera has been connected to the Umbrian town ever since, due to the fact that the production of almanacs in Foligno is the most significant here both in terms of editions and the number of items preserved. Furthermore, Barbanera almanacs have been increasingly identified with Foligno throughout the centuries, and in the 1960s a Barbanera almanac published in the USA was even defined "tipo Foligno" (Foligno-like) in its subtitle[13]. Hence, this article will focus on the different editions of Barbanera almanacs in Foligno that have tied their name to the proper long-seller. Despite having undergone a substantial evolution due to changes in demand, Barbanera is still published nowadays with decent print runs[14].

---

poranea, Torino 2010, which also contains accounts for the French, German, and Spanish historiography on cheap print.
12 *Discorso generale del famoso Barbanera per l'anno 1762* [General discourse for the year 1762] printed in Foligno by Pompeo Campana, cf. FB, call number F.1.
13 Cf. the items preserved at FB, call numbers BN 1/16.1960–1968.
14 Over 200,000 copies a year according to the more recent print runs. Such numbers are achieved also thanks to business to business policies that allow the publications of co-edited almanacs for corporate gifts.

Fig. 1: *Discorso generale del famoso Barbanera per l'anno 1762*, in "Foligno": Per il Campana stamp. vesc. pub. con lic. de' super., 1762. 1 folio: ill.; 44×32 cm - Fondazione Barbanera 1762.

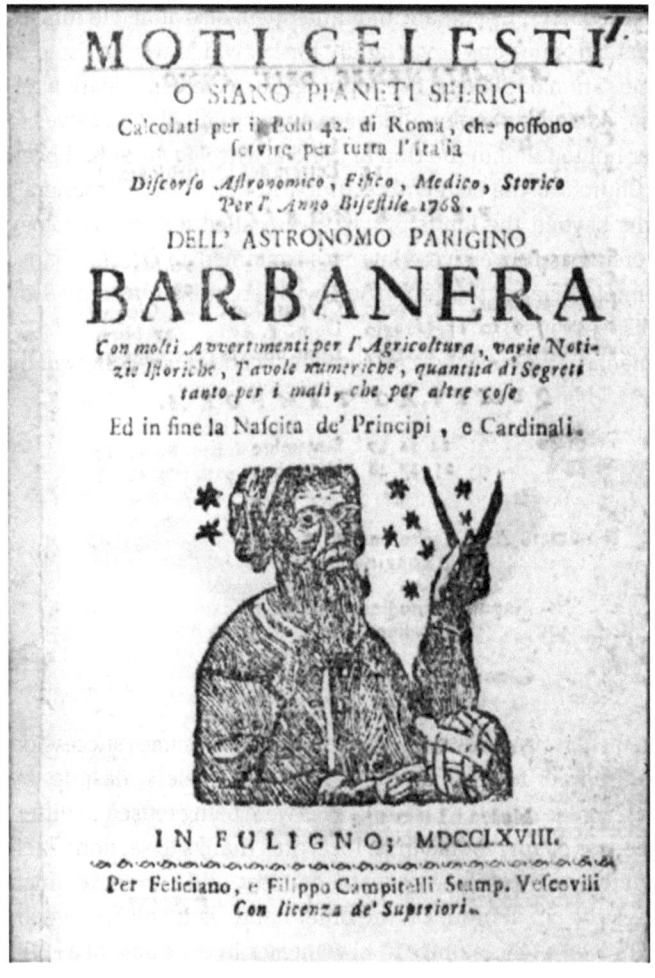

Fig. 2: *Moti Celesti O Siano Pianeti Sferici: Calcolati per il Polo 42. di Roma, che possono servire per tutta l'Italia Discorso Astronomico, Fisico, Medico, Storico Per l'Anno Bisestile 1768. Dell'Astronomo Parigino Barbanera; Con molti Avvertimenti per l'Agricoltura, varie Notizie Istoriche, Tavole numeriche, quantita di Segreti tanto per i mali, che per altre cose; Ed in fine la Nascita de' Principi, e Cardinali*, in "Fuligno": Per Feliciano e Filippo Campitelli Stamp. Vescovile, 1768. 64 p.: ill.; 16° - Staats- und Universitätsbibliothek Dresden / Digital Collections / Astron.838.

As far as some contextualization is concerned, Barbanera can be ascribed to "the predominant model"[15] in Italian eighteenth-century almanacs, specfically: a booklet containing both a calendar and astrological forecasts. Alongside these, the *discorso generale* (general discourse), in the form of a prophesy, contained predictions for the

---

15 L. Braida, *Le guide del tempo*, pp. 109–117.

year to come. These concerned not only climate and illness, but also aimed to foresee military events, natural catastrophes and royal family births, which were all said to be determined by the observation of planets' overlapping. Such elements mark a relevant difference in comparison with simpler almanacs, which limited themselves to weather forecasts in order not to fall into the trap of judicial astrology that had been banned by the Catholic Church in the sixteenth century. Nonetheless, Barbanera's tendency to predict events beyond the limits of what was called natural astrology does not have to be interpreted as subversive. Almanacs contained a *protesta* (claim) affirming that the supreme judicial authority of God was recognized, as stated by Catholic principles and dispositions[16].

As in many other almanacs, the *prognosticon* (prognostication) was followed by the following elements:
- chronology,
- calendar,
- religious holidays,
- phases of the moon,
- ephemeris,
- markets and fairs,
- currency conversion, and
- lineage.

The abovementioned elements were always presented in the same succession throughout the centuries, in order to reassure the reader. Nonetheless, despite the model being transnational, and despite the fact that titles were being reused in different areas, each publication was deeply rooted in its local area thanks to sections such as fair and market calendars, the timetable for postal delivery, and currency, which were compiled according to the circulation. On the other hand, as it will be argued, contents changed and embraced a whole range of new themes in the frame of a solid and durable structure.

2.2 Competition and agreements among almanac printers: some hypotheses

Besides Barbanera's apparent static nature, another factor that might have influenced the weak interest towards this almanac is the almost exclusive preservation of

---

[16] On the fallouts of such controversy surrounding the editing of almanacs in Italy see E. Casali, *Le spie del cielo. Oroscopi, lunari e almanacchi nell'Italia moderna*, Torino 2003, pp. 62–69. On judicial astrology in Italy cf. M. Azzolini, *The Political Uses of Astrology: Predicting the Illness and Death of Princes, Kings and Popes in the Italian Renaissance*, in "Studies in History and Philosophy of Science Part C: Studies in History and Philosophy of Biological and Biomedical Sciences", 41, 2010, 2, pp. 135–145.

copies printed in the nineteenth century. This means that it mainly concerns the late modern period, an age marked by a multifarious offer of printed products that have more easily encountered the interest of scholars. As Bollème underlines[17], the scarce number of issues preserved from the eighteenth century is another commonality across Europe. Consequently, compared to the luckier situation of calendar ephemera from the preceding and following periods, Barbanera almanacs remain partially obscure. Nonetheless, in Foligno a new interest for almanacs appears to have only emerged among publishers at the end of the eighteenth century. This was especially the case after a change in attitude towards religion during the Napoleonic occupation, when printers in the former Papal States (that were traditionally involved in religious publications), had to find new strategies to handle the market contraction[18]. Furthermore, in Foligno, they were exempt from the increasing price of paper because well-established paper mills had been present on the territory since the fourteenth century[19]. Therefore, for some printers, almanacs represented a strategy to face the decline of religious publications.

Almost all of the printers established in Foligno have published Barbanera almanacs: Pompeo Campana (eighteenth century); Feliciano Campitelli and his heirs; Giovanni Tomassini; Francesco Fofi; and Francesco Salvati (late nineteenth) were the most active within the time span of interest[20]. Even though their almanacs often contained an *avviso* (notice), where the printer stated to be patented for that very edition, it is difficult to retrace a regular correspondence between printers and the differently featured almanac issued. See Figure 3.

In fact, the main series were essentially four, two 48-page editions and two 64-page editions. Up until the twentieth century, the whole of the four editions were always published by Campitelli and Tomassini, but even in this selected corpus, a regular correspondence between a format and a publisher can only be retraced for brief periods of time. This indicates that a sort of agreement existed among printers aiming to exploit the production of almanacs. Nevertheless, no equivalent of a stationary company or printers' corporation has been tracked down in Foligno during the time in question[21].

---

17 G. Bollème, *Les Almanachs populaires*, p. 23.
18 As suggested by M. Tosti, *Strategie editoriali e famiglie di tipografi alla fine del Settecento. Le stamperie di Ottavio Sgariglia e Giovanni Tomassini*, in A. Sindoni / M. Tosti (eds.), *Vita religiosa, problemi sociali e impegno civile dei cattolici. Studi religiosi in onore di Alberto Monticoni*, Roma 2009, pp. 129–142.
19 Cf. G. Castagnari (ed.), *Carta e cartiere nelle Marche e nell'Umbria dalle manifatture medievali all'industrializzazione*, in "Proposte e ricerche – Quaderni", 13, 1995, pp. 185–208.
20 On such printers and their involvement in almanacs, see G. Brinci, *I lunari e gli almanacchi di Foligno*, Foligno 2002, and E. Marazzi, *Sotto il segno di Barbanera*, pp. 25–33.
21 Although a proper corporation existed before, as retraced in the traditional accounts of the origins of printing in the Umbrian town by M. Faloci Pulignani and T. Valenti, published in "La bibliofilia", 1–2, 1899–1901, and 27, 1926.

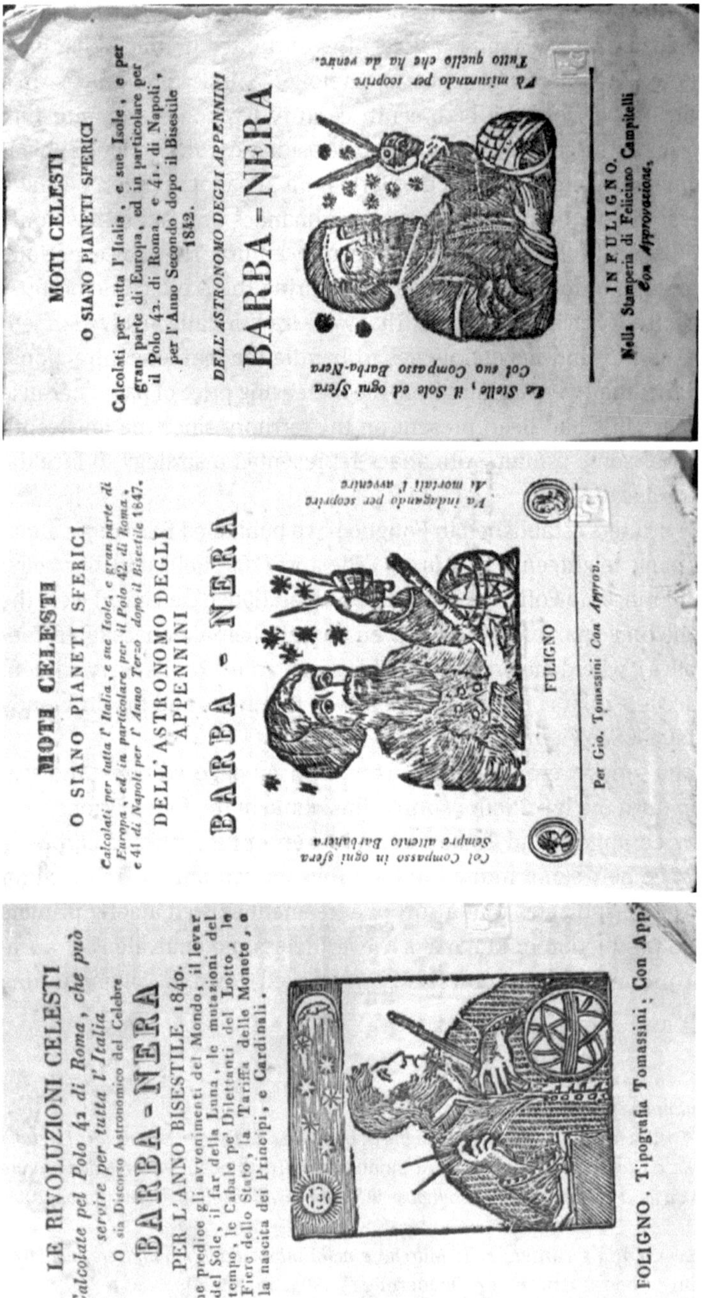

Fig. 3: Three different title pages, printed by Tomassini 1840, Tomassini 1847, Campitelli 1842 - Fondazione Barbanera 1762.

Therefore, we can only speculate on the existence of regulation such as the one in force within the London Stationer's company, which imposed shared printing of the authorized almanac. This was in place to control and to redistribute income from such a successful production[22]. Something more similar to the agreement among the London Ballad Partners[23] might have happened in Foligno, and it can be argued that a trust of printers specialized in cheap print was active in the Umbrian town. This alleged "entente cordiale entre les faiseurs d'almanachs" (friendly agreement among almanac makers) is described by Charles Nisard, a French nineteenth-century observer[24]. At the same time, in his report describing the state of the art of the so-called *littérature de colportage* in his country, Nisard depicts an ironical portrait of the plethoric productions of almanacs in a number of editions by eager printers in eighteenth- and nineteenth-century France. Such a portrait can easily be extended to the Umbrian town where Barbanera almanacs were published.

2.3 The emergence of copyright and the need for diversification

If the printers' situation reveals itself to be quite intricate, Barbanera's authors are also quite difficult to identify. Even though the "astronomer from the Appennines"[25] – whose observatory was believed to be situated in the local mountains – was represented in diverse features through woodcuts printed on the title pages, there was no accredited Barbanera. On the contrary, it can be argued that since time immemorial, it was printers and anonymous editors that brought Barbanera to life. Bernard Capp has made some considerations about the difference between British almanacs and French almanacs as far as compilers are concerned. Capp notes that the compilation of an almanac represented a form of professional affirmation for English astrologers, physicians, and quacks. Such an observation can be extended to other traditions, e.g. the Dutch almanacs[26], nevertheless in Italy and France, the editor's centrality had

---

22 Such strategies have been described by R. Meyers, *The Stationers' Company and the Almanack Trade*, in M.F. Suarez / M.L. Turner (eds.), *The Cambridge History of the Book in Britain*, vol. 5: *1695–1830*, Cambridge 2009, pp. 723–735.
23 H. Rollins, *The Black-Letter Broadside Ballad*, in "PMLA", 34, 1919, 2, pp. 258–339; T. Watt, *Cheap Print and Popular Piety, 1550–1640*, Cambridge 1991, pp. 42–50.
24 Ch. Nisard, *Histoire des livres populaires ou De la littérature du colportage depuis l'origine de l'imprimerie jusqu'à l'établissement de la commission d'examen des livres de colportage, 30 novembre 1852*, Paris, Dentu, 1864, p. 11. To benefit from a transnational perspective on the history of this genre, it could be useful to look for similar agreements in other centers of production in order to understand if the settlement of a trust was a common strategy in all popular publishing centers.
25 This mention, "astronomo degli Appennini", was recurrent in title pages and often also in the text of the almanacs published throughout the period at the focus of this article.
26 B. Capp, *Astrology and the Popular Press*, pp. 270–292. On Dutch almanacs, see J. Salman / G. Verhoeven, *The Comptoir-Almanacs*.

disappeared since the beginning of the Modern era, due to the rejection of judicial astrology[27]. In fact, since the editor was likely to receive condemnation, the cautious choice was to remain anonymous.

Nonetheless, the emergence of the concept of literary propriety, eventually set forth in Italy in 1840, caused a sort of revolution because publishers started to care about the specificity of their own editions and safeguarded their rights. Stamps of literary property together with announcements of court cases against competitors begin to appear on the covers and pages of the almanacs. Despite this, counterfeiting still proliferated, and in 1874 a brand new edition was issued in Naples that imitated the booklets from Foligno that were circulating in the central region and the southern peninsula. Nonetheless, in 1900, Luigi Chiurazzi, the farsighted Neapolitan publisher of the counterfeit edition, asserted that his almanacs had nothing to do with the one printed in Foligno. His idea was to inform everybody that his edition of the Barbanera was something newer and more accurate than the old-fashioned Umbrian almanac[28]. In this way Chiurazzi managed to benefit from the fame that by that time was strictly bound to Barbanera's name and at the same time turn his almanac into a completely different publication. This strategy led to two relevant achievements. First, the almanac does not risk being banned for copyright reasons. Second, the almanac will progressively include themes and content more likely to attract urban audiences in a city whose fabric of society is extremely different from Barbanera's original context.

The competition of the nineteenth century, triggered by an increasingly wide range of popular publications and the emergence of a bourgeois audience, laid the basis for the emergence, as far as yearly issues are concerned, of other publishing genres such as étrennes (gift books), or coffee-table books throughout Europe[29]. As far as Italy is concerned, Milan became the production center of étrennes, which represented the bourgeois evolution of almanacs par excellence; after that, illustrated press and book series would take over. This did not mean the downfall of almanacs, especially in more peripheral areas. The same phenomenon has been singled out in France during the second half of the nineteenth century, which represents an unexpected revival age for almanacs[30]. The same happened in French-speaking Switzerland up to 1925[31]. The case of Foligno is an important piece of evidence that almanacs also remained alive, healthy, and, as it will be argued in the next section, even evolved.

---

27 E. Casali, *Le spie del cielo*, pp. 62–69.
28 Cf. the item in FB, call number BN 1/6.1900.
29 The evolution of some almanacs into different book has been studied, for France, by V. Sarrazin, *L'Exemple des Étrennes Parisiennes. Succès, évolution et mutation d'un genre d'almanachs du XVIIIe au XIXe siècle*, in H.-J. Lüsebrink / Y.-G. Mix / J.-Y. Mollier / P. Sorel (eds.), *Les lectures du peuple*, pp. 39–48.
30 J.-Y. Mollier, *Les éditeurs d'almanach au XIXe siècle entre tradition et modernité*, ibid., pp. 205–223, has given an account of the same phenomenon in France.
31 Cf. F. Vallotton, *Le rôle des almanachs au sein des politiques éditoriales des éditeurs suisses romands (1750–1950)*, ibid., pp. 225–233.

3. Barbanera and the nineteenth-century publishing genres

Lodovica Braida has highlighted the direction taken by Italian almanacs at the end of the eighteenth century: from vehicles of prejudice to "powerful means of education"[32]. This happened, among other things, in the wake of Pietro Verri's idea that the almanac represented "la sola strada per potervi dire una parola così di fretta in passando" (the only way to tell you [the reader – author's note] a word in a hurry)[33]. In general, new and diverse typologies came to light that clearly show the flexibility of the genre; these included agrarian almanacs, court almanacs, and city guides in the form of almanacs[34].

A superficial review of the editions reveals that such a phenomenon seems to have involved neither Barbanera, nor other almanacs of the same typology. However, it is possible to get a different impression through a more in-depth reading, especially when it comes to the introductory section entitled *Dialogue*. This text represented a dialogue between Barbanera and his friend Silvano, who allegedly visited Barbanera every year at the end of the summer in order to let the astronomer give him the manuscript of the almanac for next year. In such a fictional context, Silvano would hurry back to Foligno and deliver Barbanera's text to the printer. But before doing this, Barbanera would talk to him briefly, instructing him about a different topic each year.

The dialogue represents the written transposition of an educational conversation. Together with other informative texts placed between the months of the calendar, this represents the main source for developing the argument of Barbanera's internal evolution. In fact, in a great number of almanacs, the dialogue texts represent the window through which the most successful coeval editorial genres entered the almanacs in the age of the so-called "reading revolution"[35].

---

[32] Cf. L. Braida, *Les almanachs italiens du XVIIIe siècle. Véhicules de "faux préjugés" ou "puissants moyens d'*éducation"?, *ibid.*, pp. 259–270.
[33] P. Verri, *Il Gran Zoroastro ossia astrologiche predizioni per l'anno bisestile 1764*, now in P. Verri, *Scritti letterari, filosofici e satirici*, Roma 2015, p. 560.
[34] Cf. L. Braida, *Les almanachs italiens. Évolutions et stéréotypes d'un genre (XVIIe–XVIIIe siècles)*, in R. Chariter / H.-J. Lüsebrink (eds.), *Colportage et lecture populaire*.
[35] On this issue cf. R. Wittmann, *Was there a Reading Revolution at the End of the Eighteenth Century?*, in G. Cavallo / R. Chartier, *A History of Reading in the West*, Amherst 1999, pp. 284–312; B. Dooley, *La seconde révolution de la lecture dans l'Italie du XVIIIe siècle*, in "Revue d'Histoire moderne et contemporaine", 49, 2002, 3, pp. 69–88; J.-F. Gilmont, *Une révolution de la lecture au XVIIIe siècle?*, in G. Petrella (ed.), *"Navigare nei mari dell'umano sapere". Biblioteche e circolazione libraria nel Trentino e nell'Italia del XVIII secolo*, Trento 2008, pp. 129–139. As far as Italy is concerned, the emergence of a proper wider, mass audience has to be postponed to the nineteenth century. Cf. M. Infelise, *Libri per tutti*, in L. Braida / M. Infelise (eds.), *Libri per tutti*, pp. 3–19.

First of all, lots of nineteenth-century almanacs contain biographies of inventors. The popularization of historical, geographical, and scientific notions was intrinsic to a great number of almanacs – from Benjamin Franklin's *Poor Richard* up to agrarian almanacs of the nineteenth century. Additionally, in previous years, from Plutarch's *Parallel Lives* (first-second century) onwards, biographies of distinguished people have been a vehicle for conveying such notions. Nevertheless it is important to remember how, in the Italian coeval publishing market, biographies and anthologies of biographies became a proper genre[36]. The Florentine Gaspero Barbera has to be mentioned as a relevant example of a publisher who believed in biographies as a means towards civic education, which should involve popular classes in the struggle for the unification of the country. After 1861, biographies remained a fruitful business if the Milanese publisher Treves, who mainly addressed urban bourgeoisie. Treves published, among others, the translation of a collection of biographies entitled *Les Héros du travail*, by the French scientist and popularizer Gustave Tissandier. The Italian adaptation addressed a diverse audience, from schoolchildren to the whole family[37].

Second, dialogues contain diverse informative notions of all sorts, among which a blatant example is worth mentioning. For example, in the almanac for 1840, Barbanera explained to Silvano what an *agenda* (diary) is, and how to use it[38]. It is not by chance that agendas represented, at the end of the eighteenth century, one path of evolution for almanacs[39]. Besides representing another expression of the self-help trend that affected all different kinds of publications addressed to lowbrow audiences – the use of an agenda is presented as a way to organize one's time and in that way improve one's quality of life – the 1840 dialogue provides a scenery for interaction between two editorial genres on the market at that time.

The topics that progressively appeared in Barbanera's dialogues throughout the nineteenth and twentieth centuries increasingly included forms and content that were typical of the coeval literature addressing less cultivated people. Health and physical exercise and other hygienic precepts were the most frequent topic addressed in the dialogues. For instance, in some almanacs an aversion emerges towards employing wet-nurses and others frequently insist on the right nutrition depending on one's daily activities. Such precepts were often to be recalled by sayings, adages,

---

36 Cf. M.P. Casalena, *Biografie. La scrittura delle vite in Italia tra politica, società e cultura (1796–1915)*, Milano 2012. See also M. Huisman, *The Written Portrait: Biographical and Autobiographical Publishing in the Nineteenth Century*, in "Quaerendo", 37, 2007, 3, pp. 226–243.

37 See also S. Lanaro, *Il Plutarco italiano: l'istruzione del 'popolo' dopo l'Unità*, in C. Vivanti (ed.), *Intellettuali e potere* (Storia d'Italia. Annali, 4), Torino 1981, pp. 551–587.

38 Cf. the item in FB, call number BN 1/7.1940.

39 Cf. L. Braida, *Dall'almanacco all'agenda. Lo spazio per le osservazioni del lettore nelle "guide del tempo" italiane (XVIII–XIX secolo)*, in A. Messerli / R. Chartier (eds.), *Lesen und Schreiben in Europa (1500–1900)*, Basel 2000, pp. 107–138.

or other brief texts that were included in the calendar section, usually at the bottom of the page.

Another frequent topic of information in the dialogue and the excerpts related to geography, sometimes it even included an account of travels and exploration, as in an 1881 item[40]. This was another trend exploited by publishers in the wake of colonial experiences. The activities of geographical societies not only fostered scientific publications, but also diverse publications, often in installments, that largely targeted low- and middlebrow audiences. The Italian readers, albeit lacking a colonial quest to follow by the means of the press, were very receptive towards narrations of this nature imported from France and England[41], which might explain why, at a certain point, they also entered almanacs.

Travel and exploration accounts can be considered part of the scientific popularization that occurred through the press and books that also met with great success from nineteenth-century readers[42]. Information regarding agricultural techniques and scientific information like the breeding of silkworms (which was a widespread activity in the region), the use of microscopes, and the invention of the lightning rod exemplify a similar trend[43]. Albeit less frequently, the dialogue also displayed self-help suggestions like the aforementioned paragraph on planning one's activities using a diary and, in an 1879 item, good manners represent the main topic[44].

To summarize, anyone who is acquainted with the most successful literary genres of that time would easily recognize them in the pages of almanacs, be it: science popularization, hygienic education, biographies of self-made people (a classic of self-help literature), travel and exploration reports, fictional narratives, and so forth[45].

Jacques Michon has argued that nineteenth-century Franco-Canadian almanacs represented a useful location for advertisements of editions by their publishers[46]. This is only partially the case of Barbanera, since its publishers were not engaged in significant publishing activities up to the twentieth century.

---

40 Item preserved at FB, call number BN 1.1881.
41 Cf. E. Marazzi, *Translating for the Common Reader. An Ongoing Research on Science and Education in the Italian Book Trade, 1865–1903*, in "Bibliothecae.it", 6, 2017, 2, doi:10.6092/issn.2283-9364/7701, accessed April 12, 2018.
42 Cf. for the Italian situation, P. Govoni, *Un pubblico per la scienza. La divulgazione scientifica nell'Italia in formazione*, Roma 2002.
43 Cf. items preserved at FB, call numbers BN 1/3.1859; BN 1/3.1861; BN 1/3.1880; BN 1.1894.
44 Item preserved at FB, call number BN 1.1879.
45 For accounts of the publishing genres in nineteenth-century Italy cf. the articles by M.I. Palazzolo / M. Infelise / A. Gigli Marchetti / A. Chemello, *La letteratura popolare e di* consumo, in G. Turi (ed.), *Storia dell'editoria nell'Italia contemporanea*, Firenze 1997. On science popularization in Italy see P. Govoni, *Un pubblico per la scienza. La divulgazione scientifica nell'Italia in formazione*, Roma 2002.
46 Cf. J. Michon, *L'almanach comme vecteur des stratégies éditoriales au Québec au temps de la naissance d'une littérature nationale (1880–1939)*, in H.-J. Lüsebrink / Y.-G. Mix / J.-Y. Mollier / P. Sorel (eds.), *Les lectures du peuple*, pp. 233–240.

This circulation of topics is not new to the transnational history of almanacs either. Bollème has argued that themes from the *Bibliothèque bleue* were part of the almanacs especially before their further specialization from the end of the eighteenth century[47]. Both in Italy and abroad, a relevant part of almanac production was to act as a tool for cultivated people and philanthropists to reach peasants and common people and to try to educate them. In Foligno no manifest evolution occurred, but the contacts with coeval literature represent a strategy of innovation by printers who ended up working as unaware mediators of a literature that would have hardly reached non-urbanized readers. It can be argued that publishers such as Campitelli, Tomassini, and later Salvati and Campi, who would lead the production of almanacs in the first half of twentieth century, were unconsciously or semi-consciously able to bring content to an audience of new readers that were unlikely to be reached by proper books, models, and other recent editorial productions. Those forms can be said to have properly crossed genres by the means of almanacs.

4 Some cues for further transnational analysis

The dialogue section is a specificity of the Barbanera almanacs printed in Foligno and represents an extremely interesting corpus for an in-depth analysis of the publication. Traces of orality in almanacs have only been studied episodically thus far[48]. Therefore it is useful to briefly linger on this topic in this section in the wake of the more recent and stimulating reflection on the role played by orality in the history of written culture[49].

On the one hand, the choice to open the publication with a paragraph organized as a dialogue between the astronomer and a peasant from Foligno easily recalls the dialogic structure of catechisms and other pedagogical tools that have been in use since the Middle Ages. On the other hand, this choice has to be considered in connection with the frequent presence of predictions in verses within the *prognosticon* and of rhymed sayings throughout the calendar. The musicality of rhymes played a relevant role in the oral circulation of chivalry romances in Italy up to the twentieth century[50], and the combination of rhymed verses and sayings with an opening paragraph delib-

---

[47] G. Bollème, *Les Almanachs populaires*, pp. 32–34.
[48] Cf. *Conclusion*, in H.-J. Lüsebrink / Y.- G. Mix / J.-Y. Mollier / P. Sorel (eds.), *Les lectures du peuple*, p. 344.
[49] Cf. S. Dall'Aglio / B. Richardson / M. Rospocher (eds.), *Voices and Texts in Early Modern Italian Society*, London 2017. On the role played by orality in the circulation of literature at diverse levels of the social ladder in Italy, see also M. Roggero, *Le carte piene di sogni. Testi e lettori in età moderna*, Bologna 2006. As far as Spain is concerned, enlightening examples are displayed in A. Castillo Gomez (ed.), *Libro y lectura en la península ibérica y América (siglos XIII a XVIII)*, Valladolid 2003.
[50] Cf. M. Roggero, *Le carte piene di sogni*, p. 38.

erately reproduces an oral exchange that allows us to suppose that the oral fruition of the more narrative parts of the almanac were taken into account by the editors. Although no evidence of oral reading practices of Barbanera almanacs has emerged to date, the presence of similar hints cannot be neglected and represents a suggestion to retrace evidence for oral fruition in a wider, transnational corpus of almanacs in order to foster research in this direction.

The interest in the oral dimensions of written culture relates to another very promising focus for a renewed study of almanacs in the wake of recent international historiography: the study of reader reception. As Robert Darnton argued in his manifesto for the history of reading[51], besides a process of abstract thinking, the act of reading is also expressed in concrete practices, places, and circumstances, which have left traces in extremely diversified sources. Such sources are increasingly rare the further we go down the social ladder. Nonetheless, due to their relationship with everyday life, almanacs provide a relatively large amount of evidence thanks to the practice of annotation, as already envisaged by Braida[52] and recently researched extensively by means of the digital humanities[53].

Barbanera almanacs represent a key to accessing the world of nineteenth-century readers because of a relatively large number of annotated copies. In an item issued in 1887, we can even retrace the first mark of possession: a stamp by a secondary school teacher who bought Barbanera almanacs throughout his long life, remaining loyal to the edition issued by the printer Campitelli, as further marks of possession show. The teacher, named Pietro A. Vasile, seems to have been interested in astronomical phenomena and checked and corrected the predictions provided in the almanacs.

What can we infer from his *marginalia*? First, an important confirmation that, even at the end of the nineteenth century and later, almanacs were bought and used by what we can define as a middle/highbrow audience (supplementary sporadic evidence is provided by other Barbanera almanacs than the ones owned by Vasile[54]). Second, there is evidence that some readers were willing to remain loyal to one particular edition. Only once was Vasile unable to avoid the pitfall of a counterfeit edition from a publisher in Rome that claimed to be the legitimate successor of the Campitelli family. Furthermore, in 1936, another reader wrote "questo è falso" (this is false) on the title page of a Barbanera almanac issued by "F.lli Campi e F.llo", a tricky

---

51 Cf. R. Darnton, *First Steps towards a History of Reading*, in "Australian Journal of French Studies", 23, 1986, pp. 5–30.
52 L. Braida, *Dall'almanacco all'agenda*.
53 See the Almanac Archive project, that will digitise annotated British almanacs dating from 1750 to 1850, http://almanacarchive.org. On this project cf. L. Eckert / J. Grandison, *The Almanac Archive: Theorizing Marginalia and "Duplicate"*, in "Copies in the Digital Realm, in Digital Humanities Quarterly", 1, 2016, 1, http://www.digitalhumanities.org/dhq/vol/10/1/000240/000240.html, accessed April 12, 2018.
54 See items preserved at FB, call numbers BN 1/7.1866; BN 1/8.1899. Further details in E. Marazzi, *Sotto il segno di Barbanera*, pp. 86–88.

formula invented by publisher Campi. In fact scarcely literate readers were very likely to misread "F.lli Campi e F.llo" and to take it for the businesses' spelling of Feliciano Campitelli[55]. Third, there is evidence of the almanacs being widespread in the center and Italy's southern peninsula given the *marginalia* written by Vasile, who was living in Trivento (which is now located in the Molise region), and by other owners of Barbanera issues.

In the end, the study of annotated almanacs allows us to reflect on the uses of writing at the lower levels of the social ladder. The examination of *marginalia* in Barbanera almanacs essentially confirms the increasing use of such printed products given that writing records important events that occurred to the owner on paper[56]. First of all, recalling what has already been said about diaries, the use of annotating future events on a calendar did not properly exist in early modern Italy. Some almanacs included blank pages since between the seventeenth and eighteenth century, but they were mainly addressed to merchants that used such booklets to keep track of debits and credits. Some readers of the Babanera almanacs would have appreciated such a choice, if it had been applied to their favorite Barbanera. Annotations are increasingly frequent in the course of the nineteenth century, so much so that in one case a reader had even pasted a piece of manually ruled paper onto the blanks of Barbanera's pages[57].

Since almanacs represent an important piece of evidence of this in earlier ages, we cannot assume that only at that point of history was the calculation of time becoming a societal imperative. Nevertheless, at the same time, the increasing acquaintance with writing must have played a relevant role in such phenomena. It is surprising to see that annotations concerned past events, despite what Barbanera had recommended about the agenda in his dialogue in 1840. People mainly registered expenses, weather, medical visits after seeing the doctor, as well as exceptional events that they wanted to fix on paper (e.g., births, deaths, departures) in almanacs. As Braida has argued for the previous century[58], past rather than present is the more frequently used tense and only in 1911 is a future appointment annotated[59].

Among the pages of Barbanera almanacs we can also find photographs, sheets, and credit notes that allow us to formulate some hypotheses on the supposed ephemeral life of almanacs. For example, we can find a note from 1857 in the Barbanera for 1854, which means that an almanac printed four years earlier was still circulating and used to keep track of events. An extremely blatant example is the "Dialogue" section of an almanac from 1870, which contains a credit note from 1948 and a later comment from 1952. Why should an almanac be used as a support for a reminder after

---

[55] See item in FB, call number BN 1/10.1936.
[56] As already highlighted by L. Braida for eighteenth-century almanacs: *Dall'almanacco all'agenda*.
[57] Item preserved at FB, call number BN 1.1895.
[58] L. Braida, *Dall'almanacco all'agenda*, p. 166.
[59] "Appuntam.o piazza della Libertà". Cf. item preserved at FB, call number BN 1/7.1911.

such a long time? The "Dialogue" section of the almanac contains a possible answer. It shows readers how to calculate two important variables used to determine the date for Easter, i.e. epact (the difference in days between solar and lunar year) and the age of the moon. It can be argued that such a text could be found useful at any time and therefore preserved in the reader's house, maybe even stored together with an up-to-date calendar. This is a possible explanation for a very unusual case that can account for almanacs being used so far beyond their apparently ephemeral use.

To conclude, the study of annotations in almanacs at the turn of the twentieth century shows how, thanks to numerous factors like mass education policies, writing and reading ceased to be separate practices in the lives of ordinary people. People who bought almanacs and read them also wrote in them. They wrote to plan actions, or, more frequently to reflect, and often to remember. Moreover, readers used almanacs as writing supports without the necessity of a calendar. Scholarly works on almanacs have often insisted on their ephemeral character, but going deeper into the collection and evaluation of annotations confirms the hypothesis that readers did not think the same, given that, for generations, such booklets represented the only contact common people had with forms of written knowledge and culture.

Reinhart Siegert

The Greatest German Book Success of the Eighteenth Century

Rudolph Zacharias Becker's "Noth- und Hülfsbüchlein" (1788/1798)
as the Prototype of Printed Volksaufklärung
and its Dissemination in Europe

1 Introduction

The *Noth- und Hülfsbüchlein* was written for people who did not read books, much less buy them. And yet, it turned into one of the most successful books of all time. The man who achieved this rare feat is not even mentioned on the title page: Rudolph Zacharias Becker[1].

Fig. 1: Title page of N&HB vol. 1, 1788   **Fig.2:** Title page of N&HB vol. 2, 1798

---

1 Only hidden: hint by anagram on the second title page (p. 61) of part 1.

Note: This contribution is the translation of my epilogue to the new issue: [R.Z. Becker], *Noth- und Hülfsbüchlein. Seitengleicher Antiqua-Neudruck der zweibändigen Erstausgabe von 1788/1798. Mit*

http://doi.org/10.1515/9783110643541-015

2 The author

Rudolph Zacharias Becker was born at Erfurt on April 9, 1752. His father was a teacher at a girls' school; his income was small but his family was large, so young Becker grew up in very humble circumstances. Life was tough. To earn his education at the grammar school at Erfurt and the universities of Erfurt and Jena, he had to work hard as a street singer, he had to copy lecture notebooks for wealthier fellow students, and he had to go hungry. Becker studied theology and *Schulwissenschaften* ("science of schooling"; education was not a formal academic discipline in Germany prior to 1779), but he was apparently rather unfocused and dissatisfied. He ultimately abandoned his studies without a degree and entered the waiting position characteristic for destitute academics of his time: he served as *Hofmeister* (private tutor). The life of a private tutor was for the most part a very difficult way to earn one's living: The position included educating the spoiled children of wealthy people of rank, often being treated with contempt, and not infrequently having to play the part of the *factotum* and erudite jester for very little money. Becker, too, uses bitter words about the years he spent in this inferior position. But at least he gained two assets this way: an in-depth experience of rural life and the acquaintance with an influential and open-minded statesman who embraced the ideas of the enlightenment, Karl Theodor von Dalberg, at the time the governor of the Electorate of Mainz at Erfurt, later *Fürstprimas*, Grand Duke, and Archbishop, who continued to promote Becker for as long as he lived.

Liberation from his oppressive social position finally arrived thanks to an unexpected personal achievement of his own. In 1779, King Frederick II of Prussia challenged the Akademie der Wissenschaften in Berlin in a contest by posing the question: "Can it be useful for the people to be deceived, either by leading them to new misconceptions or by perpetuating the ones that exist?"[2]. Prize competitions of this kind, intended to promote scholarly competition, endowed with considerable prize money and providing publication of the award-winning contributions, were very popular in the eighteenth century, and the prize competitions of the famous Academy in Berlin were renowned throughout Europe. The award ceremony of 1780 caused a sensation: for fear of political difficulties, the Academy avoided taking a stance of

---

Texten zur Vorbereitung und Programmatik, hrsg. u. kommentiert von H. Böning und R. Siegert, 2 vols. (Volksaufklärung. Ausgewählte Schriften, 9.1/9.2), Bremen 2017. This new edition presents the *Noth- und Hülfsbüchlein* (*N&HB*) in roman type, but with all woodcuts, and, for the first time since 1838, makes available vol. 2, which is much more political than vol. 1. All quotations, which have been translated for the convenience of the readers, can be looked up in the above epilogue in their original German wording. The last chapter is new.

2 In Becker's words: "Kann irgend eine Art von Täuschung den Volke zuträglich sein, sie bestehe nun darinn, daß man es zu neuen Irrthümern verleitet oder die alten eingewurzelten fortdauern läßt?"; the original question was in French: "Est-il utile au peuple d'etre trompe, sit qu'on l'induise dans de nouvelles erreurs, ou qu'on l'entretienne dans celles où il est?".

its own by dividing the prize and awarding it in equal shares to an affirmative and a negative answer. Becker gained the prize for negating the question. He negated it by making the idea of "perfectibilism" (*Perfektibilismus, Vervollkommungslehre*) key to the approach to enlightenment. Perfectibilism means that a human being is expected to see his highest God-given purpose as well as his highest satisfaction in the effort of constantly improving him- or herself and everything around him or her. A person who strives for perfectibilism strives for world improvement and is an anti-conservative on principle, whose program is the ongoing critical review of the existing conditions: Nothing is so perfect as not to have room for further improvement. A person who strives for perfectibilism is driven to unceasing progress for anthropological and religious[3] reasons. This applies to all human beings, not only to the well-educated. But what was reality like? Becker did not bite his tongue and stated in his award-winning contribution:

> All efforts are made at keeping the people in a state of misconceptions, which means to make them incapable of becoming useful to the fatherland with the help of the light that Enlightenment might spread. If this method does not taste like despotism and tyranny, at a minimum it reveals ignorance of the elementary principles of sound political wisdom [...][4].

For an enlightened nation would only stand up against a good, that is, an enlightened government if it is subjected to the highest degree of pressure; whereas a rough crowd would be game to overturn everything in exchange for a small advantage. Dalberg was not able to prevent his protégé from being excluded from any position in the civil service for this radical tutoring in government politics.

Nevertheless, Becker succeeded in turning the literary laurels gained by winning the award into a better employment. With the help of his friend Christian Gotthilf Salzmann, he found employment at the Philanthropinum Dessau, the famous reform school founded by Basedow and Wolke, where he was given the task of editing a new "Dessauische Zeitung für die Jugend" (Dessau newspaper for the youth) in the name of the Philanthropin, starting on June 1, 1782. Earning his spurs as a journalist, he used this position to establish precious acquaintances and relationships with members in the world of letters and the book trade.

When the working atmosphere at Dessau quickly proved unbearable, Becker felt strong enough to collaborate with Salzmann and become self-employed. Both then pursued the goal of founding a new Philanthropin at Schnepfenthal near Gotha (Thuringia). Whatever then happened between Salzmann and Becker will likely never be revealed. In any case, Salzmann opened the new Philanthropin under his sole

---

[3] Becker provides a religious derivation of perfectibilism that even peasants could understand in the sermon by Pfarrer Wohlgemuth (*N&HB*, vol. 1, 1788, pp. 35–44); this sermon was hailed as the model of an enlightened sermon by contemporary theologians.
[4] R.Z. Becker, *Beantwortung der Frage: Kann irgend eine Art von Täuschung dem Volke zuträglich sein [...]*, Leipzig, Crusius, 1781, p. 141.

leadership in March of 1784, whereas Becker published in Gotha as of January 1 of that same year the "Deutsche Zeitung für die Jugend", a hazardous one-man venture whose small seed capital he had raised by borrowing.

Now completely independent, Becker earned his living by writing and made it his life's work to spread the idea of perfectibilism. The "Deutsche Zeitung", a paper exclusively based on Becker's correspondence, served as his mouthpiece for promoting his standard values (progressiveness, humanity, social responsibility) among his contemporaries. Obviously, the readership he was initially able to reach was very small. Still, just one month after he had founded the paper and in the middle of all the problems that come with a new start, Becker announced a project unheard-of until then: the publication of enlightening literature even for the most uneducated and poorest – the *Noth- und Hülfsbüchlein* (Booklet of help for people in need).

The success of this project was sensational (for details see the following sections) and made Becker Germany's most prominent popular author. Four years of work on this huge venture allowed Becker to gain in-depth insight into the printing and publishing businesses, to build a network of useful connections and, eventually, a high level of awareness in Germany. By then, his economic conditions had improved substantially; titles and honorary memberships were conferred onto him. Becker promptly turned everything to good use in yet another big project: the first supra-regional advertising paper in Germany. This daily paper was designed to carry all kinds of advertisements for a fee but articles of public benefit free of charge and circulated throughout the entire German-speaking area. After he had overcome a few start-up challenges, Becker succeeded in gaining, through an imperial privilege, a monopoly position for this "Reichs-Anzeiger" in the German empire and also in making it the common newsletter for all non-profit societies in Germany. This meant that the many private efforts of Enlightenment in Germany had found a crystallization point, and Becker had built a solid financial foundation for his future enterprises. He subsequently recruited a small qualified staff, established himself officially as a publisher (under the business name of Beckersche Buchhandlung), and assumed a central position in shaping German public opinion by virtue of the *Reichsanzeiger*, the former "Deutsche Zeitung", which, in the meantime, had evolved into a high-circulation paper gentrified as "National-Zeitung der Deutschen", and the *Noth- und Hülfsbüchlein*, which continued to be disseminated in ever new editions.

With these publications, he had created an ideal base for promoting the ideas of the Enlightenment among the majority of the German population. In the meantime, however, political conditions had changed dramatically. In view of the French Revolution and especially after the execution of the French king, most German governments shrank back from an increase in national education: popular Enlightenment and revolution seemed to be fatal neighbors. The government support or at least toleration, which Becker had so far enjoyed for his project of educating the people, ceased; sales of the *Noth- und Hülfsbüchleins* declined steeply, his periodicals were submitted to censorship.

In hopes of better times, Becker hesitated for a long time to complete his system of popular reading materials. The second part of the *Noth- und Hülfsbüchlein* was released as late as 1799 (dated 1798), followed by the famous *Mildheimisches Liederbuch*, whose 588 (later on, 800) songs were meant to provide enlightened thoughts to the people for any situation in which they would be likely to sing. Being a perfectionist, Becker went so far as to provide, at bargain prices, sheet music for the piano and even for village dance bands (two violins or clarinets plus bass), a *Fragebuch für Lehrer* (Question book for teachers) for the convenient use of the *Noth- und Hülfsbüchlein* and the *Mildheimisches Liederbuch* in schools, as well as a large-sized *Mildheimische Sittentafel* (Mildheim board of morals) for attachment on the door. The physician Daniel Collenbusch supplied a *Mildheimische Gesundheitslehre* (Mildheim book of health), Becker himself subsequently a *Mildheimisches Evangelienbuch* (Mildheim book of gospels), and the parish priest R.C. Lossius a *Mildheimisches Predigtbuch* (Mildheim book of sermons). Becker even offered via his publishing house an enlightening public library, complete with catalogue and a wall cupboard that could be locked. Thanks to Becker, the common man had access to enlightened maxims for all of life's situations from the cradle to the grave.

Still, the good days for Becker's objectives were gone. The Napoleonic Wars and the economic downturn in their wake had a significant negative impact on his activities. And despite all the precautions he had taken, the French occupation power incarcerated him for 17 months in the fortress of Magdeburg – as a warning to other opinion formers. Even in the dungeon, he began to revise his popular writings; however, the high hopes he had nurtured about the post-Napoleonic peace proved to be an illusion: The *Carlsbad Decrees* (1819) were only the last proof that the limits imposed on any commitment to Enlightenment in the nineteenth century were strict. A contemporary and friend of Becker's wrote after the conclusion of peace: "Slowly enough we shall return to the good conditions we enjoyed 25 years ago"[5]. Becker himself, who remained active as a publicist and publisher to the last days of his life, was able to carry on the fight against the change in mood for only a few more years. "On the 28th of March [1822], at six o'clock in the evening, [...] few days before completing his 70th year, with the setting sun, he gently passed away from this earth"[6]. His friend's prediction, however, did not come to pass: The Mildheim period, the years before 1789, which had been supported by a massive Enlightenment spirit, never came back again.

---

[5] H.E.G. Paulus, in "Heidelbergische Jahrbücher der Litteratur", 7, 1814, Abth. 1, p. 535.
[6] "Nationalzeitung der Deutschen" (Gotha), 1822, col. 229.

3 The emergence of the "Noth- und Hülfsbüchlein"

If Becker's self-presentation is to be believed[7], the *Noth- und Hülfsbüchlein* was created in response to Becker's unease about the elitist ivory tower literature. In 1784 Becker found

> in one of our best scientific journals the announcement of a booklet on a subject of a most marginal and antiquated nature, which was continued in issues and was written in such a praising manner as if it had the power to lift science to its highest peak and to plug all sources of human misery at once. How sad it is, so I thought, that the scholars of our nation still continue to float in the air with their research projects or to dig in dusty old books, and fail to realize that all the treasures of insight and all the fruits of talent can only be of value if they benefit our society[8].

Allegedly, in a fit of rage about this attitude of the men of letters, Becker published in his "Deutsche Zeitung" the invitation to subscribe to a work, in which literature was dedicated solely to one social purpose, namely

> to present the safest and most appropriate resources known at this time for use in emergency situations that occur in human life in such a way that any peasant can understand and read it with pleasure[9].

Not a single line of this book had been put to paper yet; the announcement was only intended to provide material for a bitter mockery: Becker assumed,

> if such a book aimed at the betterment and bliss of the majority of people were to appear, our critical spokespersons would most likely not even honor its existence by mentioning it[10].

The success seemed to confirm Becker's gloomy assumption: there was next to no response in the papers, and the number of subscribed copies would have meant a third-class funeral for the well-intentioned project[11] – had Becker not spent all the more energy on it.

The idea to do something for the benefit of the peasants was at this time very much *en vogue*. There were sound reasons for the contemporary "rural movement" or even for "agromania". The pressure as a result of the population growth since the middle of eighteenth century made an increase in agricultural production both inev-

---

[7] The corresponding passages were written ten years later and apparently in a somewhat glorifying light.
[8] R.Z. Becker, *Ankündigung des zweyten Theils des Noth- und Hülfs-Büchleins und eines damit verbundenen Volks-Lieder-Buches [...]* (Announcement of the second part of the *N&HB* and a collection of folk songs relating thereto"), in "Reichsanzeiger" (Gotha), 1798, 1, col. 645–666; quotation col. 646 f.
[9] "Deutsche Zeitung" (Gotha), 1784, insert to 7. Stück (February), without page numbers.
[10] R.Z. Becker, *Ankündigung*, 1798, col. 647.
[11] According to my own search results and in conflict with Becker's later self-presentation.

itable and attractive due to the rising prices for agrarian products. Increased agricultural production was only possible by allowing peasants to be more flexible; hence the readiness of many rulers to provide a bit more education to peasants – but in a careful and controlled manner. The well-educated contemporaries read John Locke, Rousseau, and Montesquieu and watched how, for the first time since 1776, the ideas of equality and fraternity, and the right to a free development of one's personality were incorporated into a constitution. Could the peasants, and they constituted 80% of the population in Central Europe at that time, really be excluded? The philanthropic ethos of the enlightenment, which was focused on the here and now ("Auf Erden bau'n das Himmelreich"/Cultivating the kingdom of heaven on earth), nature worship, and down-to-earth national economic interests went hand in hand with an often exuberant fashion trend by the well-educated and the rulers that incorporated elements of rural life: Marie Antoinette had herself portrayed with potato flowers in her hair, Frederick II of Prussia, Louis XVI, and emperor Joseph II posed behind a plough[12], over time, ministers preached sermons on smallpox vaccination, about how to grow trefoil, and why lightning rods were godly. But Becker's notion that the peasants' conduct could be changed by literature was strange.

This notion actually required courage, considering the contemporary state of education. Compulsory schooling, if introduced at all, existed merely on paper. And whatever pupils walked away with after several years of often mindless instruction was in most cases superficial literacy, the slow and cumbersome deciphering of single letters, syllables, and words, but not working with texts. Becker anticipated this: "I desired to work for people who are not used to reading and many among them will find reading more exhausting than threshing"[13]. There is plenty of evidence that peasants read despite these poor conditions; but the share of reading peasants will most likely never be reflected in reasonably reliable numbers. If they did read, then as a "surplus attitude"; there had to be a personal interest: Most of their daily life could be managed without reading and writing. This explains why country people generally only encountered two types of printed matters: Devotional books were used for reading aloud during private devotion and served as prestigious gifts at weddings, confirmation, and the like, whereas the calendar as the sole "current" leaflet also provided, in addition to its chronological function, entertainment (calendar stories), popular medicine (dates for blood-letting), and – in modest, short articles – economic and political information. Peasants did not buy these two printed matters in a bookstore (then few and far between) but from the bookbinder on market day or at the doorstep from the peddler. Both groups of distributors were – as far as their educational level was concerned – not noticeably different from their rural customers;

---

[12] On this topic, see the seminal work by S. Richter, *Pflug und Steuerruder. Zur Verflechtung von Herrschaft und Landwirtschaft in der Aufklärung* (Beihefte zum Archiv für Kulturgeschichte, 75), Wien / Köln 2015.
[13] "Reichsanzeiger" (Gotha), 1799, 2, col. 2488.

they introduced to people in the countryside reading materials they knew from experience were marketable and were as little influenced by developments in the book market and the literary business as the customers to whom they passed their modest reading experiences. This is why they were ruled out as the prerequisite of Becker's project, i.e., "to ensure that the *Noth- und Hülfsbüchlein* actually reached the class of people for which it was created; for they are not accustomed to visit book stores and to enquire about new books"[14]. It was Becker's idea to mobilize the well-educated and to use them to bring the unsought new reading matter into the hands of the peasants – a kind of "students back to the countryside" movement two hundred years ago. This level of distributors could be reached by using the conventional cultural sector, and Becker – despite being a novice to the book trade – was so very successful that we are entitled to call the *Noth- und Hülfsbüchlein* the first "bestseller" in the history of the book trade, the first book whose sales were increased by deploying promotional materials on a massive scale and with military precision.

The first solicitation by Becker, the newcomer, in his brand-new, still little known journal faded away mainly unheard. For the second one, Becker was cleverer. He framed his ideas on popular Enlightenment by literature in a short essay, added three sample chapters of the planned chapbook, and provided them with a title page that was sensational and up-to-date (it referred to the death of Duke Leopold of Brunswick in 1785, who had lost his life by personally trying to help a poor, flood stricken women in distress and which was celebrated in the papers as an example of humanity across class differences). He presented the manuscript to four prominent experts in education, *inter alia* to his patron Dalberg, to solicit their opinion and to request the favor of publishing them. In print, they were placed in front of the essay, and the subsequent invitation to subscription was graced with a name that came with a good and well-established reputation in the book trade: Georg Joachim Göschen (who later became one of the most famous publishers of classical authors). Thus, five experts were the guarantors for sound contents, method, and economic feasibility of Becker's philanthropic project.

A trick ensured that the well-educated public had no choice but to notice his flagship, which had turned out very well. Becker had the small essay printed so lavishly to turn it into a booklet of its own. He gave it the general title *Versuch über die Aufklärung des Landmannes* (Essay on the peasant's Enlightenment) and labeled it not a prospectus but a regular book and item of the book trade. As such, the *Versuch* had to be reviewed in all review services, and because it was an inseparable combination of theory of popular lecturing and advertisement for a special hands-on project, Becker had garnered promotion in the most important papers free of charge. Just to be on the safe side, he (also) sent the booklet along with personal letters to many public figures, to rulers, magistrates, and scholars. And to win over the sceptics, Becker routinely

---

14 R.Z. Becker, *Ankündigung*, 1798, col. 653.

published the names and the orders (some of them huge) of those who already trusted in his project, including a series of rulers, who, at the same time, were testimony that his undertaking was politically sound.

It was a resounding success, the largest book subscription of the eighteenth century. Within twelve months, 18,000 copies had been ordered, and the orders continued until they reached 28,000 copies (at that time, only very few works exceeded 1,000 copies). Becker had succeeded in appealing to the well-educated: to make them believe that peasants could be influenced in the spirit of Enlightenment by a book written in an appropriate manner and that he was the right person to write this book. The book's readers and reviewers did not need to make up their own opinion as the appraisal by four education experts had already been included, and the name Göschen reassured its subscribers that their orders would be carried out reliably. Becker provided a broad section of the educated public, who were enthusiastic about the Enlightenment and eager to implement it, with an opportunity to disseminate their own philosophy of life to vast sections of the population at little expense, with a minimum order of eight copies at four Groschen each – the eight together cost less than an average novel. He incited people to buy the booklet from him, to give it away to country people, to talk about it with them, to use it in schools and churches, thereby stimulating demand from below, from the people themselves, a demand that could later be met by the usual distributors of popular prints, the bookbinders and peddlers. A theologian wrote about Becker's undertaking: "I believe this is a perfect setting for the saying 'The man who knows how to do good and does not do it is in sin'"[15].

The rapid arrival of orders got Becker in a predicament because it forced him to quickly deliver the manuscript of this comprehensive work on many different subjects. The huge number of copies caused the two entrepreneurs headaches, for an edition of this scale had never been printed before and – due to the state of printing technology at that time – could only be achieved by investing a huge amount of time. Becker and Göschen decided to issue a first edition of 30,000 copies, simultaneously produced in four printing offices on six printing presses: Becker submitted the manuscript bit by bit to a printing office at his residence in Gotha; the printed sheets were forwarded hot from the press to printing offices at Rudolstadt (Turingia), Sulzbach (Oberpfalz/Bavaria), and Schwerin (Mecklenburg), which received the page make-up ready for use. With this division of labor Becker and Göschen killed several birds with one stone: The slow and cumbersome printing process went on while Becker continued his work on the manuscript, and, in Leipzig, the wood engraver Martin Seltsam tried to keep pace with the illustrations (ultimately, several illustrations had to be omitted, because Seltsam failed to produce them properly at the first attempt and waiting would have brought printing to a standstill). At the same time, considerable

---

15 Wilhelm Friedrich Hufnagel, *Für Christentum, Aufklärung und Menschenwohl*, vol. 1, cover of issue 3, Erlangen 1786, without page numbers. The biblical quotation is from James 4:17.

numbers of copies were printed in the sales areas themselves, saving time-consuming and costly transport. In this way, the history of the book trade had gained a curiosity: There are now four (or even six, because A1/2, B, C1/2, D) authentic first editions of the *Noth- und Hülfsbüchlein*, in large part with the same text and the same woodcuts, but slightly different in print, and with slightly differing orthography, and completely different presentations in terms of vignettes and decor lines. And yet it took the four printing offices one full year to finish the giant edition. On June 6, 1788, Becker was finally in a position to announce: "The *Noth- und Hülfsbüchlein* for peasants is finished now, and the delivery of the copies to the praenumerants has already started"[16].

4 On the contents of Becker's "Noth- und Hülfsbüchlein"

Becker himself commented on the basic concept of the *Noth- und Hülfsbüchlein*:

> As I was drawing up this plan, it was my intent to provide the countryman with a system of knowledge and attitudes, which was well suited to make him happy as a human being, as a peasant, and as a citizen. I say: a system, i.e., a coherent and well-founded way of feeling, thinking, and acting with the knowledge he requires in this triple sphere of activity [...] The acquaintance with this book is meant to inspire in the countryman the urge of perfectibility that is a characteristic feature of our race. If he had this urge once, in accordance with human nature, focused on sensual objects and tasted the pleasure of satisfaction: so he should become incited by this to think about the things around him more and more and to acquire more correct concepts and better attitudes by himself – not to learn them like a schoolboy [...] I thought it would be necessary first to entice him to eat, drink, and live better, and so on, and then to guide the urge of perfectibility, which by then should be activated, to the conditions of domestic, social, and civic life up to the position of man in God's creation and his relation to the Creator [...]
>
> For these reasons I chose as the subject of this book the story of a village that is destroyed by the forces of nature and, in order to prosper again, has to overcome hurdles caused both by outdated deficiencies in the civic state and by the ignorance, passion, and malice of some individuals. This village, called Mildheim, ultimately reaches the summit of rural happiness by applying the principle that human beings must become better and better and must make everything better and better[17].

But, in his opinion, this attitude was still not sufficient. The maxim "a) Do improve yourself and everything around you at all times" needed to be complemented by another:

> b) Do act in progressing to perfection always in a way that you may within reason desire for the whole world to act in the same manner! Or else: always act justly and never unjustly! [...]

---

16 "Deutsche Zeitung" (Gotha), 1788, p. 188.
17 R.Z. Becker, *Ankündigung*, 1798, cols. 649–651.

> For that reason, I tried in the first part of the N. u. H. B. to focus the urge of perfectibility first on the needs of the senses; [...] In the second part the activated urge of perfectibility is extended to the protection of physical prosperity by civic bonds and, later on, slowly and gradually, to the cultivation of the mind and the need for morality. The Mildheimers do not succeed in becoming entirely happy just by constantly improving things: complete full happiness requires always doing the right thing and avoiding any kind of injustice. And, in the end, the multitude of moral teachings contained in the book comes together in the *Sittentafel* (moral board) to form an entire building based on said major morals[18].

Thus, the *Noth- und Hülfsbüchlein* intended to be much more than an encyclopedia of advice for the domestic and rural economy: it was intended to give the "common people" a comprehensive impulse to think independently. The booklet reveals little of this high goal at the first sight. For Becker strove to take into account the miserable educational qualifications of his half-literate target group, not only in terms of language and train of thought but also in the manner of presentation:

> I intended to work for people who are not used to reading and where there are many who consider reading a harder toil than threshing. So the book needed to have an outside appearance that piques the curiosity of this class of readers, and the first attempt to read in it had to incite them to go on and on. This explains the red title page, the woodcuts, the exciting beginning of the book with the dreadful example of a woman who wakes up in the grave and gives birth to a child, and the manifold variations of the narrative veil[19].

The small collection of advice, as it was initially announced, had turned into a voluminous work in the shape of a novel by the time it was published. The originally announced *Noth- und Hülfsbüchlein* had become – thematically significantly expanded – a book in a book. It is inserted into the *Freuden- und Trauergeschichte des Dorfs Mildheim* (The story of the pleasures and sorrows of the village of Mildheim) and got its own title page. For its part, it is divided into three sections:
1. How peasants can live cheerfully;
2. How peasants can get rich with honors;
3. How peasants can help themselves in any of life's emergencies.

Section 1 offers cooking recipes and education in nutrition, it warns against toxic plants, provides exemplary and deterring examples of housekeeping, matrimony, bringing up children, and running a farm, and promises reputation and peace of mind as a reward for exemplary conduct. Section 2 demonstrates ways of improving farm revenue by efficient management, by taking new findings into account, and by supplementary sources of income; it also broadens general education by a description of Germany (*Wilhelm Denkers Reisebeschreibung*, pp. 240 ff.), particularly taking

---

18 "Reichsanzeiger" (Gotha), 1799, 2, cols. 2485 f.
19 *Ibid.*, col. 2488.

into account regional differences in agriculture, and it tries to ridicule superstition by irony (*Ein Griff aus Wilhelm Denkers Windbeutel*, pp. 267 ff.). Section 3 contains what was originally thought to constitute the entire *Noth- und Hülfsbüchlein*, namely "the aids against most of life's emergency situations where people can help themselves with God at their side" (p. 64). It includes health rules, instruction to first aid, disaster relief, pest control, conduct in war and in legal disputes. The title page depicts the above-mentioned prototype of magnanimous aid in times of need: the rescue mission of Duke Leopold of Brunswick. To motivate his readers who were not exactly thirsting for education, Becker took great care to provide casualness and variety during their reading experience. The organization of chapters varies greatly: some start with a sensational exemplary story, some with general worldly wisdoms followed by pertinent instructions; others start out with the instructions themselves and deliver an exemplary story later. Most of the examples provide a specific location and date; they are frequently dated in the recent past, some are taken from Becker's "Deutsche Zeitung". All chapters are very short and very well organized within – therefore not discouraging even for poor and slow readers. Many woodcuts provide additional incentives for browsing and reading; very few of them serve to clarify; the majority depicts the most distinctive scene of an exemplary story, preferably one that catches the eye and invites curiosity.

Of the second volume of the *Noth- und Hülfsbüchlein*[20] roughly one third is devoted to supplements and corrections of factual information in the first volume: The people of Mildheim cover the entire *Noth- und Hülfsbüchlein* over the course of five years (!), during which experts (especially the new parish priest) present the supplements, and the peasants debate which of the general suggestions for improvement may be worth considering for their specific village. However, as much as 40% of the entire work remains for the frame story, for the *Freuden- und Trauergeschichte des Dorfs Mildheim*. This frame story is not just the wrapping that motivates to read and makes the *Noth- und Hülfsbüchlein* a novel and precursor of the *Dorfgeschichte* (story of village life) of the nineteenth century. Rather, it contains the framework for enlightenment, which the factual information is meant to promote.

The old and sick nobleman of Mildheim, lord of the village of Mildheim and owner of a manor house, is used as example to demonstrate that rank is not the decisive factor for happiness and the value of a human being. In conversations with the experienced parish priest Wohlgemuth – Becker chose this character of the novel to have himself portrayed in later editions[21] – he realizes that he is unhappy mainly for the reason that he failed to find a real vocation in life. In order to spare his son this expe-

---

20 It was published, as mentioned above, only eleven years later and was certainly not distributed as widely as volume one (political and economic circumstances had changed in the interim). Contemporaries were much more reticent in their praise; vol. 2 turned out weaker in terms of literary quality than vol. 1 due to its more abstract contents and there are far fewer illustrations.
21 For the first time in *N&HB*, 1, Gotha, Becker 1814, vol. 1, p. 1, later in all succeeding editions.

rience, he provides him with a thorough education. On the death of the old nobleman a dreadful accident is revealed (p. 6 f.), and Pastor Wohlgemuth uses this opportunity to turn the horror of the son, who had been called back from university, from personal shock into activities beneficial to the public. This accident motivates even the peasants to learn something new, and in a special meeting of the village council, the *Noth- und Hülfsbüchlein* comes into play. In an enlightened model sermon (pp. 39-44) the parish priest instills in the peasants the seed of the principle of perfectibilism (p. 42: "This principle of making things better and getting better is the real purpose for which God has created us"), and the lord of the village offers prizes for heeding the principle in real life. He leaves his village to go on a five-year educational journey – not without leaving for his peasants the *Noth- und Hülfsbüchlein*.

What they did with the *Noth- und Hülfsbüchlein* is described in the second volume, volume 1 closes with Mildheim's devastation by a disastrous thunderstorm. Over and above the details of rebuilding, this catastrophic event is also reason for tackling large and basic projects during reconstruction: agrarian reform, a local constitution, school reform, social security, etc. – the narrative is barely able to cover the superabundance of reform measures. During this time, the lord of Mildheim has to learn that even well-meant reforms are often rejected when they are implemented in an authoritarian fashion from above (enlightened absolutism!). The peasants, on the other hand, learn that openness to new developments pays off as soon as people use their own judgement and trust in the right advisers. In the end, both enlightened village lord and reform-oriented municipality along with the enlightened parish priest as the intermediary for both sides tackle all the problems, allowing the book to finish euphorically:

> Now the Lord of M[ildheim] had done everything a lord of a village can do to bring happiness to his subjects: and the people of Mildheim had accepted everything he had offered for their welfare, and they enjoyed it with thanks and love for the donor. Life at Mildheim was heaven on earth [...] People up and down the land called Mildheim the happy village, and many rulers and municipalities slowly and gradually started to copy the facilities in Mildheim as best they could, wanted, and were allowed to[22].

5 The effects of the "Noth- und Hülfsbüchlein"

"The appearance of the *Noth- und Hülfsbüchlein* is too remarkable and too charitable not to be noted when looking back to the past century"[23], writes Christian Gotthilf Salzmann at the dawn of the nineteenth century and attaches to his retrospective

---

22 *N&HB*, 2, 1798, p. 359.
23 [Christian Gotthilf Salzmann], *Taschenbuch zur Beförderung der Vaterlandsliebe auf das Jahr 1801*, Schnepfenthal, Buchhandlung der Erziehungsanstalt, 1801, p. 38; a critic even wrote about a "gift bestowed by providence on our age", "Gothaische gelehrte Zeitungen", 1788, p. 377.

entitled *Das Noth- und Hülfsbüchlein erscheint* (The N&HB appears) an engraving by Daniel Chodowiecki. The well-educated contemporaries agreed: if any book ever had the potential to be presented to "people" inexperienced in literature, it is in this manner and in this shape – nothing compares with the *Noth- und Hülfsbüchlein* for popular Enlightenment by literature. Any subsequent publication did not have an equal chance, because a) the market was saturated by the *Noth- und Hülfsbüchlein* for some time, b) popular Enlightenment had lost its economic and political support base due to the fear of revolution and the foreign policy complications since the French Revolution[24].

The methodological problems of a reception history from such a long historical distance are too diverse and serious as to allow a discussion in this contribution[25]. At a minimum, we now know the channels that were used to bring the *Noth- und Hülfsbüchlein* to the "people" – channels that some had thought to be mere inventions of enlightened wishful thinking.

Let us start with the mediating role of the well-educated (*Gebildete*), which, according to Becker's ideas, was expected to launch distribution of the work to the "people" in the first place. This initial impulse proved to be successful: a mere glance at the number, extent, and acclaiming tenor of the reviews (at that time usually not coming from professional journalists) allows to assume a strong response in this class. The subscription list and other contemporary evidence confirms that the educated class purchased the *Noth- und Hülfsbüchlein* by the tens of thousands of copies. Some of the copies they had purchased were "sucked away" by them: even the educated elite used the *Noth- und Hülfsbüchlein* as a cheap and handy non-fiction book, and its illustrations and exemplary stories also made it a popular children's book. We may assume that it formed an established part of cultural heritage among the educated in Goethe's times. And it is verified that there were many channels of distribution from there. The *Noth- und Hülfsbüchlein* was given away to peasants in large numbers by private individuals as well as by the authorities, by Masonic Lodges and non-profit organizations, often enough accompanied by oral readings to enhance its appeal or as an award (for example, it was a popular school prize book). Parish priests arranged public readings of the *Noth- und Hülfsbüchlein* and quoted the booklet in sermons, writers permuted it into other popular prints in which they referred to the *Noth- und Hülfsbüchlein*, quoted it, and replicated it in image and text. We find it in village reading societies and in lending libraries.

---

[24] Around the same time Georg Christoph Lichtenberg noted: "The saddest thing the French Revolution has brought for us is undoubtedly that any reasonable demand that can by claimed from God and the law will be considered a seed of rebellion", G.C. Lichtenberg, *Gedankenbücher*, Frankfurt a.M. / Hamburg, 1963, p. 217. In this context, it is necessary to consider the impact of the French Revolution on the reading behavior of the "people": Reading was tremendously stimulated but the subjects were more immediately political than the *N&HB* was.

[25] I refer to R. Siegert, *Aufklärung*, 1978, cols. 963–1146, where this topic is addressed in great detail.

But peasants themselves bought the *Noth- und Hülfsbüchlein* as well. Where it was introduced as an additional schoolbook, they had to buy it. Beyond this, we know about cases where enlightened parish priests succeeded in persuading most members of their parish to buy the *Noth- und Hülfsbüchlein* on their own. We also know of cases where it was given away by peasants (even the reading-abstinent classes do give away books, back then as well as today!). A number of probate inventories by peasants are testimony to this. According to well-founded estimates, about 400,000 copies of the *Noth- und Hülfsbüchlein* were in distribution in the German language area at the beginning of the nineteenth century[26]. At a (total) population of 26 million, this amounts to one *Noth- und Hülfsbüchlein* per 65 inhabitants or (taking rural conditions into account) one *Noth- und Hülfsbüchlein* per ten households. Obviously, this statistical average was not met in some places and significantly exceeded in others – this depended primarily on the local priest's enthusiasm for the enlightenment. In general, it is safe to say that the *Noth- und Hülfsbüchlein* was the most widespread secular book in Germany at around 1800, and that it was generally also accessible to half-literate or illiterate people, if social reading aloud as the most popular way of consuming literature at the time is included.

But was it really consumed? In many cases, peasants had no choice: where ever it was introduced as a school book or where Becker-sentences resounded from the pulpit. "Commoners" consumed Becker without realizing it even when they read, on their own, conventional, simple reading material: Many unsuspicious almanacs of the first half of the nineteenth century are permeated with text passages tacitly lifted from the *Noth- und Hülfsbüchlein* without labeling.

An indirect but impressive proof for this is the book trade's response to the *Noth- und Hülfsbüchlein*. Many publishers were alerted by the strong launch of the *Noth- und Hülfsbüchlein* and issued adaptations (e.g., for Catholics in individual regions) or pirated editions – to great commercial success as proven by the more than 30 editions that we have come to know by now[27]. And these editions were just ordinary items of commerce, not books subscribed by the educated and passed on to the "people" as gifts! The publishers considered the title of *Noth- und Hülfsbüchlein* in itself such a boost for sales that they published *Noth- und Hülfsbüchlein* for the sick and dying (1792), for rural school janitors (1796), for preventing cattle plagues (1797), for "ladies of easy virtue", and for people with eye diseases, etc. – almost 300 titles have been reported dating from 1791 to 1888 with nearly 500 editions. Apart from some cases where the title is used ironically (*Noth- und Hülfsbüchlein* for Napoleon, 1814, *Noth- und Hülfsbüchlein* for artists, art lovers, and art traders in the moon 1833, etc.) these are

---

26 On the translations of the *N&HB*, see the last chapter.
27 A list of all known editions of the *N&HB* is appended to its new edition (cf. introductory note) More detailed data, references, illustrations, and methodical considerations are offered in my doctoral thesis *Aufklärung und Volkslektüre. Exemplarisch dargestellt an Rudolph Zacharias Becker und seinem "Noth- und Hülfsbüchlein"*, Frankfurt a.M. 1978.

small, cheap booklets for situations where even reluctant readers like the "common people" look for a book as a last resort: cattle plagues, emigration, disease.

It is impossible to imagine the development of this unsubsidized market for the most simple reading material on factual information without an interest in reading by the "common people" who, when it came to buying printed matters, thought twice before spending the penny. This procuring of information on one's own constitutes an act of emancipation – precisely what the Enlightenment intended to set in motion.

By asking the question of whether Becker actually achieved an indoctrination of the masses by having them read the *Noth- und Hülfsbüchlein* (that this indeed happened, I tried to make credible) as he had intended, we definitively cross the possibilities of historical reception research – this is a question that can only be answered with many reservations, even in terms of current communication processes by empirical reader research (in particular questioning).

6 Popular Enlightenment: A German national specialty or a European heritage?

When Rudolph Zacharias Becker died in 1822, popular Enlightenment was weakened by the aftermath of the French Revolution, of the Napoleonic wars, including economic depression, and by the Carlsbad Decrees, yet it continued[28]. The *Noth- und Hülfsbüchlein* definitely remained the flagship of the movement[29]; its last edition appeared in 1838, a *Neues Not- und Hilfsbüchlein* was even published in 1888 by the notable economist Arwed Emminghaus (under the pen name of Dr. Karl Bernhard)[30]. Without question, it represents the greatest book success of the eighteenth century in the German-speaking areas. This raises the question about its impact in other language areas.

Proving translations into foreign languages and cultural areas is a tedious undertaking: it requires knowledge in a multitude of languages and library cultures. This is why it should be done in the recipient countries, and this is what I did for the popular Enlightenment by covering the German-speaking areas[31].

---

28 Comprehensive bibliographical proof is provided by H. Böning / R. Siegert, *Volksaufklärung. Biobibliographisches Handbuch zur Popularisierung aufklärerischen Denkens im deutschen Sprachraum von den Anfängen bis 1850*, Stuttgart / Bad Cannstatt 1990, vols. 3/1–4: R. Siegert, *Aufklärung im 19. Jahrhundert – "Überwindung" oder Diffusion?*, Stuttgart / Bad Cannstatt 2016, cf. my introduction there, translated by David Paisey.
29 Becker himself estimated its distribution at more than one million copies including pirated editions and translations, cf. R.Z. Becker, *Leiden und Freuden in siebzehnmonatlicher französischer Gefangenschaft von ihm selbst beschrieben. Ein Beytrag zur Charakteristik des Despotismus*, Gotha, 1814, p. 136.
30 Frankfurt a.M and Lahr, Schauenburg, n.d. [1888].
31 Cf. H. Böning / R. Siegert, *Volksaufklärung*, 1990/2016 passim, and summarizing vol. 3/4, 2016, Appendix "Übersetzungen", cols. 3541–3572.

As far as I know, overviews on translations of texts of the German *Volksaufklärung* (popular Enlightenment) into other languages do not exist, with the exception in some works on the Baltic states. But at least we know the languages into which three of the most popular works of the *Volksaufklärung* have been translated: the *Noth- und Hülfsbüchlein* itself (first Gotha 1788/1798), Bernhard Christoph Faust's *Gesundheitskatechismus* (Catechism of health, first Bückeburg 1792/1792), and *Das Goldmacherdorf* by Heinrich Zschokke (The goldmakers' village, first Aarau 1817).

Becker's Noth- und Hülfsbüchlein was translated into the following languages (arranged according to the four compass directions):

North: Danish, Estonian, Icelandic, Latvian (4), Swedish;

East: Czech (3 editions, two for Bohemia, one for Moravia), Hungarian (3), Polish (7), Slovenian, Wendish/Sorbian;

South: Italian;

West: Dutch (4).

These are 28 known translated editions covering 12 languages. Alleged translations into the French (soon after 1790), Icelandic, and Russian languages could not be verified; however, there is an interesting Russian counterpart: *Dereweeskoe Serkalo ili obscenarodnaja kniga socinena Ne tol'ko ctob ee citat', No ctob po nej ispolnjat*[32] (Mirror of the village or chap book, written not only for reading but also for use), vol. 1-3, St. Petersburg, Printing office of the Gouvernement 1798; 1799; 1799.

Faust's *Gesundheitskatechismus* is a small booklet designed for schoolchildren and contains nothing but medical advice. The author is a philanthropic physician and his work was propagated by many *Volksaufklärer* to improve the health of the common people; following Tissot[33] this is the widest-spread work of popular medical Enlightenment.

There are 42 known translated editions covering 14 languages:

North: Danish (7), Estonian, Icelandic, Latvian, Swedish;

East: Czech (1 for Bohemia, 1 for Moravia), Hungarian (2), Polish (4), Serbo-Croatian, Slavonic;

South: –

West: Dutch (2), English/American (17: 10 for the USA, 3 for Britain, 1 for Ireland, 3 for Scotland), French;

Others: Latin.

---

32 Transcription varies a little by country and time; in the Internet searchable under *Derevenskoe Zerkalo*; I used the copy of the British Library London: 1508/1121. The anonymous author is Michail Severgin (1765–1826).

33 S[amuel] A[uguste] D[avid] Tissot, *Avis au peuple sur sa santé*, first Lausanne, Grasset, 1761 (many editions, adaptions and translations, among them 46 editions in German).

Zschokke's *Goldmacherdorf* is a novel of popular Enlightenment, the story of a village brought to prosperity by following moral principles. There are 71 known translated editions covering 21 languages (some of them extending into the twentieth century):

North: Danish (2), Estonian (2), Finnish (4), Latvian (2, one of them Latvian/German, bilingual), Swedish (3);

East: Bulgarian (3), Czech (3), Hungarian (9), Polish, Russian (12), Serbo-Croatian (3), Slovakian (3), Slovenian (3), Ukrainian;

South: Italian (7), Rhaeto-Romance;

West: Dutch (2), English (2 for Britain, 1 for the USA), French (5);

Others: Japanese, Turkish[34].

It is obvious that the distribution of translations is very uneven. The small Baltic populations (i.e., Estonia and Latvia, whereas Lithuania does not play any role) and a multitude of small Slavic populations are overrepresented. The dissemination of works of the German popular Enlightenment in these areas may be explained by the social situation: these areas were dominated by German-speaking authorities and German-speaking well-educated people because they were part of the Russian and the Habsburg empires, respectively, lacking a national literature of their own and culturally less developed than Germany at the time. The northern European countries of Denmark (including Iceland) and Sweden are represented, but not to the same extent. So are the Netherlands, Poland (at that time divided between Prussia, Russia, and Habsburg), Bohemia, Moravia, and Hungary (then part of the Habsburg Empire). Translations into the Italian language are almost confined to the *Goldmacherdorf*, translations into Spanish or Portuguese lack completely. Russia is represented by the very interesting above-mentioned *N&HB*-counterpart and only after 1862 by translations of the *Goldmacherdorf*. Still, what is striking is the poor representation of the two main languages of the Enlightenment. The French language is almost exclusively present in titles printed in Switzerland[35] rather than in France for the French "people", and English appears in considerable numbers only in connection with Faust's *Gesundheitskatechismus*, which transported health advice but Enlightenment thoughts only implicitly.

One would think that the export of Enlightenment thoughts went in the opposite direction: from France and England to Germany. But this is not the case with popular Enlightenment. The import of titles of popular Enlightenment from foreign languages to Germany has been thoroughly explored[36]. Of 10,664 titles, there are only 312 (2.9%)

---

[34] Detailed information will be presented by myself in the transcript of the conference "Volksaufklärung im Vormärz" (Wittenberg, May 17.-19, 2018, organized by Thomas Bremer and Françoise Knopper): under the title "Übersetzungen von Volksaufklärerischen Schriften als Indikator für europäische Kulturströmungen".

[35] By far the most prominent is S.A.D. Tissot (see n. 39).

[36] As in n. 37.

translations from foreign languages into German. This does not come as a surprise in terms of countries of a less developed cultural status at that time. But just 157 translations from the French and only 74 from the English language into German is a surprise. These explanatory hypotheses are conceivable:
1) There was no popular Enlightenment in France and in Britain; as a result, nothing could be exported. But why was there no popular enlightenment? And what was the reason for not importing works of German popular Enlightenment if the deficiency was noticed?
2) France and Britain did not need popular Enlightenment because of a very high level of culture even among the "common people" – or it did not develop because of a social structure that lacked the German philanthropical concern of the well-educated for the welfare of the "common people".
3) There has not been enough research into popular Enlightenment in Britain and France to date compared to the exploration of Enlightenment heroes such as Voltaire or Hume.
4) Popular Enlightenment is the specific contribution of Germany to European enlightenment. It had gained momentum just prior to the French Revolution and by the French Revolution had lost its chance to be exported beyond the boundaries of the German-speaking areas.

At the present state of knowledge, I am inclined to favor hypothesis 4. It seems that the supporters of the Enlightenment in the decentralized German-speaking countries formed a much broader base in their societies than in Britain and France, where the "heroes" were concentrated in the salons of the capitals. Characteristic of the German Enlightenment is the tendency to make Enlightenment not only a subject of sophisticated discourse but to turn it to good use in daily life and in social conditions.

Thus, the question why *Volksaufklärung* in the German-speaking countries, in the Netherlands, and in Scandinavia was a strong movement whereas there is no counterpart known in England or France is no trifle or merely academic. In the first-mentioned countries, popular enlightenment[37] was the movement that formed the mentality that became the foundation of a modern working democracy. There is no doubt that England and France obtained this mindset as well – but how did it win over the minds of people in the absence of a corresponding phenomenon? Parallels to the modern ecological movement or to issues of development assistance are obvious, considering the combination of official and private efforts to persuade and convince, nowadays obviously using an extended spectrum of media. Thus, the answer is not just of historical interest but may be helpful in the current brain-storming efforts.

---

37 A comprehensive introduction to popular enlightenment may be found in H. Böning / H. Schmitt / R. Siegert (eds.), *Volksaufklärung. Eine praktische Reformbewegung des 18. und 19. Jahrhunderts* (Presse und Geschichte. Neue Beiträge, 27), Bremen 2007.

Rita Schlusemann
A Canon of Popular Narratives in Six European Languages between 1470 and 1900

The "Griseldis"-Tradition in German and Dutch

1 Introduction

One of the most famous literary heroines in European literature is Griseldis, a poor farmer's daughter. She marries the earl of Saluzzo who severely tests her but eventually she is rewarded. Her story is still popular today and in 2015 a children's film about Griseldis' adventures was produced for the Museo della Civiltà Cavalleresca in Saluzzo in Piemont, Italy. The novella, first told by Giovanni Boccaccio as the last of one hundred stories in his *Il Decamerone* (1349–1353), was translated, adapted, and printed in more than twenty vernaculars, among which Dutch, German, Danish, Swedish, Polish, Russian, Rumanian, Hungarian, Italian, and Spanish[1]. From the beginning, all editions emphasize Griselda's humble origins, her steadfastness, and her patience as her main character traits, as in the oldest printed Latin version (c. 1470), attributed to Ulrich Zell in Cologne: "Griseldis mulieris maxime constantie et patiencie" (*GW* M31565)[2]. Absolute *obedientia* and *constantia* as paramount character traits are reminiscent of Job, 1:21, and the sacrifice of the children reminds us of Maria and Abraham: Griseldis therefore can be called a "figura Mariae", a "figura Abraham", and a "figura Job". Griseldis' *fortitudo animi*, the strength of a soul as an anthropological character trait, has made the novella not only attractive throughout the centuries, but in many different European regions as well.

---

1 R. Morabito, *La diffusione della storia di Griselda dal XIV al XX seculo*, in "Studi sul Boccaccio", 17, 1988, pp. 237–285.
2 *Gesamtkatalog der Wiegendrucke* (*GW*); *Incunabula Short Title Catalogue* (*ISTC*). In this article, only the *GW*-numbers will be mentioned. The corresponding number in the *ISTC* can easily be found via *GW*.

Note: This article is based on two presentations, presented at a workshop and a conference organized by the research project EDPOP (The European Dimensions of Popular Print Culture, https://edpop.wp.hum.uu.nl/); the first of these was held at an international workshop in Troyes, France (May 2017) and the second at the conference in Trento, Italy (June 2017). I would like to thank Jeroen Salman for his suggestions to improve this article. A parallel article concentrates on the publication of "popular" narratives in at least four European languages (Dutch, English, French, and German) from the beginning of printing until 1600 (R. Schlusemann, *Printed Popular Narratives until 1600. Authorship and Adaptation in the Dutch and English Griseldis*, in "Journal of Dutch Literature", 10, 2019, pp. 1-23).

Griseldis was not the only narrative[3], which was very popular in a spatio-temporal dimension[4]. Between 1471, the year when *Apollonius* and *Griseldis* were the first fictional narratives being printed in German[5], and the late nineteenth century, narratives like *Melusine*, *Quatre fils Aymon*, or *Fortunatus* were printed again and again in different languages. In general, these narratives, in German or in other languages, were adaptations of older storytelling models. They became well known, not only because of their special literary qualities, but also because of their main characters and their adventures. Ulenspieghel represents a rebel, Magelone and her lover Pierre can reunite after years of separation, the seven sages of Rome prove the power of language by telling tales and therefore rescue the king's son from his stepmother's wickedness, and Griseldis shows endless patience. In order to place the status and the importance of a narrative like *Griseldis* into a broader context, this paper first presents a canon of popular fictional narratives in European languages from a German perspective. It then deals with *Griseldis* as one of the most popular narratives in Europe until the end of the nineteenth century and intends to answer the question how the German and Dutch traditions primarily differ and what the main reasons might be for these differences.

The following canon of popular fictional narratives from a German point of view is based on six criteria:
1. The narrative was published in German[6].
2. A continuous German printed tradition: at least one German edition was published each century[7].

---

[3] The term narrative is used in the following definition: "A fictional narrative presents an imaginary narrator's account of a story that happened in an imaginary world. A fictional narrative is appreciated for its entertainment and educational value, possibly also for providing a vision of characters who *might* exist or might have existed, and a vision of things that *might* happen or could have happened. Although a fictional narrative may freely refer to actual people, places and events, it cannot be used as evidence of what happened in the real world" (M. Jahn, *Narratology. A Guide to the Theory of Narrative*, English Department, University of Cologne, May 2017 [http://www.uni-koeln.de/~ame02/pppn.htm], N2.2.2).

[4] D. Bellingradt / J. Salman, *Books and Book History in Motion. Materiality, Sociality and Spatiality*, in D. Bellingradt et al. (eds.), *Books in Motion in Early Modern Europe: Beyond Production, Circulation and Consumption*, London 2017, pp. 1–10.

[5] The first editions of both texts were published by Günther Zainer in Augsburg (see *GW* 2273; *MRFH* 20180 [*Marburger Repertorium zur Übersetzungsliteratur im deutschen Frühhumanismus*; www.mrfh.de] and *GW* M31580; *MRFH* 21130).

[6] *Bevis of Hampton*, for example, was published at least in Croatian, Russian, Rumanian, French, Spanish, Italian, English, and Dutch, but not in German. Therefore, it is not taken into account in this paper.

[7] This implies that if, for example, there is no eighteenth-century edition of a certain work, it has not been taken into consideration. Therefore, a narrative like the German *Herpin*, which has not been published in the seventeenth century, is not taken into account for this corpus.

3. The narratives that form the canon of popular narratives were transmitted in (at least) six different languages. This implies that the narrative was very widely known in Europe.
4. The printed German tradition of a narrative began in the fifteenth or sixteenth century[8].
5. The printed German tradition of a narrative lasted at least until the nineteenth century[9].
6. A narrative is mentioned or published in at least one of the following important nineteenth-century publications: in Joseph Görres' survey *Die teutschen Volksbücher* (1807), in Gotthard Marbach's series "Volksbücher" in 53 volumes (1838–1849) and/or in the series by Karl Simrock "Die deutschen Volksbücher", published in 11 volumes (1845–1867)[10].

Based on these criteria the transmission data of 43 narratives printed between 1470 and 1900 were collected[11].

---

[8] Narratives with a first printed German edition not earlier than the seventeenth century, like *Hirlanda*, *Eginhard of Bohemia*, and *Genovefa*, have therefore been excluded.
[9] Narratives which were published in German only in the early centuries have not been taken into consideration, for example *Paris und Vienna*.
[10] For example, Simrock published three fictional narratives in volume 2 of his series: *Die Heimonskinder*, *Friederich Barbarossa*, and *Kaiser Octavianus*.
[11] The narratives are: *Amadis*; *Appollonius von Tyrus*; *Bevis of Hampton*; *Eginhard von Böhmen*; *Herzog Ernst*; *Esopus*; *Fierabras*; *Flavius Josephus*; *Florio und Bianccefora*; *Fortunatus*; *Fortunats Söhne*; *Friedrich Barbarossa*; *Ritter Galmy*; *Genovefa*; *Guiscard und Sigismunda*; *Griseldis*; *Haimonskinder*; *Armer Heinrich*; *Helena von Konstantinopel*; *Helias*; *Herpin*; *Hirlanda*; *Huon de Bordeaux*; *Iwain*; *Hug Schapler*; *Loher und Maller*; *Magelone*; *Sieben weise Meister*; *Melusine*; *Merlin*; *Octavian*; *Paris und Vienna*; *Pontus und Sidonia*; *Bruder Rausch*; *Reynke de vos*; *Robert der Teufel*; *Salomon und Marcolphus*; *Schildbürger*; *Siegfried*; *Tristan*; *Valentin und Orson*; *Virgilius* and *Wigalois*. A very popular text, the *Destruction of Jherusalem* by Flavius Josephus, was repeatedly printed. It was not named a popular narrative, either by Görres, Marbach, or Simrock. It is likely that texts like this, just as the *History of Troy* and the *History of Alexander*, were regarded as historical texts in later centuries. The data for the transmission of these texts in European vernaculars are based on research in *GW*, *ISTC*, *MRFH*, *Universal Short Title Catalogue* (*USTC*); C. Borchling / B. Claussen, *Niederdeutsche Bibliographie: Gesamtverzeichnis der niederdeutschen Drucke bis zum Jahre 1800*, Neumünster 1931–1936; G. Doutrepont, *Les mises en proses des épopées et des romans chevaleresques du XIVe au XVIe siècle*, Bruxelles 1939 (reprint Genève, 1969); W. Nijhoff / M.E. Kronenberg, *Nederlandsche bibliographie van 1500 tot 1540*, 's Gravenhage 1923–1971 (*NK*); R. Schenda, *Tausend deutsche populäre Drucke aus dem neunzehnten Jahrhundert*, in "Archiv für Geschichte des deutschen Buchwesens", 11, 1971, cols. 1465–1652; B. Gotzkowsky, *"Volksbücher": Prosaromane, Renaissancenovellen, Versdichtungen und Schwankbücher. Bibliographie der deutschen Drucke*, Teil 1: *Drucke des 15. und 16. Jahrhunderts*, Baden-Baden 1991; Teil 2: *Drucke des 17. Jahrhunderts. Mit Ergänzungen zu Teil I*, Baden-Baden 1991 and 1994; H.M.C.W. Blom, *"Vieux romans" et "Grand Siècle": Éditions et réceptions de la littérature chevaleresque médiévale dans la France du dix-septème siècle*, Dissertation Utrecht, 2012 (online: https://dspace.library.uu.nl/handle/1874/224190, accessed February 4, 2018). In 2014, Cuijpers presented a canon of 23 Dutch chapbooks between 1600 and 1900 (P. Cuijpers, *Van Reynaert de Vos tot Tijl Uilenspiegel:*

Of these, twelve different narratives fulfill the aforementioned criteria and are listed in Table 1[12].

What are the characteristics of these European popular narratives with regard to first editions, origin, and genre? Ten of the twelve first editions of these popular narratives were already printed until 1500, eight of them already in the 1470s, one in the 1480s, and one in the 1490s[13]. Only two were published in the first decade of the sixteenth century. Narratives with a first edition after 1515 obviously did not become that popular all over Europe. We can conclude that a narrative printed in the first decade of printing narratives had the most potential to become widespread all over Europe.

Concerning the question in which European language the first edition of a narrative was printed (tab. 1, column 3), it is noteworthy that half of these twelve popular narratives were first published in German. It is also interesting that, although a narrative like *Melusine* had a strong French manuscript tradition, the first edition of the narrative was printed in German. One of the reasons could be the overall dominance of printing and printed narratives in German towns in the 1470s and 1480s[14]. A second reason, to my mind, is that famous German authors like Thüring von Ringoltingen (*Melusine*, 1456) and Heinrich Steinhöwel (e.g. *Appolonius* [c. 1460] and *Griseldis*, [1461/62]) adapted narratives into German in manuscript, shortly before the breakthrough of the printing business. These versions formed the basis for the early printed German traditions (see, for *Griseldis* the second part of this article). Three narratives, *Griseldis*, *Guiscardo et Sigismunde,* and *Floire et Blanchefleur*, were printed in Italian first. They all have an Italian origin. A Latin adaptation – Petrarch's *Griseldis* and Leonardo Bruni's *Guiscardo et Sigismunde* – served as models for versions in other European vernaculars. Latin versions of three other narratives, *Apollonius*, *Esopus*, and *Septem sapientum*, and their adaptations in different vernaculars became popular printed narratives throughout Europe. With regard to origin, it is therefore significant that most of the popular narratives were already written in manuscript during the medieval period and were therefore known stories in different societies before they were printed.

Only two narratives with an original and rich manuscript tradition in French were also first printed in French: *Quatre fils Aymon* and *Pierre de Provence*. It is also striking that none of the twelve canonical narratives were printed in Dutch or English first.

Op zoek naar een canon van volksboeken, 1600–1900, Zutphen 2014). After my presentation of the first survey of popular narratives in at least six European vernaculars until 1900 at the international EDPOP-conference in Trento, Italy (June 2017), Helwi Blom (Nijmegen), Marie-Dominique Leclerc (Troyes), Anna Katharina Richter (Zürich), Jordi Sánchez-Martí (Alicante), Rita Schlusemann (Berlin), and Krystyna Wierzbicka (Warsaw) continued to work on the transmission history of the editions.

12 The narratives are listed in order of the first printed edition. The second column refers to the year of the first printed edition in a European language, the third the language in which a text was first printed.

13 Latin editions have not been taken into consideration.

14 See for more detail R. Schlusemann, *Printed Popular Narratives*.

Tab. 1: Canon of twelve popular narratives published in German and at least five other European vernaculars

Title	First printed edition	Language of first printed edition	Number in GW or VD16[15]	Language of first version	(Approximate) Date of first version
Griseldis[16]	(c. 1470)	Italian	GW 4440	Italian ms.	Giovanni Boccaccio, *Il Decamerone*, X,10; 1349–1353
Apollonius[17]	1471	German	GW 2273	Greek / Latin ms.	3rd century
Floire et Blancheflleur[18]	1472	Italian	GW 4462	Greek / Oriental ms.	unknown
Septem sapientum[19]	1473	German	GW 12856	Persian ms.	late antiquity
Melusine[20]	(c. 1474)	German	GW 12656	French ms.	Jean d'Arras; Coudrette, 14th century
Esopus[21]	(1476/77)	German	GW 351	Greek ms.	6th century
Guiscardo et Sigismunde[22]	(c. 1470)	Italian	GW 4440	Italian ms.	Giovanni Boccaccio, *Il Decamerone*, IV,1, 1349–1353

---

15 *Verzeichnis der im deutschen Sprachraum erschienenen Drucke des 16. Jahrhunderts* (https://opacplus.bib-bvb.de/).

16 The first edition of *Griseldis* was printed as part of *Il Decamerone* in Italian (c. 1470). A first edition of *Griseldis* as a single text was printed in German in 1471 (M31580).

17 The text was printed at least in Danish, Dutch, English, French, German, Polish, and Swedish.

18 P. Grieve, *Floire and Blancheflor and the European Romance*, Cambridge University Press, Cambridge, 1997. Boccaccio adapted it in his *Filocolo* (I. Kasten, Boccaccios "Filocolo". Zur Rezeption des Flore-Stoffs in der italienischen Frührenaissance, in I. Bennewitz / L. Auteri / M. Dallapiazza (eds.), *Giovanni Boccaccio: Italienisch-deutscher Kulturtransfer von der Frühen Neuzeit bis zur Gegenwart*, Bamberg 2015, pp. 1–23). The narrative was printed at least in Danish, Dutch, French, German, Iberian, and Italian.

19 Printed at least in Czech, Danish, Dutch, English, German, Hungarian, Iberian, Irish, Italian, Polish, Rumanian, and Swedish.

20 Printed at least in English, Estonian, French, German, Iberian, Polish, and Swedish.

21 Printed at least in Danish, Dutch, French, German, Iberian, Italian, Polish, and Swedish. The Latin tradition was used as a major source for the translations into the vernaculars.

22 Boccaccio tells the story of Tancredi and Guismunda in his *Il Decamerone* (fourth day, first story). Leonardo Bruni (also Brunus Aretinus) translated it into Latin: *De duobus amantibus Guiscardo et Sigismunde*. This version formed the basis for several adaptations into different European languages. In printed form it was first published in Italian as part of *Il Decamerone* (c. 1470). The first edition of the narrative as a single text was published in German (attributed to Johann Zainer and published in about 1476; *GW* 564210N). Printed at least in Dutch, English, French, Hungarian, Italian, and Polish.

Title	First printed edition	Language of first printed edition	Number in GW or VD16[15]	Language of first version	(Approximate) Date of first version
Pierre de Provence[23]	1477	French	GW 12703	French ms.	c. 1430
Quatre fils Aymon[24]	(c. 1480)	French	GW 3133	French ms.	late 12th century
Amadis de Gaula[25]	*1496	Spanish	–	Portugese ms.	14th century
Fortunatus[26]	1509	German	VD16 F 1928	German ed.	1509
Ulenspieghel[27]	(c. 1510)	German	VD16 ZV 2280	German ed.	(c. 1510/1512)

23 The text was printed at least in Bohemian, Czech, Danish, German, Iberian, Polish, and Swedish.
24 Printed at least in Dutch, English, French, German, Iberian, and Italian.
25 The first edition is lost, the second edition was published in 1508. The *Amadis* was printed at least in Dutch, English, French, German, Iberian, and Italian.
26 Printed at least in Czech, Dutch, English, Swedish, German, French, Italian, Hungarian, and Polish. See J. Valckx, *Das Volksbuch von Fortunatus*, in "Fabula", 16, 1975, pp. 91–112; J. Valckx, *Het volksboek van Fortunatus: Inhoud, samenstelling, verbreiding en herkomst. Proefschrift ter verkrijging van de graad van doctor in de letteren en de wijsbegeerte, afd. Germaanse filologie, aangeboden door J. Valckx*, Leuven, 1970 (unpublished dissertation).
27 The text was printed at least in Danish, Dutch, English, French, German, Polish, and Swedish.

The only two popular narratives that were not written in a manuscript version are of German origin (*Fortunatus* and *Ulenspieghel*). They first appeared in print at the beginning of the sixteenth century.

Concerning genre, the twelve narratives can be divided into three groups: 1. novellas, 2. collections of tales, 3. (longer fictional) narratives:
1. novellas: *Apollonius, Floire et Blanchefleur, Griseldis, Guiscardo et Sigismunde*
2. collections of tales: *Esopus, Septem sapientum, Ulenspieghel*
3. longer narratives: *Amadis, Quatre fils Aymon, Fortunatus, Melusine, Pierre de Provence.*

As more than half of the popular narratives are novellas and collections of tales, it is reasonable to assume that the brevity of the text also played an important role in its becoming a popular narrative. A short text can be read quite quickly and is often easier to understand than a long narrative. A collection of narratives is easier to read in portions. With regard to content, supernatural elements also seem to have increased the popularity of a narrative text[28].

All in all, there are three main factors which influenced a text's possibility of becoming a popular printed narrative throughout centuries: a) the narrative was already popular in the Middle Ages, b) there was an early printed edition in German, and c) it was relatively short or formed part of a collection. The novella *Griseldis* turned out to be one of the most popular narratives in European vernaculars. In the following the novella's German and Dutch printed traditions will be presented and compared in order to show the long-term production in different media and the spatio-temporal dimension of this European narrative for two language areas.

2 "Griseldis" in German

The novella *Griseldis* was very popular in at least 20 European vernaculars[29]. The most prominent of these are German, French, Dutch, and English. At least 99 German and at least 59 Dutch editions were published before 1900, and there were at least 44 editions in English and at least 37 in French[30]. See Table 2.

---

[28] We can think of the horse Beyaert in the *Vier heemskinderen*, the transformation of the female hero into a serpent in *Melusine*, or the water to test virginity in *Floris ende Blancheflour*.
[29] K. Laserstein, *Der Griseldisstoff in der Weltliteratur. Eine Untersuchung zu Stoff- und Stilgeschichte*, Weimar 1926; see R. Morabito, *Griselda*.
[30] The first number refers to the number of editions based on my own research, the number in brackets refers to the number of editions mentioned by R. Morabito, *Griselda*. The sources used in order to find the editions are mentioned in fn. 12. The nearly doubling of results may be due to the fact that the research situation has much improved. For the French tradition, see M.-D. Leclerc, *Les Avatars de Grisélidis*, in "Marvels and Tales", 5, 1991, pp. 200–234; M.-D. Leclerc, *Renaissance d'un thème litté-*

Tab. 2: Editions of "Griseldis" in German, French, Dutch, and English[31]

Griseldis	German	French	Dutch	English[32]
mss.	16	9	6	0
1470–1500	15 (12)	7 (7)	5 (2)	4 (0)
1501–1600	31 (19)	8 (8)	5 (3)	13 (8)
1601–1700	15 (9)	3 (3)	6 (0)	5 (5)
1701–1800	8 (7)	6 (6)	31 (19)	5 (5)
1801–1900	30 (28)	13 (13)	12 (10)	17 (17)
Total editions in print	99 (56)	37 (37)	59 (34)	44 (35)

It was also put on the market in different media: it was printed as a song (and probably sung)[33], performed and published as a dramatic text[34], it became part of didactic texts on education[35], and was written as a dramatic poem[36]. There is an enormous production of German editions in the fifteenth and sixteenth century. Peak periods are the years between 1471 and 1483 (13 editions), 1536–1556 (11 editions), 1573–1582 (7 editions), and 1589–1608 (8 editions)[37]. After the first peak, there is a breakdown of German *Griseldis*-editions, with "only" six editions in the 40 years between 1483 and 1520. Obviously, the market was saturated with *Griseldis*-editions from 1485 onwards, and in general the Reformation led to a decline in production of (mostly secular) narratives in the 1520s.

With regard to the contents of the German *Griseldis*, we can basically distinguish two different traditions: editions of Arigo's translation of Boccaccio's version in

---

raire aux XVIIe et XVIIIe siècles: La Patience de Grisélidis, in "Revue d'histoire littéraire de la France", 1991, pp. 147–176. The English tradition will be presented in R. Schlusemann, *Printed Popular Narratives*.

31 List without translations and editions of *Il Decamerone*.

32 Editions of the text, which were part of the *Canterbury Tales* have not been included.

33 For example in Dutch as *Jammerlyk liedeken van Griseldis, de verduldige vrouwe, die vyftien jaeren geduerende veel tribulatien en verdriet heeft onderstaen*, Gent, Leander van Paemel, c. 1820–1840, copy: Den Haag, Koninklijke Bibliotheek, 1700 D 1. See F. Van Duyse, *Het oude Nederlandsche lied*, vol. 1, 's Gravenhage 1903.

34 See A. Aurnhammer, *Griseldis auf dem Schultheater. Georg Mauritius Comoedia von Graff Walther von Salutz / vnd Grisolden (1582)*, in A. Aurnhammer / H.-J. Schiewer (eds), *Die deutsche Griselda. Transformationen einer literarischen Figuration von Boccaccio bis zur Moderne*, Berlin / New York 2010, pp. 153–169.

35 See K. Grubmüller, *Griseldis in der deutschen Literatur des Mittelalters*, in A. Aurnhammer / H.-J. Schiewer (eds.), *Die deutsche Griselda*, pp. 171–180.

36 See L. Reitani, *Griseldis am Artus-Hof. Friedrich Halm: Griseldis. Ein dramatisches Gedicht (1835/1837)*, in A. Aurnhammer / H.-J. Schiewer (eds.), *Die deutsche Griselda*, pp. 223–228.

37 Because of the vast number of editions and adaptations, only the developments and characteristics of some of the major German versions will be presented here.

Il Decamerone[38] and editions based on Steinhöwel's German adaptation of Petrarch's Latin version of *Griseldis*. Heinrich Steinhöwel (c. 1410/11–1479), one of the most famous late medieval German authors and translators of the fifteenth century, wrote his *Griseldis* around 1461[39]. He characterizes Griseldis as an ideal woman and her husband as an example of virtue and prudence. This image of the husband raises the question – because of the husband's cruelty towards his wife – if such an author intention is really compatible with the story itself[40]. Fifteen German *Griseldis* editions were already printed (see *GW*) in the fifteenth century – the first by Günther Zainer in 1471 (*GW* M31580)[41].

The majority of the German *Griseldis* editions from the first decades of the sixteenth century were published anonymously. These editions have a didactic focus and often stress the importance for women to be humble, patient, and obedient towards their husbands, as we see on the title page of the edition by Augustin Friess, published in Zürich in around 1545 (fig. 1). After Arigo and Steinhöwel, Hans Sachs was the third known German author in 1546. His *Comedi mit 13 personen* was the first German dramatic version of the story, emphasizing the didactic quality of the text as a lesson for marriage[42].

Hans Wilhelm Kirchhof's version with the title *Von Herzog Durando* in the fourth book of his *Wendunmuth* (chapter 86) was published six times between 1563 and 1603[43]. He ends the story with the remark that everything had been done in order to eliminate the negative aspects of the female hero's birth, to honor her, and to present her as an equal wife. Kirchhof exploits the novella as a lesson for marriage and an illustration of the Fortuna-motive of changeable luck (*ibid.*). In the following decades, there were also reprints of Hans Sachs' *Griseldis* in Nürnberg (1558; [c. 1575]).

---

38 There were two editions in the fifteenth, and fourteen in the sixteenth century, see Ch. Bertelsmeier-Kierst, *Arigo*, in *MRFH* (http://www.mrfh.de/uebersetzer0004). Arigo's version as part of *Il Decamerone* has not been taken into consideration in this article.
39 For a survey of the twelve manuscripts and the editions until 1600 see *MRFH*; see also U. Hess, *Heinrich Steinhöwels 'Griseldis': Studien zur Text- und Überlieferungsgeschichte einer frühhumanistischen Prosanovelle*, München 1975; Ch. Bertelsmeier-Kierst, *Griseldis in Deutschland: Studien zu Steinhöwel und Arigo*, Heidelberg 1988; U. Kocher, *Boccaccio und die deutsche Novellistik: Formen der Transposition italienischer "novelle" im 15. und 16. Jahrhundert*, Amsterdam / New York 2005; K. Grubmüller, *Griseldis*.
40 N. Allweier, *Griseldis-Korrektur. Liebe und Ehe in der "Griseldis" des Erhart Groß von 1432*, Freiburg i.Br. 2012, pp. 211–214.
41 Besides, there were compilations of Arigo's and Steinhöwel's versions: an anonymous version was published by Christian Egenolff in Frankfurt in 1550 and in 1563 (*MRFH* 33538 and *MRFH* 33540). Another compiled version, Georg Wachter's *Grisilla*, was published around 1540 and again before 1620 (*MRFH* 33542 and 33544).
42 M. Dallapiazza, *Hans Sachsens comedi: die gedultig und gehorsam marggräfin Griselda*, in A. Aurnhammer / H.-J. Schiewer (eds.), *Die deutsche Griselda*, pp. 143–152.
43 K. Grubmüller, *Griseldis*, stresses that the male hero Durando is presented as an "allwissender Experimentator" (p. 178) who hides his motives, thoughts, and emotions.

Besides, Jakob Frölich published Steinhöwel's novella, in later editions together with another novella by Boccaccio, *Giletta von Narbonne*[44], and entitled his edition *Zwo liebliche vnd nützliche Historien / von gehorsam / standhafftigkeyt / vnd gedult Erbarer frommen Ehefrawen* (1538; 1540; c. 1550; 1554). This title stresses three virtues of honorable and pious women: obedience, steadfastness, and patience.

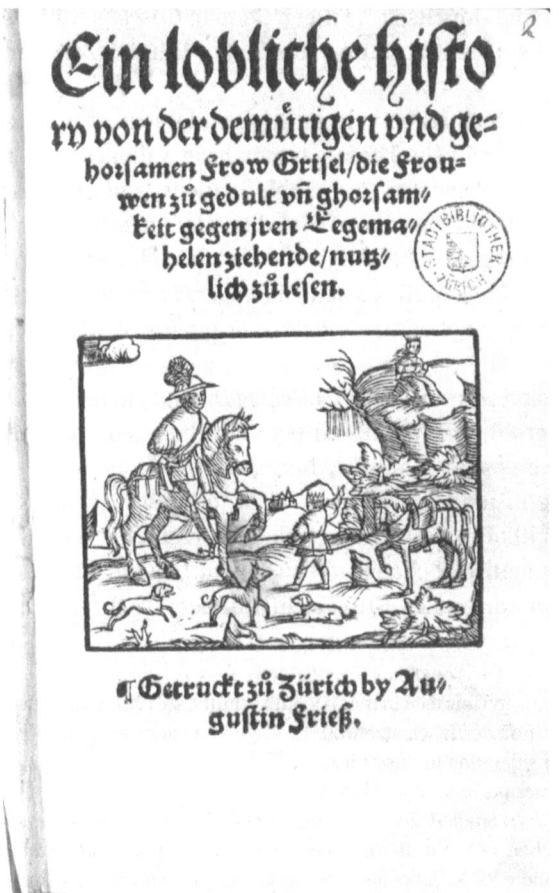

Fig. 1. *Ein lobliche history von der demütigen vnd gehorsamen Frow Grisel / die Frouwen zuo gedult vnd ghorsamkeit gegen jren Eegemahelen ziehende / nutzlich zuo lesen*, Zürich, Augustin Friess [1545], (Zürich, Zentralbibliothek, 18.2017,2, title page, https://www.e-rara.ch/doi/10.3931/e-rara-4878).

Only a few German versions were published before 1679, but from 1680–1700 onwards we find the next major stage with ten editions. In several prose editions with a title mentioning the male hero, *Schöne bewegliche und Anmuthige Historien / Von Marggraf Walthern*[45], a preface written in verse stresses that his behavior should

---

44 *Il Decamerone*, III, 9.
45 These were written and published anonymously between 1684 and approximately 1700. Sometimes, *Griseldis* was published together with the novella *Gismunda* (see *VD17* 1:694655Y; *VD17* 1:659568C; *VD17* 1:659573W; *VD17* 1: 659549X; all online).

not be condemned: "There is therefore no need for faithfulness to be tested, which sometimes tumbles badly and often rages cruelly. No reproach should be made to either him or her" (figs. 2a and 2b)[46]. This shift to the male hero in the title had already taken place in the sixteenth century, in Georg Pondo's *Historia Walthers* (1579), with the emphasis on the Welsh Earl who marries the daughter of a poor farmer, and in Georg Mauritius' *Comoedia von Graf Walther von Salutz / vnd Griselden* (1582)[47]. See Figures 2a and 2b.

In the eighteenth century, only a few German editions appeared, but between 1800 and 1820 nine German *Griseldis* editions followed. In his *Die zweyte Hochzeit* (1804) the famous author Achim von Arnim presents his *Griseldis* ballad as an ambivalent story, which ends with a seemingly unproblematic maudlin tableau, yet emphasizing the "incurable brokenness" of the female hero[48]. Another prominent reteller of the story at this time is Joseph Görres, an acquaintance of Arnim and Clemens Brentano, who also chose the name of the male hero for the title: *The Fine and Charming Story of Count Walther, His Life and Adventures* (1807)[49]. Between 1830 and 1850, the period of German Biedermeier, romantic literature, and realism, more than twenty German *Griseldis* editions were put on the market. It seems that in these decades anyone interested in narrative literature produced their own German *Griseldis* narrative. One of them was Gustav Schwab who included *Griseldis* in his book of finest stories and tales (1836)[50].

The first drama written by the Austrian poet Friedrich Halm (1806–1871) was the *Griseldis* called "dramatic poem". It was performed in Vienna on December 30, 1835 for the first time, and afterwards at least 83 times until 1864. It was not only popular in German, but also translated into different European vernaculars, for example in Dutch (1839) with the title *Griseldis: Or the Three Tests. Drama in Five Acts*. Halm sets the story at the medieval court of King Arthur. Griseldis is tested, but this time it is part of a game by Ginevra and Griseldis' husband Percival. Griseldis, who does not know that the tests are only part of a game, is shocked when she hears the truth.

---

46 "So ist es ohne Noth, daß man die Treue probt / daß manchmal übel fällt, und oftmal grausam tobt / So darf kein Vorwurf auch noch ihn, noch sie bestreichen". All translations are mine unless indicated otherwise.
47 A. Aurnhammer, *Griseldis auf dem Schultheater*.
48 D. Martin, *Griseldis in der klassisch-romantischen Ballade*, in A. Aurnhammer / H.-J. Schiewer (eds), *Die deutsche Griselda*, pp. 183–220.
49 Later C.M. Winterling also called his novella *Markgraf Walther von Salutzo* (1844).
50 G. Schwab, *Buch der schönsten Geschichten und Sagen: für Jung und Alt wieder erzählt*, vol. 1, Stuttgart, S.G. Liesching, 1836; later published with an additional second title: *Die deutschen Volksbücher: für Jung und Alt wieder erzählt*, Stuttgart, S.G. Liesching, 1843. In the nineteenth century we also find several German translations from other languages such as Italian (opera Griselda – *La virtù al cimento* by Angelo Anelli, 1798; translated by Johann Jacob Ihlee in 1811).

Fig. 2a: *Schöne bewegliche Historien / Von Marggraff Walthern / darinnen dessen Leben und Wandel / auch was sich mit ihm begeben und zugetragen / kürtzlich vor Augen gestellet: Dem günstigen Leser zugefallen mit schönen Figuren gezieret und verbessert*, s.l., 1685 (Wolfenbüttel, Herzog August Bibliothek, xb6571, fol. a1r, http://diglib.hab.de/drucke/xb-6571/start.htm).

She leaves her husband and the court for ever. The libretto for the opera *Percival und Griseldis* was based on Halm's *Griseldis*, while the text was written by Carl Heinrich Herzel and the music by Carl Schnabel[51]. The premiere of this opera was shown in Wrocław in 1851.

The *Griseldis* story was described as a "comedy" by Hans Sachs, for being very "funny and light" (1579), and as a "tragic comedy" by C.M. Winterling in 1844. On the other hand, Ludwig Heinrich von Nicolay called the story a "moralistic romance" in 1788. It was named a "melodrama" in 1841 and 1851. Several German titles emphasize Griseldis' patience, humility, and obedience (1522, 1550, before 1580, 1817, 1836, 1847), presenting the story as an example and mirror for these female virtues.

---

51 *Textbuch zu Percival und Griseldis. Große Oper in drei Akten von Carlo*, Musik von Carl Schnabel, Breslau, Graß, Barth und Comp., 1851.

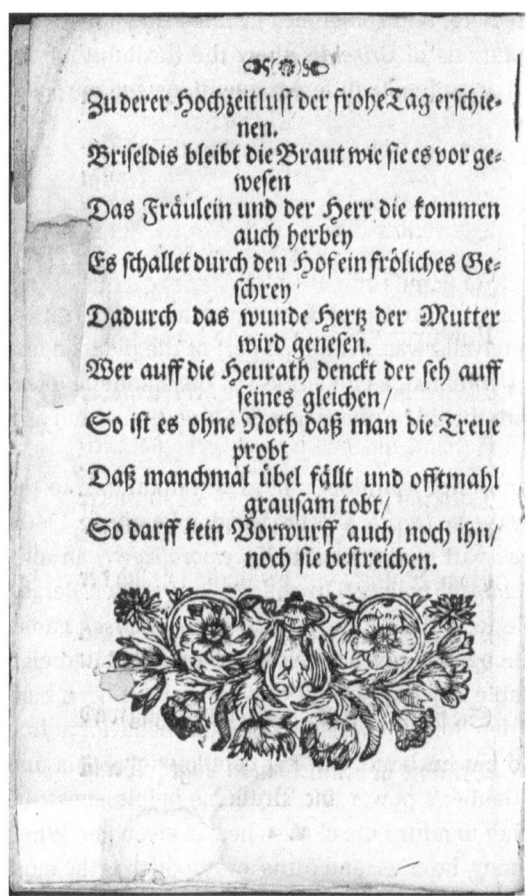

Fig. 2b: *Schöne bewegliche Historien / Von Marggraff Walthern / darinnen dessen Leben und Wandel / auch was sich mit ihm begeben und zugetragen / kürtzlich vor Augen gestellet: Dem günstigen Leser zugefallen mit schönen Figuren gezieret und verbessert*, s.l., 1685 (Wolfenbüttel, Herzog August Bibliothek, xb6571, fol. a2v, http://diglib.hab.de/drucke/xb-6571/start htm).

In his version Max Möbius choses the telling title *Die Prüfung oder das Weib wie es sein soll* (The Test or The Woman as She Should Be) (c. 1850), stressing the story's didactic purpose. All in all, the German tradition is not only characterized by a vast number of editions throughout the centuries, but by a great variance of genres – novellas, dramas, operas, and songs. *Griseldis* kept appearing under a new guise from the pen of new authors with new viewpoints, each of them writing a new *Griseldis*. These authors, most of whom were well-known, e.g. Hans Sachs, Jörg Wickram, Georg Mauritius, Ludwig Heinrich von Nicolay, Achim von Arnim, Gerhard Hauptmann, and Joseph Görres, obviously sought to write their own *Griseldis* story and show that the subject of the novella was so important and special that they had to write their own *Griseldis* version. Some of them emphasized the didactic aspects of patience and humility[52],

---

52 See also *Christliche Tugend-Schul des demüthigen Gehorsams*, Augsburg, 1731; or *Wunderbarer Demuth- und Geduldspiegel vorgestellt in der Gräfin Griseldis*, Köln, Christiaen Everaerts, c. 1800.

others changed the focus to the male hero, and sometimes justified the male hero's behavior. The German literary adaptations of *Griseldis* show the flexibility of the story and the possibility of molding it according to different intentions and purposes throughout the centuries until today[53].

3 "Griseldis in Dutch"

In Dutch, the *Griseldis* story was also produced in different media: as a narrative, a drama, and a historical song. The novella was written as part of the didactic text called *Dat kaetspel ghemoralizeert* (4 editions), as an edition of the standalone text (14 editions), as part of the trilogy with the title *Vrouwenpeerle* (36 editions), and as a historical song (3 editions)[54].

The Dutch fifteenth-century manuscript tradition is of great importance to the tradition in later centuries, especially the text written by Jan van den Berghe (c. 1360–1439) around 1431[55]. His *Griseldis* was part of *Dat Kaetspel ghemoralizeert*, an allegorical text on the handball game *kaatsen* (*bounce*). In chapter 21, Van den Berghe incorporates *Griseldis* as an example for judges. Like players in the *kaatsen* game, who sometimes leave and then join in again, judges have to deal with affairs foreign to them. *Griseldis* is told as an example illustrating that those who have been banished can be accepted again. In Van den Berghe's version, Griseldis' behavior at first sight suggests total subordination to her husband. But her combined stoicism and moral superiority eventually erode Gautier's power and stress his helplessness: he tells her to leave the court and asks her to return the clothes he has given her. When she asks him for a shirt to cover her body, he cries, and turns away, which is the most emotional reaction of the male hero in the novella. The story ends as they are reunited and emphasizes the good government of their son. The *Kaetspel* was printed for the first time in 1477 by Johann van Paderborn in Leuven (*GW* M15941)[56]. In the printed

---

[53] In November 2016 a *Griseldis* drama (1713), found at Marienberg abbey in Bozen (Italy), was staged at the abbey itself (http://www.vinschgerwind.it/archiv-beitraege-vinschgau/archiv-vinschger-wind-2016/vinschgerwind-ausgabe-21-16/9683-griseldis-einzigartig-theaterproduktion-marienberg). In June/July 2018 the theater production of *Decameron* by the Berliner Ensemble and the theater group RambaZamba was built around *Griseldis*, https://rambazamba-theater.de/inszenierungen/das-dekameron/, accessed July 5, 2018.
[54] The editions of Dirck Volkertszoon Coornhert's translation of Boccaccio's *Il Decamerone* (the first edition was published in 1564) are not discussed in this paper.
[55] For a survey of the Dutch manuscript tradition see the above-mentioned article by R. Schlusemann, *Printed Popular Narratives*; see also D.J. van der Meersch (ed.), *Die historie vander goeder vrouwen Griseldis, die een spieghel is gheweest van patientien*, Gent, C. Annoot-Braeckman, 1849.
[56] The printer is also called Johann van Westfalen. Four other editions followed: by Henrick Eckert of Homberch in Delft in 1498 (*GW* M15943), by Jacob van Liesveldt in Antwerp around 1529 (NK 0712,

version, too, the story of Griseldis is told as an example for judges to behave "ghestadich / ghetrouwe / waerachtich / ende gherechtich" (unwaveringly / faithfully / truthfully / and fairly) (1498, fol. g6v). At the end of the epilogue the narrator emphasizes that a man who is assumed to behave "gestadich ende volstandich" (unwaveringly and steadfastedly) is also more likely to suffer, a fate that in this case had befallen a woman like Griseldis[57].

Jan van den Berghe's text also formed the basis for all the Dutch editions of *Griseldis* as an individual text. The first edition was put on the market by the famous printer-publisher Gheraert Leeu in Antwerp around 1487 (*GW* M 31599). Only a small strip of the title page has been preserved, with the title: "Die hystorie van der goeder vrouwen Griseldis die een Spiegel is gheweest van Pacientien", emphasizing Griseldis' good character as a mirror for patience. In the second edition by Jacobus van Breda (not before 1492; *GW* M31600) Leeu's words are repeated verbatim, and in the prologue the novella is introduced as follows:

> Here begins the history of the good lady Griseldis, which is short but very pleasant and sweet to hear. And it tells about patience, and what a human being can gain and receive if he can endure his misfortune patiently and gently[58].

This promotion of the story in the prologue, which is repeated in the epilogue, describing the story as pleasant and sweet, and emphasizing the virtues of patience and endurance as the way to be rewarded in the end, sets the tone for all the other Dutch editions in later centuries. All in all, fourteen Dutch *Griseldis* editions were published as standalone texts until about 1820[59], all with the same contents:

1. Antwerpen, Gheraert Leeu, c. 1487
2. Deventer, Jacobus van Breda, not before 1492
3. *Delft, s.n., 1495
4. Antwerpen, Jan Wijnrijcx, 1552
5. *s.l., s.n. (1612), approbation 1612
6. Amsterdam, Jacob Brouwer, 1715
7. 's Gravenhage, Cornelis van Zanten, 1730

---

no copy), by Adriaen van Berghen in Antwerp (no date; NK 0713, no copy) and by A.M. Bergaigne in Leuven in 1551.

57 "Ende het ware veel merer redenen dat een man dye meer sculdich is te sine gestadich ende volstandich ghedoechde ende lede om rechts wille ende om godswille dan een wijf soude gedoghen om enen sterfliken man gelijc griselde gedoechde om haer man"; *Griseldis*, Antwerpen, Henrick Eckert van Homberch, 1498, fol. g6v.

58 "Hier bghint [sic] die historie vander goeder vrouwen genoemt Griseldis die welcke cort is nochtan is sy seer suuerlijc ende soet om horen: ende roert van patiencien wat een mensche al verdienen mach ende verweruen die hem in sijnen teghen spoet patientelic ende verduldelic verdragen ka"; Delft, Jacobus van Breda (not before 1492), fol. a1v.

59 There are no extant copies of the editions marked *.

8. Utrecht, Robartus Oudemeyer, 1739
9. Amsterdam, Barent Koene, 1750–1800
10. Amsterdam, Hendrik Rynders, 1751–1771, or his heirs (until 1864)
11. Amsterdam, Joannes Kannewet, 1761
12. Amsterdam, S. and W. Koene, 1801
13. Amsterdam, Barent Koene, c. 1810
14. Amsterdam, Barent Koene, c. 1820

With regard to the printing places, there are only two editions printed in the southern Netherlands (nos. 1 and 4) whereas the others were printed in the north, in Deventer, Delft, Amsterdam, The Hague, and Utrecht. Except for Leeu's edition, Jan Wijnrijcx's edition, published in Antwerp in 1552, is the only one printed in the southern Netherlands. Moreover, it is the oldest version with an illustrated title page. The woodcut under the text clearly depicts the marriage of Gautier and Griseldis (fig. 3)[60].

Fig. 3: *Dye historie van der goeder vrouwen Griseldis, die seer suyverlijck is om lesen. Ende si spreect van pacientie wat een mensche al verdienen en verwerven mach die hem in sijn tegenspoet pacientelijck ende verduldelijck draghen can*, Antwerpen, Jan Wijnrijckx, [1552], (Den Haag, Koninklijke Bibliotheek, KW 1703 B 8 [2], title page).

---

60 Wijnrijcx's edition ends with a colophon and a woodcut illustrating a couple with a child.

The next preserved edition was published more than a hundred years later, by Jacob Brouwer in Amsterdam in 1715. At least four other editions followed in the eighteenth century. The prologue, the narrative itself, and the epilogue remain the same. All editions present the "good lady" Griseldis and emphasize her patience on the title page, but the printers selected different scenes for the woodcut on the title page. In the first edition, with an illustrated title page in the Northern Netherlands, Brouwer chose the moment when the people ask the count of Saluzzo to marry. In 1761, Kannewet also used this motive. On Hendrik Rynders' title page, we see a woman kneeling. Van Zanten preferred the bust of a woman surrounded by six small decorative woodcuts. Koene selected the scene where Griseldis departs from the Count's court. With the help of these visual elements, the viewpoint shifts: from the count's duty to marry via the woman as heroine to her shameful departure.

Fig. 4: *De vrouwe-peirle ofte dryvoudige historie van Helena de Verduldige, Griseldis de Saghtmoedige, Florentine de Getrouwe*, Antwerpen, Joannes Franciscus van Soest, 1766 (Antwerpen, Erfgoedbibliotheek Hendrik Conscience, 754907, title page).

A second, unique, and very long-lasting Dutch tradition is the incorporation of *Griseldis* in a trilogy. It was called *Der Vrouwen-Peerle. Dryvoudighe Historie van Helena de Verduldighe, Griseldis de Saechtmoedighe, Florentine de ghetrouwe* (*Women's Pearl*). See Figure 4. *Gentle Griseldis* is published together with two other "histories"[61]: *Patient Helena*, the story about Sint Maarten's mother who sets off on an adventurous journey, and *Faithful Florentina*, a story about a woman dressed as a monk who rescues her husband from slavery. In all editions of the trilogy, which nearly always comprises 28 leaves, *Griseldis* forms the second part (6 leaves). The title page praises the virtues of the three heroines. The narratives are endorsed as having been taken from "old histories" and newly "gathered and much improved" for the benefit of the youth. The first edition of the trilogy is now lost. It was, according to a license by Maximilian van Eynatten on May 8, 1621[62], printed by Martinus Verdussen in Antwerp in 1621. Subsequently an edition was published by Hendrick Aertssen in Antwerp, dated between 1621 and 1658[63]. Between 1621 and 1850, at least 35 different Dutch *Vrouwenpeerle* editions were published[64]. They were nearly all printed in the southern parts of the Low Countries: in Antwerp 13, Ghent 9, Brussels 5, Bruges 2, Maastricht 2, Venlo 2, Diksmuide 1, and Lier 1; in contrast to the standalone-text editions no *Vrouwenpeerle* edition was printed in Amsterdam. There is a "dividing" line between these two traditions (fig. 5): *Griseldis* is published as a standalone text in the north and as part of a trilogy in the south. In the eighteenth and nineteenth centuries, the printers obviously acted in concert with the printers in their own regions and imitated the habits of the printers in neighboring cities.

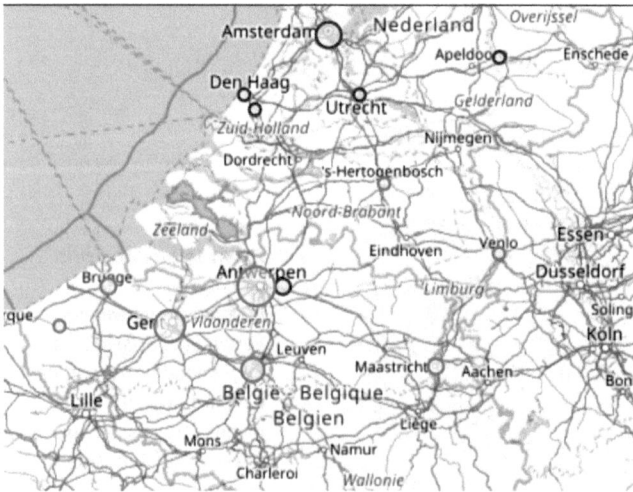

Fig. 5: Editions of *Griseldis* as an individual text (black) and as part of the trilogy "Vrouwenpeerle" (grey). Source: Software used: https://geobrowser.de.dariah.eu.

---

61 The Dutch (and English) term "historie" with the meaning "story" is widespread in early printed narratives to denominate these kinds of texts.
62 The license is still found in later editions, for example in the edition printed by Joannes Willemsens, Antwerpen, c. 1750 (Den Haag, Koninklijke Bibliotheek, 3167 H 16), or by Hieronymus Verdussen, Antwerpen 1738–1794 (Utrecht, Universiteitsbibliotheek, MAG: Moltzer 6 A 13).
63 An edition of this edition of *Vrouwenpeerle* is forthcoming.
64 R. Schlusemann, *Printed Popular Narratives* for a list of all these editions.

Regarding the chronology of all Dutch *Griseldis* editions, we can distinguish different stages throughout the centuries, as the following graph shows visually.

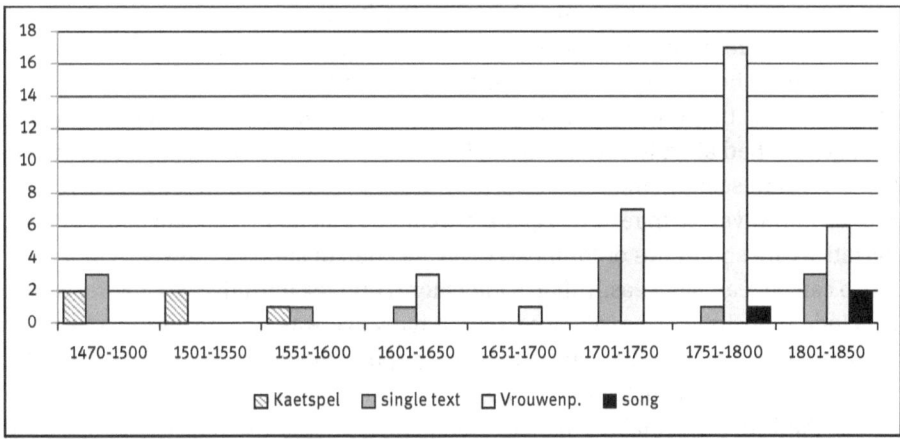

Fig. 6: Printed editions of "Griseldis" in Dutch.

Altogether there are four major "Dutch" peaks: the first was the incunabula period with editions that were part of *Kaetspel* or as a standalone text. This implies that *Griseldis* was regarded as a novella with potential for success from the beginning of printed literary texts in Dutch. A long pause follows with hardly any editions until about 1700. The second main peak can be seen in the first decades of the eighteenth century, when well-known printers such as J. Brouwer (Amsterdam), C. van Zanten (The Hague), and J. Willemsens (Antwerp) launched this novella, probably because of a plethora of "schoone historien" (nice histories), which were also printed in these decades, e.g. *The Four Sons of Aymon, The Knight with the Swan, The Seven Sages of Rome,* or *Valentyn and Oursson*. In the third peak until 1800 (especially between 1740 and 1788) all in all (at least) 21 *Griseldis* editions were published, most of them in the southern parts of the Dutch-speaking areas: e.g. in Antwerpen by F. Gaesbeeck in 1747; in Maastricht by L. Lekens, 1750–1775; in Brussel by J.B. Jorez, 1755–1786; in Antwerpen by J.F. Soest in 1766; in Ghent by J. Begyn, c. 1780; and in Brugge by M. de Sloovere, 1780.

The fourth important peak of the Dutch *Griseldis* story takes place at the beginning of the nineteenth century, when the printing house Koene (Amsterdam) published many "nice histories" as inexpensive booklets called *blauwe boekjes* (comparable to the *bibliothèque bleue*). Most editions in these decades, however, were also published in the south as part of *Vrouwenpeerle*: in Gent by P.A. Kimpe (c. 1805) and by L. van Paemel, c. 1820–1840; in Antwerp by J. Thys, c. 1816–1853; and in Diksmuide by P. Stock & Zoon, c. 1830.

4 Conclusions

From a German point of view, twelve narratives can be called the most popular printed narratives in European languages between the beginning of printing and around 1900. They were printed in at least six languages and published in German in every century from the fifteenth/sixteenth century onwards. One of the outcomes of this contribution is the conclusion that the chance for a narrative to become popular was stronger if it had already been in circulation before the media change and was therefore known in society, and if it was printed already until 1480, in the first decade of printed narratives. With regard to genre, we can see that more than half of the popular narratives are short tales or form part of a collection of short narratives. A short narrative can be read more easily than a long more complex narrative. Therefore, we can conclude that the more easily accessible a narrative was, the greater its chance to become a popular narrative. One of the most popular narratives – which perfectly fits the aforementioned conclusions – was the novella about patient Griseldis.

In the Dutch incunabula period, Gheraert Leeu was the first to recognize the potential of the story. His edition formed the basis for the text to develop as the most popular fictional narrative until 1850. The Dutch editions are characterized by a rather fixed textual narrative, emphasizing the patience of the heroine. On the whole, more or less only the illustrations of the title pages changed. The Dutch tradition, compared with the German *Griseldis* tradition, is more limited as it is mainly based on reproductions of the same story over the course of several centuries. In the Dutch tradition there are no authors intending to write their own version of the story. Instead, the printer-publishers are much more important than in the German tradition, and they obviously know that the story is successful as it is and that changes in the paratexts, especially the illustrations, are sufficient to make the narrative attractive for a new public. The success of the Dutch *Griseldis* with the combination of three prominent narratives about female heroes in the trilogy *Vrouwenpeerle* is unparalleled in a European context: this trilogy developed as a very popular edition for nearly 250 years, especially between 1725 and 1830. The trilogy was virtually only printed in the southern Netherlands, which implies that we have two distinct *Griseldis* traditions in Dutch, the tradition with *Griseldis* as a standalone text in the north and the "Women's Pearl" tradition in the south. From the seventeenth century onwards, the printers were clearly more inspired by their colleagues in the same region and chose their products as a source. This implies that, if a certain edition was popular, in this case the *Vrouwenpeerle* in the south, the printers stuck to it and did not attempt anything new and uncertain.

The German tradition of *Griseldis* differs significantly from the Dutch situation with regard to genres, titles, authors, and chronology. In contrast to the Dutch tradition, the German *Griseldis* tradition is characterized by a great degree of variation concerning the choice of titles and genres. In the beginning, it retrieves its main narrative tradition from two German late-medieval authors, Heinrich Steinhöwel and

Arigo, who produced new German versions in the fifteenth century. But in the following centuries opposing manifestations of the story were written and promoted. Many well-known authors were inclined to write a new version of the story, especially emphasizing their didactic intention, the patience and obedience of a wife towards her husband, the benefit of reading the narrative, and often shifting the focus to the male hero already present in the title. This development of new viewpoints culminated in Friedrich Halm's popular adaptation with new characters and an entirely new end. In general, the German *Griseldis* tradition, with its switch to the male hero and its more masculine expression of female obedience, compared to a more feminine tradition of the Dutch editions, commends the female hero's virtue of patience and its reward. In Dutch, the narrative remains practically unchanged throughout the centuries. A future research project should aim at finding out more detailed reasons for these different characteristics of the Dutch and German traditions and compare them to the characteristics of the *Griseldis* tradition in other European languages, and also to the traditions of other popular European narratives.

Contributors

Daniel Bellingradt, Professor at the Institute for the Study of the Book, Friedrich-Alexander-Universität Erlangen-Nürnberg

Jean-François Botrel, Emeritus professor Université Rennes 2

Flavia Bruni, Librarian at ICCU –Istituto Centrale per il Catalogo Unico delle biblioteche italiane

Rebecca Carnevali, PhD candidate in Renaissance Studies, University of Warwick

Alice Colombo, Visiting Tutor, University of Bristol

Claudia Demattè, Professor of Spanish Language and Translation, University of Trento

Juan Gomis, Catholic University of Valencia

Elisa Marazzi, Fixed-term lecturer, University of Milan, La Statale

Julia Martins, PhD candidate, King's College London

Niall Ó Ciosáin, Senior Lecturer, National University of Ireland, Galway

Goran Proot, University of Udine; Cultura Fonds Library, Dilbeek

Massimo Rospocher, Researcher, Fondazione Bruno Kessler, Istituto Storico Italo-Germanico in Trento

Jeroen Salman, Assistant-professor, Utrecht University

Hannu Salmi, Professor of Cultural History, University of Turku

Jordi Sánchez-Martí, Associate Professor of English Literature, University of Alicante

Rita Schlusemann, Private Senior Lecturer of Dutch Literature and Language, Freie Universität Berlin

Reinhart Siegert, Professor of German Studies, Albert-Ludwigs-University Freiburg im Breisgau

Francesca Tancini, Marie Skłodowska-Curie Post-Doctoral Fellow, Newcastle University

Andreas Würgler, Professor of Early Modern Swiss History, University of Geneva

Index

Aarau 261
Adams, Roger 206
Adelung, Johann 61
Aertssen, Hendrick 282
Agrigento 114, 115
Aguilar Perdomo, María del Rosario 225
Alcalá de Henares 161–162
Alciati, Petro Antonio 121
Aldermary Churchyard 136
Aldrovandi, Ulisse 24–25, 34–35
Alessio Piemontese 182–184, 188, 190–192, 194, 196–197
Alsace 54, 56
Altona 57
Amazon, river 217
Ammanati, Francesco 89
Amsterdam 14, 27, 62, 279–283
Ancona 220
Angelozzi, Angelo 119–120
Anglesea 209
Antwerp 3, 62, 89–107, 182, 190, 191, 225, 279–280, 282–283
Ar Gwenn, Yann 205
Argentina 228
Arigo 272–273, 285
Arndt, Johannes 11, 16
Arnim, Achim von 275, 277
Athens 191
Atholl 210
Audin, Stefano 148
Augsburg 266
Austria 56, 63, 275
Avanzi, Ludovico 185

Badenoch 210
Baldini, Vittorio 223
Balthasar Moretus I 92, 95–97, 100–102, 104, 106–107
Balthasar Moretus II 93, 95–97, 100–104, 106–107
Baltic States 56, 261
Bangor 212
Barbera, Gaspero 238
Barbero, Giliola 89
Barbou, Renaud, the elder 140
Barcelona 62, 168
Basedow, Johann Bernhard 247

Basel 59, 62, 110, 182, 194
Bassano del Grappa 40
Bastien, Pascal 133
Batelli, Vincenzo 148
Bavaria 253
Becker, Rudolph Zacharias 5, 245–263
Belfast 204
Belgium 56, 110
Benacci, Alessandro 34–35, 39
Benedict, Philip 21
Bergamo 114, 149
Berlin 246
Berne 60
Bernhard, Karl (pen name), see Emminghaus, Arwed
Bertarelli, Achille 47
Beyer, Jürgen 59
Bicarton, Thomas 118–120
Binotti, Lucia 166
Blom, Helwi 268
Boccaccio, Giovanni 5, 265, 269, 272, 274
Bognolo, Anna 167, 218, 220, 222
Bohemia 261–262
Bollème, Geneviève 199, 227, 233, 240
Bologna 2, 33–51, 62, 114, 140, 148, 183, 187, 229
Bonibelli, Marcantonio 221
Bonner, George 83
Bosello, Pietro 222
Boston 149, 155–156, 205
Botrel, Jean-François 131, 139
Bouchet, brothers 119
Bozen 278
Bozzola, Giovanni Battista 121
Bozzolini, Fulgenzio 148, 154
Bow Churchyard 136
Brachwitz, Peter 15
Braida, Lodovica 227, 237, 241–242
Brasov 54
Bratislava 54
Brecon 204, 207
Breda, Jacobus van 279
Bremen 63
Bremer, Thomas 262
Brentano, Clemens 275
Brest 203
Brizio, Francesco 46

Britain 72, 86, 113, 155, 263
Brittany 199–214
Brouwer, Jacob 279, 281, 283
Bruges 282
Bruni, Flavia 89
Bruni, Leonardo 268–269
Brussels 282
Bryce, David 81
Buchanan, Dugald 208
Bückeburg 261
Bullinger, Heinrich 122
Burke, Peter 24, 144
Byzantium 43

Cádiz 139
Caernarvon 211
Cagliari 114
Camarthen 204
Camerino 119
Cameron, Lucy 154
Camilli, Camillo 224
Campana, Pompeo 233
Campi, publisher 240, 242
Campitelli, Feliciano 231, 233–234, 240–242
Campitelli, Filippo 231, 241
Campomanes, Count of 134
Canada 239
Cannetus, Petrus 119–120
Canto, Francisco del 163–164
Capp, Bernard 235
Cappa, Andrea 116
Carlos III 134–135
Carlsbad 249, 260
Carnelos, Laura 109, 113
Caro Baroja, Julio 127, 130
Carolus, Johann 62
Carracci, Annibale 46, 50
Casanate, Girolamo 118
Castile 130, 163
Castillo, Manuel del 134
Catalonia 130, 148
Catania 114
Central Europe 251
Cervantes, Miguel de 159, 217
Champagne 193, 199
Chapman, Edward 74, 81, 84, 86
Charles V 218
Charlotte Elizabeth, pseud., see Tonna, Charlotte Elizabeth

Charlwood, John 175–176, 178
Chartier, Roger 193, 200
Chartres 140
Chateaubriand, François-René de 129
Cherasco 114
Chester 204, 206
Chiurazzi, Luigi 236
Chodowiecki, Daniel 258
Cicero, Marcus Tullius 55, 170
Clemente, Dionis 223
Clonmel 208
Cluj 54
Cocchi, Girolamo 35
Cochi, Bartolomeo 36–37, 39, 48, 49
Coci, Jorge 162, 218
Collenbusch, Daniel 249
Cologne 62, 265
Como 114
Constantinople 28
Cooke, Nathaniel 79
Copenhagen 54, 62
Coppa, Iacopo 47
Coppens, Christian 89–90
Córdoba 139
Coriolano, Giovan Battista 46
Cork 205
Cornuaille 205
Cortés, Hernán 217
Coudrette 269
Crane, Walter 72, 76, 78, 80, 83, 85
Creede, Thomas 177
Croce, Giulio Cesare 33–39, 41–42, 47–49
Cromberger, Jacobo 217–218, 225
Cuaz, Marco 227
Czech (Republic) 55–56

Dafydd Ddu Eryri, see Thomas, David
Dalberg, Karl Theodor von 246–247, 252
Dalle Donne, Sebastiano 224
Dalziel Brothers 82
Darnton, Robert 241
d'Arras, Jean 269
De Rubertis, Achille 155
Delft 279–280
Delicado, Francisco 165–166, 168, 170, 176
Della Porta, Giambattista 184–187
Denmark 1, 56, 262
Denucé, Jan 91
Dessau 247

Deventer 279–280
Devereux, Robert 177
Díaz del Castillo, Bernal 218
Dicey, Cluer 136–138
Diksmunde 282–283
Dingwall 211
Disraeli, Benjamin 77
Dolgellau 209, 211
Dondi, Cristina 113
Drake, Sir Francis 177
Dresden 17–20, 229, 231
Dublin 154
Dumas, Alexandre 129
Durston, Thomas 206

Eastern Europe 182
Ècija 134
Edinburgh 210–212
Eger 54
Eisenberg, Daniel 161
Elbe 20
Elizabeth I 191
Emilia Romagna 42, 119
Emminghaus, Arwed 260
England 1, 4, 18, 27, 54, 71, 75, 130, 133,
   137–138, 141, 149, 160, 174–179, 187–189,
   191, 197, 198, 200, 213, 225, 235, 239, 268,
   271
English Channel 127
Erasmus Roterodamus 55
Erfurt 246
Essex 177
Estienne, Robert 100
Estonia 262
Euston 77, 86
Evans, Edmund 72, 76, 78–80, 82–85, 207
Eynatten, Maximilian van 282

Fadini, Matteo 122, 123
Farnese, Alessandro 220
Faust, Bernhard Christoph 261
Federal Republic of Germany 56
Feinauer, Samuel 18
Felipe V 139
Fernando VI 135, 139
Ferrara 42, 219, 223
Fioravanti, Leonardo 183, 187–189, 196, 198
Fishguard 204
Flavius Josephus 267

Florence 114, 140, 148, 238
Foligno 229–230, 233, 235–236, 240
Fofi, Francesco 233
France 1, 4, 18, 53, 54, 56, 63, 71, 77, 86,
   110–112, 116–118, 130, 133, 141, 147–148,
   160, 169–174, 176, 178–179, 181–183, 185,
   190, 193–194, 198–199, 200, 213, 224, 225,
   227, 235–236, 238–239, 248–249, 258,
   260, 263, 265, 268, 271
Franceschi, Gaspare de 35
Francis I 225
Frankfurt 62, 90, 194
Franklin, Benjamin 238
Frederick II of Prussia 246, 251
Friess, Augustin 273–274
Frölich, Jakob 274

Galen 188
García de Enterría, María Cruz 131
Gardano, Angelo 48
Gascony 140
Genoa 62, 140
Gentilcore, David 190
Gentile, Barbara 119
Gerardo, Querino 161–162
German Democratic Republic 56
Germany / German-speaking areas 1, 5, 14,
   17–18, 27, 53–68, 110–111, 130, 147,
   151–152, 182, 185, 187, 191, 193–194, 197,
   224–225, 245–263, 265–285
Ghent 282–283
Giazzarelli, Anselmo 49
Gibraltar 133
Giliberti, Vittorio 147, 152
Glasgow 204, 205, 211
Goethe, Johann Wolfgang von 258
Gómez, Antonio 134
Gomis, Juan 133
Görres, Joseph 267, 275, 277
Göschen, Georg Joachim 252–253
Gotha 247–248, 253
Granada 139
Grant, Peter 208–209
Graheli, Santi 112
Greenaway, John 83
Greece 178
Greenland 149
Grendler, Paul F. 218
Groulleau, Étienne 171–173

Gundermann, Tobias 29–30
Gutenberg, Johannes 53, 65, 67, 93
Guyon, de, publisher 203

Habsburg 13, 22, 28, 262
Hachette, Louis 86–87
Hackett, Helen 177
Hague, The 280, 283
Hahn, father 19
Hall, Matthew 53
Hall, William 74, 81, 84, 86
Halm, Friedrich 275, 276, 285
Hamburg 14–16, 19, 27, 57, 62–63, 194
Happel, Eberhard Werner 15, 30
Hardy, Philip Dixon 154
Harris, Neil 109, 116, 123
Harte, Bret 78
Harvey, Naomi 206
Hauptmann, Gerhard 277
Herberay des Essarts, Nicholas de 169–171, 174, 178
Hecker, Heinrich Cornelius 20
Hering, Michael 29
Herzel, Carl Heinrich 276
Hester, John 183, 188–189, 196
Hirsch, Rudolf 123
Horosco y Covarrubias, Juan de 115
Hugo, Victor 129
Hume, David 263
Hungary 55–56, 262

Iceland 262
Ihlee, Johann Jacob 275
Île-de-France 193
Imhof, Dirk 101, 104
Ingram, Herbert 79
Inverness 208, 210–212
Ireland 111, 199–214
Italy 4, 14, 42, 54, 56–71, 100, 110, 112–113, 115–116, 118, 124, 143–157, 164–169, 176, 179, 181–198, 224, 227–243, 265, 278

Jan Moretus I 92–93, 95–97, 100–102, 104–107
Jan Moretus II 92, 95–97, 100–102, 104, 106–107
Janot, Denis 169
Jena 246
Jones, Malcolm 27
Jones, Thomas 203, 206
Joseph II 251

Kannewet, Joannes 280
Kimpe, P. A. 283
Kirchhof, Hans Wilhelm 273
Knopper, Françoise 262
Koene, Barent 280, 283
Koene, S. 280
Koene, W. 280
Krakow 54, 66

Laborda, Agustín 136–138
Lanoye, Diederik 92
Latvia 262
Lavéant, Katell
Lebens, Naomi 50
Leclerc, Marie-Dominique 268
Lédan, Alexandre 203, 205–207
Leeu, Gheraert 279, 284
Lefournier, J. B. 203
Leipzig 62, 253
Léon 205
Leonardo da Vinci 48
Leopold of Brunswick, Duke 252, 256
Lerner, Bettina 156
Leu, Urs 122
Leuven 278
Lichtenberg, Georg Christoph 258
Lier 282
Limerick 205
Lisbon 140
Lithuania 262
Liverpool 205
Livius, Titus 118
Llandwrog 212
Lock, George 76, 78, 84
Locke, John 251
London 14, 23, 50, 62–63, 79, 81, 136–137, 155, 173, 175, 188, 199–200, 203, 211, 235
Longis, Jean 169, 172
Lopane, Elisabetta 6
Lorck, Melchior 29–30
Lorraine 54
Lossius, R.C. 249
Louis XVI 251
Low Countries, the 1, 13–14, 18, 27, 54, 62, 90, 100, 110, 130, 141, 160, 183, 185, 190, 224–225, 235, 262–263, 265–285
Lucca 114
Lupton, Donald 22
Lüsebrink, Hans-Jürgen 132–133, 144

Luther, Martin 55
Luxembourg 54
Lyon 118, 174, 193

Maastricht 282
MacCoinnich, Coinneach, see McKenzie, Kenneth
Madagascar 25
Madrid 116, 129–130, 135, 139–140
Magdeburg 187, 249
Mainz 53, 246
Málaga 139
Malmierca, Lorenzo 134
Mambrino Roseo da Fabriano 167–169, 176, 220, 222–223
Mandelbrote, Maurice 89
Manchester 65
Mandrou, Robert 127, 194, 199–200
Mansel, Henry Longueville 77
Mantova 219
Manuntius, Aldus 167
Marais, Jean-Luc 200
Maravall, José Antonio 163
Marbach, Gotthard 267
Marcaria, Jacob 121–123
Marchena, José 134
Marco, Joaquín 131
Marés y Roca, José María 130
Marie Antoinette 251
Marienburg 278
Martin, Jean 170
Martín, Manuel 129
Martínez, Antonio 164, 165
Massachusetts 228
Materné, Jan 91, 98
Maugin, Jean 176
Maunoir, Julien 207
Mauritius, Georg 275, 277
Mayhew, Horace 77, 79
Mazza, Angelo 48
McKenzie, Kenneth 210–212
McMartin, Daniel 211
Mecklenburg 253
Medías, Lucía 163
Medina del Campo 163–164
Mehmed IV, Sultan 28
Meléndez Valdés, Juan 134
Merthyr Tydfil 204
Messana, Costanza 113

Meuselwitz 20
Mexico 217, 218
Michon, Jacques 239
Milan 41, 50, 114–115, 140, 147–148, 219, 236, 238
Milano, Alberto 47
Millais, John Everett 82
Missouri 149
Mitelli, Giuseppe Maria 50
Möbius, Max 277
Modena 36–37, 42–43, 45, 47–49
Molinari, Giuseppe 149
Molini, Giuseppe 148
Molise 242
Moll, Jaime 137
Montaigne, Michel de 174
Monterrubio de la Sierra 134
Montesquieu, Charles-Louis de Secondat de 251
Moraes, Francisco de 178
Moravia 261, 262
Morlaix 203, 205
Munday, Anthony 176, 177, 178
Munich 55
Murcia 139
München, see Munich

Naples 62, 114, 148, 184, 196, 219, 228, 236
Napoleon 209, 233, 249
Napoli, see Naples
Natali, publisher 149
Needham, Paul 100
Neri, Stefano 167, 222
Netherlands, see the Low Countries
Neuburg, Victor 127
Nicholson, Thomas Henry 83
Nicolay, Ludwig Heinrich von 276–277
Nicolini da Sabbio, Antonio 166
Nisard, Charles 235
Nobili, Annesio 148
North America 228
Northampton 136
Northern Europe 27, 262
Nucio, Martín, see Nuyts, Marten
Nuovo, Angela 89
Nürnberg, see Nuremberg
Nuremberg 23, 25, 30, 273
Nuyts, Marten 225
New York 228

Oberpfalz 253
Oettingen 62
Ollivier, Joseph 205–206
Ó Súilleabháin, Tadhg Gaelach 208–209
O'Sullivan, Timothy, see Ó Súilleabháin, Tadhg Gaelach
Owen, Goronwy 209
Osti, Moira 6
Ottone, Andrea 89
Oudemeyer, Robartus 280
Oursin, Friederike 6
Oxford 116, 177

Paas, John Roger 22
Paderborn, Johann van 278
Padua 114, 140
Paemel, L. van 283
Pantycelyn, see Williams, William
Palermo 114, 140, 147
Paris 62, 140, 169–173, 193, 200
Parker Willis, Nathaniel 76
Parkin, Stephen 113
Passerotti, Bartolomeo 48
Paul III 220
Perrissin, Jean 22
Perth 210–212
Petrarch 268, 273
Pettegree, Andrew 53, 109, 110
Piemont 265
Pina, Marín 221
Pistoia 114
Pizarro, Francisco 217
Plantin, Christophe 91–98, 100–103, 105–106, 183, 190, 197
Plutarch 238
Poitiers 119–120
Poland 17, 56, 262
Pondo, Georg 275
Portonotaris 223
Portugal 90, 140, 178, 262
Prussia 17, 63, 262

Quimper 200

Radziwill, Giorgio, see Radziwill, Jerzy
Radziwill, Jerzy 34–35
Rankin, Alisha 61
Rannoch 210
Ravenna 118–120

Redding Ware, James 72
Refini, Eugenio 47
Remondini, publisher 40, 49, 71
Rembertus Dodoens 92
Reuben, Percy 156
Richter, Anna Katharina 268
Riga 54
Rinaldi, Orazio 223–224
Ringoltingen, Thüring von 268
Riva del Garda 121–122
Rodríguez de Montalvo, Garci 160, 218
Rodríguez-Moñino, Antonio 130
Romania 56
Rome 18, 111, 114, 116–117, 119, 140, 148, 165, 187, 191, 219, 231, 241, 266
Rospocher, Massimo 50
Rossi, Giovanni 34, 49
Rostock 62
Rouen 193
Rousseau, Jean-Jacques 251
Routledge, George 83
Rovereto 122
Rubens, Peter Paul 20
Rudolstadt 253
Russell, Francis, Lod of Bedford 191
Russia 262
Rynders, Hendrik 280–281

's Gravenhage 279
Sachs, Hans 273, 276–277
Sadleir, Michael 73
Saint-Louis, Missouri 149
Salamanca 164
Salicato, Altobello 224
Saluzzo 265
Salvati, Francesco 233, 240
Salzberg, Rosa 11, 50
Salzmann, Christian Gotthilf 247, 257
San Donato di Sesto Calende 50
San Luca 43, 44
San Marino 113
San Petronio 44
Sánchez-Martí, Jordi 268
Sandifer, Jabez 86
Sarrant 140
Saxony 17, 20
Scandinavia 263
Schepper, Susanna de 101
Schivelbusch, Wolfgang 75

Schlögl, Rudolf 12
Schlusemann, Rita 268
Schwab, Gustav 275
Scotland 119, 199–214
Scribani, Carolus 106
Schnepfenthal 247
Schulheiss-Heinz, Sonja 15
Schwerin 253
Sebastiani, Valentina 122
Selleslach, Kristof 106
Seltsam, Martin 253
Serin, Nicolaus von 23
Sertenas, Vincent 169, 172
Seville 217, 225
Shrewsbury 203–204, 206
Sicily 115
Siena 140, 148
Silvestri, Giovanni 147–148
Simrock, Karl 267
Smith, William Henry Jr. 77, 83, 86–87
Soest, Joannes Franciscus van 281
Soliani, Bartolomeo 37, 43, 48–49
South America 228
Spain 1, 4–5, 54–55, 90, 111, 115, 116, 127–142, 154, 159–179, 217–226, 240, 262
Spey 208
Spineda, Lucio 224
Sprathspey 210
Spufford, Margaret 199–200
Squassina, Erika 89
St. Andrews 109, 119
St. Barbara 64
St. Brieuc 203
St. Catherine 64
St. Christopher 64–65
St. Francis 64, 133
St. George 64
St. Petersburg 63, 261
Stanihurst, Richard 105
Steinhöwel, Heinrich 268, 273–274, 284
Stock, P. 283
Stoker, Bram 87
Strasbourg 62, 110
Stockholm 54, 62–63
Stuttgart 62
Suárez de Figueroa, Cristóbal 163
Sulzbach 253
Swansea 204
Sweden 55, 262

Switzerland 54, 56, 59, 67, 111, 183, 236, 262

Thomas, David 209
Thorn, see Toruń
Thuringia 247, 253
Thys, J. 283
Timbs, John 156
Tipperary 208
Tissandier, Gustave 238
Toledo 134, 159, 161, 163
Tomassini, Giovanni 233–234, 240
Tonna, Charlotte Elizabeth 154
Tortorel, Jacques 22
Toruń 17–20
Toulouse 200
Tours 119
Toury, Gideon 145–146, 151–154
Tramezzino, Michele 167–168, 219–224, 226
Tredegar 204
Trefriw 204
Tréguier 205
Trentino 122–123
Trento 2, 5, 54, 121–122, 265, 268
Tréveris 140
Treves, Emilio 238
Trivento 242
Trivulzio, Cesare 165
Trollope, Anthony 82
Troyes 198–200, 265
Turin 62, 114
Tuscany 193, 196
Tyler, Charles T. 76, 78

Umbria 229, 235–236
United Kingdom 74, 111, 116
United States of America 111, 228
Utrecht 280

Vaganay, Hugues 171–172
Valencia 62, 136, 139–140
Valladolid 134
Van den Berghe, Jan 278–279
Vannes 205
Vasile, Pietro A. 241–242
Vatican 111–113, 115
Vecchi, Orazio 48
Vecchio, Antonella 6
Vecellio, Cesare 41
Veneto 196

Veneziano, Agostino 48
Venice 114, 140, 149, 165–168, 170, 181–182, 189, 198, 219, 221–223, 226
Venlo 282
Verdussen, Hieronymus 282
Verdussen, Martinus
Vere, Edward de 177
Verona 114, 220
Verri, Pietro 237
Versailles St. Quentin-en-Yvelines 228
Versendaal, Rozanne M. 116
Vervliet, Daniel 225
Vescovile 231
Vicent, Antoine 118
Vienna 28, 62, 66, 275
Voet, Leon 91, 93
Voltaire 263

Wachter, Georg 273
Wales 199–214
Ward, Ebenezer 76, 78, 84
Ward, William 191
Warne, Frederick 80, 84–85
Warsaw 54
Washington D.C. 175
Wecker, Johann Jacob 183–184, 188, 196
Weichsel 20
Weidmann, Sandra 122

Weygand, Zina 140
Whitehead, Maurice 89
Wickram, Jörg 277
Wierbicka, Krystyna 268
Wiering, Thomas von 14, 27–31
Wight, Thomas 191
Wijnrijcx, Jan 279–280
Willemsens, Joannes 282–283
Williams, William (Pantycelyn) 206–209
Winterling, C.M. 276
Wolfenbüttel 62, 122, 276–277
Wolke, Christian Heinrich 247
Wood, John George 85
Wrexham 204
Wrocław 276

Young, Francis, of Brent Pelham 177
Young, Susan 177

Zainer, Günther 266, 273
Zanten, Cornelis van 279, 281, 283
Zaragoza 218
Zell, Ulrich 265
Zschokke, Heinrich 261–262
Zülpich 140
Zurich 59, 62, 122, 274
Zwierlein, Cornel 13